Sociological Philosophy of Education

Sociological Philosophy of Education

Yogendra K. Sharma

KANISHKA PUBLISHERS, DISTRIBUTORS
New Delhi 110 002

KANISHKA PUBLISHERS, DISTRIBUTORS
4697/5-21A, Ansari Road, Daryaganj
New Delhi -110 002
Phones : 2327 0497, 2328 8285
Fax : 011-2328 8285
E-mail : kanishka_publishing@yahoo.co.in

Sociological Philosophy of Education
First Published 2002
Edition-2021

ISBN: 978-81-7391-528-8

PRINTED IN INDIA

Published by Madan Sachdeva for Kanishka Publishers, Distributors, 4697/5-21A, Ansari Road, Daryaganj, New Delhi-110 002, Typeset by Sunshine Graphics, Delhi, and Printed at Rajdhani Printers, Delhi.

Preface

The work at hand is a result of the appreciation and admiration of my previous works, on the following subjects by the learned scholars and students:

1. *History and Problems of Education*, Vols. I and II.
2. *Foundatons in Sociology of Education.*
3. *Doctrines of Great Western Educators.*
4. *Fundamentals of Educational Technology.*

Hence, I feel duty-bound to express my heartfelt thanks, gratitude and indebtness to the learned readers of my works. I trust that the present work will fulfil the needs, requirements and expectations of the scholars and students of the subject.

The present work captioned as *Sociological Philosophy of Education*, among several books, published in India, claims to be the most comprehensive. This lays down the basic concepts of Sociological Foundations of Education as required to be understood by every specialist of the subject.

This book contains point analysis and description of the subject in Indian socio-educational context. It covers the syllabi of all the Indian universities on the subject in simple and lucid language drawing examples from the Indian society.

Part one of this book lays down the Fundamentals of Education required to be understood by every scholar and student of the subject alike. It includes Basic Aspects of Education; Educational Values; Educational Aims, Functions and Priorities; Institutions and Agencies of Education; Distinction between Training, Instructions and Teaching and Education as well as Curriculum of Education.

Part two of this book deals with Sociological Foundations of Education, which discusses various aspects of the subject in 27 chapters. The emphasis has been laid on the nature of educational sociology, education and society, education in Indian social context, social mobility, child's socialisation, social change, social control, culture and place of family, community, social values, modernisation as well as religious and moral values in education.

Due emphasis has been laid on national policy on education—science education, vocational and technological education as well as role of mass-media in education and concepts of freedom, descipline and responsibility in education in social context.

Since India is a socialistic and secularistic democracy, due emphasis has been laid on education for democracy, nationalism, internationalism, national integration, as well as education for political conduct and economic growth in socio-national context.

Due to some defects in the educational system, in almost all the nations of the world, some intellectuals advocate for a deschooled society which is a unwanted, anti-social and anti-educational concept, therefore, we have included one chapter on this aspect as well but to counter this concept we have included another chapter, in this book, the thoughts of Karl Mannheim on the future of sociology of education—the concept, to the best of my knowledge, is not found in any Indian book on the subject. Thus, this book is unique.

Planned as a text book for the students and reference for the scholars and teachers, this book is critical and constructive appraisal of the subject. While I have tried my best to make this book the best on the subject, the students, scholars, teachers, and other general readers are the best judge of its merits.

Suggestions for improvement are, therefore, cordially invited.

Yogendra K. Sharma

Contents

PART ONE
FOUNDATIONS OF EDUCATION

1

Basic Aspects of Education

The scope of this book is to discuss the sociological foundations of education but to understand sociological foundations of education. One must have the basic knowledge of the fundamentals of education, therefore, in part one of this book, we will discuss the fundamentals of education which will enable the reader to understand sociological foundations of education, which are being discussed in part two of this book. In first chapter, basic aspects of education are given briefly as under:

INTRODUCTION

The new born infant is a helpless human being. He has neither friends nor enemies. He is not aware of the social customs and traditions. He is not even keen to achieve any ideal or value. But as he grows older, he is influenced by the informal and formal agencies of education. He develops his physical, mental and emotional self and social feelings. By and by, he develops a sense of responsibility like his elders. He solves the problems of life successfully.

Thus, education instils in the child a sense of maturity and responsibility by bringing in him the desired changes according to his needs and demands of ever changing society, of which he is an integral part. Education bestows immense benefits upon a person. A well educated person is known all over the region. He is able to meet the conflicting challenges. He tides over all the difficulties which confront him in day to day living.

Education culturises the individual and helps him to fulfil his needs. Education develops the individual like a flower which distributes its fragrance all over the environment. Thus, education is a conducive process which develops child's individuality in all its aspects—physical, mental, emotional and social.

With this all-round development, he becomes a responsible, dynamic, resourceful and enterprising citizen of strong good moral character who uses all his capacities to develop his own self, his society and his nation to the highest extent by contributing his best to national honour, national glory, national culture and national civilization of which he is an integral part.

On one hand, education develops personality of an individual in all fields and aspects making him intelligent, learned, bold, courageous and possessing strong good character, on the other hand, it contributes to growth and development of society. It is only through education that moral ideals and spiritual values, as aspiration of the nation and its cultural heritage is transferred from one generation to another for preservation, purification and sublimation into higher and higher achievements.

With the growth and development of individual, the society also develops to higher and higher levels of attainments. Thus, education is essential for the growth and development of individual as well as society.

ETYMOLOGICAL MEANING OF EDUCATION

The Latin word 'Educatum' means to train. 'E' means from inside and 'Duco' means to draw out, to lead out or to bring up. By combining the two, education comes to mean to draw from within. Education is a process which draws from within. Each child is born with some innate tendencies, capacities and inherent powers. Education draws these powers out and develop them to the full.

Latin words 'Educare' and 'Educere' mean to bring up, to lead out and to develop etc. In this way, the word education means to develop the inborn qualities of a child to the full.

Thus, education is a process of development. To understand

its nature and rate of progress, one must know the data of education.

Data of Education

The data of education consists of the following four factors—

1. The child.
2. Heredity.
3. Environment.
4. Time.

1. The child. The foremost data of education is the child. Each child has certain innate powers. His natural development is possible only according to these native endowments. As such the child's nature should be known to those who provide education for his development.

2. Heredity. Hereditarians believe that education of a child is predetermined by heredity. According to them, hereditary impressions influence a child from his infancy before any formal education begins. As the impressions are often indelible, therefore, education has to follow the lines laid down by these impressions generated and formed by parents and other related elders of society.

These innate tendencies and qualities are the firm foundation for his education. These also delimit and define the highest achievements to be achieved by him. Thus, to hereditarians, education is development according to lines pre-determined and prelaid by the heredity of a child.

3. Environment. Another factor of education is environment. Every child is born in a family at a particular place and time. His upbringing also takes place in a specific environment. This environment is either controlled or uncontrolled. Both types of environment exert their influence upon the growing child in different ways.

Controlled environment leads to controlled growth and uncontrolled environment promotes uncontrolled growth. According to environmentalists, heredity factor is only a myth. They assert that if the environment is not desirable, no amount of heredity will be able to develop the child according to desirable lines and standards of growth.

According to them, environment is a powerful factor which influences the development of child. One cannot escape its influence at any cost. The environmentalists hold that as the child gradually comes into contact with the physical and social environment, his innate tendencies flower out and his behaviour begins to change.

In this sense, it is the environment and not the heredity which makes a child a musician or an artist. Thus, according to environmentalists education is a process based on and conditioned by the environment in which the child is brought up.

4. Time. During the process of development, specific activities are indulged by the child at specific times. To understand this process of development, one must have a clear understanding of the various stages of development. As different and specific tendencies sprout out of these various stages, education must correspond its plans and programmes to these budding capacities. Then only, the development of the child will be normal and natural. Any discord or imbalance will result in stunted growth or no growth at all.

Hence, education should correspond and suit the mental level of the child, otherwise it will create complexes and mar the development.

Both the hereditarians and the environmentalists assert one side of the truth. The two factors are not contradictory. They are mutually complementary and supplementary. Both work together to develop the child smoothly and in a balanced way. Both are essential for the proper development of a child.

EDUCATION IN NARROW SENSE

In its narrow sense school instruction is called education. In this process, the elders of society strive to attain predetermined aims during a specified time by providing pre-structured titbits of knowledge to children through set methods of teaching. The purpose is to achieve mental development of children entering school.

In this process, the teacher is the most important factor and the child is assigned a subsidiary role. The teacher is expected to instil ready made dozes of knowledge in the child's mind. By this, the child cannot attain the wholesome development of his personality. Such knowledge strangles the natural development of the child and hence, is of no use to him for his actual future life.

In spite of this, school education has merits of its own. In the words of John Stuart Mill—"The culture which each generation purposefully gives to those who are to be its successors, in order to qualify them for at least keeping up, and if possible for raising the level of improvement which has been attained."

Following opinions of some educationists represent the narrow meaning of education:

1. "In narrow sense, education may be taken to mean any consciously directed effort to develop and cultivate our powers."

—*S.S. Mackenzi*

2. "Education is a process in which and by which knowledge, character and behaviour of the young are shaped and moulded."

—*Prof. Drever*

3. "The influence of the environment on the individual with a view to producing a permanent change in his habits of behaviour, of thought and attitude." —*G.H. Thompson*

EDUCATION IN ANALYTICAL SENSE

Following are the constituent fields of education:

1. Not limited to knowledge imparted in schools. Education can not be confined to the processes of giving knowledge to children in schools. Its programme goes on from birth till death. Every one learns something or the other throughout life by various experience and activities. All this is education.

2. Education as the development of child's innate power. Education is developing the native endowments of a child rather than something forced into the mind from outside. Addison has rightly remarked, "Education when it works upon noble mind, draws out to view every latent virtue and perfection which without such help are never able to make their appearance."

3. Education as a dynamic process. Education is not a static but a dynamic process which develops the child according to changing situation and times. It is a purposive activity always pursuing some aim of life to which an individual devotes himself fully.

4. Education as a bipolar process. In his book "Evolution of Educational Theory" Adams has interpreted education as a bipolar process. He analysed education as under:

(i) "It (Education) is a bipolar process in which one personality acts upon another in order to modify the development of the other."

(ii) "The process is not only a conscious one but a deliberate one. The educator has the clearly realized intention of modifying the development of the educand."

(iii) "The means by which the development of the educand is to be modified are two folds: *(a)* The direct application of the educator's personality to the personality of the educand, and *(b)* The use of knowledge in its various forms."

According to Adams, the bipolar education has two poles. At one end is the teacher and at the other is the child. Both are equally important in education. If the teacher instructs, the child follows. If the teacher gives, the child receives.

Thus, in the process of education there is interaction between the teacher and the child. The teacher tries to mould and modify the behaviour of the child so that the latter develops his personality to the full. With the active cooperation of the teacher and the child, the process of education goes on smoothly and efficiently.

5. Education as a tripolar process. Like Adams, John Dewey also regards education as a process of development. But, while accepting the psychological view, Adams emphasizes the importance of teacher and the child, John Dewey emphasizes the sociological view point.

Hence, according to John Dewey, education has two aspects—(1) Psychological, and (2) Sociological. He accepts the contention that education of the child should be according to his native endowments. He further asserts that the development of a child does not take place in a vacuum. It takes place in and through the society in which the teacher and the child both live.

It is the society which will determine the aims, contents and methods of teaching. In this way, the process of education contains three poles, namely—(1) The teacher, (2) The child, and (3) The society. These three factors actively co-operate in the efficient and successful working of the educational process.

EDUCATION IN WIDER SENSE

In its wider sense, education is not the communication of information by the teacher or the acquisition of knowledge by the child but the total development of the personality. Education consists of all those experiences which affect the individual from birth till death.

Thus, education is the process by which an individual freely develops his self according to his nature in a free and uncontrolled environment. It is a life-long process of growth and development. It is not confined to the limits of time, place and individual.

Any person who gives the child a new experience is a teacher and any place where this giving and receiving takes place may be termed as a school.

Thus, education is essentially a process of growth and development which goes on throughout the whole life. Rousseau developed his philosophy of naturalism keeping this wider concept of education in his view-point. Following eminent scholars interpret education in the wider context:

(1) "In the wider sense, it is a process that goes on throughout life, and is promoted by almost every experience in life." —*S.S. Mackenzi*

(2) "By education, I mean the all round drawing out of the best in child and man—body, mind and soul."

—*M.K. Gandhi*

(3) "Education in its widest sense includes all the influences which at upon an individual during his passage from cradle to the grave." —*Dumvile*

CONCEPT OF EDUCATION IN INDIA AND IN THE WEST

The system of education changes according to time and cultural conditions, therefore, hereunder we first mention Indian concepts of education:

Indian Concept of Education

Indian approach includes the spiritual aspect as a part of the development by education. In fact, Indian thinkers have placed special emphasis upon this. Yajnavalkya opined that only that is education which gives a sterling character to an individual and renders him useful for the world.

Shankaracharya said that education is that which leads to salvation. Even the more recent educationists have stressed the importance of the spiritual aspect.

In the words of A.S. Altekar, "Education has always been regarded in India as a source of illumination and power which transforms and ennobles our nature by the progressive and harmonious development of our physical, mental, intellectual and spiritual powers and faculties."

This spiritual tradition has been carried on by contemporary Indian philosophers of education in their integral approach, synthesis of idealism and pragmatism, rationalism and humanism, diversity in unity and harmony of the individual and society.

It was due to this emphasis on the spiritual meaning of education that Vivekanand said, "Religion is the inner most core of education."

In the words of Sri Aurobindo, "The child's education ought to be an outpouring of all that is best, most powerful, most intimate and living in his nature, the mould into which the man's action and development ought to run is that of his innate quality and power. He must acquire new things but he will acquire them best, most wholly on the basis of his own developed type and inborn force."

M.K. Gandhi expressed the same idea when he defined education by saying, "By education, I mean an all round drawing out of the best in child and man, body, mind and spirit. Literacy is not the end of education not even the beginning. It is one of the means whereby man and woman can be educated. Literacy in itself is no education."

Western Concept of Education

Educational thinking, like every other branch of knowledge, started in the philosophical deliberation of the ancient Greek philosophers. Thus, the meaning of education in west is initially available in the works of Plato. It is interesting to note that thousand of years ago, Plato gave a meaning to education which is even now followed in the West with slight changes here and there.

Plato defined education as a life-long process starting, "from the first years of childhood and lasting to the very end of the life." He used the term education in a very wide sense, "which makes a man eagerly pursue the ideal perfection of citizenship and teaches him how rightly to rule and how to obey."

Education not only provides knowledge and skills but also inculcates values, training of instincts, fostering right attitude and habits. In, Plato points out that, "true education, whatever that may be, will have the greatest tendency to civilize and humanise them in their relation to one another and to those who are under their protection." This humanist definition of education propounded by Plato is still the most widely accepted meaning of education in the West.

Education everywhere has been taken as a process of inculcating values. As Plato said," Now, I mean by education that training which is given by suitable habits to the first instincts of virtue in children." These views of Plato have been universally accepted in West as well as in the East.

Education has been defined differently by the idealist, the pragmatist, the naturalist and the realist philosophers. However, its meaning has been generally idealistic. Without some sort of idealism, there can be no education worth the name.

In the words of Robert R. Rusk, "We may accept, the aim of education is the enhancement or enrichment of personality, the differentiating feature of which is the embodiment of universal values." The Western educational philosophers have generally agreed that the growth of the human child is the essence of education.

In the words of A.G. Hughes, "The essence of discipline is, thus, not forced subordination to the will is hated tyrants, but submission to the example of admired superiors." In the middle ages, Comenius declared education to be a process whereby an individual developed qualities relating to religion, knowledge and morality and thereby established his claim to be called a human being.

"The fundamental principles of education", according to Froebel, "instruction and teaching should be passive and protective not directive and interfering." The principle of liberty has found most eloquent expression in the definition of education given by Rousseau when he said, "Let us obey the call of Nature. We shall see that her yoke is easy and when we give heed to her voice, we find the joy in the answer of a good conscience."

Other have laid emphasis upon the social meaning of education whereby it aims at making an individual fit in the society. It was in this sense that Aldous Huxley said," A perfect education is one which trains up every human being to fit into the place he or she is to occupy in the social hierarchy, but without, in the process, destroying his or her in individuality."

All the foregoing definitions have stated that education is the process of development. It, therefore, becomes necessary to discover what is implied in this development.

Although the ability to learn depends upon development, but development is not synonymous with education. Development means the gradual and continuous progress of mind and body. Through this development the child acquires the following elements:

1. Knowledge of the environment by which he is surrounded.
2. The necessary motor control to fulfil his individual needs.
3. Linguistic abilities to enable him to converse.
4. Some knowledge of individual and collective relationship.

The development of all these elements begins at home itself. The educator's task is to continue this process and to encourage it while the child is at school.

In fact, this process of development continues right through an individual's life time. Consequently, it is accepted that education in its general sense continues throughout a man's natural span of life. Even the successful teacher or educator himself remains a students throughout his life.

On the one hand, he teaches certain things to some people but at the same time he learns something from them. All successful educators experience that the development undergone by their thoughts, personalities and abilities would have been impossible otherwise. In much the same way, people other than the educator, teach and learn simultaneously.

SYNTHESISED CONCEPT OF EDUCATION

It is clear from the above discussion of the meaning of education in West and India, ancient and modern that it may be synthesised since all these accept some common characteristics of education. The following points concerning the meaning of education emerge from a review of the meaning of education in the West and in India.

1. A Life long process. Education according to most of the philosophers continues from birth to death. As Madam Paul Richard pointed out the education of man "should begin at his very birth and it is to continue the whole length of his life."

2. Unfolding. Education is a gradual unfolding. In his 'Allegory of the Cave', Plato observed that "the power and capacity of learning exists in the soul already, and just as the eye was unable to turn from darkness of light, without the whole body, so too, the instrument of knowledge can only, by the movement of the whole soul, be turned from the world of the becoming into that of being and learn by degrees to endure the sight of being and of the brightest and best of being or in other words of the good." It is in the same sense that Sri Aurobindo said, "The chief aim of education should be to help the growing soul to draw out that in itself which is best and make it perfect for a noble use."

3. Based on child psychology. Western thinkers unanimously agree that true education should be based on child psychology. This again has been accepted by Indian philosophers of education.

According to Sri Aurobindo, "Nothing can be taught to the mind which is not already concealed as potential knowledge in the unfolding soul of creature."

Educational theory must be based on sound psychology. As Sri Aurobindo points out, "The true basis of education is the study of the human mind, infant, adolescent and adult."

4. Individual as well as social. True education is individual as well as social. Plato brought out a scheme of education according to each individual's capacities to serve the society. Philosophers in the West have everywhere laid emphasis upon individual as well as social aims of education.

Contemporary Indian philosophers also exhibit this tendency. M.K. Gandhi said," I value individual freedom, but you must not forget that man is essentially a social being. He has risen to his present status by learning to adjust his individuality to the requirements of social progress."

5. Total development. Thus, education by general agreement is a total development, physical, mental and spiritual, individual as well as social. This total development is the meaning of self-realisation. This synthesis of the different aspects of man's development is characteristic of not only idealism but also naturalism, pragmatism and realism. It is again the meaning of perfection, acclaimed as the aim of education by so many thinkers. It is also what is known as complete education. It is again the humanist meaning of education since man is a complex being several aspects of his personality all of which require full development.

According to Sri Aurobindo, education should help the individual to grow, "into a fullness of physical and vital energy and utmost breadth, depth and height of his emotional, his intellectual and his spiritual being."

The total development lays equal emphasis upon physical as well as spiritual growth. Without physical culture, mental training has been considered as one-sided.

In the words of Aldous Huxley, "Where the body is maladjusted and under strain, the mind's relations, sensory, emotional, intellectual, conative, with external realty are likely to be unsatisfactory." Education aims at an all-round and total perfection of the individual and society. Hence, physical culture should form an important part of the educational process. As Sri Aurobindo puts it, "If seeking is for a total perfection of the being, the physical part of it can not be left aside, for the body is the material basis, the body is the instrument which we have to use."

Similar quotations may be hunted from other philosophers of education in West and East. The total development involves character development, development of social virtues and individual skills. It includes all the various aims of education. It involves all the functions of education in human life such as development of natural abilities, character building, personality integration, preparation for adult life, control and sublimation of basic instincts, creation of useful citizens, development of a sense of community, progress of culture and civilization, social welfare, use of leisure and synthesis of national as well as international consciousness.

TRUE DEFINITION OF EDUCATION

The different meanings and definitions of education as given in this chapter lead us to the conclusion that education should have a comprehensive definition.

Thus, education may be defined as a purposive, conscious or unconscious psychological, sociological, scientific and philosophical process which brings about the development of the individual to the fullest extent and also the maximum development of society in such a way that both enjoy maximum happiness and prosperity.

In short, education is the development of individual according to his needs and demands of society, of which he is an integral part.

T. Raymont has rightly remarked, "Education is that process of development in which consists the passage of human being from infancy to maturity, the process whereby he adapts himself gradually in various ways to his physical, social and spiritual environment."

MODERN CONCEPT OF EDUCATION

To understand the modern concept of education, one has to make a comparative study of the old and modern concepts. Following are the differences between the old and the new concepts:

1. Meaning of education. Education is derived from the Latin word 'Educatum' which means to draw out, to foster growth and to develop. Hence, the modern concept of education seeks to develop the inherent capacities of a child in the social environment. In the old concept, education was taken to mean as a process to thrust ready made titbits of knowledge into the mind of a child as if it was an empty vessel.

The old concept has exploded under the weight of psychological researches and democratic values. The mind is a dynamic self-adjusting and self-learning force needing proper guidance for wholesome growth and development modern education seeks to develop the mind according to its own inherent capacities in a social environment.

2. Aims of education. Ancient education emphasized scholarship and mental development. It kept an indifferent attitude towards other aspects of personality. Acquiring more and more knowledge was regarded as the prime aim.

On the contrary, modern educationists lay equal stress upon other aspects of development viz., physical, mental, emotional and social. Thus, the aim of modern education is to develop individuality to the full and attain social efficiency and dynamism.

*3. **Curriculum.*** In the old curriculum, only subjects promoting mental development were included and emphasized. Thus, old curriculum got rigid and stratified. It was confined mostly to classroom activities and experiences.

Modern curriculum is flexible, varied and progressive in the sense that it tries to meet the needs of the developing child as well as demands of ever changing modern society.

*4. **Methods of teaching.*** As the methods emphasized cramming and stimulated rote memorization education was a lifeless, dull and drab process.

Modern methods condemn rote memorization and promote the adoption of lively and effective methods like Play-way, Learning by doing, Learning by experience etc. These methods stimulate motivation, interest and attention.

*5. **Discipline.*** Old concept of discipline emphasized the use of rode and punishments to enforce obedience and discipline in children. This concept of enforced discipline through repression has now been given up. The modern concept is self-discipline leading to natural obedience.

*6. **Examination.*** The old method of essay type examination encouraged cramming and rote memorization. Modern techniques evaluate as well as examine. These include objective tests, progress reports, cumulative records, interviews and practical performances.

*7. **Agencies of education.*** According to old beliefs, school was the only agency for the education of children. According to modern views all formal and informal agencies are harnessed to the task of education.

*8. **Teacher.*** Old education put the teacher at the top of the educational process. In modern times a teacher is considered as a friend, philosopher and guide.

*9. **Child.*** According to old concept, the child was a mere passive recipient of whatever the teacher instructed. Modern education is child centred. The entire educational process is to cater to his needs and develop him according to his nature. He is to interact actively with the teacher and his class mates to achieve effective learning promoting his own development and the development of the society of which he is an integral part.

(10) School. According to old concept, school served as a shop for selling knowledge. Everything was pre-planned in advance. Teachers were concerned with the input and bothered little about output. Modern concept of education regards school as a miniature of society laying emphasis more on output in comparison with input.

(11) Education as a discipline. In ancient times, education meant only training of something for some aim. Modern education is a separate discipline of deep study, investigation, and research. It is a very important process of human development in all fields of human activities. It has its own distinct special features and factors to promote it as a vital formative process.

The following chart clarifies the modern concept of education:

Serial Number	*Aspects of Education*	*Old Concept of Education*	*Modern Concept of Education*
1.	Meaning	Instruction	Development
2.	Aims	Knowledge	(1) Development of total personality, (2) Social efficiency.
3.	Curriculum	Subject-centered	Activity-centered, social efficiency.
4.	Methods	Rote memorization	Learning by doing, project etc.
5.	Discipline	Rigid, repressionistic	Self-discipline.
6.	Examination	Essay type tests	Objective type tests, evaluation.
7.	Agencies	Formal (School)	Formal and informal both.
8.	Teacher	Instructor	Friend, philosopher and guide.
9.	Child	Passive recipient	Active, dynamic.
10.	School	Teaching shops	Miniature of society.

EDUCATION—A TRIPOLAR PROCESS

According to John Dewey, education is a tripolar process. It has three important ingredients:

(1) The teacher,

(2) The learner, and

(3) The curriculum.

1. The teacher. In ancient times, the teacher had the main role to pay while the leaner's role was subsidiary. In modern time, the role has been reversed. Though the place of teacher has now become secondary, yet his responsibility has increased because a teacher is not only an important factor in the educational environment of the learner, he is also a builder of the whole educational environment which is very comprehensive and all inclusive.

In the process of education, a teacher's role is two fold. Firstly, being the important factor of the educational environment, he influences the personality of the learner through his own magnetic personality. Secondly, as a builder of the educational environment, he provides suitable experiences to the learner to develop and use fully his skills and capacities to achieve the good of his ownself and the welfare of his society, of which he is an integral part.

Besides, by his own attitudes and behaviour, the teacher builds the character of learners and infuses in them respect for moral and spiritual values. This is only possible when the teacher is himself a man of strong moral character. He must be well aware of the modern strategies, tactics and techniques of teaching. He should be capable of using them to the best of his knowledge to make teaching learning most effective.

Thus, to develop the learner as well as the society, a teacher is a very important factor in the educational process of today.

2. The learner. According to psychological findings and democratic feeling, education starts from the child. Thus, education has become child-centred today.

Adams was the first educationist to point out this truth by his remark, "The teacher teaches Latin to John." John is more important than Latin. Modern educationists are unanimous about the importance of child in the educational process.

Education should develop the personality of the learner according to his interests, inclinations, abilities, and capacities.

Everything concerning education is now child-centred.

Aims, curriculum and methods keep the child at the centre of their formulation and planning of educational programmes. No teacher can be successful in his activities, if he fails to understand the learner with which he is to deal.

To make teaching-learning normal, natural and effective the teacher should not be the master of content only but also know fully well the stages of child development and their characteristics.

3. Curriculum. The essential link between the teacher and the child is the curriculum. It serves as a vehicle for the realization of educational aims. The teacher uses the items of curriculum according to modern methods of teaching to educate children to realize the predetermined aims of education. In the wider sense, curriculum means all the experiences and activities from which a child learns something or the other.

The teacher and the child both co-operate in building and formulating experiences conducive to learning. Curriculum is structured according to the ever growing needs of children and changing demands of dynamic society. This is the difference between the curriculum of despotic as well as democratic countries. In the former type, all activities are rigid, predetermined and fully controlled by the state, while in the latter pattern, there is flexibility, freedom and adjustment.

FORMS OF EDUCATION

Education is a comprehensive concept which comprehends the knowledge obtained through various other means, in addition to the formal education provided in colleges. The average individual interprets the term in the sense of college education, which is obviously different from the education obtained from the other sources. Educationists have distinguished between the various types of education in order to remove this confusion. Briefly, education is of the following kinds:

1. General education. As is evident from the name itself, general education is the minimal education required by an individual to satisfy all his various needs. It aims at developing the general qualities of the child, so that its personality can develop and it can become capable of adjusting to its environment.

It also enables him to earn his livelihood and to behave properly, in accordance with his age. It is generally believed that this general education continues upto the eighth class. All modern states make general education compulsory for all children, and in many cases it is provided free of charge.

2. Specific education. General education which is outlined above, is a supplement to specific education, which, as is evident trains the child to pursue some specific profession or job. The modern age is a period of specialization.

As long as an individual cannot perform some particular task better than any other person, he will find it difficult to make a place for himself in society. It is for this reason that nowadays individuals are given vocational guidance in order to help them to take up professions for which their abilities are best suited.

General education is more liberal while specific education is comparatively narrow. It is not so closely connected with the development of the person's general personality and character. This is the task of general education. Specific education is spread over a long period of time and is often centred in specialized institutions such as medical colleges, engineering colleges, technical institutes, etc.

In each case, the aim is to make the individual proficient in a particular skill, be it curing sick people, designing or repairing machines, growing crops or anything else. Besides, specific education is also often more expensive than general education.

Specific education, on the contrary, can be really profitable only if the individual possesses mental and physical qualities commensurate with that profession. Specific education plays a very important role in a nation's development because it provides specially trained personnel in every field who can serve society and enhance the welfare of the nation.

3. Formal education. In another classification, education is divided into the formal and the informal. The former comprehends education as it is provided in educational institutions according to a particular pattern. In the school, the educator educates the educands according to a specific programme aiming at particular goal. He follows a predetermined syllabus.

In this formal kind of education, the time and place of teaching are fixed, and the educand has to arrive at that place and at that specific time to receive education. The length of such education is also fixed in terms of years. Both the kinds of education mentioned earlier can be included under the formal classification because both are often provided in schools.

The advantages of the formal kind of education lie in that it can be specifically and consistently provided to a large number of children simultaneously. The objectives of this education are also determined beforehand. Although, of course, education in one form or the other continues as long as a person lives, education in its more common meaning starts at the age of four or five and continues to the age of twenty five. During this period the individual passes through a succession of institutions of primary, secondary and advanced education in the form of schools, colleges and universities.

At all these place of learning, he receives formal education, provided on a pattern determined by syllabus which is itself framed with a view to achieving certain fixed targets. The fact that it can be provided to a large number of people is an advantage but also a drawback.

Because of its completely of formal nature, formal education often fails to touch certain aspects of one's personality and leaves it completely undeveloped. At times, it can also become so detached from reality that it hinders rather than helps the educand in satisfying his needs.

This fact can be seen in the case of the contemporary pattern of formal education in India. It would not be inaccurate to state that, in India, the more formal education a person receives after a certain stage, the more useless he becomes in facing the problems of real life. His adjustment deteriorates instead of improving.

4. Informal education. Informal education complements the formal education outlined above, without which formal education remains incomplete. Education of this kind has no specific time or place at which it is provided. Even the educator is not fixed. All fixed syllabi, rules, formalities are absent from it.

Education of this kind is the education one receives while

playing in field, talking to family members in the house, roaming around somewhere, in fact, everywhere. This kind of education never comes to an end, and it teaches the individual more than he can ever learn through his formal education.

A child learns many things when he comes in contact with new people. He discovers many new worlds when he goes to new places. This education that he receives cannot be evaluated as formal education can.

Formal education can be evaluated by some specific techniques, and the quality and quantity of education imbibed by the educand can be known. But this is not true of informal education for there is no standard of measure in its case. It also does not provide the recipient with a certificate or a degree.

Informal education is a gradual process, for people learn a few things after years of experience. But the things learnt in this manner prove to be more valuable than all the degrees accumulated through formal education. Formal education provides education on specific subjects while informal education is more general in nature.

5. Direct education. In another classification, education is divided into the direct and indirect classes. Direct education is the equivalent of formal education and specific education. In its form of education, the educator and the educand are in direct contact whence education on a specific subject is disseminated.

Its chief advantage lies in the material learnt by the educand more by the example of the educator's personality and character than by the formal material he seeks to impart. It is for this reason that direct education was very much in vogue in India in the past. The student lived with the teacher and learnt various skills and sciences.

Direct education becomes difficult when the number of students becomes very large, or education itself becomes very mechanical and purely vocational. It then loses the advantages of the direct contact between the educator and the educand.

If the pattern of direct education is to be maintained, then the number of teachers must be very large, for one teacher can establish rapport only with a small number of educands. Once the value of direct education was realized, educationists stressed the importance of limiting the size of a class.

6. Indirect education. Direct education was efficacious and practicable in the past when the population was not too large and life had not become as complex as it is today. With the present increase in population, it is no longer possible to provide direct education to all the people. In the past, this kind of education was popular also because of the comparative primitive forms of communication. Such modern developments as the printing press, radio, television, etc., have made it possible to communicate the ideas of the greatest thinkers to those people who have never come into direct contact with the thinkers themselves. For this reason, in the present context, indirect education has come to acquire greater significance than direct education.

Many universities have undertaken to conduct correspondence courses, which are a fine example of indirect education. In this form of education, the subject of a lecture is printed and posted to the student. The student is required to answer certain questions sent along with the lecture. These answers are sent by him to the university where they are evaluated and returned to the student with the appropriate guidance. As this kind of indirect education offers a better and more practical adjustment to the circumstances of a very large number of individuals, it is becoming increasingly popular, particularly in the west.

All the books that are written by the greatest thinkers and read by a vast audience are an excellent example of its indirect education. It cannot be denied that irrespective of the abilities of the educator, he cannot provide complete education to the educator, he cannot provide complete education to the educand without turning to books for assistance.

For this reason the scope and field of indirect education is increasing steadily. In the last few years, teaching through the medium of radio and television is becoming more popular and reaching a higher level of sophistication. In India, the All India Radio regularly broadcasts lectures and programmes on musical education, cultural education and the like. By this many millions of individuals gain some kind of education.

7. Individual education. Education is also classified into the individual and the collective groups. Many of the modern educational psychologists have stressed the importance of individual difference between people and suggested that the educator should pay individual attention to each educand, remove his difficulties and, if necessary, modify the syllabi and teaching programme to suit the specific abilities and traits of the educand.

Scientifically considered, this advice is very good, and if arrangements can be made to provide individual education at this level, nothing could be better. Kindergarten, Montessori and Project methods, all of which are modern methods of child education, attempt to provide the highest degree of individual attention possible.

But where education is to be provided to a very large number of individuals, the most expensive kind of education yet devised since one educator can pay attention to the specific needs of only a very small number of students. The experiment conducted by Rabindra Nath succeeded as an experiment, but if it is accepted as a pattern for large scale education, it would be completely impractical. That is why arrangements are made for collective education, although the value of individual education can be clearly visualized.

8. Collective education. Collective education is provided to a group of individuals collected at one place. Formal education is often also collective education. Keeping in mind the obvious advantages of individual education, efforts are made to restrict the size of the group of educands. The very meaning of education would be lost if the educator lost all contact with the educands, if they are in too large a number.

This form of education is comparatively economical of time and money because one single educator can teach a large number of educands. In view of the present size of the population, and the possibilities of its growing further, collective education is the only practicable answer to the need for universal education.

9. Conscious education. Education is also divided into the conscious and the unconscious kind. The conscious kind of education is the education which is provided with a full knowledge of the objectives to be achieved through it. College education is of this kind. It is intended to fulfil certain pre-determined objectives. Conscious education is arranged for the child by his parents and by the state, but the child deliberately receives conscious education.

10. Unconscious education. An individual does not learn all the things he actually knows consciously. Many of the important facts that a child learns are absorbed unconsciously from his natural and social environment which surrounds him. This kind of education is informal and since it supplements the education received consciously, neither can be said to be more or less important than the other.

Of the various classifications listed above, the division into the formal and informal classes is the most common. All the other classifications are based on some specific approaches to education, although most of them resemble each other. For example, formal education is also collective education.

This classification of education into different kinds has been made by different educationists according to their individual standpoint. A study of each one of these can help to throw much light on the vast field of education and on the various aspects of it. In every classification, both the kinds described, supplement each other because the process of education is many sided and synthesizing. It takes place at all times and places, but it does not remain the same in every circumstance. It has a multiplicity of forms, means, quantity and quality. It is imbibed both consciously and unconsciously by the individual.

NON-FORMAL EDUCATION

In July, 1979, the Central Board of Secondary Education, New Delhi started the Open School—the first of its kind in the country. It is an institution set up to bring the flexibility and openness in the educational system and to extend educational opportunities to the weaker and disadvantaged sections of the society. The main objectives of the Open School are the following:

1. To offer a parallel non-formal system as an alternative to a formal schooling.
2. To provide the opportunity of education to out-of-school learners, school drop-outs, working adults, housewives and learners from disadvantaged section of society living in remote areas of the country.
3. To offer bridge/preparatory courses for enabling learners to take up secondary level courses.
4. To offer Secondary, Senior Secondary, Technical,

Vocational and Life-enrichment courses through distance teaching methods.

5. To promote an open distance-learning system of education through research, publication and information dissemination.

This is an example of non-formal education.

Non-formal education is an arrangement wherein flexibility is the key-word. Such a system is an open one with regards to various aspects of education, *i.e.,* admissions, curriculum, place of instruction, mode of instruction and the time and duration of instruction. Various examples of such a system are the Open School and Open University, Open Learning and the Correspondence Courses.

Definitions of Non-Formal Education

Non-formal education includes adult education, continuing education and on the job education, etc. Philip Coombs talked about it in 1968. However, until 1970 it had not been defined. Non-formal education is a new concept for an ancient phenomenon. Some of its definitions are as follows:

1. Coombs and Ahmed (1974). "Any organized, systematic, educational activity carried on outside the framework of the formal system to provide selected types of learning to particular sub-groups in the population, adults as well as children."

2. La Bella (1975). Non-formal education refers to "organized out-of-school educational programmes designed to provide specific target population."

3. Illich and Freire. "Non-formal education is anti-formal education."

4. Moti Lal Sharma. "In brief, one could say that non-formal education is an active, critical dialectical educational programme which aims at helping people to learn, to help themselves, to place them in consciously critical confrontation with their problems. To develop integrated authentic human beings who can contribute to the development of the society is the aim of Non-formal education. In this not only the individuals but also the total social system learns, adding up to a true learning society."

Non-formal education is the "missing ingredient" in accelerated social and economic development schemes that do not work. Therefore, it has its own valid claim to reality. It is deliberate, planned, staffed, financially supported life formal education. It is functional, unrestricted as to time and place and in general responsive to needs like informal education. It is much more responsive to needs and change.

Thus, it is more effective tool for rural development. It unlocks the doors of development plans. According to Malcolm A. Adiseshiah, "Non-formal education should be marketable and vocationalised. It should lay emphasis on the self-learning pattern." According to H.S.S. Lawrence, "Non-formal education system was not rival to the formal educational system but it was complementary to the latter. The common ingredients in both should be identified and an integrated system evolved."

Non-Formal Education and Adult Education

Explaining the difference between non-formal and adult education, writes Anil Bordia, "The New Non-Formal Education Plan differs from previous adult education programmes, in that it provides for adequate administrative and resource support and emphasizes need-based curricula and teaching and learning materials; but it is unique in emphasizing evaluation at all stages on a continuing basis. All training programmes and teaching and learning materials are to be pre-tested and also subjected to impact studies."

Nature of Non-Formal Education

After the World War II, in the post colonial period new nations, one after another, scrambled for expanded and improved formal education. By the late sixties, there was a growing uneasiness that expansion in the facilities in formal education was not the whole answer. The traditional two-fold categorisation of education into formal and informal education leaves a big gap.

Studies by Philip Coombs and other revealed that as societies developed a third kind of education emerged which could be labelled as non-formal education. This non-formal education accounts for much of the highly functional, development and short-term related needs of a rapidly changing society.

Advantages of Non-Formal Education

To sum up, non-formal education is needed on account of the following advantages:

1. Universalisation or primary education.
2. Eradication of adult literacy.
3. Meeting the omissions of formal education.
4. Meeting the enormous and imperative challenges of democratic set up.
5. Enabling the pupils to learn and earn.
6. Enabling those students to study who had to discontinue formal education owing to pecuniary and other circumstances.
7. Enabling the students in geographically remote areas to get education because the formal education can not be within their easy reach.
8. Enabling individuals to refresh and update their knowledge.
9. Rectifying the educational imbalance between those who live in villages and those who live in towns.
10. Providing educational facilities to social and economically neglected sectors of society.

Objectives of Non-Formal Education

Following are the three sets of objectives of non-formal education:

(i) The immediate objective is the removal of illiteracy.

(ii) The middle-range objective is the application of 'new' knowledge to resolve economic, cultural and social problems.

(iii) The long-range objective is to provide for life-long education.

Types of Non-Formal Education Programmes

1. Adult Functional Literacy Programmes
2. Correspondence Courses
3. Open School Studies
4. Satellite Instructional Television Programme
5. Programme for drop-outs in the age group 6-14.

Persons' Benefits by Non-Formal Education

Non-formal education is particularly useful for the following categories of persons.

1. People of all ages. Those who never had the opportunity to follow any formal education programme.

2. Students. Those who are not in position to complete primary, middle or secondary school.

3. Learners. Learners of different stages of education who feel the need for deeper and more comprehensive knowledge in a subject of particular interest.

4. Labourers. Both in urban and rural areas young workers, small farmers, landless labourers, small entrepreneurs, etc., who need up-to-date knowledge related to their jobs particularly related to latest technological improvements.

5. Educated unemployed. Unemployed educated persons of various age groups whose no-relevant education needs to be made more relevant in order to increase their chances of employment.

6. Graduates, professionals, intellectuals. Those who need a refreshment or orientation to make themselves up-to-date in their knowledge.

7. Other persons. Those who require programmes for personal satisfaction like recreation, leisure time activities, cultural or artistic programmes, etc.

Agencies of Non-Formal Education

The various agencies for organising programmes for non-formal education are as follow:

1. Institutions for formal education.
2. Special agencies for non-formal education such as Nehru Yuvak Kendras, training centres in factories, public libraries, centres of correspondence education, etc.
3. Voluntary non-governmental organization like club and societies.
4. Radio and television.

Non-formal education is one of the modes of education, others are formal and informal. Therefore, non-formal education ought to be perceived and designed in coordination with formal and informal systems. It will prove an insufficient and an ineffective mechanism for solving the complex problems or for achieving concrete goals, if organised in isolation.

Again, it must not be limited to the imparting of basic skills only. It must be designed as an integrated systems in the context of the total socio-economic environment. To make it effective in modern societal context, a more integrated community based programme of innovation and change is needed to which various forms of education may contribute. This requires filling the gaps between the learning systems and the community needs.

Formal v/s Non-Formal Education

Formal Education	*Non-formal Education*
1. Limited to a period of being taught.	1. Life-long and not limited to any period of being taught.
2. Generally not integrated with work.	2. Integrated with work.
3. Has fixed points of entry and exit.	3. Has flexible points of entry, exit re-entry and re-exit. In fact, it continues throughout the life-span of the individual.
4. Has fixed curriculum.	4. Has a diversified and varied curriculum.
5. In it the 'giver' dominates and the 'receiver' is rather passive.	5. A process of sharing, exploring, analysing and judging together.
6. Geared to knowledge acquisition.	6. A process of enabling the individual understand his needs, the environmental situation and mutual relationships.
7. Fosters an uncritical obedience.	7. An open-end process of education which develops self-reliant awareness.
8. Works within a fixed social change.	8. Anticipates and prepares for change.
9. Associated with traditional schooling—schooling confined to a school or a college, etc.	9. Not confined to any educational set-up.
10. Rigid with regard to various aspects of education, *i.e.*, admissions, curriculum, place of instruction, mode of instruction, the time and duration of instruction.	10. Very flexible in regard to various aspects of education.

One should try to avert the danger of education being isolated from the subject matter of life experience. Hence, one of the weightiest problems with which the philosophy of education has to cope with is the method of keeping a proper balance between the informal, the formal and non-formal, the incidental and the international modes of education. It may be remembered that one should try to incorporate the virtues of informal education as far as he can and also to keep away the dangers of too much formal education.

QUESTIONS FOR ANSWER

1. Define education and explain its scope.
2. Differentiate between instruction and education.
3. Explain the various aspects of education according to modern concept of education.
4. "Education has been defined and interpreted in many ways, but these definitions are mostly complementary rather than contradictory." Explain this statement with suitable examples.
5. Write a short note on 'Forms of Education'.
6. *(a)* Describe the meaning of formal education.
   (b) Describe the meaning of informal education.
   (c) Describe the meaning of non-formal education.
7. Define education as a process and a system and explain why it is necessary to educate the human being?
8. What do you mean by education? Differentiate between under and narrower meaning of education.
9. What do you understand by formal, non-formal and informal education? Explain their differences.
10. "Education is the process of Human Resources Development." Discuss this statement in the light of nature and scope of education.
11. "A system of education is a response to the changing needs of the society it serves." Critically discuss the above statement, giving examples.

2

Educational Values

Personal and social values are attempted to be gained through education and these values are termed as educational values which are considered vital in opting for an educational aim and formulating the curriculum. Here we discuss 'Educational Values' very briefly.

MEANING OF EDUCATIONAL VALUES

Educational values are related to those activities which are good, useful and valuable from the point of view of education and has already been pointed out that according to Adams, it is a bipolar process which has two parts— (1) the teacher, and (2) the child.

The teacher, in order to mould and modify the behaviour of the child employs various strategies and tactics to achieve the desired behavioural change in the child. He performs all these activities, because he thinks them as valuable for the purpose in view. As the teacher provides an environment of utility and value to the child, in the same manner, the child participates only in those activities which he considers useful and valuable to him.

Thus, the teacher and the child participate only in those activities which they consider as educationally useful and valuable. According to Cunningham educational values become aims of education.

According to these qualities, abilities and capacities are

promoted in the individuals, which are inherently values of life. Brubacher speaks out this as— "To state one's aim of education is at once to state his educational values."

VIEWS ABOUT EDUCATIONAL VALUES

There are two views about educational values. They are: (1) Have these values an independent existence, and (2) Are these values dependent upon the individual who does evaluation. The nature of these are of two kinds as under:

(1) Internal and subjective.

(2) External and objective.

1. Internal and subjective. Some educationists are of opinion that values depend upon personal ideas and experiences. In other words, a value is born out of a mind's power of imagination. They hold that those things are of any use to human beings which have values inherent in them. Things are of no use which have no value.

Hence, educational values are internal and subjective. According to these educationists, curriculum construction, selection of educational aids, strategies and tactics all depend upon the teacher and the child. They determine their values according to their utility.

2. External and objective. Some educationists firmly hold that values are inherent in objects and activities in accordance with their qualities and attributes. According to their view, the social environment influences the quality or the value of an object. In other words, it is the social environment which assigns any value to an object.

Hence, each social value according to environment enters an objects and becomes a part of it. These educationists do not regard a value as something internal and subjective, but assert that it is external and objective.

According to them, curriculum construction, selection of strategies, tactics and teaching aids are all used with relevance to the social environment in which the teacher as well as the child live.

The above discussion makes it clear that some educationists hold values as internal and subjective whereas others believe that they are external and objective. It should be borne in mind that either of them are one-sided and reveal only one side of truth.

The first group of educationists neglects the external social environment and the other remains indifferent to the interests inclinations, aptitudes and capacities of the child. In fact, the internal and external social environment and the other remains indifferent to the interests inclinations, aptitudes and capacities of the child. In fact, the internal and external values are essential for an effective and wholesome process of education.

Thus, educational values should be created keeping into consideration the nature of the child together with the nature of the objects and activities. In short, an educational value is created out of a synthesis of both—the subjectivity and the objectivity.

KINDS OF EDUCATIONAL VALUES

About educational values Urban, McDougall, Brubacher and other educationists have expressed different views of which those of Brubacher need mention. In his book 'Modern Philosophies of Education' he has divided educational values into two categories as under:

1. Related to likes or immediate.
2. Related to intelligent likes or remote.

1. Related to likes or immediate values. These values are those which fulfil the biological and psychological needs of children. Only immediate objects satisfy these values. The remote ones have no relevance. For example, a child, having an interest and liking for fine arts, shall be able to satisfy his artistic taste by practising artistic activities only. In short, these values are related to immediate needs and their fulfilment to achieve immediate self-satisfaction.

2. Related to intelligent likes or remote values. These values are closely related to intelligent and rational needs. It is a matter of common experience that each programme of school satisfies the diverse needs of teachers and children, but of these needs, only some are important. It is also a fact that all these needs are not likely to be satisfied.

Thus, each individual has to make an intelligent selection out of all these needs and try to achieve maximum advantage from all the activities of the school. Hence, these values are related to intelligently selected likes and needs. These values can be divided further into two categories as under:

(i) Instrumental values

(ii) Intrinsic values

(i) Instrumental values. In the words of Brubacher, "Instrumental values are values that are judged good, because they are good for something." These values are useful in themselves and they are also instrumental in realizing some other values. For example, if a child wants to become a noted musician, knowledge of 'Tal' and 'Swar' will be useful to him to realise his chief objective.

This knowledge of 'Swar' and 'Tal' is an instrumental value for some higher values. These instrumental values are subjective and change according to change in circumstances. Thus, instrumental values are of no use in other vocations and professions.

(ii) Intrinsic values. Again in the words of Brubacher, "Intrinsic values are values, which are judged good, not for something else, but in and of themselves." These values are complete in themselves and are not dependent upon any thing external. For example, furniture of a class is useful to the teaching process. Hence, furniture has a value in itself. It may be borne in mind that intrinsic values are not subjective but objective in nature.

In the above lines, we have discussed the instrumental and intrinsic values with examples. Still there are many objects which are valuable from the point of view of both the categories.

Aesthetic values. Values which give us pleasure and happiness are known as aesthetic values. Some educationists delimit these values upto the domain of fine arts only. Other educationists of the day hold that pleasure and happiness may be derived from other subjects of the curriculum also besides fine arts.

It should be borne in mind that aesthetic experiences are vitally composed of feelings of heart as well as mind. Hence, teacher should strive to familiarize children with various curricular as well as co-curricular activities to develop the aesthetic values more and more.

HIERARCHY OF EDUCATIONAL VALUES

As discussed above, J.S. Brubacher has divided values into two categories *viz.*, (1) Related to likes or immediate, and (2) Related to intelligent likes or remote. Most of the educatonists regard the intelligent likes or remote values as of higher nature than the immediate ones. Even in the latter category, they hold intrinsic value as of greater importance than the instrumental values. This is because instrumental values are subjective conditioned by time and place while intrinsic values are universal, relatively permanent and objective.

Be it noted that there are some educationists, mostly materialists, who rate instrumental values higher than the intrinsic values.

This controversy poses a problem in curriculum construction as whether subjects related to instrumental values should be assigned any place above or below or near the subjects connected with intrinsic values. As a matter of fact, both kind of values are interrelated, mutually complimentary, supplementary and are essential for the progressive growth and development of children.

Hence, hierarchy of educational values is not of great significance. For a wholesome and proper development of children, all values are essential inspite of the undoubted greater significance of intrinsic values.

EDUCATIONAL VALUES ARE THE DETERMINENTS OF EDUCATIONAL AIMS

Educational aims are determined by educational values. As are the values, so shall be the aims of education. In other words, educational values take the form of educational aims.

In this process of transformation, we have to depend upon some bases which according to J.S. Brubacher are as under:

(1) Historical Analysis
(2) Scientific Analysis of Current Life
(3) Activity Analysis of Child and Adults
(4) Psychological Analysis of Human Nature
(5) Job Analysis
(6) Personal Opinion
(7) General Opinion
(8) Philosopher's Opinion.

Out of all the above bases, philosopher's opinion is regarded as the most important base for the determination of educational aims. This is because all the other bases are conditioned by time, place, circumstances and situations while the views of philosophers are relatively permanent for all times and places and in addition, can point out towards directions of reform and modification of the prevalent aims.

But there is a controversy overhere also as different philosophers emphasize different values. Some think intrinsic values higher to instrument values and others *vice versa*. But inspite of these differences in approach and view points, one thing is of utmost importance, that educational aims depend on and are based upon educational values.

Educationists have divided these aims into two categories as under:

1. General and ultimate aims.
2. Specific and related aims.

1. General and ultimate aims. The formation of general and ultimate aims of education is done on the basis of natural and intrinsic values of life. For example, if the aim of education is self-realization, then the first step towards its attainment will be to understand the nature of the child and after correct scrutiny try to know well his basic tendencies, capacities and abilities.

After this, educational activities and programmes should be so organized that the basic capacities and abilities are developed to the fullest extent and the child is able to realize his self completely. In short, ultimate aims are determined on the natural and essential basis of intrinsic values.

2. Specific and related aims. Specific or immediate aims of education are determined on the basis of instrumental values. Though the general and ultimate aims of education possess an all pervading importance, yet the teacher should try to break up a general aim into subsidiary aims which are quite specific, clear and definite.

This will make the educational process very effective and purposeful. For example, according to Herbart Spencer, the ultimate aim of education is—"Complete Living." He has divided this broad aim into five specific categories and has assigned appropriate activities to each category. In the same way, to realize this aim of 'Complete Living'.

The National Education Association of America has divided this aim into seven specific aims of education in the following manner:

(i) Health
(ii) Command of Fundamental Processes notably the three R's
(iii) Worthy Home Membership
(iv) Vocation
(v) Civic Functions
(vi) Worthy use of Leisure Time
(vii) Ethical Character.

The above discussion clearly points out that the ultimate aim of education is 'Self-realization'. All the subsidiary specific aims contribute towards its realization to the fullest possible extent.

In the words of J.S. Brubacher, "Aims, there must be tailor made for the occasion. We can not publish a list of them in advance... Hence, there are no educational aims which are unalterably or eternally."

QUESTIONS FOR ANSWER

1. What do you understand by the phrase 'Educational values'? Write a note on the kinds of educational values.
2. Educational aims are determined by educational values. Discuss with examples.
3. Write short notes on:
   (a) Hierarchy of educational values.
   (b) Specific and related aims of education.

3

Educational Aims, Functions and Priorities

The knowledge of educational aims, functions and priorities will enable the educands to understand how these elements have their foundations in sociology, to be discussed in part two of this book.

INTRODUCTION

The aims of education are determined by human life. Putting it differently, the aims of education are formulated after deciding the kind of life we want human beings to lead. In addition to this, the aims of education are also determined by the kind of life human beings live. It can, thus, be said that the aims of education are based upon human nature.

Any system of education which seeks to fulfil its aims must provide for the development of all these aspects. In view of the complex social and economic structure of human society, every adult human being is faced with the necessity of earning his bread and of fulfilling his various needs. In view of this permanent necessity of human life, one of the aims of education has always been to equip the individual to earn his livelihood.

Man has to fight with nature to ensure his own existence, and in this process he needs his physical abilities and powers. For this reason, children are taught to maintain their health not only in civilized societies but even in the most primitive ones.

Education is also made to conform to the changing environment of a particular social group so that its later generations may be able to adjust better. For this reason, one finds distinct differences in the pattern of education in societies living near the coast and societies living inland.

HUMAN LIFE AND EDUCATIONAL AIMS

Human beings always live in groups because they cannot fulfil many of their needs alone. Without a family group, a human child cannot be born and neither can it survive. Social life of some kind is essential for everyone. Social life is based upon the fulfilment of certain duties and obligations and upon facing certain responsibilities. Hence, one of the most common objectives of education is to train the individual to lead a fruitful social life.

One finds some form of political organisation in civilized as well as in primitive societies. These serve to control and to systematize the life of individuals. Most political systems aim at the greatest good of the greatest number and it is considered essential that individuals should obey the rules of the state and be aware of their responsibilities towards it.

Most of the modern political states have taken the responsibility of education upon themselves. For this reason, the state plays a prominent part in the individual's life, and training an individual to become a responsible citizen is one of the aims of education.

It is evident from the above description that the aims of education are intimately connected with human life. Following points can be made in this connection.

1. Livelihood. As has been already pointed out, livelihood is essential for human life everywhere. Hence, one of the main aims of education is to train men and women according to their abilities so that they can earn their own livelihood.

2. Development of personality. A balanced development of personality is essential for the individual's private and social life, for without this he can neither satisfy all his needs nor lead a successful life. Consequently, all modern educationists unanimously agree that education must aim at the complete development of human personality.

3. Intellectual development. Man is distinct among all living beings because of his intelligence. It is on the basis of his intelligence that he has become superior to all other forms of life. Through his intelligence, he developed the sciences and by using them has gained mastery over nature. It will, therefore, be quite in order to state that all his future progress depends to an extent upon his intellectual development.

4. Physical development. In the struggle for survival, man needs a healthy and strong body, for without it, he cannot either live or satisfy his requirements. Hence, education must also aim at developing the individual's body.

5. Moral development. Ethical and moral values are considered the most important in human life. Character is the most valuable thing an individual can possess. Success, in human life in every sphere, be it the family, the neighbourhood, society at large depends very much upon the possession of moral qualities and upon obedience of moral laws. The importance of moral values is even more evident in the modern world since the unprecedented improvement in the means of transport and communications and the remarkable power of destruction possessed by modern weapons.

In the absence of ethical values there would be little to prevent the world from being destroyed in catastrophic wars. For this reason, moral and ethical development has also become an important object of education.

6. Aesthetic development. As other living beings are, man is not satisfied merely by maintaining his existence. He seeks to raise his life above the level of survival, and the things he needs for his requirements must not only be useful but also be attractive and aesthetically satisfying.

Cultural development includes development of sensibilities, awareness of the aesthetically satisfying in art and literature. Education also seeks to develop the aesthetic sensibility.

7. Social development. Most of man's life is spent in a social environment, and in order to accommodate to this environment, the individual requires many social qualities. Education tries to develop these social qualities to facilitate the child's social adjustments.

8. Cultural development. When human beings are to be distinguished from other living beings, they are said to be cultured. Culture is man's prerogative, since it is not found among other animals. It is culture which maintains a man's relationship with the succeeding generations. He gets it as his social heritage and passes it on. Cultural development is also an important aspect of education.

9. Spiritual development. Another distinctive feature of human life is the presence of the spiritual element. It is for this reason that Indian religious texts state that human life is granted to the soul after it has lived the life of other living beings. Man's superiority is, thus, the result of his spirituality.

He is not merely a more efficient animal. He even seeks to identify himself with the divine power. His future depends to a large extent upon this spiritual development. Thus, spiritual development is also accepted as one of the aims of human education. Religious education is introduced solely for this purpose.

10. Total development. Man is a complex being, made up of such physiological parts as the motor organ, sense organs, nervous system, etc., such processes as intelligence, emotions, feelings, etc., the social, cultural and other aspects of personality.

In view of this complexity, it is believed that education must seek to develop every aspect of the human individual. He is trained to make the best use of his body. Efforts are made to develop his intellectual, moral, aesthetic, social and cultural aspects. Some people believe that this is the ideal of human perfection.

11. Training for civic life. It has already been explained that, in civilized societies, human life is identical with social life. Hence, education seeks to train the individual to live as a citizen and to fulfil all his obligations to society.

12. Training in international living. The individual of today is not restricted in his movement by the boundaries of his country. In the West, in particular, people commonly move from one country to another. It is now commonly felt that if man is to rise above his present level, he must be prepared to discard his narrow nationalistic leanings and adopt more universal or international attitude.

THE AIMS OF EDUCATION AND SOCIAL IDEALS AND LIFE

A single glance at the history of education in any country will reveal that the aims of education have invariably gone hand in hand with the aims and ideals of social life. One can take the case of education in India. In ancient times, the Aryans believed that the objective of human life was to lead a prosperous and varied life in a natural environment and to aim at total development. In the Upanishadic period, salvation was believed to be the ideal of life and hence it was felt that anything which led to salvation was educative.

Thus, spiritual development was the objective of education in ancient India because it was also the social ideal of the time. Clarifying the aims of Vedic education, Altekar has commented that the aims of Vedic education were workshop of God and a feeling of religiosity, building of character, development of personality, training in the fulfilment of civic and social duties, improvement in social skills, the protection and further propagation of national culture.

During the Buddha period, Gautama Buddha established a new set of religious ideals which differed from the Brahman ideals. He placed the greatest emphasis upon religion, and consequently one of the main aims of education in the Buddhist monasteries was religious training. In other educational institutions, the students were also given training in other skills necessary for life.

Buddhist education was more practical and useful than Brahmanic teaching but it did not include military training. Education was open to men and women both. It was imparted by the Buddhist monks, whose only aim was to spread their own religion.

During the Muslim period as well as British period, the social ideals and mode of life in the country underwent considerable change due to rulers influence.

After India had won independence, the pattern of society and its ideals underwent another change. Education no longer aimed at the propagation of a particular religion or at strengthening the roots of a foreign administration.

The establishment of democracy helped to import democratic

ideals into education also. Education was given the aim of achieving the all round development of the nation. It, therefore sought to provide education in the art and sciences, business and commerce, law and medicine, in fact, in every sphere of activity calculated to promote the nation's interests.

Education at all levels, primary, intermediate and college levels, was reconsidered and reframed in order to help in achieving the national goal. It was oriented to the needs of the nation. Various committees were set up to examine the pattern of education and to redefine its aims and objectives in the light of the new aims of the society and the nation.

All the notable educationists—Sri Aurobindo, Mahatma Gandhi, Rabindranath, Vivekanada, Radha Krishnan, Dayananda, and others—suggested the need for a comprehensive education based upon human psychology.

Education in India, today represents a synthesis between utility and idealism, keeping in view the need and aims of modern India. The present pattern of education allows the presence of various kinds of syllabi. It stresses the importance of national values, and aims of a synthesis between the individual and the social good.

The casual survey of the history of education in India is adequate to illustrate that the "ideals of education are linked with the social ideals", and hence, they change when the social ideals change.

In the modern era, it is the political organisation which determines the pattern of social life. Life and social ideals under communist government differ from those under democratic or despotic governments. J.F. Brown astutely remarks, "Education in any country and at all periods reflects values of the ruling class."

It cannot be denied that, at times, educationists have raised their voice against educational patterns set down by the state, but all such efforts have been futile until the social ideals themselves have changed and accommodated the ideas of the rebels. Irrespective of the form of the government, it is the state which lays down the objectives of education. One main reason for this is that, in any case, the state exercises considerable control over education in most countries.

In fact, without such control and governmental assistance,

it would be impossible to provide all kinds of education. This is true of India also. Here, too, the objectives of primary, intermediate and university education have been determined by committees formed and empowered by the state. Education in America, for example, is oriented towards propagation of the democratic ideal while education in China aims to spread the communist concepts.

Democratic education teaches the individual to prepare for democratic citizenship while education under communist or dictatorial regimes is concerned primarily with instilling in the individual a healthy respect and obedience to the rules and mandates of the government.

It is clear from the foregoing discussion that social life and ideals influence educational objectives to a very great extent. This subject will now be subjected to more detailed analysis—effect of social life on the aims of education, and effect of social ideals on the aims of education.

(a) Social life and the aims of education. In the history of human civilization, one can see considerable changes in the pattern and form of social life, as new attitudes and scientific and technological developments made their impact. Social life today is so different from the primitive social life because of technology. As a consequence, one of the aims recently given to education, in most civilized countries, is to provide technical and professional training.

In addition to the technological developments, economic changes have also influenced social life considerably. Industrialization and urbanization have influenced economic change. Increase in population have only added to the complexity of economic problems.

The democratic values of equality, fraternity and liberty are now part of social life in almost every country of the world. The social instinct of most people refuses to discriminate between one person and another on the basis of caste, class, creed, community, and sex, etc.

Everyone wants freedom and demands an equal share of the opportunities in every sphere of life. It has been experienced everywhere that true liberty and equality are impossible without spreading the feeling of fraternity. Consequently, one of the chief responsibilities of modern education is to generate a character when will help the educand to become a useful member of a democratic society.

(b) Relation between social ideals and the aims of education. In any country the social ideals are determined by the form of government and the ideas of its great individuals. In modern India, social ideals have been formed by the ideas of such great individuals as Aurobindo, Vivekananda, Rabindranath, Mahatama Gandhi, Dayananda, on the one hand, and by the suggestion of various government committees on the other.

Much the same can be seen in the care of the civilized countries as England, America, Germany, France, etc. The objectives of education are formulated by the ideas of leading thinkers and the plans of the government.

The influence of social ideals can also be seen in the form of the prevailing social philosophy. This social philosophy is seen in the form of materialism, utilitarianism, idealism, fascism, communism, democracy, and other philosophical attitudes. These social philosophies influence and change the ideals of education. This is as follows:

1. Idealism. In idealistic societies, of which one example is ancient Indian Vedic society, the greatest emphasis is laid upon the propagation of religious, moral and spiritual ideals. In this case, the more permanent objectives are considered more important than the more immediate ones. Efforts are made to achieve a complete development of the human personality, and also to create the best possible synthesis between the basic elements of the individual and the society. Most of this objectives of the kind of the education tend to be universal.

2. Realism. The philosophy of realism suggests that in determining the objectives of education, the immediate needs of society should be kept in view. The attitude encourages technological, economic and scientific education which can help in the material development of the nation.

3. Materialism. A society accepts the materialistic philosophy sets no store by moral, religious or spiritual values. Consequently, education is fashioned to achieved the physical and mental development of the individual.

4. Pragmatism. Pragmatic thinking encourages a pattern of education in which every individual gets the opportunity to develop all his abilities and capabilities to their fullest extent.

5. Fascism. Fascism accepts the complete authority of the state, and argue that the state is the end, and the individual only the means to that end. Consequently, education is designed to train the individual merely to serve as the instrument of the state. In this case, he is taught to work in the interests of the state and to be prepared for the greatest sacrifices he is called upon to perform.

6. Communism. Communist societies normally stress the value of the realistic aims of education. Communist thinking is primarily materialistic in its value orientation, with the result that idealistic objectives are considered unimportant. Labour is accorded the greatest importance.

The aim of education is concerned with labour from every aspect: the economic, political, social and even aesthetic. Educational institutions are mere instruments of state policy. The ideas of the state are propagated among the educands everywhere, and no one has the liberty to oppose or to criticise them. Consequently, the objective of education is to propound communist ideals to the educands.

7. Democracy. One example of a democratic society is the modern American society. The two fundamental principles of democracy are that the individual is an end in himself and that he should comport himself in such a way that his conduct promotes the welfare of all.

Liberty, equality and fraternity are the ideals of democracy. Such a society allows the greatest possible freedom to its members and tries to provide equal opportunities to all. The aim of democratic society is the maximum good of the maximum number. Consequently, education has the following objectives in a democratic society:

(i) Creating respect for human personality in the new generation.

(ii) Assisting the students to obtain control over the means of education and, according to the time and ability available, to gain control over the greatest possible extent of social heritage.

(iii) Helping the student to pay attention to general welfare and to learn the difficult art of self-development.

(iv) Developing in each individual is the ability to think in terms of the established categories of truth.

(v) Assisting the students in understanding the nature of democracy and in aiming at the progress of society as the goal of life.

It is thus seen, that educational objectives in a democratic society are framed to assist in the spread of democratic ideals. India is a democratic republic. Here, also, education aims at instilling the ideal of democratic life in the educands at every stage of education.

From the foregoing account of the various forms of social life and social ideals, and the objectives of education conforming to each one of them, it is evident that the aims of education are not permanent but changeable. Hence, it follows that if we want to create a particular pattern of social life and social ideals in a society, it is necessary that the educational pattern should conform to that kind of social life.

VOCATIONAL AIM OF EDUCATION

Dewey, an American educationist, has commented that education is meaningful only when it aims at some vocation or employment. In the present age, some kind of educational qualification is essential for almost every job. As a result, very extensive educational qualification becomes necessary for good jobs which carry big salaries. Economic independence is essential in the present day world, and for this reason parents are determined to educate their children so that they can become economically independent.

It is clear from the above description that the vocational objective of education is an important aspect of it, and it has the following advantages:

1. Solution of economic problems. India is today facing such grave problems as unemployment, poverty, famine, etc. Our economic problems are our greatest difficulties. On the other hand, most of the Western and Asian nations accept the vocational aspect of education, and it is seen that these nations are self-dependent and prosperous. They enjoy great respect and power in the world. Hence, technical and vocational training is of the greatest importance, since only such training can help to solve the economic problems of any country.

2. Dynamism. The principle of activity applies to the

vocational aim of education. Dewey has commented that education imported in this way makes use of the child's tendencies and habits, pays attention to their interests and awakens their minds. It tests the mind, excites the intelligence and puts an end to lethargy and inactivity.

*3. **Moral, intellectual and cultural development.*** As far as the vocational aspect of education is concerned, it is connected with earning money. For this reason, one can expert a high moral, intellectual and cultural level from an educated individual. If the educated individual fails to win economic independence, he tends to be immoral in his behaviour, degenerate in his intellectuality and indifferent to the art and sciences.

In view of these advantages of vocational objectives, most educationists in India are in favour of it. Efforts are being made to expand the facilities for technical and professional training in the country. Even the kind of basic education suggested by Mahatma Gandhi aimed at making the individual financially independent. But if the earning of one's bread is considered the sole aim of education, it leads to many difficulties. The major ones are the following:

*1. **Absence of liberal education.*** Liberal education plays an important part in the individual's development, since it alone is responsible for his intellectual and cultural development.

*2. **One sided attitude**.* Although vocational guidance and professional training aimed at economic independence are important forms of education, it can not be denied that education must also be responsible for the individual's character development, etc. If education aims only at vocational proficiency, it represents a one-sided approach.

*3. **Materialism.*** If education has vocational proficiency as its only objective, it becomes materialistic, at the cost of religious, moral and intellectual values. Materialism also leads to an increase in self-interest, violence and cut-throat competition which are detrimental to society and individual both.

It is evident from the foregoing discussion of the vocational objective of education that although it is an important objective, it cannot be considered the sole aim of education, even if it is considered the most important.

CHARACTER DEVELOPMENT

Philosophers of education have always considered character formation as one of the most important objectives of education. Among these philosophers are Plato, Aristotle, Herbart and Pestalozzi. Herbart has gone to the length of saying that the very fundamental nature of education is implicit in morality. He argues that education is essential for moral development since the moral individual must be free. Independence is bestowed by reason, and reason is obtained by education.

The educational system in ancient India laid great stress upon forming the character of the students. Yajnavalkya suggested that only that is education which enhances the individual's usefulness for society and provides him with a good character. Even today, educationists agree that education must aim at forming the character of the individual.

But it must be remembered that no two thinkers have defined character in the same way. McDougall, the psychologist, defines it as an organisation of sentiments, in which one particular sentiments governs all the other sentiments of the individual. From the psychological point of view, an individual whose sentiments are not governed by a governing or driving passion, has a disorganised personality. The higher the governing passion, the higher is the individual's character.

The Hindi equivalent of this word refers, to a great extent, to the qualities of the personality. Values which a person considers important are concerned with his sentiments. For example, the sentiments of patriotism, love for mother or philanthropy are concerned with the values of sacrifice, service or kindness.

The sentiment of self-respect plays an important role in character formation. Most of the qualities concerned with the development of character are acquired by the individual, as he lives his life in society. This process of character formation starts in childhood. The child's environment, made up of his family life the society and culture to which he is exposed, plays an important part in his character formation.

There can be no two opinions about accepting character formation as the objective of education. Now that the world has been made much smaller by rapid transport and communication, the obedience of ethical rules is important not only in an individual's conduct but also in the behaviour of nations.

With the development of nuclear weapons, man possesses fantastic destructive power, which has endangered the existence of the very race. In the absence of morality he may be inspired to use these weapons. Wars can be avoided not by the rules of an international agency but by the morality of the leaders of the more powerful nations. In these conditions, it is imperative that education in every part of the world aims at the development of moral character.

Even if character is interpreted in more liberal terms, without limiting it to the concept of a moral character, it remains one of the major aims of education. Man cannot develop, if his character is allowed to remain dormant. Character is the basis of his individual qualities, since he expresses his individuality through his character. Character is, thus, an essential characteristic of a developed individual.

It is evident from the foregoing discussion that the major objective of education should be the formation of character. But in India's present condition, education should also aim at enabling the individual to earn his livelihood. Education cannot aim exclusively at character formation. If character formation is accepted as the major aim of education, it would benefit society, but education must also seek to enhance the individuality.

It is evident from this that character formation is an important objective of education, but by no means the only one.

THE UNIVERSAL AIMS OF EDUCATION

Roughly speaking, education has two kinds of aims—the universal aims, and the specific aims. Universal aims tend to remain the same, irrespective of the time and place. One of the universally accepted objectives of education is the comprehensive development of the human personality.

Human nature does not change with time and latitude, and for that reason education has some universal aims. To take one example, the principle that a healthy mind needs a healthy body is a universal maxim, and a universal aim of education.

For this reason, education everywhere includes mental and physical training.

And, since man lives in society, it is essential that there should be adjustment between one man and another, because without it society cannot survive. Education, therefore, must ensure that men and society develop in such a manner that the occasions of clash and conflict are reduced to a minimum. Clearly, then, there are certain objectives of education which remain the same in all places and at all times.

1. Specific aims of education. But, the aims of education are also conditioned by the social ideas, circumstances and changes that occur at a particular place and time. Hence, the aims of education also change with the circumstances. This change and adjustment is essential because education is the tool with which the society and the individuals in it, can be made more efficient, satisfied and adjusted. And this can be possible only if the aims of education are changed to suit the circumstances. The example of India will clearly establish this.

2. Aim of education in ancient India. The attitude prevailing in ancient times was that education should indicate the ways and means of defeating the pains created the man's passions. Self-knowledge was believed to be the only way of becoming independent of one's passions. Yajnavalkya, one of the greatest philosophers in the period of the Upanishads, believed that education must aim at developing a moral character. This attitude is best explained by Shankaracharya who believed that only that which brings liberation or salvation in education.

3. Aims of education in modern India. The old attitude outlined above cannot be applied to the present period in India. One reason for this is that the contemporary political, social and economic conditions differ completely from those existing in the past. In the past, India was considered the golden bird because there was no shortage of food for Indian population. Today half of Indians are below poverty line. Therefore, aims of education have changed state and the society, with the result that the scholarly educator could devote his entire life of mental and spiritual development. Today, India is one of the backward countries in which there is a shortage of the means of survival. Before worrying about achieving complete literacy, the nation is more concerned with arriving at a stage of economic independence. Almost everybody has to wage a terrible battle against others to satisfy his own physical needs. If education does not prepare the man to earn his own bread and that of his family, and to fulfil the common needs of his dependents, his education will be useless, however spiritual it may be.

EDUCATION FOR A DEMOCRATIC NATION

The objective of education in India is to try to achieve the aims laid down in the Constitution. A democratic nation aims at instilling a love of liberty, equality and fraternity in its people. And, if India is to be made a truly democratic nation, education should aim at developing these qualities. Hence, education aims at the total and independent of the individual. But in this development it is essential that personal liberty should be in consonance with social justice. Social justice is based on equality. It provides every citizen with the opportunity to pursue his own development without prejudicing the interests of others. One implication is that the government must provide the poor people with the opportunity and the help to get an education which will raise them to same level as the others, because without this help they cannot secure such education for themselves. And without it, equality will have no meaning.

The most important democratic objective and ideal of education is the evolution of the sense of fraternity because democratic life is impossible without it. This feeling of brotherhood makes little of the differences generated by caste, race, class, profession, sex and nation etc., and gives rise to a genuine love of humanity and human beings. The future of any democracy depends entirely upon its future citizens and the quality of leadership. Hence, one of the important functions of education is that it should train the educands in democratic leadership. It is a truism that students are the future leaders of the nation. Education, therefore, must evolve ways and means of training these prospective leaders in the norms of democratic life. For this, it is essential that the student community itself must evolve a democratic pattern, and it must be burdened with much of the responsibilities of running the educational institutions in order to get practical training in social living.

EDUCATION FOR CREATING A PROSPEROUS NATION

If India is to develop into a prosperous nation, education must pay attention to the following objectives:

1. Professional training. Education must see to it that the educand is provided various kinds of scientific and technical education so that he can make a positive contribution to the nation's economic and technological progress. For this, technical and scientific education is required.

2. Character building. The prosperity of a nation depends upon the character of its citizens, not upon their individual and respective knowledge. One of the reasons of the widespread and endemic corruption that is seen in the Indian economic sphere today is the lack of character. Hence, education must also seek to develop social and moral qualities in the eudcand so that he should be inspired to employ his talents for the benefit of society. Patriotism is an important element in character building. At present, there are many Indians who have got the opportunity to receive scientific and technical education in foreign countries at the cost of their own nation. But these people do not return home to put their talents at the disposal of the country, because they sell themselves for the remuneration they receive abroad. The attitude reflects the absence of love for one's country. What is required is that the training received at the cost of the nation's wealth should be employed for the benefit of the nation. Besides, this training should be put to the best possible use. For example, if the doctors of the country refuse to go and live in the villages where they are most required, there is little hope of the nation become prosperous.

3. Proper utilization of leisure time. It has been found that the average Indian villager makes no sensible and profitable use of the spare time at his disposal. If this time is put to constructive use, it will help in the development of the individual's personality and also contribute to the nation's prosperity.

4. Military training. One important condition of developing India into a prosperous democratic nation is that it must have the capacity to face and rebuff any military challenge. For this it is desirable that education must help every young man and woman to receive military training. Such a training will help in time of national emergency because trained men and women will be able to form an effective second line of defence. Besides, this training has its uses in peace time also since it helps in evolving such social qualities as discipline, self-control, obedience, interest in community projects, etc.

It is evident from the foregoing account that education in India should aim at evolving democratic qualities, providing professional, industrial, scientific and military education.

EDUCATION FOR SOCIAL CHANGE

Any system of education is profoundly influenced by the processes of social change. In the present period, one can clearly see the impact of such tendencies of social change, as industrialization and westernization, on the society as a whole and consequently on the pattern of education. A tendency towards westernization, an imitation of the western mode of life, is one of the most notable trends in Indian society. As a consequence, one can see this change in the ways of living of thinking and even in the ideals and values of life of the students at the secondary and higher levels of education. Many people are of the opinion that the aim of education is to facilitate the educand's adjustment to a changing society.

Hence, education is a means to continuity as well as to change and progress. On the one hand, it is influenced by social changes, but on the other, it must keep a level head amid chaos, and guide future social emancipation.

EDUCATION FOR LEISURE

Some people are of the opinion that the best education is the one which teaches the educand many ways of spending his leisure usefully and constructively. Although many people never tire of delivering lengthy speeches on the importance and nobility of work, it is seen that all that is best, permanent and really valuable in human life is the creation of leisure.

If all the people of the world devote themselves to brutish effort, it might lead to physical development, but it would negate cultural development. Hence, now it is believed that apart from the material pursuits of life, the individual must have sufficient leisure so that he may do something in the direction of self-development. The importance of leisure for human life is, thus evident.

But cultural development does not automatically follow if leisure is provided. The role of education will be seen here. One can perceive the difference if one observes the different ways in which the educated and the uneducated people around one spend their leisure hours.

The uneducated can be seen consuming their leisure in useless gossiping, smoking, quarrelling, sleeping, indulging in school or at the most spending their time in visits to the cinema or rarely the theatre. On the other, the educated individual puts his leisure to better use because, in addition to the physical needs of earning money, eating, satisfaction of the sex, drive the educated person also feels the need for increasing his knowledge, self-development, discretion and religious contemplation, etc.

Evidently, then, it is only the educated person who can utilize his leisure properly. And, in fact, only those nations have led the others in cultural activities where individuals have enjoyed the proper proportion of occupation and leisure.

Education trains one in the proper use of leisure. One of the best example of this is old age. After people have retired from their professions, the educated people spend their leisure in a much better way than their uneducated counterparts. The same is true of old woman. Uneducated people often find it difficult to pass time while the educated people have so much work that they are always conscious of a shortage of time. But here, it must be remembered that the term 'educated' does not mean holding a formal education consisting of degrees obtained from colleges and universities. The truth of the matter is that the term 'educated' should be used only for those people who spend their leisure time properly. Proper utilization of leisure includes such activities as self-development, religious activities, activities leading to intellectual, development literature, interest in and devotion to the arts, social service, etc.

But the above description is not intended to create the impression that the sole aim of education is to teach the proper utilization of leisure. It is one of the many objectives of education. If the proper use of leisure is accepted as the chief aim of education, then the following three difficulties crop up:

(1) This circumscribes the field of education, for it is limited only to those who have leisure, while, in fact, it should be provided to every one in a democratic society.

(2) Education must also have certain other objectives, such as training an individual to earn his livelihood, achieving a balanced development of personality self-consciousness, cultural development, etc.

(3) As has already been pointed out, even many formally educated individuals can be seen misusing or wasting their leisure.

Despite the above criticism, the proper use of leisure and training for it is an important aspect of education. In this connection the following things should be kept in mind:

(1) The educated person has a larger choice of activities to pursue in his leisure time, such as literature, music, arts, etc., which are closed to the uneducated individual.

(2) Evidently, this objective of education encourages cultural development.

(3) Education helps to improve the constructive ability of individuals so that they can contribute to the progress of society.

(4) If it is accepted as an objective of education, it will be seen that education improves the interests of individuals and develops the mind.

Hence, training in the proper use of leisure is one of the important aims of education, though not the only one.

AIMS ACCORDING TO SECONDARY EDUCATION COMMISSION

In cogitating upon the aims of education, the Secondary Education Commission, in 1952, attached the maximum importance to the development of democratic citizenship. In its report, the Commission commented that, "The educational system must make its contribution to the development of habits, aptitudes and qualities of character which will enable its citizens to bear the responsibilities of democratic citizenship and counteract all those fissiparous tendencies which hinder the emergence of a broad national and secular outlook."

Another one of the aims recognised by the Education

Commission was the training for leadership. This, too, is an important objective of education because the future of democracy depends upon the quality of leadership provided to the masses. These leaders are elected by the citizens. But if the citizens do not have adequate training in citizenship, they fail to elect the right leaders. It is for this reason that universal and compulsory education has been accepted as the fundamental condition of a democracy. On the other hand, it has been granted that education must also train men and women in leadership so that they can guide the country in various spheres.

These ideas were reiterated by the Kothari Commission in 1964, for it is said that education must aim at strengthening democracy. And this is possible only when education imparts training in responsible democratic citizenship.

EDUCATION FOR CITIZENSHIP

It is evident from the foregoing discussion that accepting citizenship as one of the major aims of education is of particular importance for democratic nations.

Bertrand Russell astutely observed that democracy should not even be thought of in a country in which the masses are uneducated. If democracy is to be a success, it is essential that the people of the country be educated in responsible citizenship.

It must be remembered that the training in citizenship is provided not so much by schools and other educational institutions as much as by lectures, radio, television, newspapers and institutions of self-government. Even the different political parties can make a lot of positive contribution in this direction.

ESSENTIAL ELEMENTS IN EDUCATION FOR CITIZENSHIP

In order to fully comprehend training in citizenship as an important objective of education, it is essential to understand the qualities and abilities that such an education must seek to generate in the educand. Some important aspects are the following:

1. General knowledge of the various problems of individual and social life. Man's life, whether personal or social, is beset with various kinds of problems in all its aspects and forms such as the economic, political, moral, spiritual, physiological, mental, etc. Education should aim at equipping the individual with some general knowledge regarding all these problems so that he may not have any extraordinary difficulty in facing them. General knowledge in itself is important in democratic countries, because the individual citizens are expected to help in the progress of the country in every sphere.

2. Socialization. Socialization is the prerequisite for evolving the qualities of responsible citizenship. In the absence of socialization, the individual cannot fulfil his responsibilities as a citizen. In fact, he has little obligation to discharge his duties in the first place. After the home, the college or the university is the next important medium of socialization. Here various programmes can be organised to develop such qualities as mutual cooperation, friendship, social service, sacrifice, sympathy, etc. These help in individual's socialization and thus prepare him for the role of the citizen.

3. Total development. Every democratic nation must provide for the comprehensive development of its masses if it wants ideal citizens. Hence, education should aim at the all round development. Only then they can be expected to devote themselves to the task of serving their nation, of making an honest contribution to the nation's economic and spiritual progress.

4. Fulfilment of political responsibility. Only he is a good citizen who honestly and zealously fulfils his political irresponsibility along with the other obligations he has to society. For example, in an election, it is the duty of every adult man and woman to elect the best possible candidate to represent this electorate, so that the country may get the best leaders. Citizens should be aware of their responsibilities, be prepared to defend their rights and be willing to fulfil their obligations. Walker has commented, education in a democracy does not imply that the individual should become a tool of the government. He has himself to be an administrator or prepare others for this role. Hence, individuals must be trained to become leaders themselves and also to elect leaders.

EDUCATION FOR CULTURE

One of the accepted objectives of education is cultural

development. Before trying to understand this objective, it is essential to understand the meaning of the term culture. Indian philosophical tradition interprets culture as the series of impressions impinging on the individual which help to prepare him for various functions in life.

Marriage for example, is a ceremony which impresses upon the individual the responsibilities of procreating and then looking after his progeny. In this manner, cultural is a means of socialization, but it can also be interpreted as the end result of socialization, in which case it is a purifying process.

Western tradition interprets culture as social attraction and intellectual superiority. According to Sorokin and MacIver, culture implies man's moral, spiritual and intellectual superiority and attainment. In the words of Bogardus, "Culture is composed of integrated customs, traditions and current behaviour-patterns of a human group. Culture is the stock-in-trade of a group. It is an antecedent complex of values into which every individual is born. It is a medium within which individuals develop and mature." Hence, culture comprehends all that is implied in social heritage.

Alexander A. Goldenweiser has expressed it, "Our attitudes, beliefs and our judgements and values, our institutions—political and legal, religious and economic, our ethical codes and codes of etiquette; our books and machines, our sciences, philosophies and philosophers, all of these and many other things and beings within themselves and in their multi-form interrelations." This definition of culture contains a detailed account of all factors. Culture is generated and acquired. It is a unique quality of the human race, and it is transmitted from one generation to the next, as a mental phenomenon, it is social rather than individual, and it helps to satisfy certain needs.

CULTURAL OBJECTIVE OF EDUCATION

It is clear from the foregoing explanation of the term culture, that if culture is accepted as the objective of education, then certain specific things may be expected of education. The first factor in the cultural objective of education is the transmission of the social heritage from one generation to the next.

Education aims at imparting the values, traditions, customs, pattern of life, etc., of the particular social group to the child, so that he can conform to these patterns and make his own contribution to the cultural development of his group. In the second place, the objective of education is to lend sophistication, grace and polish to the child's behaviour.

But in this respect there are differences of opinion. Hinting at this difference, Vivekanand commented to an American lady, "Madam! In your country, it is the tailor who makes a man cultured and gentleman but in may country it is the character which makes a man cultured and gentlemen."

Recognised patterns of behaviour, such as greeting a stronger, showing respect to one's elders, showing love and affection etc., vary from culture to culture.

Hence, education aims at acquainting the child with the patterns recognised in his own society. Obviously, then, culture can be interpreted liberally as well as narrow-mindedly. In its more superficial and limited sense, culture implies the mode of dress, external manifestations of behaviour, etc. But in its broader and more liberal sense, culture implies values, thinking, self-development, etc.

Consequently, the possession of a certificate of formal education is no guarantee of culture, because culture can be found only in the individual who has achieved some degree of self-development, both mental and spiritual, and has some notion of the values of life. From this standpoint, it is possible to distinguish between various levels of cultural attainment.

SYNTHESIS OF VARIOUS AIMS OF EDUCATION

Even the educationists of the fairly remote past were interested in the various objectives of education, and consequently, many different aims were ascribed to education. On the other hand, there has always been a distinct tendency to synthesize all these various aims into a single comprehensive aim. One example of the inclination is the aim Herbert Spencer ascribed to education, the aim of providing completeness to life. In general, other educationists have accepted that the general aim of education is a balanced development.

Certain other educationists believe that education should aim at the complete development of human personality, but by including social qualities in this they also hint at the development of the social aspect which promotes adjustment between the individual and society.

Hence, it is evident, that the various aims of education are not mutually exclusive or contradictory and it is, therefore, possible to synthesize the different aims and arrive at a single objective. But for this, it is necessary to glance at the various possibilities and alternatives.

COMPLETE LIVING

Herbert Spencer believed that the general aim of education was training for complete living. He pointed out that education must be so designed as to develop every aspect of human life and to enable the individual to adjust to every possible circumstance. He must have knowledge of the various responsibilities that he must fulfil towards himself, his friends, his society and his nation. He must also be taught to fend for himself in the economic jungle, also to spend his leisure time concretively.

If one has to understand the concept of complete living properly, one must understand the concept of life. Spencer uses the term 'life' to imply five kinds of activities—the action of self defence, the action of apparently protecting life, the action of protecting one's progeny, the action of safeguarding society and the action of spending one's leisure.

HARMONIOUS DEVELOPMENT AIM

The harmonious development of the various aspects of human beings is the aim of education suggested by some philosophers. The human personality is made up of many aspects, such as the physiological, the mental, etc. In addition to this, each individual is born possessed of certain instincts.

Education, according to this approach, must aim at a harmonious development of these aspects and instincts. Such a development amounts to a balanced development. The possibility of the greater development of any one aspect at the expense of another leads to the creation of a balanced personality.

Apparently, this aim of education appears to be very attractive because it cannot be doubted that there are many facets of the human personality. It is, therefore, desirable that education should seek to develop each one adequately.

SOCIAL AIMS OF EDUCATION

Since man cannot hope to exist outside society, it is desirable that education must have some social aim also. Certain scholars have insisted upon this aspect of education to such an extent that they have denied any importance to the individual aspect. Hegel believes in the complete sovereignty of the state and permits it complete authority over the individual.

Spartan leaders were primarily concerned with strengthening their country through education of this kind, so that they could defend their territorial integrity. Literature and the arts did not concern them to any great extent. Much of the nation's energy was consumed in imparting military training to every young man.

Hence, their educational system aimed at producing soldiers. This practice was carried to extremes, inasmuch as all infants thought to be incapable to engage in physical exercise of every kind. Independent thinking of any kind was looked down upon. Administration was given great attention. Briefly, they desired to generate and develop all those qualities which are required in physical conflict. There was a very rigorous system of punishment.

Literary education was considered to be of secondary importance, while training in music extended only to patriotic songs. The education of women was also given some attention, but their importance lay only as sources of good soldiers.

Education of this kind came to the front again in modern Germany. After the defeat of Germany in 1806, German thinkers mediated upon ways of saving their country. They concluded that this could only be done through education. This feeling spread to the field of education, and expressed itself through the insistence upon the teaching of national history and imparting of military training.

Thinkers like Hegel and Fichte stressed the sovereign and supreme authority of the state, in direct opposition to any individual rights. Education became a medium of disseminating the ideas of the government among the educands. This trend culminated in the establishment of the Nazi cult and government, and later on in occurrence of the world war. Education on this pattern is seen emerging at various points of history in many different countries.

INDIVIDUAL AIMS IN EDUCATION

It is evident from the foregoing description that the social aims of education should not be stressed to the utter exclusion to the individual aims, since it leads to many distressing consequences.

Contrary to this, many thinkers have been influenced by numerous factors to stress the importance of their individual aims of education. Development of the individual's personality was an accepted aim of education both in Ancient Greece and India.

The modern period has seen a resurgence of this interest in the individual. It is manifested in an education which is completely child-oriented. Factors influencing this are the following:

1. Effect of biological science. The biological sciences suggest that every living being is distinct from every other living being, that each one has certain peculiar and unique characteristics, that its natural development means only the development of these unique characteristics. Hence, education aim at development of the individual abilities of each child.

2. Effect of psychology. Modern psychology places a lot of emphasis upon individual differences. Every child differs from every other child in respect of its colour, form, nature, interest and mental abilities such as intelligence, thinking etc., and its personality.

The aim of education is to develop each child in conformity with its special abilities. Success in life depends to a great extent upon development of this kind. As the result of this psychological concept, it is believed that education must seek to develop the individual abilities of each individual. Consequently, education has become child-oriented.

3. Influence of the progressive. According to T.P. Nunn, the progress of the world is rooted in the development and progress of the individual personality. The world has progressed only because some individuals have contributed to it according to their special abilities. If such gifted individuals had not existed, progress in any sphere of activity would have been impossible. Hence, education should aim at individual development, if it seeks to contribute to social progress.

In the words of T.P. Nunn, "Nothing good enters into the human world except in and through the activities of individual men and women and educational practice must be shaped to accord with this truth." Hence, the aim of education is to develop the abilities of men and women as individuals. Only this can help the world in progressing. And this alone will produce the leaders in various spheres and make progress possible.

4. Effect of democratic ideas. Democracy stresses the freedom of the individual. American educationists attach the greatest importance to the independent development of the individual, and hence they concede very few rights to the state to interfere in this matter. Democracy aims at providing the greatest freedom and equality to all individuals.

Hence, it is believed that the democratic state should provide facilities for all individuals to develop in any direction they conceive to be useful to themselves. The state has to pay particular attention to that class of individuals who cannot get education of their own accord. For this reason, democratic societies make special arrangements for the education of the backward, orphaned and physically handicapped children.

Teachers and students in educational institutions are free to think and express their own ideas, because, as Bertrand Russell has suggested, "Education for the individual is a finer thing than the education of the citizen." Education must not only seek to produce fine citizens but also fine individuals. The educational system should be so designed that it helps to develop the individuality of the child.

THE SYNTHESIS

The emphasis that is nowadays placed on the individual aims of education does not imply total neglect of the social aims. It is, in fact, a synthesis of the individual and social aims. It is impossible to conceive of one in the total absence of the other. There is no human being outside society and society is made up of human beings. Hence, even if education is designed to aim at social service or training for citizenship, it implicitly promotes the interest and the individuality of the human being. It will be in keeping with the context to recount the ideas of some eminent educationists.

THE CONCEPT OF SOCIAL SKILL

In America, Professor Bagley believes that social skill is the aim of educational behaviour. Explaining the concept of social skill he has pointed out the following qualities which can be said to characterize the socially skillful individual:

(1) Economic efficiency or the ability to bear one's own financial burden.

(2) Prohibitive or negative morality, or the willingness, on the part of the individual, to sacrifice those wishes, the satisfaction of which would endanger or hinder the fulfilment of economic skill of other people.

(3) Willingness to desist from the satisfaction of those drives and desires which make no direct or indirect contribution to social progress.

In this approach to education, the individual's activities are evaluated from the standpoint of social duties. After the first world war, American thinking on the subject has inclined towards the individual's contribution to society. Social service has been the recognised aim of education even since. Educational institutions felt it necessary to acquaint the individual with the duties and responsibilities of the citizen, while even the teaching of history was oriented to the fostering of social consciousness. Considerable stress was placed on cooperation and sacrifice. Much the same thing can be said about India too.

SELF-REALIZATION

Self-realization, as the aim of education, presents a synthesized ideal which comprehends the individual and social ideals, since both aspects of self-realization are important. Self-realization is not merely the manifestation of one's self but the complete development of the individual. Individualism should not be considered a contradiction of the social environment because the social aspect can not be separated from human nature. In fact, the concept of a spiritual personality comprehends both the social and the individual aims of education.

J.S. Ross has argued, "The only meaning of the individual aim in education that is worthy of our acceptation is the development of valuable personality and spiritual individuality."

Euken suggests that the aim of education is to make the personality superior. The adjustment or synthesis between the individual and the society is possible only in a democratic structure.

J.M. Baldwin has commented, "The real self is the bipolar self..." Personality develops only in society, since outside society it is possible to evolve those characteristics which are unique in human beings. Personality has no meaning when it is separated from the social environment. And social service is the finest medium of achieving self-realization. Only free and independent individuals can achieve social ideals. The Christian religion accepts this concept of personality. Indian religions also stress the unbreakable bonds between society and the individual.

FUNCTIONS OF EDUCATION IN HUMAN LIFE

Whatever is acquired in human life is the result of formal or informal education. When the child is born, he has no knowledge of his surroundings. Gradually, he comes to recognize his environment by using his sense organs and by coming in contact with other people. Many ideas and habits he learns merely by observing others.

But in no civilized society it is believed possible for an individual to be fit for adult life, if he does not have some degree of formal education. For this reason, one finds arrangements for education everywhere. Not only in civilized societies, but even in primitive societies the adults try to educate adolescents in the ways of adult life.

Among the tribals of India, this social education of the young girls and boys takes place at the dormitories. To put it briefly, the individual's character, personality, culture, thinking, commonsense, skills, habits and even the other less significant things of life depend upon education.

The importance of education in human life is thus evident. This importance is further clarified, if we look at the following functions of education:

1. Development of natural abilities. When the child is born, he is already possessed of many kinds of natural abilities. As the body grows of mind also grows, but the innate abilities and qualities do not develop quite so naturally and without aid. It is often said that if the mind is not exercised its abilities cannot be developed.

Hence, the first aim of education is to try to develop such abilities as power of imagination, of thinking etc., by providing appropriate opportunities and stimuli. It is for this reason that, as a part of child education, one of the first steps is to put various kinds of instruments and apparata before the child so that he can learn to use his sense organs. This is called education of senses.

The child is also made to improve his power of thinking by presenting many different kinds of problems.

His imagination is allowed to develop through the medium of various arts and skills. He is taught to concentrate by using many kinds of techniques to attract his attention. The various methods of learning are brought to his notice by letting him do different kinds of work. He is also taught to make adequate use of the different parts of his body by various games and sports.

Such basic requirements of life as eating, sleeping, sitting and walking, moving ground, are taught to the child by the family itself. All these activities are part of the child's early education.

2. Character building. Psychologists contend that the foundation of the child's character is laid in the first few years of his life. The impressions about behaviour and conduct that fall upon the infants's mind are later exhibited in the form of his character. The importance of character is hardly a subject to be discussed. It is developed by education, mainly informal education.

Putting it differently, the infant's character is built up not so much by lectures and lessons as by the examples presented to him in the family, school neighbourhood, group, etc. Character is the organisation of various sentiments. The focus of this organisation is the sentiment of self-regard. And it is upto the teacher and the child's parents to develop this sentiment of self-regard in the child. Once this is developed, the child can then move further on the road to self-development.

Education is of particular significance in the development of a moral character because the child is not naturally endowed with the power of distinguishing between the right and the wrong. The difference between right and wrong is taught by adults.

Socialization is an important factor in the development of a moral character. This is aided by story-telling, setting good examples and providing education of social life. In fact, many educationists believe that the aim of education is to develop a moral character. As Herbart has expressed it, the development of a good moral character amounts to education.

3. Development of personality. The patterns of behaviours that a child chooses in his adjustment with the individuals and objects in his environment depend upon his personality. It is the development of personality which leads to a development of individuality, which is an inevitable characteristic of an educated individual. The informal development of the personality takes place through his family, neighbourhood, the conditions of work, etc., but educationists believe that one important objective of education is to develop personality.

Hence, the child is given opportunities of performing different kinds of work so that his personality may develop. Games play an important role in personality development. His personality achieves integration and strength in facing the many kinds of problems which make up a game.

The social aspect of his personality is developed in the communal life of the school. Social customs, traditions, the forms of social control, cultural element, etc., also play an important role in developing the personality. It is for this reason that distinct differences can be seen in the personalities of individuals belonging to different cultures and societies.

The first and most permanent influence upon the child's personality development is the family. Such things as his order of birth in the family, his place among his brothers and sisters, the social and economic status of the family, the parents' behaviour towards the child, the mutual behaviour of the parents themselves, their profession influence his personality. It is said that parental education plays a large part in building the personality of great men.

Apart from this, the child's personality is influenced by many kinds of literature such as biographies of great men, stories, novels, essays, etc. It is believed that it is the duty of the teacher to prevent his wards from developing bad habits and also to see if the wards are developing balanced personalities.

The teacher can take the assistance of the psychologist and also of the parents in ensuring a healthy development of personality. If the child does not develop a balanced personality, it can be said that his education is incomplete.

4. Preparation for adult life. Livelihood is believed to be the aim of education. Economic factors controlling life in the present day world, have become so complex that no one who is not properly educated can hope to successfully earn his living. In the past, most people pursued agriculture, which does not demand such a high degree of hospitalization. For them education was not so essential.

But the recent developments in science and the increasing hospitalization of all professions has made it impossible for an individual to perform any job without previous training and education. As a general rule, highly paid jobs require specialized training of a very high calibre. The ability to earn enough is not the only factor to be considered in the preparation for adult life. Earning money is one of the aspects of adult life, another is marriage and children.

If Education aims at training the individual to earn his livelihood, to marry, to bring forth children, to fulfil his duties towards other individuals and society in general. In fact, if the child is helped to develop a balanced personality and a good character, there can be no better preparation for adult life.

5. Control and sublimation of basic instincts. Every living being is born into the world possessed of certain basic instincts. There may be difference of opinion about the instincts that the child is born with, but there can be no doubt about the presence of some instincts. The child's mind is not a blank tablet on which anything can be written. Psychologists have demonstrated that not only does the human infant possess some instincts, but also that there are individual differences in respect of these instincts.

Human beings live in groups, and hence it becomes necessary for them to control some instincts and to change the mode of expression of other instincts in such a manner that they do not injure other people. Besides, there are certain instincts which can be fulfilled only with the co-operation of another human being. Sex is one such instinct. Since, from the moral standpoint, the individuality and the humanity of every individual must be respected, it becomes necessary for people to control their instincts in all forms of communal life, such as marriage.

Civilized life would become completely impossible if such instincts as aggressiveness and sex were not sublimated. Education helps in the control, sublimation and change of instincts. Various kinds of arts are used as a medium of sublimation. Education in social life helps the child to learn how to control his instincts.

6. Creation of useful citizens. Although many thinkers have dreamt of a society without government, in actual fact no such society exists. Individuals who have been deprived of their citizenship or have never been granted this, make all kinds of efforts to get the citizenship of one nation or another. If they cannot obtain it, they have to face all kinds of difficulties.

Hence, the relationship between the individual and the state is universal. In this relationship, the status of the individual is called the status of citizenship. Hence, it is desirable that the individual should be trained in behaving as a citizen so that he can fulfil his duties to the state. In the present age, this function of education is emphasized very much because most states themselves are responsible for providing education. In democratic systems, the public also plays a hand in guiding the educational system.

The thinkers of ancient Greece believed that this is the most important function of education. Nowadays, almost all the thinkers agree that true democracy in any country is possible only when almost all its citizens are properly educated. Education in responsible citizenship is also given through the medium of political parties, radio, television, newspapers, magazines, etc.

7. Development of a sense of community. The statement that man is a social animal means no more than that he lives in society. It does not imply that the human child is possessed of social qualities at birth. These social qualities are acquired and taught. One major objective of education, therefore, is the teaching of social qualities and development of a sense of community. This community feeling urges the child to co-operate with the fellows, to make sacrifices if they become necessary, to rise above the considerations of caste and creed and develop a sense of oneness with the nation, etc. The development of this feeling depends upon opportunities provided in family life, play groups and schools and colleges.

This feeling is the basis of national unity. The efforts being made in India today to evolve an emotional unity are in fact efforts to develop this feeling of community.

*8. **Protection and increase of culture and civilization.*** As compared to other animals, man has progressed more because human society has succeeded in protecting its knowledge and in conveying it to future generations. This has been done through the medium of culture and civilization. A child born in the present time does not think of everything from the beginning. His thinking and modes of behaviour are determined by customs, traditions and social institutions, which are repositories of the experience and thinking of his ancestors.

For this reason, societies which have a more ancient culture show signs of greater organisation and systematization, greater stability. Hence, it is now universally accepted that culture and civilization should be protected and allowed to grow through new developments. This is mainly achieved through education. The child receives the social heritage in the form of education. Then, through education the child develops his own knowledge, character and personality thus becoming capable of contributing to the literary, cultural and social life of his society.

For its reason, many contemporary thinkers in India have suggested that teaching of Indian culture should be made compulsory in all universities.

*9. **Encouragement to social welfare.*** Both formal and informal education helps the individual to evolve a critical attitude which helps him to analyse everything presented to him. If he finds any faults in it, he exercises his mind to find some ways of removing the faults. In this manner, education has been the basis of all social welfare programmes.

When English education was introduced in India, it brought along with it the western tendencies of individualism, rationalism, etc. As a consequence all educated people in the country were impelled to re-examine ancient Indian traditions and institutions. This led to the development of such institutions as the Brahmo Samaj, Arya Samaj, Prarthana Samaj, Theosophical

Society. Each one aimed at social welfare. And the inspiration for each of these institutions came from highly educated individuals. Education thus leads to a continuous analysis of the various constituents of society, its institutions, modes of social control, etc., and inspires efforts to make improvements where they are needed.

10. National development. The overall development of all national groups is essential for the development and progress of human society, but this is not possible without universal education. It is for this reason that the U.N.O. is making efforts to provide education to the backward countries. In every country, efforts are made to develop a feeling of belonging among its citizens, the sense of nationality. It helps to induce the individual to do his best for the nation. Besides, almost every nation has its own plan of national education which seeks to fulfil the aims of that nation.

11. Use of leisure. One of the main aims of education is to teach an individual to make the best use of leisure. Using leisure time in educational activities is itself useful. On the other hand, education itself guides the individual to utilize his leisure time properly.

Educated people can use their leisure time effectively by devoting themselves to magazines, arts, etc. Even the standard of their normal conversation, discussions, etc., is higher than that of the uneducated person. Education helps to develop various kinds of interests so that leisure itself does not become a burden.

12. Increasing consciousness of other cultures. In countries in which many different cultural groups co-exist, education helps to increase consciousness of these other cultures and of cultural exchange. This helps individuals to understand each other, thus increasing national unity. There are many different cultures in the world today. As long as education cannot create a feeling of cooperation and of mutual love, the ideal of a unified world cannot be realized.

13. Improving emotional unity. At the present time, many disintegrating forces such as regionalism, casteism, communalism, linguism, etc., are working towards a complete disintegration of the country. If the nation is to be saved from complete fragmentation, it is necessary to generate a sense of emotional unity in all men and women. Then individuals can be expected to feel that they are members of the same nation and to behave in the interests of the nation. Education can help to create this emotional unity. Many educationists have given valuable suggestions for achieving this.

14. Developing an international feeling. As a result of the unprecedented improvements in the means of transport and communications, people of different nations are constantly coming into contact with each other. All kinds of people are also realizing the importance of internationalism, after having witnessed the havoc caused by the two recent world wars.

All contemporary educationists in India, including Sri Aurobindo, Rabindra Nath, Vivekanand, have stressed the importance of creating this feeling of internationalism in all educands. In the present context, therefore, one of the main tasks of education is to generate this feeling in the student community.

From the foregoing description of the functions of education in human life, it is evident that the functions of education are the same as its objectives. To put it differently, the objectives which have been assigned to education by various thinkers are the tasks it has to do. It need hardly he stressed that the functions of education change when ideals governing it undergo changes. Nevertheless, the fundamental elements of human life are the same today as they were in Plato's and Aristotle's times.

Hence, such aims of education as character-building, development of personality, social welfare, proper use of leisure, protection of culture and civilization, development of communal feeling, creating able citizens, preparation for adult life, development of innate qualities, etc., are permanent objectives which will remain the same in future also.

FUNCTIONS OF EDUCATION IN NATIONAL LIFE

The functions of education in national life differ somewhat from its functions in normal life because human life is possible even without a nation. Primitive societies still do not possess any kind of nation. Nations are found in more civilized societies. Before examining the role of education in a national life, it is necessary to discover the nature of a nation.

Nation is a group of human beings which lives in a country

delimited by geographical boundaries. This group is possessed of a desire to be bound by common traditions, common interests, similar political ambitions and political unity.

The important aspects of national life can be understood from this description. For national life to be possible, it is essential that its members should have common traditions, interests, sentiments and political ambitions, and an emotional unity. Education aims at creating and maintaining all these various elements, and thus it contributes to national life. The following points are to be considered in this connection:

1. Maintaining communal interests and traditions. The main objective in applying a uniform system of education to an entire nation is that a similarity of interests and traditions may be generated among the people. For India, this is of even greater importance, because the nation is composed of many different cultural and linguistic groups. Education achieves this similarity and identity through its prescribed syllabi and various kinds of extra-curricular programmes.

2. Similarity of political ambitions. If different groups within a single nation are found to possess various and contradictory political ambitions, it becomes difficult to maintain that nation's independence and unity. One chief objective of education, thus, is to propagate similar political ambitions among all classes and groups of people.

In India, young men and women who received English education studied the history of Western nations and concluded that India must also win its freedom. Once this political awakening spread among the educated classes and led to similarity of political ambitions, national movement took shape and the demand for a free India was put forward.

In the more recent context, education should aim at creating a desire for complete and comprehensive development of the nation so that people may rise above their own narrow interests and work in the interests of the nation as a whole.

3. A diffusion of emotional unity. It is obvious that one task of education is to diffuse a feeling of emotional unity in the younger generation so that all its members may feel identified with the nation and be inspired to work for its improvement.

Such forces of disintegration as communalism, casteism,

linguism, regionalism, etc., can be countered only when emotional unity is increased. For this, the educational programme should insist on the teaching of the same history, same cultural heritage, etc. Sense of community is an essential part of nationalism and the foundations of sense of belonging to a community are laid in schools.

Hence, efforts should be made to create such an atmosphere in school that the students may have a sense of belonging, not of alienation.

4. Development of a national language. Although the development of many different languages and the common use of them does not hinder national unity in any way, the absence of a single common language hinders it considerably since language is the medium through which thoughts and emotions are expressed. Just as thoughts and language are intimately connected, nationalism and language are also intimately related to each other.

Hence, one objective of education is the development of a national language. In India, the Constitution has laid down Hindi as the national language and it has been accepted in principle that this language must be spread over the entire country. But it is regrettable that the work of giving this status to Hindi is not progressing as fast as is desirable. If greater efforts are not made in this direction, it may create a danger to national unity in the country. Hence, it is desirable that the teaching of Hindi should be compulsory at all stages of education.

5. Respect to all religions. India is a secular state in that it grants equal status and importance to every religion, and refuses to discriminate between citizens on the basic of their religious beliefs, but despite this provision of the Constitution, the poison of communalism is found in greater abundance in the country, and it has been impossible to remove it despite the greatest efforts. One way of achieving this is to indoctrinate the children through education that every religion deserves equal respect and that one's own religion is not necessarily the best. Education must see to eliminate all such prejudices. Hence, in a country like India, one task to education is to generate respect for all religions.

6. Training for leadership. Proper development in any sphere can be achieved only if there is adequate leadership. A country can progress only if it has able leaders in the social, economic, political, literary, cultural, artistic, industrial and moral fields. Education can provide such leaders.

Hence, one of the objectives of education is to bring forth leaders in various spheres and to train them to perform their tasks efficiently. This can be done by encouraging student participation in various kinds of extracurricular programmes in the colleges so that the student's capabilities can find expression. This also helps to train him in leadership.

7. Fulfilling the need for skilled workers. In addition to leaders, every sphere needs the dedication and cooperation of skilled and efficient workers. Such workers are required not only in industry and commerce, but also in the social and political spheres. This need can be fulfilled by education.

During the process of education, it is possible to discover the sphere for which a particular individual is best suited. Once this has been found out, he can then be trained in his particular profession.

8. Consciousness of duties. If a nation is to progress, it is essential that its citizens should be aware of their duties and responsibilities. Education can spread this awareness among the people. In schools the students are told of their responsibilities as members of the nations. This awareness of their duties is created in them, and they are also taught how they can fulfil these duties. This role of education is of the greatest importance in democratic states.

9. Evolution of a national feeling. The strength of national feeling in an individual is judged by the extent to which he can subjugate his personal and narrow class interests in favour of the wider national interest and the extent to which he is prepared to work for the national interests. For this, it is essential that the individual should be conscious of his duties to the nation as well as capable of rising above narrow interests of regionalism, communalism, casteism, etc. Both these can be made possible through education.

National feeling is generated among the students in the colleges through various extra-curricular programmes and syllabi. But in fact the informal modes of education, such as family, newspapers, magazines, radio, television, etc., play an important role in generating a national feeling. National education programmes should pay particular attention to these and to the creation of a national literature.

It is evident from the work of education in national life that the members of the nation should be educated in such a way, through the teaching of national history, the national language, different kinds of programmes, etc., that a national sentiment should be created in them. They should begin to consider national interests as higher than any other interest, and they should be prepared to make any sacrifice for the nation.

EDUCATIONAL AIMS OF MODERN INDIA

India is a land of spirituality. Ancient Indian educational systems aimed to achieve the following aims:

1. Infusion of piety and religiousness.
2. Character formation.
3. Development of personality.
4. Inculcation of civic and social duties.
5. Promotion of social efficiency and happiness.
6. Preservation and spread of culture.

In India during Islamic and British period above aims were almost forgotten. But after independence we are moving in the right directions.

INDIA'S EDUCATIONAL PRIORITIES

India attained its freedom on 15th August, 1947. The dawn of liberty brought a great responsibility on Indian shoulders to shape the future of our country according to our plans. For this, India needed a vast army of leaders in all spheres of activity and all areas of human life. The continuous development of our country demands that generations of capable and devoted persons should be coming up to shoulder the responsibilities of national development. Education is the only means to achieve this high ideal of national service. Hence, formulation of suitable aims of education and organization of an efficient working system to achieve those aims is the foremost and prime need of the day Keeping into consideration, the dominant needs of the country, the Government of India responded to this crying need of the nation by appointing the following Commissions to formulate suitable aims of education.

1. University Commission 1948

The University Commission recommended the following aims of education:

(*i*) To develop a sense of discrimination.
(*ii*) To motivate for more and more knowledge.
(*iii*) To know the real meaning of life.
(*iv*) To provide vocational education.

2. Secondary Education Commission (1952-53)

Considering the dominant needs of India, the Secondary Education Commission recommended the following aims of education:

(a) Development of democratic citizenship. India is a secular, socialistic democratic republic. To make the Indian democracy successful, the first aim of education is to produce dynamic, resourceful and enterprising citizens. Citizenship is a challenging responsibility in democracy, because each individual in democratic nation has to form his independent judgement on all social, economic and political issues and also decide his own course of action. For this, each child should have a correct ideology, correct attitudes and correct mode of behaviour. Education should develop in children a capacity of clear and correct thinking and receptivity to new ideas so that they are not misled by false propaganda or become slaves to outmoded customs, traditions and beliefs but are able to develop the intellectual ability to sift the right from the wrong and also the strength of character to reject the improper and the unwholesome. Besides a scientific attitude towards life and the nation, children must possess the ability to express themselves in press or on platform so that they are able to assist in the formation of a healthy public opinion by free discussions, persuation and exchange of ideas.

(b) Training in the art of living efficiently. A child cannot live and develop alone. So far for his wholesome development and the benefit of society, education should develop in him a spirit of accommodation, the necessary conditions of which are discipline, cooperation, social sensitiveness and tolerance. With the development of these socially desirable qualities, he will be able to lead an efficient life with others in happy union and undertake plans of national reconstruction with the help of other fellow beings.

(c) Improvement of vocational efficiency. To achieve the improvement of vocational efficiency of every child vocational training is necessary. Appreciation of the dignity of all types of work should be inculcated in all children from the very beginning so that they are able to take pride in doing every work as thoroughly and efficiently as they can. At the same time, due emphasis should be laid on craft work. Each subject should be given proper place in the curriculum so that each child may choose the vocation of his interest which he wants to follow after finishing his studies. This will provide skilled labour to various vocations and ensure the industrial development of the country.

(d) Development of personality. By development of whole personality is meant the development of all aspects namely—physical, mental, social, moral and spiritual. For this, education should provide creative and constructive activities to be done by the child so that he is able to develop his literary, artistic and cultural interests. The development of these interests will lead to the development of the whole personality of the child. The child should be motivated to participate in various creative and constructive plans of national development so that he is able to develop his personality to the full extent.

(e) Education for leadership. India needs ideal leadership at all levels and in all spheres of life. To achieve education for leadership education should inculcate certain socially desirable qualities namely—discipline, tolerance, sacrifice and social service etc., so that as capable and devoted citizens people feel their responsibility and lead the country ahead on the road of progress and prosperity.

3. Kothari Commission (1964-66)

Kothari Commission recommended the following aims of education:

(a) To increase productivity. The first aim of education in Indian democratic set up is to increase production by leaps and bounds matching with the increasing population. Unfortunately the picture is just the reverse. While population is increasing at an alarmingly high rate production in all fields is lagging behind. Indians should try to increase production in all fields as much as possible. To achieve this important aim, we should try to vocationalise secondary education besides emphasizing agricultural and technical education. The commission has suggested some specific plans to increase production.

(b) To develop social and national unity. National unity is an essential need for national reconstruction. In the absence of national unity, self-centred individuals try to achieve their own motives without caring for the interests of the nation. This makes the nation weak and backward. Thus, national unity is greatly essential for national reconstruction. But the sense of national unity can be developed through education only. Hence, the aim of education should be to develop social and national unity.

(c) To consolidate democracy. Education is necessary for the success of democracy. To consolidate democracy, education should be so organized as to provide more and more effective experiences to children to inculcate in them the qualities of democratic living. Then only, national consciousness will stimulate national outlook, sense of national character and responsibility. The commission has suggested specific measures to consolidate democracy.

(d) To modernise the country. The fourth aim of education is to modernise the country. In this age of science, new researches are made by all advanced countries of the world in all fields of human life. Due to these researches old customs, traditions and beliefs are breaking yielding place to new and useful ideologies and techniques of production. On account of this change a new society is in the making. Unfortunately, in our country the old customs, traditions and techniques of production still exist with the result that India is taken to be a backward country in the community of other nations of the world. If we wish to bring our country in the line with the advanced countries of the world, our people should learn various kinds of scientific knowledge together with useful techniques of production and use them intelligently to boost our production bringing about a desired change in our old ideologies. This modernization of our country depends upon education.

(e) To develop social, moral and spiritual values. To develop social, moral and spiritual values and modernize the country, skilled labour is greatly essential. Hence, prime importance should be given to scientific subjects in the curriculum. But scientific subjects may not always lead to the development of character and human values. Thus, the commission recommends that besides scientific subjects, humanities should also be included in the curriculum so that industrial development and human values continue to develop simultaneously. Human values should be inculcated in the children to enable them to become human beings in the real sense of the term. Besides becoming as advanced as possible and developing our economy to the highest level, we should not give up our cultural foundations which have withstood the ravages of adverse times from time immemorial.

QUESTIONS FOR ANSWER

1. What were the aims of education in Ancient India? Discuss.
2. In view of the modern social and economic conditions of India, what should be the aims of best education?
3. Briefly define various aims of education.
4. Write a note on 'Human Life and Educational Aims.'
5. Explain the relationship between 'Social Ideal' and 'Aims of Education.'
6. Write short notes on the following:
   (a) Vocational education.
   (b) Character development.
   (c) Education for citizenship.
7. Write a note on social and individual aims of education.
8. Write a brief note on various functions of education in human and national life.
9. Explain educational priority of modern India.

4

Institutions and Agencies of Education

INTRODUCTION

Education is a very comprehensive process which is unending and every experience serves as a education, therefore institutions and agencies of education are large in number. Sir Godfrey Thomson has written, "The whole of environment is the instrument of man's education in the widest sense. But in that environment certain factors are distinguishable as more particularly concerned; then home, the school, the church, the press, the vocation, public life, amusement and hobbies."

Generally, of course, the process of education continues from birth to death, but some specific institutions play a more important part in it. All of these institutions are the agencies of education, and they include all those factors, bases, places or institutions, which have an educative influence upon the child.

Hence, the institutions, agencies and bases of education mean the same thing, and should be interpreted as such. These institutions of education have been variously classified by different educationists. Some of the major classifications are the following:

Classification of all the Agencies of Education

First Classification of all the Agencies of Education

Active Agencies	*Passive Agencies*
(The Family, the School, the Community, the Religion, the State, Social clubs, Organized games, Entertainment programmes, etc.)	(Cinema, T.V., Radio, Newspapers, Magazines and Market places etc.)

Second Classification of all the Agencies of Education

Formal	*Informal*	*Commercial*	*Non-Commercial*
(1) School	(1) The family	(1) Radio	(1) Sports club
(2) Religious institutions	(2) General games	(2) T.V.	(2) Social welfare centres
(3) Library	(3) The State	(3) Cinema	(3) Dramatic clubs
(4) Museum	(4) The community or society	(4) Clubs	(4) Scouting and guiding
(5) Zoo		(5) Theatres	(5) Youth welfare clubs
(6) Art galleries		(6) Newspapers	(6) Adult education centres
(7) Organized games		(7) The press	
(8) Educational programmes			

Third Classification of all the Agencies of Education

Formal Agencies	*Informal Agencies*
(School, Organised entertaiment centres, Libraries, Picture galleries, Games, Cinema, Educational programmes on Radio and T.V. etc.)	(Family, Community, Religion, Free play, Market place, Fairs and exhibitions etc.)

1. Active and passive agencies. Among the active agencies of education are home, schools, religious institutions, society, state, club, social welfare centres, etc. Here the educator and the educand, the audience and the speaker, the citizen and the leader, deliberately come into contact with each other and also react to each other. Consequently, the process of education forges ahead.

Among the passive agencies of eduction can be enumerated radio, television, films, newspapers, magazines, etc. These are called passive because the process of education set into motion by them is not mutual but one sided, because only the audience, or educand is actively participating. The other element, the agency itself, remains inactive, and hence only the educand is himself influenced without influencing the source of his education.

2. Brown's classification. In addition to the formal and informal classification, to be mentioned later, Brown has divided the agencies of education into the commercial objective while the uncommercial have social welfare as their objective.

Hence, the press, films, radio, television, magazines, etc., are the commercial agencies of education. On the other hand, sports clubs, scout and guides institutions, adult education centres and social welfare centres, etc., are the uncommercial agencies of education.

3. Formal and informal agencies. The most recognised and well known classification is the division into the formal and informal agencies of education.

(a) Formal agencies. In the words of Henderson, "As the child watches, imitates, participates, in the activities of living he is being informally educated. When he is being consciously and intentionally taught, that is formal education." In this manner informal education is unconscious whereas formal education is conscious and deliberately imbibed.

Informal education is unsystematic while formal education is systematized. Among the agencies of formal education are those institutions which have a predetermined location, time, plan and curriculum as well as trained educators. The best example of such institutions is the school.

Such agencies are brought into existence by the state or society. In such institutions discipline and administration is created by the application of set rules. It is possible to use such agencies to provide education to a large number of educands simultaneously, according to a predetermined plan.

At least specific education cannot be provided in the absence of these institutions, but it must be realized that education provided through these agencies is rather lifeless and theoretical, or bookish. It sometimes takes the educand for away from the realities of life.

In addition to schools, libraries, lecture theatres, recreation centres, museums, etc., are also enumerated among the formal agencies of education. Pointing out the significance of the formal agencies, Dewey has remarked, "Without formal education it is not possible to transmit all the resources and achievements of a complex society. It also opens a way to a kind of experience which would not be accessible to the young, if they were left to pick up their training informal association with others, since books and the symbols of knowledge are mastered."

(b) Informal agencies. The informal agencies of education are those in which education is provided informally and unconsciously. These lack all formality, rules, systematization, pre-planning, premeditation or training. All of them perform the function of educating the educand indirectly. Most of them are independent of the control of any individual or institution.

Education provided by them does not follow any set pattern. Besides providing education, they also perform certain other functions and fulfil many other needs. Education provided by them is devoid of any pretension, formality. It is natural and subtle.

Among the agencies of informal education are family, society, state, radio, press, cinema, magazines, television, etc. Dewey believes that the informal agencies of education are more important than the formal ones, for he believes that they are natural. One example of this is education through communal living. Living in a group, the child thinks of many things. The sphere of his experience is being rapidly enlarged, for he is being subjected to many new stimuli.

Under these circumstances his imagination develops and he becomes conscious of new responsibilities which provoke him to think. Even though the influence of these informal agencies is subtle, it is definitely very comprehensive. In the development of the child's personality and character, the informal agencies play a very significant role. The major benefit derived from them is that they do not restrict the child in any way. The child develops naturally.

Despite these advantages, the informal agencies cannot

completely replace the formal ones, because in the absence of a definite plan of education, much time and energy is wasted over things which ultimately prove useless. Besides, these informal agencies cannot be employed to give specific education or knowledge of a very complex kind. Again, definite and certified education cannot be provided through informal means.

It is evident from the foregoing account of the advantages and disadvantages of formal and informal agencies of education that both are essential for the development of the individual and of society. As social structure becomes progressively more complex and population increases, the importance of the formal and informal educational agencies also increases.

Consequently, it has come to be believed that there is intimate relationship between the formal and informal means and agencies of education. When formal education increases to a great extent, it tends toward abstraction and lifelessness and then it needs the assistance of the informal agencies to infuse new life into it. For this reason, modern educationists believe that college and family are complementary factors in the child's education.

Dewey has correctly commented that in the modern age, "One of the weightiest problems with which the philosophy of education has to cope today is the method of keeping a proper balance between the informal and the formal, the incidental and intentional modes of education."

Neither of the two should be stressed at the cost of the other. On the one hand, various kinds of schools and colleges should be established to provide formal education, while on the other the informal agencies must also be exploited to make up any deficiencies left in the formal mode.

Even in colleges and schools, excessive emphasis should not be upon book learning. It is for this reason that modern schools design their curriculum so that sufficient time is given to extra-curricular and social activities. For the same reason, it has been found desirable that educators and parents should meet from time to time.

Here, we are discussing formal and informal agencies of education, but most important formal and informal agencies such as family, school, community, religion and the state are being discussed in greater detail at the end of this chapter.

FORMAL AGENCIES OF EDUCATION

The different kinds of schools and colleges are enumerated among the formal means of education. The English word 'school' is derived from the Greek 'skhole', which means leisure. Hence, school implies a place of leisure where people gather during their leisure time for the purpose of developing themselves.

In Ancient Greece, young men and women used to collect in schools during their leisure time to receive education from famed scholars and philosophers. These same schools, later on took the form they have at present. In a school eduction is imparted to the educand by trained educators, at a fixed time and place, according to a predetermined syllabus.

Different schools are intended for different kinds and levels of education, for example, primary, secondary and higher education, university education, etc. Among professional institutions are medical colleges, engineering colleges, etc. The function of the school is to achieve the physical, mental and character development of the educand, to develop in him a social consciousness, the qualities of citizenship. It must also aim at cultural development and the imparting of professional or industrial training.

From this standpoint, it is seen that schools in India suffer from many defects, which have to be removed. If a school is to be successful in achieving its aims in the present age, it must have intimate relationship with the family on the one hand and the state or government on the other. Both must give it their wholehearted support and cooperation.

INFORMAL AGENCIES OF EDUCATION

1. Library. There is little need to elaborate the role played by libraries in disseminating education. Libraries are the collection of the knowledge of centuries summarised in books. Many people maintain personal libraries but these do not fulfil all needs. Hence, the state and local self-governing bodies undertake the responsibility of establishing libraries. In almost all countries modern governments spend vast sums of money to establish big libraries.

2. Reading Room. In most modern towns, one finds reading rooms in addition to the libraries. These are established by the state and other institutions. These reading rooms provide many daily, weekly and monthly newspapers, all kinds of magazines, which are available to the public who can come there and read them. It is not possible for every individual to subscribe individually to such a large number of magazines. For this reason, the reading room plays a significant role in education.

3. Museums. Museums are very useful in imparting education in such subjects as history, geography, biology, anthropology, etc. It is for this reason that one finds well stocked museums and zoos in many big cities of the world. The knowledge that an individual can gain by roaming around in these institutions is not available to him anywhere else. It is a psychological principle that the thing seen is remembered than the thing heard. For this reason, museums can contribute a lot to an individual's education. There are many museums and zoos in many Indian cities.

4. Cinema. Cinema is one of the important informal agencies of education in the modern world, for it is an important form of audio-visual education. By means of this it is possible to see incidents, individuals and objects as if with the eye itself. It is therefore very useful when one wants to acquaint the educand with things, places and incidents occurring in foreign countries. It can be done by taking the educand to any cinema hall and exhibiting the appropriate film.

It is evident, therefore, that this agency can easily be employed for the teaching of history, geography, civics, political science and comparable subjects. The government in India has inspired and financed the production of many entertaining and informative film documentaries concerning the revolution in agriculture and industry that is taking place in the country today. Newsreels also help in the dissemination of news and ideas. For example, the cinema has played an important role in educating the illiterate public about family planning.

Apart from newsreels, even the commercial films have a tremendous impact upon the personality, character, behaviour and many smaller things of the young men and women of the country. It has been seen in America that the incidence of crime has gone up after films about crime became popular there. In India also a comparable trend is noticeable.

Most films being produced today are concerned with the exhibition of the latest fashions, and this has had a detrimental effect upon the thinking of the younger generation. Hence, the government is faced with the task of encouraging the production of good, illuminating and elevating films, and also with the responsibility of preventing the production of films which cater to the baser instincts of men and women, films concerning sex, crime, etc. In many states, students have been legally barred from seeing films during the matinee show. This is not a very psychological way of shielding the younger generation from the ill-effects and bad influences of film going. They can see the same films later in the evening and still imbibe the same ideas. Preventing students from seeing films during college hours will achieve nothing more than to increase attendance in colleges.

There is no doubt at all that cinema has comprehensive influence upon the moral, religious and intellectual development of adolescents. The main cause of this is that in viewing the film, the members of the audience unconsciously identify themselves with the hero or the heroine and hence suffer the same experience through which the hero or the heroine passes.

They can be observed exhibiting the same emotions which are controlling the figure on the screen. It would be no exaggeration to say that if the cinema is exploited to the greatest extent as a medium of education, then there is no other informal agency which can be more influential than the cinema.

5. Drama. Although the popularity of the cinema has done much to reduce public interest in drama, in fact cinema can never completely replace dramatic performance. In a dramatic performance the actor, through his concrete presence and acting, arouses certain emotions in his audience.

The drama can be a very effective medium for the powerful presentation of many ideas and behaviour patterns. But from the educational standpoint, drama is more significant from the point of view of those children who can take active part in it. It does not compare in this respect with films because children cannot participate in films.

For this reason, almost all colleges and schools have some or the other dramatic society in which the educands produce plays. Acting is itself an art, and it can only be learnt through drama. Besides, drama also promotes interest in singing and dancing. Participating in drama is useful because it helps a person to outgrow stage fright, or the fear of appearing before an audience.

This promotes the ability to work in group. Acting also helps to reflect clearly the differences in the personalities of the actors and actresses. In certain cases, it has been seen that proximity of boys and girls during stage performances has led to certain undesirable consequences, but such incidents can, by and large, be prevented if the educators are conscious of their responsibility and handle the situations psychologically.

Drama has also proved to be a useful medium for letting out or expressing many repressed drives and feelings. In the form of Psycho-drama, dramatic performances can actually be used to get rid of many of the child's abnormalities.

Finally, the teacher himself, in order to be a successful educator, must indulge in some acting, because only then can he present his subject forcefully to the class and influence his audience.

6. Newspapers and magazines. The contribution of newspapers and magazines to the education of people in general is far greater than that of any other informal agency because they can be circulated over a far larger area than can be covered by films, dramatic societies, television, etc.

Today, the progress of education in a country is computed by the number and quality of magazines and newspapers published there. It is a matter of no little pride that after independence, the number of newspapers and magazines, in English and in local languages has been going up steadily. This has been made possible by the rapid increase of literacy among the people. In the last few years many children's magazines have been published. These play a considerable part in child's education.

Magazines concerning sports and games provide considerable information in that sphere, while certain magazines provide information about health and how it can be maintained. There has been literally a flood of magazines concerning films, although it is difficult to class these among the better magazines.

Besides these, a considerable number of weekly, monthly and magazines of other frequency add to the knowledge of the people. Apart from English and Hindi newspapers,

newspapers in almost all regional languages are being published in the country, the latter having the advantage of being able to reach the masses living in the villages. And in fact, newspapers play the greatest role in making democracy a success. No other form of informal education can be compared with these as far as political, economic and social education is concerned.

*7. **Radio.*** In the West, the radio has been almost completely supplanted by the television, but in India it is still very much in vogue. It is pleasant to note that transistor radios can now be seen in even the remotest villages, and have become so common that they are carried everywhere, to work, to play, to social gatherings, to travel. The radio amuses as well as instructs.

The All India Radio, the national radio network, has conceived and executed a number of programmes to achieve these ends, amusement, pleasure and education. Among their programmes many are aimed at the agriculturists, children, uneducated women, students, those inclined towards light or classical music, towards humour and laughter, towards serious discussions on current topics and scientific subjects, etc.

Most of the programmes broadcast over the radio are so full of information and also effective that if one only has the patience to listen to them, one would find unprecedented progress in one's education. Aware of this significance of the part that the radio can play, the Indian government has provided public radio sets for each panchayat so that the villagers can collect in the building housing the panchayat and listen to various programmes of interest to them.

Radio is a very good medium of political education, in particular. Before the last general elections, the All India Radio arranged for the leaders of various political parties to speak on the radio and explain the aims, objectives and plans of their respective organisations so that the uneducated people could assess the merits of each party and select the representative of the party most aligned to their own way of thinking.

This was an important step forward in the political eduction of the electorate. As a consequence, one finds the opposition parties creating an uproar whenever it seems that the broadcasting system is becoming unduly sympathetic towards the ruling party. Efforts are being made to neutralize the broadcasting organisation, politically, so that it should not become an organ of the ruling party alone, but should develop into an agency for disseminating information, knowledge and amusement.

By means of the radio, people who are separated by long distances from the centre of things can listen to all kinds of cultural programmes while relaxing at home. In this it is not even necessary to open one's eyes or to sit up, as is necessary in the case of television or cinema. But if the radio is to be made an effective agency of informal education, there is considerable need for overhauling its programmes. AIR pays considerable attention to the suggestions put forward by its listeners in this connection, and it also consults experts from time to time.

8. Television. As has already been mentioned, television has become an important means of informal education in most advanced countries. Colour television has also been introduced so that it has now come nearer to reality. Most men and women spend their leisure time in front of the television, and thus absorb a lot of knowledge and information without having to make any great effort.

Most of the programmes exhibited over the television are so life-like that one hears of people dying of heart failure while watching boxing matches and other exciting events. Television was extensively used to inform people about man's recent journey to the moon. The launching and various other stages were televised for the benefit of the people. In India, the effective range of television is far too small at present, and most of the programmes put on the screen have a long way to go.

Faster development in this direction would be very much desirable, but progress has been hampered by many difficulties. Once these are removed, it will be observed that television is the most effective means of imparting social, economic, political and even professional training.

Closed circuit television, a more modern form of television exhibition, is being extensively used in the training of medical students. In this the operation taking place in the operation theatre is televised so that students sitting in the classroom can view it. In this way more students can be accommodated than would be possible in any operation theatre.

9. Scouting and girl guides. The scouting and girl guide movement has made an important contribution to the education of young boys and girls, for it teaches them social service through giving first aid, swimming, cooking, guiding the physically handicapped, pitching camps, returning lost children to their parents in big fairs, etc.

This helps the child to understand the human body, to develop his personality and character and also contributes to his moral progress. Such institutions can be seen in school the world over. They are even more useful in that they do not indulge in political discrimination.

10. Social welfare centre. In addition to the scouting and girl guide movement, Brown considers social welfare centres as media of informal education. Social welfare centres and social education centres have been set up in India as part of the community development projects. These have been established in rural as well as urban areas. By taking part in it, men and women receive education of different kinds, learn various skills and thus generate the ability to achieve financial independence.

11. Educational tours. Now-a-days, much importance is being attached to educational tours as means of providing education in history and geography. In such tours the educands accompany the educator to far away places of historical or geographical significance. This has its entertainment value, apart from the information it provides.

In many universities, educational tours have been made a compulsory part of education in history so that this education may become more life-like. Educational tours awake in the educand a greater awareness of the various movements occurring within the country, and also help to bring him nearer to nature. Tours are also considered an important part of industrial training, for the educand learns much by visiting industrial establishments.

OTHER INFORMAL AGENCIES

In addition to the above agencies of informal education, different societies also have other institutions which are doing valuable work in this direction. Labour welfare committees, women welfare committees, cooperative societies, village panchayats, development block committees, and the like are concrete examples of this.

Apart from this exhibitions of various kinds—art, science, industry, railways, postal etc., do much to increase awareness of these spheres among the public. Now-a-days international exhibitions have also become very popular. In such exhibitions, nations put up their respective pavilions to show their achievements and progress in various directions so that people viewing them can learn how far a particular country has progressed in a particular direction.

One such exhibition was organised in Japan in 1970. The cause of higher education is also served by the committees and associations for various subjects—mathematics, history, biology, philosophy, etc., which hold international meetings from time to time in order to exchange views. And, the coffee houses in many large towns are no less important than educational institutions because among their clientelle are leading doctors, lawyers, literary figures, artists, impoverished politicians, who gather together to discuss all kinds of things. This helps to disseminate information and improve understanding of all affairs.

Many towns also have literary associations which do much valuable work by encouraging and felicitating important literary figures. Professional associations, one example of which is the Indian Chamber of Commerce and Industry, also play a significant role in educating public opinion by holding seminars and discussions. So, in this manner, different institutions contribute to the cause of education in their own way by providing information to the people.

MOST IMPORTANT AGENCIES OF EDUCATION

1. Home or Family (An Active and Informal Agency)

The family is the oldest, basic and fundamental unit of human society and therefore the most effective agency of education, though it is most informal yet very effective and hence vital in the education of the child.

Importance of Family in Education

Mazzinni was quite correct in saying that the child's first training in citizenship is in the mother's lap and the father's affection.

Accepting the importance of the family as a factor in the child's education, Montessori called his schools the home of children. Locke attached greater importance to education at home than to school education. Comenious opined that the home is the centre of all kinds of education for the child. Froebel is correct when he says that the education imparted at home is both effective and natural. Pestalozzi also felt that the home is the child's first school.

Raymont says, "Two children may attend the same school, may come under the influence of the same teachers and the same organisation, may pursue the same studies and perform the same exercise; and yet may differ *totocaelo* as regards their general knowledge, their interests, their speech, their bearing, and their moral tone, according to the homes they come from."

The family looks after the child's physical development, lays the foundations of his character, gives him religious education, acquaints him with the realities of life and provides the right kind of environment for the development of his interests, tendencies, motivations, intelligence and other processes. It is the most important agency of the child's socialization.

Besides, in many families some kind of professional and practical education is also imparted to the child. It is for this reason that cooperation between the family and the school is considered an important aspect of the child's education.

Meaning and Definition of Family

Meaning of family. The family is the oldest, basic and fundamental unit of human society. It consists of the husband, wife, children together with all the young and old dependents. They are related to one another in one way or the other. In some old societies even servants were included in the family. Thus, family may be regarded as a small social group consisting of a few related persons. In our country, the picture of a family is more or less the same.

Definition of family. To make the meaning of family more clear we are giving some important definitions given by some well-known persons as under:

(1) "The family is a group defined by sex relationship

sufficiently precise and enduring to provide for the procreation and upbringing of children." —*MacIver & Page*

(2) "By family we mean a system of relationship existing between parents and children." —*Clare*

(3) "A family is a group of persons united by the ties of marriage, blood or adoption constituting a single household interacting and in intercommunication with each other in their respective social role of husband and wife, mother and father, son and daughter, brother and sister creating and maintaining a common culture." —*Burgess & Locke*

The above definitions make it clear that a family consists of interrelated persons who interact with one another in different ways. Not only this, each family has its own distinct habits of clothing, eating, thinking, talking and living. These are the items of that family's culture. This culture has to be preserved and transmitted by each family from generation.

Main Elements of Family

The following are the essential elements of a family:

(1) Sexual intercourse of a man and a woman.

(2) Marriage is the basis of these connections by social sanction.

(3) Their progeny is known to belong to them and to their family's name by the sanction of state which guarantees their legality and status.

(4) Each member contributes something to the family welfare, joint sharing of income to meet the needs and joint responsibility in all spheres of activities.

(5) Shared use and joint ownership of house and all attached facilities are guaranteed.

Functions of Family

The functions of family are given below:

1. Physical development. To develop the child physically is first function of family. Parents and other members of the family are always careful about the health and well-being of the child. For this purpose useful physical experiences, exercises and other activities are provided to the child. In other words, regular physical exercises, habits of cleanliness and vigorous living is fostered in the child. Not only this, wholesome food containing all the ingredients of a balanced diet is also provided to the child to achieve his maximum physical development.

*2. **Emotional development.*** The influence of family greatly affects the emotional development of the child. Home environment, its upkeep, sanitation and decoration all influence the emotional growth of the child. Amity and good fellow-feeling in the members of a family affect the emotional make up of the child and develop in him healthy and passive emotions namely; sympathy, courage, affection and love etc. On the contrary, disunity and maladjustment in a broken home or family develop in the child negative emotions namely; fear, anger, jealousy, and worry, etc.

*3. **Development of language.*** The child learns his mother tongue in a natural way in his family. Schools only reform it and add to the vocabulary. We observe that children belonging to educated and cultured families pronounce the words correctly in comparison with those who come out from backward and illiterate families. Schools are able to reform very little in such cases.

*4. **Development of innate tendencies.*** Congenial and conductive environment of the family brings out and develops the innate tendencies of the child. If these tendencies do not have a natural outlet, they turn into complexes and the child becomes maladjusted. Mention may here be made that the unfoldment of innate tendencies begins in the family and is evident during early childhood. Parents and other members of the family should be very careful about this and provide all facilities to the child for his self-assertion and proper development.

*5. **Mental development.*** Mental development of the child is the second important function of family. By mental development we mean the development of mental powers namely; thinking, feeling, reasoning, discrimination, judgement and memory. To develop these powers parents provide adequate opportunities and experiences to the child. In comparison with poor families, well-to-do families are able to provide better opportunities and experiences for their children to receive better education.

*6. **Social development.*** However, it is the function of school to ensure the social development of the child, but we must not forget that family is also a miniature of society—in which the child learns all the socially desirable values namely; sympathy, love, co-operation, tolerance, responsibility and justice by living democratically with all the other members of the family.

*7. **Development of interests and habits.*** Good or bad habits and interests of a child spring up and develop in the family in which he lives. These good or bad habits and interests form the character of the child. If parents and other members of the family are unmindful and indifferent towards the activities of their child, he develops such bad habits and interests that plague him all through his life and do great harm to his family members also. Therefore, parents should be ever vigilant to know the activities of their children otherwise their children and they themselves shall have to suffer in the long run. We observe that those parents who are indifferent and careless about their children, the latter are getting more indisciplined, work-shirkers, careless and mischievous in schools.

*8. **Transmission of culture.*** Though it is the duty of school to preserve, transmit and develop the culture of the race, but it does not mean that family, as an agency of education, has nothing to do in this connection. As a matter of fact, each society has its own culture. That culture is still practised in families. In schools, culture is taught whereas in families it is caught. That is why, Hindu culture is alive in Hindu families and Muslim culture is fresh in Muslim families. In short, the child of particular family imbibes the culture of his family consciously or unconsciously.

*9. **Development of morality and character.*** A family develops moral and ethical values in the child. These values lead to the formation of habits and attitudes which build character, the backbone of life. Other institutions can only help in this connection. Thus, it is the family alone which originates and fosters these values in the early childhood. A child learns these values through imitation. As he grows older, he learns the desired moral and social values through insight. In short, family is a cradle where character of the child takes roots upto the age of six years. Other institutions only develop it further.

*10. **Religious development.*** Family is the only institution where religious development of the child can be ensured. In a secular state like India, it is the duty of family alone to impart religious education to the child. In the religious environment of the family, the child learns to follow the principles of a particular religion with the result that religious, moral and ethical values develop in him without any difficulty.

11. Development of individuality. Though other institutions are also responsible to see that the child develops his individuality on proper lines, yet this development start in the family. The seeds begin to sprout out during early childhood in the environment of the family. The responsibility of parents is utmost here and for this they are ever vigilant and considerate in this respect.

12. Provision of practical and vocational education. Attitudes to labour, hard work and practical work also develop in the family during early childhood. The child gets his first lesson of further vocation in the family from those who are engaged in the family vocation. The child becomes a sort of apprentice and in future may adopt the family vocation.

Indian Families—Their Effects upon Children

Joint family system has been the chief characteristic of Indian family. With the active cooperation, love and sympathy of father, mother, uncle, aunt, grandfather and grandmother together with other close relations, the child imbibes the habits and thoughts of his elders in a natural way.

Due to various reasons the old joint family system is gradually disintegrating into smaller and smaller individual families. The result is that children do not get, now those all pervading, comprehensive and broad experiences necessary to shape their desirable attitudes and strong good character.

Poor families are not in a position even to provide adequate diet and other necessities of life to their young ones. Even the well-to-do families are often found to be quite indifferent towards the proper nurture and education of their children. These conditions need to be changed if the family has to play its shaping and formative role.

Measures to Make Indian Family an Effective Agency of Education

We are suggesting some measures to make Indian family an

effective agency of education as under:

1. *Provision for physical development.* The following elements are essential for the physical development of the child.

(a) Residence of family. Residence of family should be open to light and air. It should be clean and its entire environment should be peaceful and conducive to physical well-being. It has been well said that where open air and sunlight is not available, the doctor will be necessary. Thus, the locality round about the residence should be very clean and open.

(b) Food. Good food is essential for good health. Hence, the diet given to children should be clean, wholesome and health-giving containing a balanced combination of fats, vitamins, proteins, carbohydrates, mineral, salts and water.

(c) Clothes. Tight fitted clothes lead to physical discomfort and sometimes injure the body to the child also. These days we find that fashion is playing havoc with the health. It is undesirable. Hence, clothes of children should be such which permit sufficient air circulation and free movements.

(d) Provision of play and rest. Play is a form of exercise which is very essential for sound health. Hence, children should be encouraged to play in parks or open places. Parents should also play with their children to give them natural encouragement from their activities. After play or exercise, rest is equally essential to ward off fatigue. Physical development of children will be very conducive, if a balance in four factors namely—exercise, rest, diet and study is established upto the mark.

(e) Personal cleanliness. Personal cleanliness is very necessary for personal health. Hence, good habits of personal cleanliness such as regular cleaning of teeth, cutting of nails, daily bathing, wearing clean clothes, polishing shoes and other articles should be inculcated in children from the early childhood. These good habits remain with children throughout their lives and keep them physically healthy.

2. *Development to intellectual, aesthetic and practical interests.* Family should develop the intellectual, aesthetic and practical interests of the child from the early childhood. In this connection we are suggesting some measures as under:

(a) Intellectual development. For the intellectual development of the child, the family environment should be intellectual. In this connection quiz games, intelligent play devices, word

building games, action songs, toys and sketches etc., should be provided to children. Further, curiosity is the basis of motivation for learning and deeper understanding.

Hence, the natural instinct of curiosity should never be discouraged even if it leads to some loss or expenditure and waste. Parents and elders should always encourage children to read stories and complete the home work given to them by their teachers.

(b) Aesthetic development. Aesthetic taste of children is developed by various kinds of hand work, sketching, drawing of sceneries and designs etc. Observation of star studded sky and other natural scenes and sights, singing, dancing and fancy dress etc., also stimulate the child's aesthetic sense. Parents should try to develop the aesthetic sense of their children as much as possible.

(c) Provision for practical knowledge. Children should be provided full opportunities to learn practical knowledge. They learn many small courtesies by observation and practice. Hence, showing courtesies to guests and receptive behaviour to strangers and other small cultural activities should be taught to children through actual work and behaviour of parents and other elder members of the family.

3. Provision of constructive activities. The family should provide constructive activities to develop the constructive tendencies of child. Knowledge acquired through constructive activities remains permanent and helps in the selection of a suitable vocation also. Hence, family should provide such constructive activities before the child which may help him to develop his constructive energies as far as possible. To encourage the maximum self-expression of children, the family should arrange for newspapers, monthly magazines and other useful literature.

4. Development of character and training of responsibility. The character of a child is developed in family by inculcating in him self-confidence and training of responsibility. Hence, parents should encourage children to plan and execute small projects of home decoration, table setting and garden planting etc. This will develop in them self- confidence and a sense of responsibility.

5. Development of individual needs, capacities and interests. Psychology has proved that each individual is not a carbon copy of another. In other words, each individual has his own individuality. Hence, members of family should provide suitable opportunities to each child to develop his individuality according to his needs, capacities and interests. The defect of teaching in school will also be supplemented and complemented by individual development at home under family environment.

6. Impartial treatment. Parents should behave fairly and impartially with all the children of family. There should be no sex discrimination between boys and girls as is found in some of the Indian families. Both boys and girls of today are the citizens of tomorrow. In their capacity as citizens they will not only enjoy the fundamental rights equally but also form a sound national government. Hence, the family should break the old artificial walls and provide equal opportunities to boys and girls for their richer, happier and better development.

7. Religious education. The family should provide suitable opportunities before the child to receive religious education also. One can not deny the fact that a child cannot understand the conflicting elements of religion but he can certainly receive religious education in the wider sense through religious books, religious tales and other religious activities.

Such religious education shall inculcate in the child all the desirable values namely—love, sympathy, service, sacrifice and fellow-feeling. In a secular state like India, it is the sacred duty of family to provide religious education to each child so that he may grow into a responsible citizen of the state.

8. All-round development. The family should ensure the all-round development to the child. In India, most of the families are satisfied only with partial development of their children. They neglect the other aspects of development. Jacks in his book 'Total Education' has classified such families into three categories. In one type of competitive families children are developed into one set direction upto set limits only. The other aspects are neglected. In other type of families cultural activities and interests are made fun of with the result that children remain deficient in emotional and cultural aspects of development.

The third type of families are known as emotionally

refrigerator families. In such families socially desirably qualities namely; love, affection and sympathy etc., are looked down upon by their members with the result that the behaviour of children belonging to such families becomes static and undesirable. In reality, a family should look to all sides of child's personality— physical, mental, emotional and social. Then only, the wholesome and full development of child will be possible. For this purpose, no aspect of development is to be neglected. Parents should provide all the desirable experiences and activities to their children duly planned and structured in advance.

2. The Community (An Active and Informal Agency of Education)

The community is also an important informal agency for the child's education. Moving out of the family, the child automatically takes up the membership of various groups in community and through them develops various aspects of his character and personality. Playing in the group, he develops his mind and body. He also experiences moral, social and cultural development. Many institutions in the society provide him with professional and vocational training, while political groups look after his political training.

Definition of Community

To make the meaning of community more clear, some definitions are given below:

(1) "A community may be thought of as the total organization of social life within a limited area."

—*Ogburn & Nimkoff*

(2) "A community is the smallest territorial group that can embrace all aspects of social life."

—*K. Davis*

(3) "By community is to be understood a group of social beings living a common life including all the infinite variety and complexity of relations which result from common life or constitute it." —*Ginsberg*

Community as an Agency of Education

Every community has its various needs and glaring problems.

When these needs are met and problems solved, the standard of community rises higher and higher. This progress goes on gradually and continually. On the contrary, a community which is unable to provide right type of education to its members, it remains cramped up and stagnant with the result that its progress is blocked and stunted.

Therefore, each community tries to plan its progress and development by providing purposeful and effective education to its members especially children. In other words, a community tries to mould education according to its social, economic and political needs or aspirations. This is an ongoing and continuing process.

The school run by a community is therefore called a miniature of society. In short, the community, as an agency of education, influences its children both formally and informally. In the lines to follow, we are throwing light on the importance, influences and functions of community.

Importance of Community in the Education to the Child

Community is an important informal and active agency of education. Just as the family and the school have a great influence upon the child, much in the same way the community also modifies the behaviour of child through social contacts, group activities and group dynamics in such a way that he begins to participate in all the desirable activities of the community of which he is an integral part.

It is why we still hear the saying that children of a community develop as the adults of that community wish them to become. In fact, the child does not develop in the environment of his family alone, the environment of the community also moulds and modifies the behaviour of the child according to its ideas, ideals and goals. It is the miracle of community environment alone in which the child develops his innate and inherent tendencies according to his nature and learns his language, and standard of living.

In brief, the community environment exerts its impressions upon the developing children in all perceptible and imperceptible ways. Since each community has its own culture, we find a great difference in the culture and behaviour patterns of children belonging to different communities. A Yeoger has rightly remarks—"Since man by nature is a social being, he has learnt through the years that the personality as well as group activities can be best developed through community."

Educational Functions of Community

Now we discuss below the formal influences which a community exerts upon children—

1. Establishment of school. The community establishes various types of schools so that the culture of the community may be preserved, developed and transmitted to its children. Many communities establish their own communal schools to train their children for the welfare and advancement of their community interests.

2. Formulation of aims and control on education. The community determines the aims of education. It also supervises and guides the educational process followed in the schools established by it.

3. Provision of universal education. The community determines the various stages of education. At the same time, it strives to provide universal education.

4. Construction of curriculum. For the purpose of achieving the aims of education, suitable curriculum is constructed. Hence, the community prepares an outline of curriculum to be followed in its school.

5. Provision of vocational and industrial education. In modern age, there is a great demand for vocational and industrial education. Hence, the community establishes vocational, industrial and technical schools according to its needs.

6. Adult education. Community welfare and its development needs that adults should also be educated. Thus, the community makes provision for adult education also.

7. Finance of schools. To shoulder the responsibility of running the schools smoothly and efficiently arrangement of required finance is essential. The community makes necessary provision of finance for school building, furniture and salary of teachers.

8. Co-operation between citizens and school leaders. Close cooperation between citizens and leaders of schools is necessary. Hence, the community tries to maintain as much close co-operation as possible between the members to the managing committees and school teachers.

From the above discussion, it is clear that the community tries to influence the education of its children both informally and formally. Crow and Crow has rightly remarked—"A community cannot expect something for nothing. If it wishes its young people to serve their community well, it must provide whatever educational advantages are needed by the young people, individually and collectively, to prepare themselves for that service." —*Crow and Crow*

3. The State (An Active and Informal Agency of Education)

The modern welfare state is responsible for the over all development of all its citizens. That is why modern states pay so much attention to education and formulate national policies for education. The state shoulders the responsibility of establishing different kinds of schools.

In many states, free and compulsory education is provided, and even where this is not so, almost all educational institutions are aided by the state in one way or the other. The state provides able and trained teachers by establishing training colleges for them.

The state also provides military training. Besides, research cannot be carried on without the help of the state. In a democracy, the state trains every individual in responsible citizenship. Although most sociologists oppose complete governmental control over education, every one agrees that without state's help education would fail.

State also plays an important role by retaining control over literature and encouraging it to evolve along acceptable lines. The state also looks after the education of physically and mentally handicapped children by establishing special institutions for such children.

"We observe that education, like other beneficial influences at work in a civilized community, may be conducted by all or any of the three means, first by voluntary efforts with a view to profit; secondary by voluntary efforts arising from philanthropic or religious motives; thirdly by the agency of state." —*Raymont*

Influence of State on Education

Each state has its distinct political set up, its culture and civilization, its industry and commerce and various other needs. They are quite different from those of others. All the above mentioned factors influence and shape the system of education of that state. Hence, each state tries to influence and control its education in some way or the other. State may be classified as under:

1. Totalitarian state
2. Democratic state

1. Totalitarian state. The supporters of totalitarian state believe that state is omnipotent and supremely sovereign in all fields of life. It has a superior and higher entity than that of those who form and organise it. As such, it can have absolute control over all its citizens. As able and capable citizens form and run a state efficiently and only education develops such citizens, therefore the state must have complete control over education for its existence and advancement.

In short, the supporters of the totalitarian ideology emphasize that the whole educational system must be centralized. Hence, in a totalitarian state education is completely centralized with the result that all aspects of education, namely; aims, curriculum, methods of teaching and discipline etc. are all closely guided and supervised by the central government.

2. Democratic state. The inherent powers of a democratic state are limited and well-defined. The state distributes its absolute power amongst its citizens by decentralization. This means that people become responsible for their own welfare. They plan for their own good and execute the plans themselves.

The state provides more and more opportunities to its citizens to plan and execute such plans for their happier, richer and better development. In the following lines we are throwing light on the relation between state and education, keeping into consideration the pattern of a democratic state.

Relation between State and Education

There are two views about the relation of state and education as under:

1. Individualism, and
2. Collectivism.

1. Individualism. Locke, Mill and Bentham etc., individualist thinkers firmly believe that the function of the state is only to protect and guide its people. It should not interfere in the sphere of education in any way. This is known as the 'Doctrine of Laissezfaire'. According to this doctrine, the individual has accepted the discipline of organized society for some definite objectives only. It does not mean that he has subordinated his freedom and liberty objectively and in toto. There are many spheres of life where he is completely free to choose and act. Education is one such sphere. In this way, according to individualist thinkers, state should not interfere in the sphere of education at all otherwise it will bring more harm than good.

2. Collectivism. Mathew Arnold, Carlyle and Ruskin etc., are the supporters of collectivism. They hold the view that the function of the state is not only to protest its citizens from internal or external dangers alone but also to control the education as well.

Since the progress and development of state depends upon educated citizens possessing desirable habits, competence and sound character, in the opinion of Mathew Arnold, "State must have full control even on higher education." In short, the advocates of collectivism firmly believe that full control over education by the State will be advantageous and beneficial to all its citizens in all respects.

State Control on Education and its Merits

State control on education will ensure the following merits:

(1) State control will ensure universal, compulsory and free education to all children of a certain age group and put a certain standard.

(2) Children having a minimum quantum of education will grow into capable and dynamic citizens imbued with social and national consciousness.

(3) Education imparted by the State will be better than education given by other agencies.

(4) Education of all children will be uniform confronting to the principle of the equality.

(5) Scheme of national education will be achieved successfully.

The above discussion reinforces the arguments of collectivists. Thus, the Russian thinker Pinkvich speaks out, "Public education aiming to mould the future citizens is a mighty instrument which government cannot pass to others."

State Control on Education and its Demerits

State control on education may bring the following harms:

(1) Politics will enter the domain of education.

(2) Instead of acting as a welfare oriented agency, State will turn into an instrument of indoctrination, brain washing and brain storming. Spartan education emphasised only physical development neglecting all the other aspects of personality.

(3) Committed teachers will be appointed by the state. Such teachers will turn out the same models.

(4) The real importance and aim of education will be set at naught.

(5) Complete development of individuality shall be impossible. Hence, the individual shall not be able to make his original contribution to the variegated whole of human life.

(6) Children will not get education according to their nature.

(7) The family will be deprived of its fundamental right.

(8) The principles of equality and freedom will be thrown to the winds because state will regiment the development of children. This is against the spirit of democracy.

(9) Under such a regimented system of education, only servants or slaves can be prepared to serve the state blindly. It will stop all scientific progress as that depends upon original thinking, free experimentation and expression.

Golden Mean

The individualists and the collectivists both insist on their extreme ideologies. Modern thinkers neither favour the doctrine of Laissezfaire alone nor accept the rigid control on education by the state. They regard both the ideologies as extremes and wish to strike a balance between the two. According to them, the task of education is so important that the co-operation of all the agencies is essential to complete it.

No doubt, State is an important agency of education but

it is not all in itself. Hence, the state should neither show complete neutrality towards the education of its citizens nor try to control it in toto but must work in active cooperation of all other agencies namely; the family, the community and the church.

Hence, whereas on one hand, the family, the community and the church should be allowed to help education in their own way, the state on the other hand should also guide and supervise the various stages of education through its policy of limited interference.

In this connection Raymont has rightly remarked, "The function of the state is to protect and promote, not to absorb or take the place of family and the individual. In the sphere of education it is the state's right, and even duty to protect the interior right of the family and the church.

Similarly, the state ought to make good the deficiency due to incapacity, unworthiness or other defects of parents and generally to protect, according to rules of reason and the faith, the moral and religious education of the young by moving any public impediment. The national state can rightfully demand and ensure that the citizens have a proper knowledge of their civil and national duties and attain a certain standard of intellectual and moral culture."

Educational Functions of State

Following are the main functions of education in a democratic state:

1. Construction of a national scheme of education. In a democratic state, education is just like the soul in a body. Thus, each state constructs a national scheme of education, keeping into consideration the multifarious needs of its citizens, after detailed discussion with its prominent educationists, educational philosophers and ministers.

After the construction of such a comprehensive scheme of education, it is cooked out and executed in such a way that no one is discriminated on the basis of colour, caste, sex as well as economic and social status. In other words, each individual gets equal opportunities to grow and develop.

2. Training in citizenship. The progress of state depends upon the ability, capacity and strength of character of its citizens.

Hence, the second function of a democratic state is to provide political, social, cultural and economic training to its citizens so that they are able to grow into dynamic, resourceful and national-minded individuals to serve their nation with full sincerity, zeal and devotion.

Political training or training regarding the political ideology of the state is given by way of free film shows, military demonstrations, radio, magazines, newspapers and television shows. Social training is given through social service programmes, social functions and other variety programmes.

Cultural training is given by establishing various institutions like museums, picture galleries, exhibitions, zoos, clubs for entertainment and arranging national tours, national fairs and free film shows. Much in the same way, economic training is given by imparting best possible vocational and technical training.

3. Provision of schools. The third function of state is to establish primary, secondary and various types of other schools. A democratic state establishes such schools and also the voluntary agencies run such schools to fulfil the needs of its citizens.

4. Adult education. The fourth function of state is to provide adult education for the uneducated and illiterate adults. It is really a matter of great pleasure that India has very recently launched such a scheme on a very huge scale.

5. Finance of schools. Financing is greatly essential to establish schools of various types and stages. The state provides adequate financial assistance to all the schools established either by the state or run by other voluntary agencies.

6. Universal, compulsory and free education. The success of a democratic state depends upon those citizens who make use of their rights and discharge duties correctly. Therefore, each democratic state provides universal, compulsory and free education upto a certain standard.

7. Encouragement to guardians. Opening more and more schools does not bring in them all the children of the nation. To achieve this objective, the state motivates the parents in such a way that they begin to take interest to educate their children.

8. Provision of efficient teachers. Establishing various types of schools, provision of universal, compulsory and free education upto a certain level requires the services of a large number of competent and efficient teachers to run those schools and to work out those schemes successfully. The state opens more and more training colleges and various types of training institutions to make available the vast army of capable teachers.

9. Provision of military education. In this modern age of conflict each citizen is expected to defend the state against a foreign invasion. Hence, the state provides military education in all the schools and colleges so that in times of emergency the trained citizens are able to be vigilant and defend the state.

10. Provision of standard books. Good education depends upon the availability of good and standard books. The state persuades authors and publishers to prepare good and standard books of reasonable price.

11. Provision of scholarships. Many talented, gifted and intelligent children of indigent means cannot pursue their education properly and go ahead further. The state provides scholarships and stipends to the needy and deserving ones without any discrimination of colour, cast, creed or sex.

12. General control and direction of school system. Each state determines the aims, curriculum and methods of teaching various subjects together with the evaluation system keeping into consideration its own demands and needs of its citizens. Not only this, it extends proper guidance and keeps close supervision in such a way that the entire educational system runs on the right track. The defaulting institutions are brought to book reformed and made to run on proper lines with motives of public good and national service.

13. Organisation of boards and committees. The state organizes committees and boards for determining the aims, curriculum, methods, the examination system and other relevant activities concerning education.

14. Appointment of commission. Sometimes, the state appoints commissions of enquiry to know about the working, deficiencies and drawbacks of schools and suggests measures for improvement and progress. The Secondary Education Commission and the Kothari Commission were appointed in India for this purpose and the government is executing the recommendations of these Commissions gradually.

15. Encouragement to education research. The modern age is an age of research. Hence, each state encourages educational research according to its needs and requirements to solve its own problems and explore new areas of improvement. We, in India, are beginning to realize its importance and schemes of research are coming up over here also.

4. Religion
(An Active and Informal Agency of Education)

From very ancient times, various educational institutions in almost every country have been shouldering the responsibility of educating the populace. In India, most schools were organised either within or very near the places of worship, for example temples, mosques, etc. All the education was imparted by the chaplain of these places of worship. Although almost all modern welfare states are also secular, it is an acceptable practice to assist religious institutions where they contribute to the educational effort.

"Religion and education are natural allies. Both recognize and have to do with the spiritual as against an exclusively material attention to the physical. Both seek to emancipate man from contact with his environment, but from slavery to it, to enlarge his horizon and quicken his aspiration."

—*E.D. Burton (Education in Democratic World)*

Importance and Values of Religion in Human Life and Society

Following are the main advantages of religion:

(1) Religion inculcates in children the essential moral and human qualities of courtesy, tolerance, sympathy, fellow-feeling, equality and fraternity etc. These qualities stimulate spirit of service and sacrifice which forms a noble character of man and develops his personality.

(2) Religion infuses hope and faith in man. He gets mental peace and develops in him sufficient courage and self-confidence to face the problems of life successfully.

(3) Religion is that dynamic aspect of culture which infuses in human being moral qualities. These qualities are expressed in all fields of human life.

(4) Religion sublimates and redirects our sex instinct into desirable channels. It is so potent a factor that influences all aspects of human life and society of which he is an integral part. Prof. H. Kabir has rightly remarked—"Religion resolves many of the conflicts. It releases energies that recognise neither difficulties nor defeat."

The above discussion makes it crystal clear that religion is essential both to man and society.

Religion and Education

There is a very intimate relation between religion and education. An effective educational system inculcates only those values in human beings which are valued and recognised by all the philosophies of the world. According to E.D. Burton— "Religion and education are close and real friends. Both are related to spiritualism in contrast to physical and material phenomenon. Both try to free the human being not from his physical surroundings but try to free him from the slavery to physical environment." Education broadens human outlook. It tries to modify human behaviour according to those ideals and values which are recognised by religion as of worth and importance. Thus, proper placing of religion in the system of education gives us those powers and capacities which develops human beings and the society to which they belong.

Religion inculcates those moral qualities which mould the educational system on democratic lines. The democratic and secular policy which aims at providing equal opportunities for all the citizens of our country is rightly based on true religion. It is why we inculcate in our children a spirit of self-discipline, sense of duty and responsibility so that they are able to rise above their selfish motives and work for the welfare of others with a spirit of devotion and dedication.

Education is intimately related also to culture which is an inseparable part of religion. The curriculum which incorporates cultural values and ideals in the educational system naturally gives due place to religious values and ideals.

In the complicated and complex society of today, naturalism and pragmatism cannot preserve the moral and spiritual values of life. Both these philosophies advocate material values and prosperity quite unrelated to the values of human life. The need of the day is that education and philosophy should lead man to higher and higher towards achieving the noble and immortal ideals of truth, beauty and goodness so that he leads a peaceful life and ultimately realizes God in himself. The philosophy of idealism serves as a sound basis for noble ideals and value which an educational system should incorporate. Thus, idealism is an integral part of religion and as such idealistic values are the real religious values.

From the above discussion, it becomes clear that both religion and education aim at the wholesome and fullest development of human personality which includes mental as well as spiritual development. To achieve this aim religion and education are closely related from ancient times. We see that in ancient times religious persons were teachers also. They taught children to discharge their duties to self and society both and thus developed their personalities to the full so that they were able to lead their lives happily and peacefully. In short, the aim of religion and education being the same both are very intimately related to each other.

Historical Retrospect

A cursory view of past history of the world clearly brings out that from ancient times the religious and moral principles have influenced the aims, curriculum and techniques of education. In those times, religion held sway in almost all the western countries. It was only through religious education that people were taught to live in unity, peace and co-operation. The 'Reformation Movement' in England had left the work of education entirely on churches and other religious institutes.

In the nineteenth century, gradually, the concept and practice of secular education began to hold the field and replaced religious education which used to be monopolised by a particular sector mission. In the 20th century 'The Religious School Movement' in America replaced the old pattern of education by general and liberal education with the result that the policy of 'Religious Neutrality' was in incorporated in the American Democratic Principles and Policy.

In India and other Eastern countries, education has been religious since ancient times. According to McDonell, Indian education bears the imprint of religion since very early ages of human history. In those days, religious persons used to be teachers also. They inculcated moral and religious values in the minds of children.

During Muslim rule also, education maintained its religious character and form. But during the British rule, religious naturality was practised by the rulers. This policy of religious naturality was opposed tooth and nails by Indians with the result that denominational schools began to be opened. The Hindus insisted firmly that education devoid of religion will destroy their religion and culture. Hence, from 'Hunter Commission' of 1882 to The 'Punjab University Commission' various commissions and committees recommended some sort of religious education to be associated with the general and common system of education in India.

Position of Religious Education in a Secular State like India

On 15th August, 1947 we achieved our freedom. As our country is a country of diverse religions, castes and creeds, our leaders adopted the ideal of secular education. They thought that any kind of narrow, bigoted and communal education would create divisions and dissensions in the nation due to which our very independence would be in jeopardy.

Hence, they separated religious education of any sort from the national pattern and propagate the ideal of secular liberal education. Viewing the defects of religious education, our Indian Constitution also emphasizes the secular ideal. According to article 19, all citizens are free to follow any creed or sect. No religious tax can be imposed on them.

According to article 22 no religious education can be imparted in any Government school. Only those institutions can impart religious education which are founded by some 'Trusts' for this purpose. Even in such schools there is no compulsion on any child who does not like to opt for that education. In short, our country is committed to the ideal of secularism.

The Secondary Education Commission Report (1952-53) also opines, "In view of the provision in the Constitution, religious instruction cannot be given in schools except on a voluntary basis and outside the regular school hours: such instructions should be given to children of a particular faith and with the consent of the parents and management concerned. In making this recommendation we wish to emphasise that all unhealthy trends or disunity, rancour, religious hatred and bigotry should be discouraged."

From the above, it is clear that the State has no religion. It is committed to democratic ideals and beliefs. As a matter of fact, religion and democracy are same. Both strive to develop the innate tendencies and capacities of the child to the full. This is true of the religion and democracy all over the world. Both are committed to foster individual good and the good of the society.

Precautions While Introducing Religious Education in Schools

Following precautions should be taken, while introducing religious education in schools—

(1) Narrow religious education prepares the child for the other world. It neglects the needs of individual and demands of society. This should not be allowed to happen.

(2) In the garb of religious education narrow communal or sectarian education is provided. This spoils the natural development of the child. Thus, healthy principles and virtues of all religions should be incorporated in the education so that fanaticism, bigotry and blind beliefs are avoided.

(3) To impart the education of all the virtues of all the religions of the world, the school environment should be so congenial and conducive that children receive virtuous education in a natural way. No compulsory indoctrination of dogmatic education should be allowed at all.

(4) No child should be compelled to receive any kind of religious education directly or indirectly.

(5) Life of teacher should be so ideal that children are inspired to imbibe the ideals of good conduct and character in a natural way.

(6) Religious education should not receive so much emphasis that schools become temples, guruduaras, churches and mosques.

(7) Religious education should be imparted only to those children who wish to opt it after receiving the permission of their parents or guardians.

(8) Life histories of great persons of the world, stories of moral greatness, examples of patriotism, fellow-feeling, service and sacrifice should find place in the educational system as the same naturally and imperceptibly inculcate religious and moral values.

(9) Critical outlook of adolescents should be developed so that they themselves avoid blind beliefs and rationalize their faith and action.

(10) The ideals and values of true religion should be imbibed by children in a natural way. For this, the activities of the school should reflect all the higher moral ideals and values.

(11) Unity of all religions should be emphasised in the education of the school. Since all religions have virtues, therefore, they should be discussed in the right earnest. In the words of M.K. Gandhi, "The fundamental principles of ethics are common to all religions. These should be certainly taught to students."

5. The School
(An Active and Formal Agency of Education)

The school is the most important formal agency of education as is evident from the following definitions:

1. "A school is a vibrant community centre, radiating life and energy all-round, a school is a wonderful edifice, resting on the foundation of good will, good will of the public, good will of the parents, good will of the pupils. In a word, a well conducted school is a happy home, a sacred shrine, a social centre, a state in miniature and bewitching Brindavan, all beautifully blended into a synthetic structure."

—*S. Bala Krishna Joshi*

2. "School is a special environment, where a certain quality of life and certain types of activities and occupations are provided with the object of securing the child's development along desirable lines." —*John Dewey*

3. "Schools are institutions devised by civilized man for the purpose of aiding in the preparation of the young for well-adjusted and efficient members of society." —*J.S. Ross*

Need of School

In the ancient times human life was very simple. Knowledge

had not grown so vast as it is today. Human needs were very simple and could be easily fulfilled by informal agencies like the family and the community. Gradually, with the development of vast and varied knowledge and growth of over-population needs of man increased and the form of culture and civilization also became so complex and complicated that it became almost impossible for parents to transmit it to their children.

Further, most of the parents and other members of the family became so busily engaged in their own vocations or other professions that they were not capable enough to educate their young ones diverse subjects of the curriculum.

Hence, the need was felt for some such institution which could preserve, transmit and develop the cultural heritage. In short, the formal agency of education, namely the school came into existence on account of a rapid rise in the means of transport and communication, urbanization of growing population and the position of women as wage earners.

Mention may here be made that in the beginning, the school benefited the rich and well-to-do people only. It is the modern democratic society of today which has begun to cater to the educational needs of the poor and the neglected. In almost all the countries to the world namely; China, Egypt, Greece, Rome, Babylonia and India, the schools came into existence by the same process and the same circumstances of society.

Concept of School

There are two concepts about school. They are—(1) Traditional, and (2) Progressive. In the following lines, we are throwing light on both the concepts.

Traditional School

Traditional school imparts only formal education. Such schools came into existence when family failed to impart the needed education to its children. In early times, the church and the state were not separate institutions. In those days, the priests used to be teachers also and their places of imparting education were the premises to the churches. Those priests or teachers had made the education so costly that children belonging to well-to-do families only could receive it.

Later on, the state separated from the church and democratic trends began to appear in the working of the state. Gradually, with the availability of paper in the 13th century and invention of printing press in the 15th century more and more opportunities came to be available for more and more people to receive education. Today, these traditional schools have become the teaching shops where teachers are the sellers of knowledge and the children its purchasers.

In other words, the teachers in such schools, try to thrust upon the minds of children the ready-made titbits of knowledge by employing unpsychological methods and techniques without caring for their interests, inclinations, aptitudes, needs and capacities.

Discussing about such traditional school, Pestalozzi has rightly remarked— "Our unpsychological schools are essentially only artificial strifling machines for destroying all the results on the power and experience, that nature herself brings the life in them (children). We tyranically stop the delightful course of their unrestricted freedom, pen them up like sheep, pitiously chain them for hours, days, weeks, months, years to the contemplation of unnatural and unattractive letters."

Modern or Progressive School

Like Pestalozzi, other educationists namely Herbart, Froebel, Montessori, Nunn, Parkhurst, Tagore and others have emphasized child-centred education. All these educationists have opposed the traditional schools in which ready-made knowledge is thrust upon the minds of children forcibly without caring for their individual differences. They make numerous psychological experiments regarding the education to children. As a result of these experiments, progressive schools came into existence. In short, progressive schools developed in contrast to the unpsychological tendency in traditional schools.

Distinctive Features of Progressive School

The distinctive features of progressive school are as under:

1. Importance of child's personality. In traditional schools more importance is given to subject-matter in comparison with the child. Hence, dozes of content are forced down into the minds of children without paying any attention to their interests, inclinations and capacities. In other words, more importance is given to child rather than the curriculum. In progressive schools the personality of each child is honoured.

Hence, each child is provided such congenial and conducive environment in which he develops his personality according to his innate tendencies, capabilities and speed. In the words of Prof. K.G. Saiyidain—"Thus, the modern school seeks to replace information by experience and chooses the most significant and abiding aspects of experiences for its subject-matter and thereby makes school life active and meaningful."

2. Importance of the principal of activity in education. In traditional schools a child receives education as a passive listener whereas progressive schools stimulate and motivate children to self-choosing and self-learning which is the best way of learning. It infuses a sense of serious and sincere efforts together with heart-felt responsibility.

In the words of Prof. John Dewey—"The environment of a progressive school is simplified, purified and balanced. Under such an atmosphere the child is afforded ample opportunities to experiment for himself and acquire many social ideas."

3. Emphasis on practical knowledge. In contrast to traditional schools which impart bookish and theoretical knowledge curbing the innate tendencies of a child, progressive schools impart useful, constructive and practical knowledge to the child. In these schools, the curriculum is based upon real life experiences. The child recreates such learning experiences himself and learns out of such experiences the solutions to his real needs and problems of life. Such schools are playing their part very well in western countries. They are coming into existence gradually in our country also.

4. Emphasis on social values. Traditional schools are too much academic and monastic. They are cut away from real life and hence, they are of little value to the child in actual day to day living. On the other hand, progressive schools work under the light of social ideals and develop the child with reference to such ideals and aims. These schools encourage children to come in active contact with the libraries and youth welfare centres organized or run by the community or government.

The miniature school life is brought into active and lively contact with the wider world outside. Children are made actively conscious of their obligations to the community, society and the nation. Not only this, they are led and guided in such ways that they develop their personalities to the full in active and vital correlation with the development of society to which they belong.

5. Emphasis on the development of personality. Traditional schools emphasize only the mental development which is only one aspect of the whole process. On the other hand, progressive schools try to develop the whole personality to the child. This includes physical, mental, emotional and social development. This is real development.

In the words of F. Tracey—"The true end of all education is the complete realization of the ideal personality. The ideal product to the educational process is balanced personality."

6. Centre of community life. A community opens schools for its own good and progress. As such, it is the chief function of schools to impart such education which develops the child's personality in intimate relation with the development of the community. Traditional schools carry out their teaching work keeping the children away from the real life of the community.

On the other hand, progressive schools are such centres of community life where children are developed according to the demands of community. In the words of Prof. K.G. Saiyidain—"Since, these demands are always changing and modifying themselves, it is necessary that the school should be in vital rapport the life outside the school."

In India we find traditional schools. Now we need to replace these traditional schools by progressive schools. We hope that with the realization of democratic ideals and practices, more and more schools of the type will come into existence. We see that the process of change has started and now we should accelerate it as soon as possible.

Functions of School

Functions of school may be divided as—(1) Formal, and (2) Informal. We discuss below these two categories separately in some detail.

Formal Functions of School

Formal functions are mainly concerned with the mental development of the child. In this connection, following are the functions of school:

1. Development of mental powers. The first formal function of school is to develop the mental powers of the child so that he is able to think freely, clearly and logically. To complete this function the school structures such experiences for the child that he is able to develop his inherent mental faculties according to his needs, interests and capabilities for his own good and good of the society.

2. Cultivation of a dynamic and adaptable mind. The second formal function of school is to impart such knowledge to the child which is not an end in itself but a means to achieve some end. The end is cultivation of a dynamic and adaptable mind which is resourceful and able to create new value for future life.

3. Preservation, improvement and transmission of culture. The third formal function of school is to preserve and improve the national culture and then, transmit it to the rising generation.

4. Vocational and industrial education. The fourth formal function of school is to impart vocational and industrial education to children according to the demands of society. In a poor and developing country like India the school must be alert to impart vocational and industrial education to children according to their interests and capabilities so that they are able to support themselves and serve the country with sincerity.

5. Re-organization and reconstruction of human experiences. The fifth formal function of school is to re-organize and reconstruct human experiences. As a matter of fact, the function of school is not to preserve the continuity to society only. It has to meet social problems, to reform the society and ultimately to purge it off its dead wood. For this, a continuous process of research in all the higher branches of knowledge is a must and the school should be equipped to do it.

6. Development of citizenship. The sixth formal function of school is to develop in children the essential qualities of citizenship so that they may become active and responsible citizens imbued with qualities of leadership leading the nation on the path of progress in all spheres of national life.

*7. **Development of character.*** The most important formal function of school is to develop children morally and socially so that they are able to acquire firm and noble character. In early times the family and the church developed the character of children jointly, but now it has become the function of school to develop the character of children by allowing them to participate in such moral, ethical and social activities which may inculcate in them the socially desirable values and lead to the formation of a strong good character.

Informal Functions of School

Informal functions of a school relate to the physical, social and emotional development of children. We discuss them in some detail as under:

*1. **Physical development.*** The first informal function of school is to develop the child physically. For this, the entire environment of school should be such which leads to the physical well-being to children.

*2. **Development of social feeling.*** The second informal function of school is the development of social feeling in all the children of school. As a matter of fact, school is a miniature of society. Hence, the school should provide such a social environment before children by organizing students' unions, social service camps, social functions and parent-teacher associations etc., so that all the socially desirable values namely sympathy, cooperation, tolerance, social awakening and above all discipline develop in them in a natural way.

*3. **Emotional development.*** The third most important informal function of school is to develop the child emotionally. For this, the entire environment of school must be artistic. In other words, there should be garden, flower plants and other beautiful natural objects. The school building and the campus should be neat and clean. The walls of the rooms should be white-washed annually and the rooms be decorated tastefully. Trips, tours, exhibitions and debates also stimulate the emotional and aesthetic sense of children who can further be infused with a sense of admiration towards truth, beauty and goodness, the high ideals of human life.

School the Most Important Agency of Education

The school is considered the most important agency of education on the basis of the following arguments:

1. School is the sole agency of education as this term is generally interpreted. It is difficult to call a person educated if it is known that he has never been through school or college. Even if the individual does not take the trouble of obtaining he highest degrees, he should have been to school to gain elementary knowledge of mathematics and language.

2. Schools and educational institutions are believed to be the only media through which the national educational policy can be put into actual practice. When a national educational policy was laid down after independence in India, main attention was paid towards increasing the number of schools.

3. Without the assistance of the school, the family cannot by itself perform the task of educating child, and for this reason alone do parents send their children to schools. Earning one's livelihood is one important objective of education, and for this the child has no alternative but to go to school.

It is not at all surprising that family businesses and occupations should have come to an end and that women should also be going out of the home in search of jobs. In consequence, it is no longer possible for the parents to educate their children without external help. It is better therefore to leave this task to the school.

4. Most of other means of education are capable of being turned to ulterior use, of use as the means of spreading political thought of a particular school, while school is the only one which provides real education. Schools and colleges have no aim but education.

Magazines, radio, films, newspapers, etc., can be perverted as media of political propaganda of a definite school of thought. This reduces their importance as agencies of education.

5. School is the only educational agency which seeks to develop the individual's body, mind, morals, religious thinking and spiritual contemplation. It aims at complete development. Most of the other agencies can hope to develop any one or the other aspects of a person's personality.

Libraries and reading rooms provide only mental education. The radio does not help in improving the body but schools and colleges also provide opportunities for physical, mental, moral and spiritual development.

6. School are also the chief media of conscious or intentional education. Their sole aim is to provide education, just as it is the sole aim of the educators, men and women, who work there. These educators are professional people trained to educate. These individuals devote much thought to the objectives and means of education, analyse the novel experiences which fall to their lot during the course of actual teaching, and make use of such experiences to improve their efficiency. No other individual can find or even hope to find so much time to devote to education. Neither is such a person an expert in teaching. Obviously, the school should be accepted as the best medium of imparting education.

7. In the case of certain specialized forms of education, it is impossible to achieve anything in the absence of schools and colleges, for example, medical, engineering and technical education. Colleges are the only media of providing training in these specialised spheres and in academic learning at the highest level.

8. One criterion of the importance of an agency of education is the extent to which it makes a contribution to education, but another criterion is the possibility of its being substituted by another. If this criterion is applied to the various agencies of education, it will be seen that school is the only one for which there is no substitute, and hence it is indispensable.

The state, family, library, cinema, social welfare centres, infact none of these agencies can hope to replace the school. Even if the child is educated within the family, such education is limited to primary education or training in the hereditary occupation.

The family cannot provide more education than this. On the other hand, even some agency of education is not available after formal education has been completed, the absence does not constitute such a great handicap. Hence, school is the most important agency of education.

RELATIONSHIP BETWEEN THE FORMAL AND INFORMAL AGENCIES

Finally, it is necessary to keep in mind that the formal and informal agencies of education are complementary. Those aspects of education which are not attended to in schools are taken care of by the informal agencies. Even educational institutions employ many of the informal agencies for education—reading rooms, libraries, dramatic societies, cinema, films, institutions for military training, scouting and girl guides, etc.

Besides, a school education is definitely incomplete if it is not complemented by education at home. For this reason, it is now an axiom of education that parents and educators should be given opportunities to meet each other so that they can consider the problems of their wards and think up ways of solving them.

Many schools now celebrate parents day in which the parents of educands come to the school, meet teachers and discuss the various problems that face both the parents and the educators.

In addition to this, school must also take the assistance of the community in spreading education, because the school is a special association created by the community through which it passes its acquired and accumulated knowledge to the younger generation.

Without the cooperation of the state, it is difficult to establish or maintain an educational institution. Not only does the state make arrangements for the training of teachers and establishment of various institutions of special education, it also provides financial help to institutions otherwise not concerned with it.

Inspectors appointed by the government inspect even the non-governmental institutions in order to ensure a uniform standard of education. In the absence of such control, most educational institutions would probably go the dogs. In the field of higher education, most universities and research scholars would probably stop work if the government did not establish national libraries and provide grants for the creation of local libraries.

It is therefore evident, that the formal and informal means

of education supplement each other's effort, and both should be exploited to the fullest extent to help the cause of education.

QUESTIONS FOR ANSWER

1. Write a note on the relationship between formal and informal agencies of education.
2. Discuss the functions of a family as an agency of education.
3. "School is the most important and most effective agency of education." Justify.
4. Explain traditional and progressive school system and enumerate their distinctual features.
5. Critically evaluate the educational functions of community.
6. What is the position of religious education in a secular state like India.
7. Explain the main functions of education in India.

5

Distinction between Training, Instruction, Teaching and Education

Commonly the terms training, instruction, teaching and education are not distinguished from each other but for educators they have different meaning and society must accept it. Therefore, hereunder, an attempt is being made to make the same clear.

TRAINING

This word which we often meet in educational discussion has a certain clear connotation and carries with it also often a number of derogatory implications. First of all it can refer to the actual drill or practice which a person may undertake to prepare him for an improved performance, the training which an athlete or an apprentice may undergo, the reference being to the preparation itself whether it be running or gymnastics or the repetition of supervised practice with tools or some other such.

However, the additional element which differentiates repitition of this kind from practice is that it is done in the framework of some sort of programme and that there is in the minds of the person supervising the work a goal to the attainment of which each of the steps is part of the preparation. You need to have repitition, improvement and purpose for the word 'training' to have meaning.

It may be that the goal to be aimed at exists in the mind of the instructor or that in the case of someone training himself, the same person is both the instructor and the apprentice according to the way in which he looks at his own programme. The trainee may also become his own trainer.

This word has often been mischievous in educational discussion. It is associated with the tricks of the trade, with dependent attitudes and with a limited understanding of the purpose of any activity.

It is significant, for example, that we speak of 'teacher training' and 'training colleges'. At the universities in England, for some years the official title for the department of education was 'The University Training Department.' The official title now is 'The University Department of Education.' The training colleges, however, still have this word associated with them. In intellectual activity it is a mark of esteem that you have something more or less independent and individual to say.

Training places emphasise upon a man's dependence, upon being taught by others, upon learning within the framework of a known programme.

In the early part of the 19th century in Scotland, David Stow elaborated a programme of preparation for teaching and founded what he specifically termed 'the training system', and in this practical work in classroom played a large part. The Normal School was the accompaniment of this training system—the school from which the norms or standards of practical teaching could be obtained.

We are told in proverbs that if we train a child in the way he should go, when he is old he will not depart from it. This emphasis upon laying down and establishing ways of acting, a routine, a procedure, a solution to all eventualities on the basis of practice, represents on the one hand a necessary part of anyone's mastery of a subject, of a trade, but on the other, in the case of relationships to ideas or to people, it may be too rigid to be creditable.

Here, then, we have a word 'training' which is legitimate in that it defines the skills and practices which have to be understood and mastered but which does not include the equally important principle of independence, the necessity to improvise with all the overtones of judgement, intelligence and freedom which this suggests.

It is interesting to notice that training is probably linked with vocational preparation, and education is linked with liberal preparation. Technical education is often thought of as representing the training tradition but technology may give more room for liberal traditions.

INSTRUCTION

This word represents the passing on of information. The emphasis here is upon what is communicated and its importance. This is another word which represents part of the educational process but which very often produces confusion in discussion. We can see this sort of difficulty arising in such a sentence as 'children should profit from the instruction of their elders.' The emphasis in instruction is upon the factual material which is being presented by an instructor.

The implication is that the material is clearly understood by the instructor, has been ordered for presentation by him and is presented to the pupil. Perhaps it could be summed up by saying that this term represents a state of affairs something like the following 'here is material which has been sorted out to be presented to you. You should absorb it—take it or leave it.'

TEACHING

There is a two-fold difference between instruction and teaching which is not easy to disentangle. First, the emphasis in teaching is upon a relationship between people, the teacher and his pupils. Secondly, there is an implication of the necessity for follow-up so that the teacher may be assured that what he has presented has, in fact, been understood and learned.

It is quite true that teaching, like training and like instruction rests to some extent upon certain methods, techniques, tricks of the trade. However, in addition teaching presupposes an interest in the learning process of the pupils and the interaction of the minds of teacher and taught.

It is to be expected that the emphasis in this interchange will be now upon the teacher, what he has to say and how he says it, now upon the learners, his growth in understanding and his mental initiative in grasping and transforming what is being presented to him.

The word 'teaching' has also other references arising from historical associations. For example, in England, the term 'teacher' has to be differentiated from 'schoolmaster.' The word schoolmistress, for various reasons of association, is very often thought to be slightly less advantageous in relation to schoolteacher than the word schoolmaster. It is sufficient at this stage to have indicated that while the words 'teaching' and 'teacher' have certain associations with the relationship between people and the learning process involved, the shadings of repute can be very subtle and fluctuating.

EDUCATION

It is now commonly held that this word derives from educare which refers to the bringing-up of children physically and mentally. It is a word of such wide reference that at times, it is of necessity. For example, we read that it is concerned with all the qualities which are acquired through individual instruction and social training, which further the happiness, efficiency and capacity for social service of the person educated.

Adams points out that education has for its aim not merely to supply a certain amount of knowledge but also to modify the nature of the pupil. It is noticeable that in the history of the development of the institution of school we have been moving steadily away from the narrower concept of school instruction, of training in specific knowledge or techniques, towards the notion of the school and other agencies as part of an educative society. This is to be detected in the shift and enrichment of the meaning of the word 'education' itself.

It would be wise at this stage to distinguish between the narrower and wider senses in which this term is used.

Wilhelm Dilthey speaks of education as the planful activity of grown-ups to shape the mind of the younger generation, and Adams takes this farther in his examination of the bi-polar process mentioned above. Here one personality acts upon another in order to modify the development of the other. That is to say, that the process is not only conscious but deliberate, for the educator has the clearly realized intention of shaping and modifying the development of the pupil.

Indeed, we have the curious and inverted view characteristic of some university opinion, and particularly at the older universities, that it is almost an advantage to have mastered your knowledge despite the teaching which you had to undergo.

Dilthey and Adams have this in common, that they see in education the influence of person upon person in which the older generation wishes to prepare the younger generation in terms of idea, knowledge and attitudes. In the foreground of this activity stands the school as an institution in which there is concentrated the purpose of presenting knowledge deliberately and on the basis of a consciously planned programme.

Only relatively recently, with the entry of psychological considerations, has the importance of emotional factors in learning and indeed the educational significance of the emotions at large been thought to be important.

This may lead us now to consider the broader concept of education. One of the classical statements of this wider and necessarily vaguer view of education is contained in J.S. Mill's address as Rector of St. Andrews University, Mill said, "Whatever we do for ourselves and whatever is done for us by others for the express purpose of bringing us somewhat nearer to the perfection of nature (education) does more: in its largest acceptation it comprehends even the indirect effects produced on character and on human faculties by things of which the direct purposes are different, by forms of government, by the industrial arts, by modes of social life: nay, even by physical facts not dependent on human will, by climate, soil and local position."

This is the assumption that education represents the organization of forces and influences which are to lead to a higher standard of behaviour and values—Mill speaks of the effects produced on character.

Education can only arise out of a social situation. Robinson Crusoe could teach himself to adapt to the needs of survival but the heritage of his training and experience as a member of society before he was wrecked on his island gave him resources which he developed with admirable ingenuity and good sense.

If the need for education arises out of people living together, one of its aims has to be to enable them to live together more successfully in the widest sense of these terms. Where societies or communities develop, normal ways of organizing their life develop, too, and these the sociologist calls the institutions of a society. Institutions come about from the clash and interplay of individual interests and when they have come into existence they in their turn help to define the area of acceptable conflict and harmony, that is to say they make their contribution to the development of the social and individual aspects of character, where character represents how a man behaves and what his motivation is to behave in that way.

Education, then is dynamic on both sides in that it deals with adaptable development of individuals and equally with a changing and developing society.

QUESTIONS FOR ANSWER

1. Draw a distinction between training and teaching.
2. Draw a distinction between teaching and education.
3. Draw a distinction between instruction and teaching as well as between instruction and education.

6

Curriculum

Educational values effect the formulation of educational aims which determine the curriculum of education and the curriculum thus becomes practical aspect of educational system of the society.

CURRICULUM AND EDUCATION

Education has to integrate the two processes—the individual process and the social process. In the former sense, it is identical with individual growth and the development of latent power in the child. From the latter point of view, it is identical with socialisation adjustment of environment and imbibing of culture. Both the processes are integrated.

While education is a process, curriculum is a means to the process. While education is learning, curriculum signifies situations for learning. While education deals with 'how' and 'when', curriculum deals with 'what.' While education is the product curriculum is the plan.

OBJECTIVES OF THE CURRICULUM

(1) To draw out, cultivate, excite and inspire the full development of each student.
(2) To create an atmosphere in which students will learn to think critically and constructively and seek truth and solve problems.
(3) To help students in establishing values through intimate acquaintance with the humanities, the arts, the natural

sciences, the social sciences and religion.

(4) To develop the character of students—integrity, honesty, judgement, co-operation, friendliness and goodwill.

(5) To prepare men and women for citizenship in a democratic society where freedom and liberty go hand in hand with law and justice and where responsibility, national and international, is a characteristic of the individual.

(6) To meet the needs not only of more students, but of students with wide range of ability aptitudes and interests.

PRINCIPLES OF CURRICULUM CONSTRUCTION

1. Child Centred Education

Curriculum should be child centred. The interests, needs, capacities, abilities, age and the level of intelligence of children should be kept in full view and close attention while constructing a suitable curriculum.

2. Relation with Life

Only those subjects should be included in the curriculum which are directly relevant to actual living because of its irrelevance to the actual living conditions of children. The old and prevalent curriculum is under heavy fire.

3. Utilizing Creative and Constructive Powers

Those subjects should be assigned prominent place in the curriculum which develop the creative and constructive capacities and abilities of children.

Raymont rightly says, "In a curriculum that is suited to the needs of today and of the future, there must be a definite bias towards definite creative subjects."

4. Interrelation of Play and Work Activities

The learning activities and experiences should be made so much interesting while constructing a curriculum that a child gains knowledge and learning from them in the play way spirit, finding them very interesting and captivating.

According to Crow and Crow, "The aim of those who guide the learning process should be so as to plan learning activities that the play attitude is introduced."

5. Knowledge of Culture and Civilization

Those subjects, activities and experiences should be included in the curriculum which convey to the children the knowledge and understanding of their cultural values and civilization. The curriculum should preserve and develop culture and civilization.

6. Totality of Experience

The integrated whole of human experiences should be included in the curriculum as one unit. The curriculum should include both the literary and academic subjects as well as the sum total of varied human experiences which a child receives in the school campus, in the class rooms, on the playing fields, in the libraries and laboratories and through the various informal contacts with the teachers and other educationists.

The Secondary Education Commission Report lays down, "Curriculum does not mean only the academic subjects, but it includes the totality of experiences."

7. Achievement of Wholesome Behaviour Pattern

Curriculum subjects, activities and experiences should inculcate in the children social and moral qualities which shape courteous behaviour towards others.

Crow and Crow remarks, "The curriculum should be so framed that it may help the children in the achievement of wholesome behaviour patterns."

8. Utility

Curriculum should include those subjects, activities and experiences which are useful to the present as well as the future life of children. Irrelevant and useless material should find no place in the curriculum. The dead wood in the present curriculum should be removed and replaced by needful and relevant materials.

9. Forward Look

Curriculum subjects and materials should be forward looking so that the child is able to solve the various problems coming before him in the immediate as well as remote future, and also to find out suitable solutions and achieve harmonious adjustment with the changing conditions and situations of life in a progressive ways. This capacity for adjustment should also enable the child to modify the environment according to his needs.

10. Variety and Flexibility

Different children have different inherent interests, aptitudes, urges, tendencies, capacities and abilities. Due to these variations and differences, there should be enough flexibility and elasticity in the curriculum to suit the varieties.

The Secondary Education Commission Report (1952-53) says, "There should be enough variety and elasticity in the curriculum to allow for individual differences and adaptation to individual needs and interests."

11. Education for Leisure

The problem of utilizing leisure time gainfully is of considerable magnitude in modern times. It is generally noticed that people have no plan to spend this time effectively. They often waste it or rather kill it. A good curriculum should develop capacities in the children to spend their leisure time in a useful manner.

12. Inclusion of All Life Activities

According to Herbert Spencer, the prime aim of education is to achieve complete development of individuality. Hence all those activities and subjects should be included in the curriculum which promote physical, mental, moral, social and political development of a child in a harmonious manner.

13. Relationship with Community Life

Full consideration of local needs and situations should be kept in mind while constructing curriculum. All those social beliefs, attitudes, traditions and problems of community life should be given due place to make children understand them well and realize their responsibility towards them.

The Secondary Education Commission Report lays down, "The curriculum should be vitally and organically related to community life."

14. Developing Democratic Spirit

As India has accepted the ideal of a democratic republic, curriculum should contain and emphasize those activities and experiences which promote democratic spirit, feelings and attitudes in the children together with democratic behaviour patterns based on democratic ideals and values.

15. Correlation

The impact and importance of a curriculum is destroyed if it is broken into unrelated fragments and unconnected units. On the other hand if the integrated approach is employed in teaching various subjects, then this correlation leads to wider and deeper understanding and wholesome knowledge. Hence the curriculum should keep various units interrelated and lay stress upon correlation.

BASIS OF CURRICULUM CONSTRUCTION

1. Psychological Basis of Curriculum Construction

Psychological basis of education emphasizes that child is the centre of educational process. Education is for the child and child is not for education. Psychology has established the fact that a child develops through various stages.

There are individual differences in the interests, impulses, urges, needs, capacities and abilities among children. Therefore curriculum should be so flexible to meet the individual differences effectively and allow each child to develop along his natural path and progress at his own speed according to his natural directions of development. For this, the curriculum should contain various games, sports, creative activities and useful developing experiences.

2. Scientific Basis of Curriculum Construction

Scientific tendency in education or scientific basis of education emphasizes that the main and important place in the curriculum should be given to scientific subjects and secondary place should be given to the academic disciplines.

The credit of introducing and developing the scientific tendency in education goes to Herbert Spencer, according to whom the development of a human being should not be one-sided but complete in all aspects. Education should so achieve this complete development that an individual is able to solve all the problems and thus lead a happy life.

Thus, the main aim of education should be to prepare the

individual for complete living. Herbert Spencer divided human activities into five categories and in order of their priority and prescribed definite subjects for each category.

In the first category are those activities which promote self-preservation directly. In the second category are those activities which promote self-protection indirectly. In the third category are those activities which promote human progeny and its protection. In the fourth category are activities which secure social and political protection. Fifth category are included activities concerned with the proper utilization of leisure time.

According to Spencer for the first category—Physiology, Hygiene, Physics and Chemistry, for the second category—Maths, Biology, Sociology and Physics, for the third category—Physiology Domestic Science and Psychology, for the fourth category—History, Politics, Economics and for the fifth category—Art, Music and Poetry should find proper place in the curriculum.

3. Sociological Basis of Curriculum Construction

According to sociological basis of education, the individual needs, propensities, interests, capacities and tendencies should be moulded through education to achieve social welfare and social development. Only those subjects and activities should be included in the curriculum which are useful from the point of view of society.

The curriculum should be constructed in accordance with the needs, requirements, conditions and aspirations of society so that qualities of sociability and citizenship are inculcated in each child. The curriculum should contain Language, Arithmetic, Health education, Physical education, Social studies, General science, subjects to enable children to earn livelihood, Experimental arts, Music and such other socially useful subjects which develop the individual side by side with the society.

CURRICULUM RECONSTRUCTION IN INDIA

In free India number of attempts were made to renovate and revamp the curriculum to make it suitable to the growing needs, aspirations and demands of a modernising egalitarian society.

Basic Education (1937)

The first major attempt in curriculum reconstruction in India was made in 1937 when Gandhiji propounded the idea of Basic Education. Dr. Zakir Hussain Committee elaborated it in the scheme of studies of Basic Education. After independence the Basic System of education was accepted as the national system of education at the primary stage.

The entire instructional programme was to centre round a craft. Besides craft, physical and social environment were also considered to be important factors in the curriculum. Correlation of various subjects was to be achieved through craft and social and physical environment.

University Education Commission (1949)

In 1948, a year after the attainment of independence, a University Education Commission was set up under the Chairmanship of Dr. S. Radhakrishnan which recommended the adoption of Three-years degree course and suggested suitable curriculum for this stage, in 1949.

Secondary Education Commission (1952-53)

With Dr. A. Lakshmanaswamy Mudaliar as the Chairman the Secondary Education Commission made faithful analysis of the curriculum, revealed its defects, formulated principles and suggested the need reforms, which were not properly implemented and the Education Commission (1964-1966) was appointed.

The Education Commission (1964-66)

For the first time in the educational history of the country, the Government of India decided to review the entire educational structure of the country by setting up the Education Commission 1964-66 under the Chairmanship of Dr. D. S. Kothari.

The Kothari Commission made a detailed survey of the curriculum followed in the country. It came to the conclusion that the curriculum was inadequate, out-moded and not properly designed to the needs of the modern times. There was widespread dissatisfaction with the curriculum due to tremendous expansion of knowledge in recent years. There was a good deal of 'Useless Education Lumber' in the school courses. There was an urgent need to raise, upgrade and improve the school curriculum.

Recommendations

(i) School curriculum should be upgraded through research in curriculum development by University Departments of Education, Colleges of Education and other such agencies. Research is also needed in the preparation of textbooks and learning materials.

(ii) The teacher should be oriented to the revised curriculum through 'in-service education.'

(iii) The schools should be free to devise the experiment with new curricula suited to their needs.

(iv) The State Boards of School Education should prepare advanced curricula in all subjects and introduce them in a phased manner in schools.

(v) In general or non-vocational school common curricula of general education should be provided for the first 10 years, and diversification of studies and specialisation should begin only at the Higher Secondary Stage. An unified approach should be made to the curriculum synthesising general education with specialised course.

(vi) The standard of attainment should be clearly defined at the end of each substage.

(vii) Science education should be given special importance. "Science and Mathematics", says the Commission, "should be compulsory in the first 10 years of schooling." Science teaching should be linked with agriculture in the rural areas and with technology in the urban areas.

(viii) The study of Mathematics should be emphasised in view of the importance of qualification on the advent of automation in the scientific and industrial revolution.

(ix) Teaching of Social Studies must be made effective for the development of good citizenship and emotional integration. The syllabus in Social Studies must stress the idea of national unity and the unity of man.

(x) The three language formula should be modified, and a new plan presented. It suggested that three languages (Mother tongue, Hindi and English) should be studied

from class VIII, but, do not on compulsory basis. A classical language also should be introduced on optional basis from class VIII.

(xi) Emphasis should be laid on 'Work Experience'. Manual work should be emphasised at all the stages. It may take the form of hand work in lower primary, craft in upper primary, workshop training in lower secondary and experience in school workshop, farm or commercial or industrial establishment at the higher secondary stage.

Suggestions

In addition to the above recommendations, the following are also suggested:

(i) Programme of social service and participation in community development should be organised at all levels as suited to the different age groups.

(ii) Labour and social service camps should be run throughout the year and for this purpose, a special organisation to be set up in each district.

(iii) Physical education should be provided for the physical fitness and efficiency, mental alertness and the development of certain qualities of character. Hence, physical education programme should be re-examined and re-designed.

(iv) Organised attempt should be made for imparting moral education and inculcating spiritual values in schools through direct and indirect methods with the help of the ethical teachings of great religions.

(v) The Government of India should appoint committee of experts to survey the present situation of art education, and explore all possibilities for its extension and systematic development. Art departments should be set up in selected university centres to carry research in art education. A variety of co-curricular activities should be organised to provide pupils an opportunity for creative self-expression.

(vi) The recommendations of the Hansa Mehta Committee should be endorsed that there should be no differentiation of curricula on the basis of sex. Home science should be provided as an optional subject but

not made compulsory for girls. Larger provision should be made for music and fine arts, and the study of mathematics and science should be encouraged.

(vii) The essential principle of basic education, namely: productive activity, correlation of curriculum with productive activity and environment and contact with local community should guide and shape the educational system at all levels. No single stage of education should be designated as basic education.

NATIONAL POLICY ON EDUCATION (1968)

The Government of India considered the recommendations of Education Commission and adopted a National Policy on Education in 1968 which identified national goals of education. The policy resolution stated that the educational system must produce young men and women of character and ability committed to national service and development. The following five goals were clearly mentioned:

1. Relating education to the needs of the society.
2. Promotion of national integration.
3. Equalisation of educational opportunity.
4. Linking education with productivity and national development.
5. Acceleration of social transformation.

10+2+3 PATTERN

National Policy. A new programme of curriculum development should be undertaken by the adoption of a broadly uniform pattern popularly known as 10+2+3 pattern throughout the country. This pattern meant 10 years of general education followed by diversified Higher Secondary Education and then 2 or 3 years of University Education.

QUESTIONS FOR ANSWER

1. Discuss the meaning and objectives of curriculum.
2. What are the important basis of curriculum? Explain.
3. Write a note on the principles of curriculum construction.

PART TWO

SOCIOLOGICAL FOUNDATIONS OF EDUCATION

7

Educational Sociology

Education is now regarded as a social dynamic and progressive process which aims at achieving social planning, social change and social reconstruction. Therefore, social consciousness is the essential base of education. All these aspects belong to educational sociology.

DEFINITION OF EDUCATIONAL SOCIOLOGY

Following definitions of some well-known scholars make the meaning of educational sociology clear:

(1) "Educational Sociology is the study of interaction of the individual and his cultural environment including other individuals several groups and pattern of behaviour."

—*Brown*

(2) "Educational Sociology starts with the assumption that education is an activity which goes on in society and the society in turn determines the nature of education."

—*Ottaway*

(3) "Educational Sociology is the scientific study of how people live in social groups, especially including the study of education that is obtained by the living in the social groups, and education that is needed by the members to live efficiently in social groups."

—*Good*

AIMS OF EDUCATIONAL SOCIOLOGY

According to Harington, following are the aims of educational sociology:

(1) To acquire knowledge about school work and the work of teachers in relation to society and social progress.

(2) To study the effects of social elements on the school.

(3) To acquire knowledge about the effects of social elements on individual.

(4) To construct a curriculum of education with full understanding of the economic and cultural tendencies of society.

(5) To gain knowledge about the democratic ideologies.

(6) To employ research techniques for achieving the aims of educational sociology.

SCOPE OF EDUCATIONAL SOCIOLOGY

Educational sociology is a wide and comprehensive subject which deals with the influences of education process on social relationship and the effects of sociological processes on education.

Following are the important issues of study for educational sociology:

1. Mutual relations of teachers and students.
2. The place of a teacher in society.
3. Social problems, needs and aspirations.
4. Small units of society and their interrelation.
5. School and its relations with local social institutions.
6. Effect of social life upon individuals and school.
7. Progress of democratic feelings in school.
8. Necessary modifications in the curriculum for individual and social growth.
9. Encouragement to critical thinking and investigation.
10. Evaluation of radio, television and press as medium of social progress.
11. Determination of teaching methods of the development of child.
12. Investigation of all the sources of social restrictions and social advancement.

EDUCATION FROM SOCIOLOGICAL POINT OF VIEW

1. Meaning of Education

An individual is born with some animal instincts. He begins to interact with the environment in order to develop these instincts in a natural way. By this interaction he learns some habits of behaviour all by himself. He learns some other patterns of behaviour after coming into contact with his relations, friends and other persons of society. Sociologists call this learning by social contacts as real education. It is a continuous process.

Interaction between the individual and the society leads to the progress and development of both. Thus education is a life-long process of interaction, growth and development which results in the modification of behaviour of the individual by more and more social interaction leading to the socialization of individuals.

In the words of Brown, "Education is the consciously controlled process whereby changes in behaviour are produced in the person and through the person within the group."

2. Aims of Education

The development of sociological tendency in education led to the important role of educational sociology in the process of determining the following aims of education:

(i) To develop social feelings, social attitudes, social qualities and democratic ideals. Individuals are able to achieve harmonious adjustment with their environment developing society to higher and higher levels by performing their obligations and using their rights. This development eventually leads to international brotherhood and international welfare. Hence education for efficient dynamic citizenship is the main aim of education.

(ii) Social efficiency and self-reliance. Hence the second important aim of education is to provide vocational education to children.

(iii) Effective and gainful use of leisure time. Hence proper utilization of leisure time is the third aim of education.

3. Functions of Education

In his famous book *Brief Course in the History of Education*, Monroe has laid down the following four main functions of education:

(i) Diffusion of knowledge. The first function of education is to prepare an individual for active participation in social activities, so that both the individual and the society grow and develop higher and higher. But the development of individual and society depends upon intelligence which requires considerable knowledge.

The function of education is to diffuse more and more knowledge creating intelligent, useful and dynamic citizens contributing their best to the advancement of society.

(ii) Education as a means of social control. In addition to the preparation of intelligent citizens, education also devices means for social control and guidance. Proper education inculcates in children moral consciousness, sentiments of self-control, service and sacrifice which develop the capacity to face all problems squarely and find effective solutions for them. Thus social control through education is an important function of education.

(iii) Security and transmission of social heritage. Another important function of education is to protect, preserve and transmit the valuable heritage of human culture and civilization to successive generations. Neither preservation nor transmission of culture to successive generations without a sound and effective system of education. In the absence of this wholesome influence, harmonious adjustment will not be achieved. Consequently the process of social decay will set in.

(iv) Social progress. The development of an individual is possible only in a developed and progressive society. In India, since the attainment of independence, the old and traditional structure of our society is increasingly becoming irrelevant under the impact of modern ideals and values of life. We need a social structure according to this changing social life, which is able to meet the demands of modern society.

Only education can re-structure Indian society, modify and modernize our thinking and behaviour in all spheres of human activity. Without this essential remodelling and restructuring, Indian society runs the risk of total decay and destruction.

(v) Constructive and creative role. According to George Payne, "Besides Assimilation of Traditions and Development of New Social patterns, the most important function of education is to develop the creative and constructive capacities of the individuals."

Education enables an individual to think independently, take independent judgements and act in an independent manner. This ability inspires and develops his creative and constructive capacities.

Cultural wealth and civilization grow and develop with the contribution of all individuals engaged in creative and constructive activities.

4. Construction of Curriculum

Moore, Brown, Cole and other sociologists have prescribed the following principles to guide curriculum construction:

(i) It should be flexible and changeable.
(ii) It should be confirm to the level of child development.
(iii) It should inspire children to become responsible.
(iv) It should include variety of social services.
(v) It should make children capable for their livelihood.
(vi) It should emphasize educational plans and schemes.
(vii) It should be constructed in confirmity with social ideals and values.
(viii) It should include more and more subjects of sociological value to promote international understanding.

Thus, a comprehensive and wholesome curriculum should have Language, Social studies, Arithmetic, Biology, Science, Elementary science, Physical training, Health education, Experiemental arts, Music, Literature and subjects promoting vocational efficiency for livelihood and successful happy life.

5. Methods of Teaching

George Payne has laid down the following three principles for formulating effective methods of teaching:

(i) Methods of teaching can be effective only when the knowledge gained in the class room is practically used in social activities and experiences.

(ii) Efficient methods of teaching should emphasize social behaviour.

(iii) Methods of teaching should make full use of social activities, social powers and capacities operating in society.

6. Efficient Method of Teaching

It should possess the following traits:

(i) It should try to develop in children social qualities through social influences and effects.

(ii) It should employ available social powers to the full to achieve wholesome social adjustment.

(iii) It should emphasize social values and social patterns of behaviour to the utmost limit.

(iv) It should develop efficient social abilities so that children well understand social plans and also are able to formulate such plans.

(v) It should promote democratic feelings, ideals and values.

7. Discipline

Before the advent and development of sociological tendency, individual development was valued as most important to the total neglect of the social aspect. Since the growth of sociological tendency in education, the sense of social discipline has come to be valued as most effective and most desirable form of discipline. In contrast to the sense of individual discipline, the famous educationist John Dewey has laid great stress upon social discipline.

This sense of social discipline is born out of social activities and experiences in school and active participation of children in such activities and experiences. With the development of this sense of social discipline a child controls himself and exercises self-discipline without doing any harm to others or to the society in general.

8. School

The school is only one agency in society concerned with education. It takes its place with the home, the industrial order, the church, the voluntary agencies, the social services, the mass media. We can draw a fairly useful distinction between formal and informal education, but we should recognize that while we give the school a place of great importance which it deserves, the total effect of education is not to be found only through the formal agencies. Indeed, part of the responsibility of the school will be to enable its pupils to detect more and more of the informal influences which are flitting incessantly but quickly through their field of consciousness.

According to sociological thinking, a school is a society in miniature. In modern times, a school is a living organism bringing into being various useful social activities and experiences which promote the development of social qualities in the individuals. Thus, educands become social beings in the true sense of the term.

To sum up, education should be organized according to sociological basis all its activities and processes promoting social qualities, ideals and values in children so that they develop their personality to the full and achieve the utmost development of society of which they are inseparable and integral parts.

MEANING OF SOCIOLOGICAL TENDENCY

Sociological tendency in education means the inculcation of social qualities in children so that while developing their own individualities, they also contribute their best to social welfare and advancement.

SOCIOLOGICAL TENDENCY AND OTHER TENDENCIES IN EDUCATION

1. Psychological and Sociological Tendencies

The aim of sociological tendency is to develop society. Pestalozzi, Herbart, and Froebel were three main propounders of psychological tendency. Pestalozzi wished to improve the condition of society. He emphasized the development of child according to his interests, needs and natural disposition, so that he is able to adopt a profession of his choice and lead his life happily. He regarded education as a vehicle of social uplift and thus stimulated the development of sociological tendency.

Froebel laid emphasis on the social development aim of education to enable an individual to achieve happiness in his life. Identifying the school as a miniature of society, he advocated social education through his kindergarten method. Men were led to believe that there is a great similarity between the psychological and sociological tendencies.

2. Sociological and Scientific Tendency

Like sociological tendency, scientific tendency also aims to achieve social good and welfare. Both the tendencies aim to bring about social reform and regeneration by keeping human good and growth in view scientific tendency gives impetus to individualism because of its emphasis upon science, education and scientific subjects.

Happy individuals constitute a happy society. Both sociological and scientific tendencies have common aim of social reform and social welfare. Both advocate essential changes in the curriculum to make education an effective means of all-round development and welfare.

CAUSES OF THE DEVELOPMENT OF SOCIOLOGICAL TENDENCY

1. Social Aim

The social aim of education maintains that education ought to transmit the heritage of human culture and civilization from one generation to another. Thus laid the foundation of sociological tendency and reinforced by educational processes and procedures.

2. Philosophy of Naturalism

In his philosophy of Naturalism based on the natural development of child, Rousseau advocated child-centred education. It brought about social good and development promoting the welfare of people in general and inculcating in the individuals a social attitude and social mentality.

3. Psychological and Scientific Tendencies

The psychological and scientific tendencies have given a great impetus to the development of sociological tendency. Pestalozzi, Herbart and Froebel laid emphasis on social growth and development of moral values. All these contributed to the development of sociological tendency in their own ways.

4. Industrial Revolution

The great industrial revolution of the 18th and 19th centuries changed the whole economic set up of society. Based on various trades and professions new communities sprang up. Due to these changed circumstances and new social problems politicians, writers, social thinkers and workers began to change their traditional modes of thinking of solve the evergrowing social problems of living in a changed world.

5. Development of Democratic Feelings

Democratic feelings began to develop all over the world during the 18th and 19th centuries. Most and more countries took the form of political democracy. The statesmen and political thinkers began to realize that democratic ideals and values can not be developed on sound and permanent footing without public education. Education was accepted as the only effective means to inculcated the democratic ideals and values in the individuals so that they may be able to develop their individuality to the full and also consider their duty to bring about social reconstruction and social welfare. This put the democratic set up on a sound footing to see that democracy succeeds and develops more and more.

6. Introduction of Sociology

Inspired by the above mentioned development George Payne developed a new discipline of Sociology called Educational Sociology. In his famous book "The Principles of Educational Sociology", he laid stress on the fact that education and community life have profound influence on each other.

In his book *Democracy and Education* John Dewey gave a very prominent position to sociological tendency. The sociologists of France, England, America and Germany determined the various aspects of education according to Educational Sociology. Thus educational sociology reinforced the already sound foundations of sociological tendency.

CHIEF CHARACTERISTICS OF SOCIOLOGICAL TENDENCY

1. Modifying Individual's Behaviour according to Environment

Sociological tendency emphasizes the development of a child's inherent tendencies. It also lays stress upon the adjustment of a child's thinking and behaviour in harmony with the environmental conditions and circumstances.

2. Preparation for Successful Social Life

Sociological tendency seeks to create dynamic citizens conscious of their rights and duties and discharging their obligations to the utmost extent by participating in the economic, political and social activities of the country to lead their own lives successfully and contribute their best to the social good.

3. Opposition of Individualism

Sociological tendency corrected the imbalance generated by excessive adherence to Individualism of the 17th century. It emphasized social welfare over individual development.

4. Development of Social Values

Sociological tendency lays stress upon the development of social qualities in children. By understanding their social obligations, they are able to lead their lives happily.

5. Importance of Social Subjects in the Curriculum

Sociological tendency advocates the inclusion in the curriculum of those subjects the study of which builds the capacity to meet social needs and solve social problems. Assigning lesser importance to academic subjects, this tendency attaches great value to the study of natural sciences and social sciences. It emphasizes the necessity of enlarging the scope and orientation of education to include the wide range of modern life rather than to delimit it to the study of a few disciplines only.

6. Free and Compulsory Education

Contribution of all individuals is essential for social welfare and development education is the only effective means to develop this feeling. Hence, sociological tendency lays emphasis upon free, compulsory and universal education.

7. State Education System

Sociological tendency believes in the democratic set up of state for the success of which education of the masses is essential. This tendency advocates an efficient state system of education for the good of one and all. It has inspired the organization of a state system for all levels of education.

8. Understanding the Complexities of Life

Sociological tendency lays emphasis upon the fact that children should understand that complexities of modern life. A clear understanding of these will enable them to choose freely their own paths and directions.

9. Study of Problems Connected with Practical Life

Sociological tendency brings out into prominence the need of enabling children to understand the intricacies and problems of actual and practical life in modern items. This will enable them to face the challenges of life boldly and contribute their best to social welfare.

10. Emphasis on Vocational Education

Like scientific tendency, sociological tendency also emphasizes the need and importance of vocational, technical and industrial education so that, after receiving such education, children are able to earn their livelihood by their own efforts and contribute their best to social welfare and advancement.

IMPACT OF SOCIOLOGICAL TENDENCY ON EDUCATION

1. Philanthropic School

Under the impact of sociological tendency, a movement for social welfare was launched by social reformers and educationists. Schools began to be opened to educate more and more children. These schools were opened by individual persons with the object of promoting public good through education.

Gradually, these private schools were included in the list of government aided institutions. The credit of opening such schools goes to Basedow who got an aid from Leopold, the ruler of Desseau to open such a school in 1777 AD. He named it 'Philanthropinum.' Inspired by its method of working, social welfare societies opened many such schools at many places with the object of promoting public good.

In England also a number of 'Charity schools' and 'Sunday schools' were opened with great zeal, imparting free education and providing free books, dresses and diet to the children.

2. State System of Education

Inspired by this tendency, a number of States found education a very powerful means to consolidate and develop the power of State. They decided to accept it their first duty to provide a State system of education. Germany was the first country to start a State system of education of its citizens. Later on France, England, USA and other countries started the system of public education.

3. Use of Monitorial System

Sociological tendency inspired many public utility association to open more and more schools for public. Gradually the number of schools multiplied by leaps and bounds. Dearth of teachers was felt to meet this situation. Dr. Andrw Bell propagated the old Indian system of pupil-teachers co-operative teaching popularly known as monitorial system of education.

He had studied this monitorial system thoroughly when he worked as a clergy man at Madras in India. These schools could be called in single teacher schools, where senior students helped the teacher teaching lower classes. This system worked successfully in England. Influenced by its success Joseph Lancaster started Monitorial schools. Gradually, more and more schools began to be opened on its plan making education social and worldly.

4. Establishment of Public Schools

Sociological tendency also stimulated the movement for infant indication. Its aim was to remove the evils of factory life and improve the poor living conditions of the working people. In those days even women and children were compelled to work for 12 or 13 hours a day.

These adverse conditions of work were debated in the Parliament of Great Britain and suitable laws were passed or providing education to small children. The credit of this awakening goes to Robert Owen who by his sincere and untiring efforts achieved success in the form of schools for even the poorest infants.

This movement travelled to USA and other progressive countries where astonishing success was achieved by social workers. By the end of 19th century numerous infant schools were opened in Europe and America by the states.

5. Provision of Vocational Education

State system of education came into being in the 19th century. The State began to realize that only economically well people can co-operate with the government in national services. Hence the need for vocational and industrial education was keenly felt. In modern age in almost all progressive countries of the world provision for various types of vocational, technical and industrial education is made to meet the growing needs and demands of efficient and skilled workers.

6. Diffusion of Adult Education

Sociological tendency inspired a social consciousness in the people. It began to be realized everywhere that good of the society at large could be achieved only through education. Hence schemes of adult education, education of the physically handicapped, training to the mentally retarded and to children of special category, began to be devised and implemented by the State as well as public associations. In India also were emphasized socialistic ideals, social work and public services. Hence Janta colleges, Night schools, part time schools and various types of social institutes have been opened in more and more number in India with the aim of achieving social welfare.

QUESTIONS FOR ANSWER

1. Explain the sociological basis of education.
2. What do you mean by educational sociology? Define it and discuss its utility.
3. Elaborate the relationship between education and sociology.
4. Discuss the various aspects of education in the light of sociological point of view.
5. The main aim of education is to remodel and restructure the old Indian social structure into a modern one. How far do you agree with it?
6. What do you mean by sociological tendency in education? How did it develop? Discuss its chief characteristics.

8

Education and Society

INTRODUCTION

Society, sociology and educational sociology are intimately connected with education. Hence each society, keeping in view its own needs, ideals and aspirations organizes its education in such a manner that it is able to realize its ideals and develop its individuals into dynamic citizens.

Hence, a society, in confirmity with the times and circumstances, determines the kind of education its members are to receive to develop themselves into able and useful members to make the society strong, stable and powerful in all spheres. It is crystal clear that education is a very powerful medium of change in the hands of society to organize and mould its educational pattern to suit its aims, ideals and purposes.

As discussed above, education and society are intimately related. It is the society which determines and formulates the pattern of its education according to its needs, ideals and ambition. In other words, as is the society so is its education. Thus, education follows and tries to realize the ideals of society which it serves.

The changing pattern of a society brings about corresponding changes in the educational processes and patterns. Following are some of the relevant examples in this connection:

1. Ancient and Medieval Society

During ancient and medieval times religion had its sway over society. Consequently, education was also of religious nature.

Thus, in confirmity to religious tenets, ceremonies and rituals were emphasized to develop character, attitude and behaviour of individuals.

2. Modern Society

Science has a powerful impact upon modern society. Hence, education tries to promote thinking, reasoning, discrimination, judgement together with other mental powers of individuals to the maximum. It may be noted that present day society has various forms. Each type of society organizes its education according to its needs and ideals.

Hereunder, we are trying to discuss the forms of educational organization in confirmity with the type of society which it tries to serve:

3. Idealistic Society

In an idealistic society, great importance is attached to ideals and intelligence and education is organized to achieve the ideal of spiritual development. Hence, in such a society, education emphasizes character formation and moral development.

4. Materialistic Society

In a materialistic society, material welfare and affluence are greatly emphasized. Hence, the whole educational pattern is organized to develop abilities in the individuals to achieve more and more physical pleasure and material welfare in all fields of life.

5. Pragmatic Society

Pragmatists believe that truth is related to times, circumstances and places and hence, it changes to suit the changing conditions of life and society. The test of truth is, therefore, its verification by experiment and application. Hence, pragmatists lay great stress upon education to develop capacities to create new values to suit the changing pattern of social conditions and situations.

6. Fascist Society

In a fascist society, state is all powerful. In such a state, the individual is of little significance. Hence, in a fascist society, an individual is expected to sacrifice his all, even his life for the sake of the state. Thus, education is organized in such a way as to promote absolute obedience and an attitude of complete surrender for the state. In such a society the masses are generally discouraged to have any education worth the name.

7. Democratic Society

In a democratic society, freedom and full development of all individuals are valued most. One and all are allowed full opportunities to develop their individuality to the fullest extent. For this, each individual is provided education according to his needs, nature and requirements. Nothing is forced from outside and nothing is imposed by virtue of any authority. Social and moral qualities together with human sentiments are developed through wholesome and harmonious education so that all individuals develop their fullest personalities and are able to contribute their utmost to social good and international welfare.

IMPACT OF SOCIETY ON EDUCATION

1. Influence of Social Structure and Ideals

It has already been made clear that the ideals of a society determine the ideals and values which education is to achieve. A closed and despotic society will have its organizational pattern of education to develop qualities of absolute and meek obedience together with attitudes of complete and unquestioning self-surrender; while open and democratic societies will advocate education to promote free thinking, free reasoning, eager co-operation, initiative and self-discipline together with other self-experiences and activities according to one's own needs, nature activities and inherent capacities. Such societies plan and encourage mass educational schemes to the fullest possible extent.

2. Influence of Political Conditions

Political ideologies also influence education to a great deal. We see that political doctrines and set up of states organize education according to their political aims and ideals which are to be achieved through educational processes and programmes. The purpose is just to prepare citizens for political confirmity.

3. Influence of Economic Conditions

Economic condition of society exerts its great influence upon the educational pattern. It is because of the fact that educational activities and programmes require a great amount of financial support. Those societies which are affluent and plentiful provide liberally to educational plans of mass education and also provide various types of education to increasing number of children. On the other hand, poor societies, as our country is still, are not able to provide for all types of education to its citizens who need all types of vocational, technical, professional, commercial and agricultural education to achieve their own development and the development of society.

4. Influence of Religious Conditions

Religious ideas and beliefs of a society influence the educational pattern to a great extent. Those societies which hold fanatical religious beliefs, plan their education in their own way and deny free thinking and liberal attitudes to be inculcated in their children. On the other hand, societies which believe in free thinking, liberal attitudes and respect for all religious provide education on a secular and liberal basis and promote liberal attitudes and respect for all religions emphasizing only moral basis for educational processes and programmes.

5. Influence of Social Thought

Social point of view has its own unavoidable impact upon education. In a society where old customs and traditions reign supreme, education is planned in the old traditional ways emphasizing traditional ideals and values. On the other hand, societies where progressive attitudes of people gain their hold, devise progressive modern aims, curriculum and even adopt newer and newer progressive techniques and devices of education.

6. Influence of Social Changes

Society changes with the change of social ideals, attitudes and values of people. Linked as education is with the society, changes also occur in the educational patterns, procedures, policies and programmes. For example, in our country some sixty years back, education was provided for the chosen few among the society. Even women were discouraged from being educated. But now under the impact of modern democratic and progressive ideals of life, the portals of education have been thrown open to all the individuals without any distinction of colour, caste, creed and sex.

IMPACT OF EDUCATION ON SOCIETY

As society influences education, too, exerts its influence on society in the following areas:

1. Preservation of Social Heritage

Education preserves social and cultural heritage. As a matter of fact, each society has its own customs, traditions together with moral and religious creeds which are the society's achievements since early times. Really speaking, each society has a legitimatic pride over its social heritage which it never allows to decay and die out.

2. Awakening of Social Feeling

An individual is very closely related to society. He can achieve his development in and through society promoting the good of other fellow-beings. Without society an individual cannot exist. Therefore, development of social awareness, social feelings and social attitudes is very essential from all points of view. In fact, it is education which inculcates such social attitudes, ideals and values together with a spirit of service and sacrifice for the cause of others. Varieties of educational programmes, processes, activities, experiences and active participation in them make the individual social-minded and service-oriented.

3. Political Development of Society

Education helps in an important manner in the political development of society. It is through education that an individual is able to gain knowledge about various political ideologies operating in the world. One can acquire a balanced outlook after a comparative study to different political doctrines with that of his own state. In this way, education spreads political awakening in the people developing civic sense of their rights and duties for the promotion of their own good and good of society. In short, education helps the political development of society.

4. Economic Development of Society

Education develops society economically also. To achieve this goal, education provides various types of vocational training to children to uplift themselves and bring about economic progress and prosperity of society to which they belong. Without education, a society remains economically backward and consequently poor.

5. Social Control

Education exposes evil customs and harmful traditions of society. Not only this, it creates public opinion against social evils and succeeds in elimination them from society for the good of the individuals as well as the good of whole society. In other words, education is greatly essential for social control. Without social control, no reformation in society is possible.

6. Social Change

Ottaway has rightly asserted that education brings about social changes of very important nature. We see that due to modern science, new researches and techniques, revolutionary changes are occurring in all fields of human activities. Education imparts knowledge of these latest developments to the individuals and provides adequate inspiration for their use which in turn bring about the creation of new ideals, values and goals which society gradually adopts.

7. Social Reform

Education brings about social change and social reform in a continuous manner. It does not only achieve identification and adjustment with the present social state of affairs but also develops intelligence, insight and capability to remove what is evil and bad from about the desirable changes and reform of the social fabric for the good of the individual as well as for the welfare of society too.

8. Socialization of Child

Education socializes a child. In the school, a child comes into contact with other children and comes to know about and interacts with their ideas, ideals, cultural values and patterns of behaviour. In this way, he develops himself socially and culturally. He imbibes the cultural values and ideals of society of which he is an integral part.

The above discussion clearly proves the close and intimate relationship of society and education. Both are mutually interdependent and complimentary. In other words, as is the society so is its education. Much in the same way, as is the education so is society. It is because of this fact that society organizes education according to its needs, ideals and aspirations and education in turn constructs and often reconstructs the social structure.

DUTIES OF SOCIETY TOWARDS EDUCATION

Development of a society is possible only when its individual members also grow and develop. Because education develops the individuals, so it is the bounden duty of society to organize proper education for its individuals to grow and develop more and more. In the following lines, we are discussing the important duties of a society towards education:

1. Establishment of Schools

It is the prime duty to establish and maintain schools for all the age groups of children, provide able and trained teachers to work in these schools and make available all aids and educational resources to achieve complete and harmonious development of all children of schools by organizing an effective system of education. In other words, establishing schools, appointing trained teachers and providing financial assistance to all schools is the first duty of society.

2. Provision of Vocational Education

The second duty of a society is the provision of vocational, technical, professional, agricultural and other types of education for all children so that they develop themselves according to their interests, aptitudes and inherent capacities to the fullest extent and contribute effectively to the progress and prosperity of society. Hence, each and every society should be very conscious of its obligations towards such provisions in the educational processes and programmes.

3. Establishment of Libraries

For the mental progress and development of individuals, society is duty-bound to establish and maintain more and more reading-rooms and libraries where newspapers, magazines and periodicals of all types are available to educate the readers in national and international trends and affairs.

4. Building Gymnasium

Physical well-being and development of individuals is equally important and essential. Hence, society should provide adequate physical education through lectures, gymnasium, games and sports for all children, youngmen and adults.

5. Provision of Academic and Cultural Education

The fifth essential duty of a society is to promote the cultural and academic development of individuals through proper education. It may be noted that schools and other educational centres established by society can contribute a great deal in this connection. However, academic and cultural functions together with conferences should also be organized frequently to achieve these purposes.

6. Provision of Adult Education

The sixth essential duty of society is to make adequate provision for adult education. It may be noted that all societies are quite conscious of providing education for school going children, but they are quite indifferent towards their grown-up adult who could not receive any education in their early and middle ages of life.

Thus, adult education should be of different types motivating and useful to the grown-up. Only then the adults will do their best to promote social welfare and social development.

7. Enlisting Co-operation of Other Agencies

The society should try to enlist the co-operation of all agencies in organizing its educational programmes, policies and procedures. The family, the church, the school, the community and other formal together with informal agencies should be inspired to co-operate with the educational efforts and activities in all aspects and in all fields of growth and development.

DUTIES OF EDUCATION TOWARDS SOCIETY

Duties of education towards society are given below:

1. Preservation of Culture and Civilization

The primary duty of education towards society is to preserve its culture and civilization. In fact, customs, traditions, beliefs, morality, ideals, language and accepted patterns of behaviour are the bases of education and culture.

2. Maintenance of Culture and Civilization

The second important duty of education is to promote and develop the culture and civilization of society. In this connection, education should not only impart knowledge of these cultural excellences and achievements of civilization, but it should see that these values become part of the behaviour patterns of the individuals.

3. Development of Culture and Civilization of Society

Education should not only perserve and maintain but also develop more and more the cultural heritage and civilizational achievements of society. If education fails to perform this important duty, society will become static and may stagnate. Hence, education should enable individuals to become dynamic, proceed towards higher and higher heights of excellence.

4. Fulfilment of Social Needs

Education should fulfil the needs and meet the requirements of society. It may be remembered well that needs of society change with the changing times, circumstances and situations. Education should understand these needs well and devise plans and programmes to meet these demands. It should be a continual ongoing process.

5. Importance in Curriculum

The fifth duty of education is to formulate a curriculum suited to the modern needs of society. Without a suitable and effective curriculum, education will fail in its duty of developing individuals to face the challenges of life and solve the emerging problems with courage, boldness, fortitude and conviction. Hence, education should always remain conscious and sensitive towards this purpose.

6. Development of Constructive Powers

The sixth important duty of education is to promote and develop more and more the creative and constructive faculties of individuals. Only then they will be able to develop their personalities in a harmonious manner and contribute towards the development of society bringing about national welfare as well.

QUESTIONS FOR ANSWER

1. Explain the relation between society and education. Critically evaluate this relationship.
2. What is the influence of education on society? Discuss.

9

Education in Indian Social Context

INTRODUCTION

On the one hand, one finds numerous groups in contemporary Indian society, distinguished from each other on the basis of language, religion, race, caste, tribe, geographical location, etc., while on the other, one also finds distinct economic classes. The processes of secularization, westernization, acculturation, industrialization and urbanization have led to remarkable changes everywhere. The impact of the West is evident enough, but it is accompanied by frantic attempts to rejuvenate ancient Indian values.

Increasing political awareness in another factor which is clearly evident. The most clear outcome of the interaction of all these tendencies is that the young generation has been presented with a fantastic variety of alternatives and differences of opinion.

This disorganization of values is manifested through such undesirable activities as indiscipline, juvenile delinquency, pessimism, destructive and murderous tendencies, etc.

In such a situation, the first duty of the educational organisation is to supplement the clear presentation of all possible alternatives before the younger generation with active encouragement in the choice of one alternative, so that there is some positive guidance.

Hence, education must not merely inculcate secularism, realism and liberality in the educand, but must also provide him with the ability to distinguish the right from the wrong.

The young people are subject to a multiplicity of influences emanating from various sources, and for this reason it is essential that there should be some unity in all this diversity.

The first step in this direction is the creation of character, which will grant an adolescent the determination to be guided by his own opinion. It is essential that old and traditional values be explained to the younger generation in the interest of continuity with the older generation, but this should not preclude consideration of new values which can lead to progress and development. Education can thus fulfil the needs of society only if it adopts a comprehensive and dynamic curriculum, a dynamic methodology of teaching and a dynamic philosophy of education.

TRADITIONAL NATURE OF INDIAN SOCIETY

In the traditional aspect of Indian society, various groups stand out in bold relief. In ancient times, these groups played a very important role, but in the modern context, they have become irrelevant and often harmful creating numerous hindrances in the progress of society. The various groups of Indian traditional society are as under:

(1) Social groups, (2) Castes, (3) Occupational groups, (4) Religious groups, and (5) Other social classes—higher, middle and lower classes.

HISTORICAL NATURE OF INDIAN SOCIETY

For a fuller and proper understanding of the nature of modern Indian society, we review its historical background as under:

(A) Indian Society in Ancient India

During the Vedic period, Indian society was very simple. The whole society was divided into four varnas namely—(1) Brahmins, (2) Kashtriyas, (3) Vaishyas, and (4) Shudras. The religion of people was also very simple. 'Havans' and 'Yagyas' were performed to appease the God. Men and women were equal in developing themselves to the utmost extent and women were respected at all occasions and the family considered wife as entitled to half the prestige and claims due to a family. The main profession was agriculture and cattle were the important items of wealth and property of individuals.

During the Brahmanical period, two epics namely—(1) The

'Ramayan', and (2) the 'Mahabharat' were composed. Brahmins were given great regard and the society moved in the same Vedic pattern.

During the Buddhistic period, the superior status of the Brahmins was challenged and caste system was decried as an evil. But Buddha also could not transform the traditional society in any aspect. In those days a village was the smallest social unit and the towns were gradually developing as centres of commerce and seats of political power.

(B) Indian Society During the Muslim Period

Muslim rulers were generally pleasure loving. As a consequence permissiveness pervaded the society in the form of prostitution, drinking and gambling. There was a great tension among Hindus and Muslims. Early marriage of very young girls and boys became a vogue to avoid forced snatchings and abductions of young Hindu girls by Muslims. Many Hindu women had to commit mass suicide or 'Johar'. Muslims believed in polygamy. Out of fear, Hindus adopted evil practices of 'Sati', child marriage, forced widowhood and even polygamy in some sects. Guru Nanak and Kabir preached the cult of 'Bagti'. This 'Bagti' movement became very popular among Hindus. Later on, Meera and Chaitanya etc. preached the divine cult of devotion of God.

Inspite of their pleasure loving lives, the Mughal rulers did much to encourage architecture, fine arts and literature and bestowed even powers of significance to Hindu artists and musicians. The state of religion and society during the Mughal period remained the same with the result that lower sections of Hindu society sank deeper and deeper into social and moral degradation.

(C) Indian Society During British Rule

Together with the British rule, British culture also came to India. Thus, whole Indian society in all its aspects got influenced by British culture. Raja Ram Mohan Roy condemned Sati ceremony, Idol worship and Caste system showing indifference to British education. Side by side with his crusading mission, the preachings of Theosophical Society, 1857, Arya Samaj, Ram Krishan Mission and other such associations heralded reformation and renaissance in Indian society awakening national consciousness. Many other saints, saviours, social thinkers and reformers did their utmost for the uplift, growth and progress of Indian society. The Indian National Congress led the struggle for freedom from the British rule. This mission of freedom invited more and more Indian men and women to join the struggle of independence. Schemes of Harijan uplift, abolishing of untouchability and economic uplift through Swdeshi movement were launched by Gandhiji. Indian philosophers, social reformers and educationists also tried to develop Indian society socially, economically and culturally. The total effect of all these movements charged the face of Indian society greatly and gave it a modern orientation. In the words of Jado Nath Sarkar—"We cannot fail to see that revolutionary change has been made by it in our society." The following are some of the important changes brought about in Indian society by these movements during the British rule:

(i) Equality for all, irrespective of religion or race.
(ii) Raising the labourers, peasants from semi-servile condition to full citizenship.
(iii) Growth of a vast and most influential middle class.
(iv) Rise of a capitalist class.
(v) Uplift to women from a degraded status.
(vi) Disintegration of the castes system.
(vii) Gradual disappearance of provincial, linguistic, and sectarian differences of mentality.

SOCIO-ECONOMIC PROBLEMS OF MODERN INDIA

Our own national leaders, after a careful consideration, decided to transform our country into a Socialistic Democratic Republic. We adopted our own Constitution on 26th January, 1950. Now, the main task before the Government is to educate the masses to feel their national responsibilities. Education is the most effective means to solve the various national problems, the most important ones are the following:

1. Poverty

There is poverty in the country everywhere. This impoverishment has led to the feelings of insecurity and awful helplessness which degenerate character, individual as well as the nation.

2. Lack of Confidence in Religion

India has been from time immemorial a land of religion. But

due to many factors, general people are turning away from religion, moral ideals and faith in divine powers. New values and ideals are yet to be established and accepted. This state of indecision has led to corruption and moral degradation.

3. Unemployment

Unemployment is one of the most serious problems being faced by our country. The consequence of this is widespread lawlessness and criminal tendencies in all spheres of life.

4. Encouragement to Fissiparous Tendencies

In our country, population is increasing more than the growth of agriculture and industry. This has given encouragement to fissiparous tendencies due to which the condition of Indian society is going from bad to worse day by day.

5. Competition for High Posts

It is an age of competition. Hence, there is very unhealthy competition for grabbing lucrative jobs and high status in Indian society. This has led to rivalries, leg pulling, back biting and all sorts of moral degradation and social disintegration.

6. High Aspirations

In modern age, the needs and aspirations of all people are increasing day by day to lead a life of ease and pleasure. To fulfil these needs and aspirations, an individual tries to grab more and more affluence and pleasure by any means, fair or foul. This has created terror in the entire social environment of Indian society.

7. Early Marriage and Dowry System

Early marriage and dowry system are eating away the very vitals of Indian society. Because of these social evils all kinds of vices and foul play are rampant. Not only this, defiance of law has also become general.

8. Disintegration of Joint Family

The old joint family system is disintegrating day by day. Thus, people are not in a position to enjoy the merits of this system.

9. Low Standard of Living

The smallest unit of our Indian society is the village. We see that the standard of living of people, living in village, is still very low. Though the Government is doing its best to raise this standard, yet our standard of living is still very poor.

The above discussion makes it clear that the nature of modern Indian society is still not convincing in comparison with other countries of the world. To ensure its development higher and higher, we should dedicate ourselves to national service and democratic values of life.

CHARACTERISTICS OF MODERN INDIAN SOCIETY

To understand the sociological foundations of our society, one must know the characteristics of Indian society. The main features of Indian society are as follows, but since they are self-explanatory, therefore, we think further details are not needed because we feel every Indian is aware of the meaning of these features:

1. The caste system.
2. Social classes—Higher, Middle, and Lower classes.
3. Relgious Group: Hindus, Muslims, Christians, Parsis, and many sub-religions, such as Jains, Buddhists in Hindus and Shias and Sunnis in Muslims.
4. Variety of Languages.
5. Many cultures.
6. Excessive population.
7. Poverty.
8. Disorganization of joint family.
9. Disorganization of values.
10. Marital disorganization.
11. Materialism.
12. Politicization.
13. Social disorganization.
14. Economic difficulties.
15. Unemployment.
16. Uneducated masses.

IMPACT OF INDIAN SOCIETY ON CHILD

Indian society is still a backward society consisting of diverse castes, creeds, religions and languages which are best with many social evils and harmful traditions. These multifarious diversities influence the development of child in one way or the other. This influence may either be good or bad. Let us discuss this impact in the following lines:

1. Impact on Child's Physical Development

Children of our society are provided with various opportunities in schools in the form of games, sports, scouting, girl-guiding, PAC, NCC and gymnasium etc. Every year National Organizations organise youth festivals, tournaments and welfare programmes for children. But the fact is that our children do not avail of these facilities fully and effectively, because various types of evil influences and bad habits plague their physical well-being. There are various kinds of evil entertainments, pernicious fashions and snobbish activities which spoil the health of our children. Society should be very careful and cautious about this state of affairs.

2. Impact on Child's Mental Development

Our Constitution has guaranteed full freedom for the mental development of all citizens irrespective of colour, caste, creed and sex. Various states provide universal, compulsory and free primary education to children. Not only this, professional colleges, universities and academic colleges are open to all children who join entrance in them by merit. Yet these facilities are sometimes abused and misused for selfish ends ignoring the good of the society which is greatly essential.

3. Impact on Child's Moral and Spiritual Development

Moral and spiritual development of a child is achieved through religion. India always held aloft the banner of human religion and moral ideas. But it is the matter of regret that these days, religious and moral values are utterly neglected from our education in the false propaganda of secularism, with the result that materialistic outlook and habits of physical enjoyment are increasing by leaps and bounds. We see that outlook of the people is gradually drifting from our cultural ideals and values of life. The result is that our society is sinking deeper and deeper into moral corruption and degradation.

4. Impact on Child's Emotional Development

The pernicious disintegrating tendencies are raising their sinister heads to lead our society to conflicts and strifes. Diversities of religions, languages, castes and narrow loyalties are hindering the growth of national outlook and national character which are based on unity and emotional integration. These healthy and wholesome ideals remain a dream in the face of these fissiparous tendencies and narrow outlooks. Education should bring this unity in diversity and face the challenges of evil tendencies successfully. It is unfortunate that inspite of the work done by Emotional Integration Committee and National Integration Council, our education is far from promoting these desirable ideals of emotional integration and national unity.

5. Social Development

The ideal of seeing oneself in all others has been part and parcel of Indian culture for ages, and as a consequence one finds that in India, particularly in the rural areas, there is a considerably high level of social exchange, organisation and adjustment. This is more true of the past than of the present because in more recent years the detrimental effects of communalism, linguism, regionalism, etc., have been evident. They have cut into this social exchange and destroyed social feeling. Poverty and corruption have helped this disruptive process, and as a consequence one finds a very high incidence of disagreement civil litigation, violence, theft, dacoity, prostitution, etc., in the villages and sometimes, even in the towns and cities. Social control practically ceased to exist, and has been replaced by selfishness and individualism. Materialism has practically replaced interest in religion. One finds that educated or literate villagers have even less of the social consciousness than their uneducated counterparts because they are less amenable to social control. This effects childs social development.

6. Effect on Aesthetic Development

The child's aesthetic development depends very much upon the beauty of the surroundings in which he is brought up, the beauty of the home, the school, the neighbourhood. In school his aesthetic development is helped along by some elementary training in the various arts, drawing and painting, singing, music, dramatics, etc. Many schools in the country provide specialized training in the arts. Efforts are also sometimes made to make the school buildings attractive and aesthetically appealing. But in actual fact the paucity of means makes such steps difficult and often colleges are not able to maintain beautiful buildings or lawns. In many cases one finds that the school or college present an appearance little better than some factory. Yet, it must be remembered that it is the home which plays a larger part in the aesthetic development of the child, and in this respect the home of a majority of children compares unfavourably with the school these children attend. Leaving aside the deliberate attempts at beautification, which require a definite economic standard, one finds that frequently children come from homes which do not even provide sufficient space for the large family to live cleanly and in normal privacy. In villages, one often finds the family and the domestic animals practically sharing a common shed, thus living in almost inconceivably unhygienic surroundings. How much aesthetic development can one expect from the child who spends much of his day playing naked in the dirty and dusty street outside his house.

7. Spiritual Development

It has been the fond belief of many generations that Indian culture is basically spiritual, and that this inherent spirituality is steadily vanishing under the impact of such modern tendencies as westernization, urbanization, industrialization, that spiritual values are being rapidly replaced by more material and secular values. This process is also being hastened by other cooperating factors such as endemic poverty, illiteracy, corruption, a numbing dirtyness, widespread communalism. Some educationists have advised the adoption of some kind of religious instruction in schools, and have been trying to convince the government that this would not constitute a violation of secularism, but most of the political parties are against it, therefore, spiritual development of the child is not properly advanced.

8. Effect on Cultural Development

In the good old days of ancient India, education sought first of all to make the child cultured and civilized, but in the present day, educational institutions are concerned merely with acquainting the child with the various subjects put on the syllabus. The institutions care little whether the child acquires any culture in the process of education or not. Besides, the shortcomings that could be made up at home are not compensated because of the consistently widening generation gap and absence of social and family control. Society in general also provides a model only for such disruptive tendencies as classism, individualism, all of which promote selfishness, absolute liberty and disregard of laws. One finds little consideration and respect in the relations between teachers and students, parents and children, adults and young. Freedom and the rights of the individual are the call of the day, and they are only excuses for unbridled violence and indiscipline. Again, selfish politicians are encouraging instead or trying to arrest the process. Cultural development suffers another setback when the young see their elders raising their voice and hands against constituted authority in the form of the government. Even the social, educational, political and other circumstances obtaining in the country are not conductive to cultural development of any kind. Hence, one finds almost no cultural development in the present generation of children.

There are some other elements also which influence the development of our children. We are discussing them as under:

1. Impact of poverty. India is a poor country. Most of its social groups live a life of extreme misery without even the essentials of life available to them. A vast majority of people live in slums and extremely filthy surroundings. They remain below the poverty line and lead a life of starvation. Under these conditions, they are too poor to think and avail of any education at all. This is the reason of our great percentage of illiteracy and ignorance.

2. Impact of family disorganization. Family is the most important agency of education. Here, the child gets affection as well as lessons of socialization. He develops his character and habits in a family atmosphere and social qualities are developed in him. But in modern times disintegration and general discord in family life have led to great mental stress and strains with the result that this important agency of education has failed to educate the child.

3. Impact of crimes. After the attainment of independence, criminal tendencies are developing day by day. People do not hesitate to kill one another on petty matters. These criminal tendencies have a great impact on our children also. We see that schools have also become the centres of committing crimes. Educationists should be seriously and sincerely concerned to meet this challenge.

Having considered the impact of the Indian environment on the various aspects of the child's development, it is evident that considerable social reform will have to be undertaken, if the child's comprehensive development is to be ensured. This entire treatise was not to say that such conditions obtain in India alone, because such defective environment exists in many countries. Yet, instead of deriving consolation from this fact, it is better to try to improve things in our own country as best as we can.

INDIAN SOCIETY AND EDUCATION

We have discussed above that the present Indian society is influencing the development of an individual very powerfully in various ways. It is a matter of regret that these influences are directed towards evils and various criminal tendencies which plague our society and are increasing day by day threatening the very stability of our social structure. Education is the only means to meet these sinister challenges and stop this gradual decay. In other words, education should promote higher social and moral ideals developing desirable habits so that our society is saved from impending decay and destruction. It is through education alone that the great ideal of emotional integration, unity in diversities, national consciousness and national glory are realized. Let us all dedicate ourselves for these great ideals of life and social living.

QUESTIONS FOR ANSWER

1. Explain the impact of Indian society on child.
2. Write a note on the nature of Indian society since ancient period till date.
3. Write short notes on:
   (a) Traditional Nature of Indian Society.
   (b) Characteristics of Modern Indian Society.

10

Social Mobility and Education

Social mobility is the movement of an individual or a group in a social structure. It means transformation in social status, which may be upward or downward according to his or their desire and efforts. The material change or physical movement from one place to another is not social mobility but promotion from poor or middle to higher class or otherwise is social mobility.

DEFINITION OF SOCIAL MOBILITY

1. "By social mobility is meant any transition of an individual from one position to another in a constellation of social group and strata."

2. "Social mobility is any change in social position, such as occupational changes where persons move up or down the occupational scale, or election to office whereby a follower becomes a leader, or a leap from a low economic class to a high one, or vice versa."

3. According to P.A. Sorokin, "Social mobility is either horizontal or vertical. Horizontal mobility is the process of making changes on the same status level, while vertical mobility is the process of changing from one status to another, either to a higher or lower level."

Sorokin distinguishes between the following two forms of social mobility:

(A) Horizontal Social Mobility.
(B) Vertical Social Mobility.

(A) Horizontal Social Mobility

While some groups of persons have similar status some are placed in lower or higher status in a society. In horizontal social mobility, the position of an individual may change, but his salary, grade, prestige and other privileges remain the same. Thus, his social status remains the same. For example, transfer of a district magistrate to a post in Secretariat in the same grade does not affect his social status. Sorokin has differentiated between the following forms of horizontal social mobility.

1. Inter-group mobility in race, sex and age groups. Generally, there is no mobility among people of the same race, sex and age groups because nobody can change his or her race, sex or age according to his or her own will. But when sections of population grow and develop as social groups, horizontal mobility is liable to occur among them. Thus, social mixing and social interdynamics promote horizontal social mobility.

2. Occupational mobility. Occupational mobility is change from one occupation to another of the similar nature, conditions and circumstances. Occupational mobility is non-existent in closed societies because of rigid restrictions and limitations. On the other hand, occupational mobility gets an impetus in open stratification and during crisis or economic prosperity.

3. Inter-religious mobility. Religious mobility is change from one religious faith to another or conversion from one religion to another. It generally occurs under compulsions of force or allurements of various kinds among poor and ignorant sections of society only.

4. Political mobility. Leaving one political party and joining another is political mobility, which occurs because of self- interests, allurements, political instability and lack of moral character.

5. Family and kinship mobility. Marriage or remarriage, adoption of a child or divorce encourages this type of mobility, which happens more in society where polygamy is practised.

6. Territorial mobility. Leaving a particular territory by a group of people and entry into another territory is called territorial mobility. For example, groups of villagers seasonally migrate to towns for better living conditions. Territorial mobility is more frequent in towns, government services, industrial services in men and young persons. In times of harvest failures, epidemics, wars and critical circumstances of security and safety, territorial mobility occurs very rapidly.

*7. **International mobility.*** Encouraged by better prospects, more affluence and better living conditions, many persons migrate from underdeveloped countries to developed and progressive countries. This is international mobility which also increases when people of over populated countries migrate to other countries.

(B) Vertical Mobility

P.A. Sorokin says, "By vertical mobility, I mean the relations involved in a transition of an individual (or social object) from one social stratum to another." All social groups are not equal in social status. Some are higher and some are lower in social prestige. Vertical mobility achievement of higher status and prestige by an individual or a group of lower status and in the same manner degradation of an individual or group from higher status or prestige to lower status.

Sorokin has discussed the following forms of vertical mobility:

*1. **Ascending mobility.*** It refers to the movement from lower to higher position. It means the entry of persons from lower strata and prestige to higher status and prestige groups. Promotion of a clerk to an officer, of a lecturer to readership or professorship are examples of ascending mobility.

*2. **Descending mobility.*** It means descending or going down of a person from higher position prestige and status to lower ones. Occurring in government and private services, it is generally the outcome of some sort of inefficiency or acts of criminal tendencies and moral turpitude. Degradation of a minister to the status of a voter is an example of descending mobility.

Thus, the higher development of an individual or group of persons and their degradation denotes vertical mobility in both the directions. Some societies have insulated, restricted and rigid mobility, there is no mobility either way. They try to maintain their status and position for all times. An example is the caste system. On the contrary, developing groups have vertical mobility. Vertical mobility of the ascending type is found in affluent and aristocratic families of modern times. Descending mobility is common in weaker sections of society particularly in women and in backward societies.

DIMENSIONS OF SOCIAL MOBILITY

According to Lipset and Zitterberg the following are the areas of social mobility:

1. Occupational Ranking

Occupation is a common ground of social mobility. It may be noted that occupations which have similar social and economic foundations, they are called an occupational class. It is a matter of experience that each occupational class has its distinct social prestige and status. Not only this, there is a great difference in the ideals, values, feelings and habits of persons engaged in different occupations. Thus, persons engaged in comparatively less prestigious occupations strive to move towards occupations comprising greater prestige and social distinction. In this sense, entry of a skilled worker in the white collared jobs or occupations is called occupational mobility.

2. Social Class

It is comparatively easier for an individual to shift from one occupation to another, but is very difficult almost impossible for any one to shift from one social class to another. In this connection, it is essential to note that people of elite sections of society do not associate with persons of inferior social status. Hence, the social status and social class of a person can only be ascertained by social status and prestige group of his friends and companions.

3. Consumption Ranking

According to Lipset and Zitterberg, there is difference between occupational status and economic status. Business status is ranked according to income whereas economic status is ascertained according to expenditure. Because expenditure is directly related to styles and habits of living, therefore, people having the same or similar living styles and habits of life are known as same consumer's group of society. Generally, it is seen that life of persons of the same occupation have different modes of social life. To cite an example, individuals of lower strata of society, after getting good education and entering good profession or good business shift to higher social status equivalent to middle class of society and sometimes equal to higher classes. It proves that not income alone but expenditure and styles of living determine social status and social prestige.

4. Power Ranking

Role relationship of the individuals with reference to the society determines their power ranking. Thus, persons of the same power impact form a power group. These power groups are independent. For example, the ward of a union leader can easily obtain the occupational status and prestige of a middle section ward. In the same way, even a poor labour leader can achieve greater political power and influence.

CAUSES OF SOCIAL MOBILITY

Lipset and Zitterberg have discussed the following causes of social mobility:

1. Supply of Vacant Statuses

The first cause of social mobility is to fill the blanks in the social statues in a society. In every social structure, positions of statuses are in a constant state of influx. In modern times, in governmental, managerial and official work more and more white-collared persons and skilled workers are in need whereas there is a progressive decline in the positions of unskilled labourers. Demographic compulsion also helps in the increase of positions of higher strata of society because of their lower birth rate and greater demand of business, government and private services. More and more persons from lower strata get upwards to fill the increasing need and requirements of society. This promotes social mobility.

2. Interchange of Ranks

Another cause of social mobility is the interchangeability of ranks. The more a society offers opportunities for the lower ranks to compete with those of the higher ranks, the more likelihood is there for social mobility promoted by those competitions which are open to all sections of society. Under such circumstances, if all people of a society are able to develop vocational and professional efficiency, then vocational mobility will definitely be promoted. The following are the important factors of interchangeability of ranks:

(i) Motivational factors. For social mobility through interchangeability of ranks, motivation and ambition, to push upward play a very important role. According to Verblen, every

individual by nature desires to push himself upward. In this connection, one thing is to be kept in mind that evaluation of a person by others influences his self-evaluation to a great extent. He tries to go higher and higher in his own estimation. In this way, ambitions for higher and higher status and prestige promotes more and more social mobility.

(ii) Structural factors. Structural factors also play an important part to influence social mobility. In all societies, positions of higher social status and prestige cannot either be changed or obtained by mere wish of an individual. Persons belonging to middle class group employed in government services strive to give costly and higher education to their children with the purpose to promote and make them eligible for higher status jobs, but they cannot give higher positions to their wards according to their wish. It is just possible, that failing in their efforts, they unwillingly push their wards to lower ranks whereas wards of lower ranks are able to achieve those positions of status, power and prestige. Because of those structural factors, ascending and descending social mobility becomes a common phenomenon and experience.

FACTORS AFFECTING SOCIAL MOBILITY

The following factors influence social mobility:

1. Opportunity Structure

Opportunity structure or structure of society powerfully influences the process of social mobility. Societies are of two kinds—(1) closed societies, and (2) open societies. Closed societies have a social structure based upon birth and heredity due to which individuals in such societies do not get opportunities for ascending and descending vertical social mobility. On the other hand, in open societies, every individual gets full freedom and opportunities to both kinds of vertical social mobility according to their own efforts of development or downfall. In India, caste structure is deeply rooted and even today people of higher castes look down upon the people of lower castes. It is a pleasure that through education and promotion of progressive democratic ideas, caste rigidity is loosing and the path of social mobility is getting free of the stronghold of caste system now.

2. Demographic Structure

Social mobility is closely connected with diffusion of population, its size and density. Birth rate and migration of village folks towards towns and cities are closely connected to social mobility. When people migrate to places of greater density of population, persons of higher status gladly accept even menial jobs and thus local population rises higher status. Much in the same way, people belonging to lower status get jobs of people having less children. After the attainment of independence, revolutionary progress has occurred in India in the fields of industry as well as agriculture. Thus, more and more people are migrating to cities and industrial centres from villages to take jobs in factories and mills. This has greatly promoted social mobility.

3. Economic Success

From economic point of view, there are three sections of society namely—(1) Rich class, (2) Middle class, and (3) Lower class. Out of these three classes, rich people receive greater respect and prestige. Hence, each individual irrespective of his group strives more and more to earn more and more money in order to achieve higher status and social prestige. This makes it clear that economic success influences social mobility from one group to another group.

4. Occupational Improvement

Some occupations are associated with greater social status and prestige in comparison with others. Hence, people engaged in occupations of lower status and prestige try to achieve occupations and positions of higher social status and greater social prestige. This accelerates social mobility. In India, occupational improvement is increasing day by day. Hence, social mobility is also going up and up.

5. Education

Development, propagation and spread of education also promotes social mobility. Those persons who receive more and more education achieve higher and higher social status. This gives an impetus to the growth of social mobility in a normal and natural way.

6. Administration

Administration set up of a country is related very closely to social mobility. In a democratic society greater opportunities are provided for social mobility in comparison with other types of administrative societies. The reason behind this is that democratic set up pre-supposes open societies which are oriented towards greater development of its members. Hence, democratic administration promotes social mobility in greater degree.

7. Effects of Automation

Automation in industry renders unemployment to a number of people who go elsewhere for jobs. Not only this, automation promotes opportunities for white-collared jobs. In both cases social mobility operates.

8. Aspirational Level

In a society, some people are ambitious by nature and some are inspired and encouraged to achieve higher positions of status which promotes social mobility. The more ambitious the people in a society are, the more social mobility grows.

MOBILITY OF TEACHERS AND STUDENTS

Education is a social process. An educated person gets recognition, position and prestige in society. Education abolishes social rigidity of structure, removes discrimination based on birth and destroys rigid stratification. It also strives to achieve higher ideals, obtains higher positions of prestige; formation of good habits and inculcation of permanent values. In short, education seeks to develop ability and capacity in the individual to gain higher statuses and positions of prestige. This promotes effective social mobility. Following are the causes of the mobility of teachers and students:

1. Teacher's Mobility

Most teachers try to achieve their social position and status in their own professional associations and organizations composed of teachers, lecturers, readers, professors, principals, chairmen, deans and vice-chancellors. Promotion from one position to a higher one promotes social status and prestige. In ancient times, the status of teachers was very high in society. But today, the teacher has fallen from that high status of respect and prestige due to the following causes:

(i) Dissemination of general education.
(ii) Increase in the number of students.
(iii) Less emoluments than in other professions.
(iv) Opportunities to achieve higher position among students.
(v) Indiscipline among students.

2. Social Mobility of Students

Education is a means to achieve higher social status and position in society. All students try to obtain more and more education to gain higher and higher social status. Achievement of higher status or social mobility is not possible without education. The following elements play an important part in the social mobility of students:

(i) Amount of education. Schools, colleges and universities impart education of different levels. Any student liable to receive education upto a particular level, obtains social status and prestige suited to that level.

(ii) Content of education. Educational curriculum also influences social mobility. Different subjects have different importance and value. In comparison with Humanities, Scientific subjects like engineering, medicine and technology are rated higher. Therefore, persons having knowledge of science get higher social status and social prestige. Therefore, there is intimate relationship between type of curriculum and social mobility.

(iii) Research degrees in specialized areas. Some scholars are able to achieve higher social status by their academic and research work in various fields of study. Thus, higher the academic achievements, greater is the social mobility.

(iv) Importance of college and university. Students of colleges and universities having a higher recognition and greater academic rating among institutions of higher education get higher jobs in comparison of students receiving education in other institutions. Oxford and Cambridge Universities in England are famous for higher education.

EDUCATION AND DOWNWARD MOBILITY

Education and social mobility are closely related. Education is capable to promote the growth and remove the backwardness of a country. In modern times, there are some developed countries where due to advanced technology no further development is possible. In other words, advanced technology has achieved saturation of development with respect to some well-developed and affluent countries. In such countries the process of social mobility operates very little. But in under-developed and developing countries like our own, social mobility has unlimited possibilities. In such countries the more useful and productive is the education, the more is the social mobility. Here it may be borne in mind that in such developing or under-developed countries, only capable children will go up whereas the incapable and mentally retarded will go down. Education will achieve both these processes and attain a balance between the two kinds of social mobility—the upward and the downward.

MERITS AND DEMERITS OF SOCIAL MOBILITY

Merits

Following are the merits of social mobility:

(i) Full and wholesome development of individual.
(ii) Higher positions to deserving persons.
(iii) Growth of social efficiency and social progress.
(iv) Remedy of mal-adjustment.
(v) Promotion of national solidarity and plenty.
(vi) Progress of society towards stability.
(vii) Development of welfare and happiness.

Demerits

Following are the demerits of social mobility:

(i) Disorder in rural and urban societies.
(ii) Development of pride and snobbery in individuals.
(iii) Constant discontent of individual with social order.

QUESTIONS FOR ANSWER

1. What is social mobility? Discuss its causes and the factors which promote social mobility.
2. Bring out the relationship between education and social mobility and discuss how does education affect social mobility?
3. What is the position today in India about: (1) Social mobility, and (2) Methods of this social mobility. How does education affect the two aspects?

11

Child's Socialization

Socialization is the process of making an individual social, which fall within the scope of interaction or the social act and this makes him well adjusted with his family, neighbours and other social groups so that he himself becomes a true social being in the true sense of the term.

DEFINITION OF SOCIALIZATION

To make the meaning of socialization more clear, the following definitions are adduced:

(1) "Socialization is the development of we-feeling in associates and the growth in their capacity and will to act together." —*J.S. Ross*

(2) "Socialization is the process by which children learn the ways of their society and make these ways part of their own personality." —*Havighurst and Newgarton*

(3) "Socialization is the process whereby persons learn to behave dependably together on behalf of human welfare and in so doing experiences social self-control, social responsibility and balanced personalities." —*Bogardus*

PROCESS OF SOCIALIZATION

As discussed above, the process of socialization makes a child social. Among the various factors which play a vital role in this process, the following are the prominent ones:

1. Child rearing. The upbringing of a child plays a

significant role in the socialization of a child. As the way in which the parents bring up the child and as the atmosphere which is available to the child in his early childhood, accordingly the feelings and experiences develop in the child. It means that improper upbringing of a child leads to the growth of anti-social tendencies in him because of social mal-adjustment. Hence, for wholesome socialization, healthy and proper upbringing is essential.

*2. **Sympathy.*** Like upbringing, sympathy also plays an important role in the socialization of a child. It may be noted that during infancy, a child is fully dependent on his family for the fulfilment of all his needs and requirements. Not only the fulfilment of need is enough, other should also show full and real sympathy with the child. It is sympathy which develops we-feeling in the child and he learns to discriminate between his real well-wishers and other members of society.

*3. **Co-operation.*** Society makes the child social. In other words, the co-operation of society plays an important part to socialize the child. As the child receives co-operation of others towards him, he also begins to extend his hearty co-operation towards other members of society.

*4. **Suggestion.*** Social suggestion powerfully influences the socialization of a child. It is a natural fact that a child acts according to the suggestion received from his well-wishers. Thus, suggestion determines the direction of social behaviour.

*5. **Identification.*** Sympathy, love and suggestion of parents, relations and well-wishers develop in the child a feeling of identification with others. Those who behave with the child sympathetically, the child considering them as his well-wisher, begins to act according to their ideals, language and standard of living.

*6. **Imitation.*** The basic factor in socialization is the process of imitation. This is the most potent way of learning by a child. He imitates the behaviour, impulses and feelings of his family members. In this way, learning by imitation is the most powerful means of socializing a child.

*7. **Social teaching.*** Besides imitation, social teaching also influences the socialization of a child. It may be noted that social teaching takes place in the family, among friends and relations who guide the child in one way or the other.

8. Reward and punishment. Reward and punishment have a great influence on the socialization of a child. When a child behaves according to the ideals and beliefs of society, people appreciate and approve his behaviour. On the contrary, when he does some anti-social act, he is criticized and condemned by society. This type of punishment weans the child away from unsocial activities leading towards proper socialization.

FACTORS LEADING TO THE SOCIALIZATION OF A CHILD

At the time of birth a human child is no more than a mere animal. As he gradually comes into contact with other children and participates more and more in joint social activities and experiences, he imbibes social ideas, social attitudes and social habits. This process of socialization is a continuing process and goes on throughout life. Now, we are discussing the important factors leading to the socialization of a child in the following lines:

1. Family. Family plays a pivotal role in the socialization of a child. Every child is born in a family where he comes in close contact with his parents and other members of the family. As he grows older, he learns number of socially desirable qualities namely—love, sympathy, tolerance and cooperation etc. Not only this, living in his family he gradually learns the ideals, values, beliefs, customs and traditions of the family directly or indirectly. In short, the socialization of the child, through wholesome interaction with the members of family, goes on continually.

2. Neighbourhood. Neighbourhood also is like a wider and enlarged family. Children living in the same locality interact among themselves and gain norms of behaviour, habits of living and co-operative attitudes to solve their immediate simple problems of day to day living. In this sense, if the neighbourhood is wholesome and conducive, socialization will be desirable. On the contrary, bad neighbourhood is likely to spoil the desirable development and socialization of children. Hence, people belonging to good families prefer to live with good neighbours.

3. School. After the family and the neighbourhood, school is a place where socialization of a child takes place. In school, children belonging to different families read together, interact in various patterns and imbibe various traditions of society. Besides this, their participation in educational and social functions of the school also inculcates in children social qualities, attitudes, habits and patterns of behaviour which brings about their socialization.

4. Games and sports. Every child is fond of play. We see that there is more effective interaction in games and sports than organised teaching in a class. In other words, while playing various social qualities namely—sympathy, co-operation, fellow-feeling, selfless service, sacrifice, team spirit and many other socially desirable values develop in children to make their socialization more effective and purposeful.

5. Scouting and girl-guiding. Scouting and girl-guiding also lead to effective socialization. The motto of these organizations is service of society and service of self. They motivate and inspire children to launch and pursue social service projects and programmes through co-operative efforts, sacrifice, sympathy, fellow-feeling, selfless service of others and many other human qualities, so essential to effective socialization.

6. Caste. The main purpose of a caste is to socialize the child. It may be noted that each caste has its specific customs, traditions, achievements, cultural values and ideals of life different from those of others. Hence, each caste tries to socialize its children according to its specific ideals, attitudes and values.

7. Community or society. Community or society also plays a vital role in the socialization of a child. Various social functions and community programmes provide ample opportunities to children to participate in them whole heartedly and develop socially desirable qualities.

8. Religion. Religion has important contribution with regard to the socialization of a child. Each religion has its specific virtues, rituals, dogmas and cosmologies. As the child interacts with children belonging to his own religion and people having faith in other religions, this interaction inculcates in him sympathy, co-operation, respect for the sentiments of others, fellow-feeling and attitude of adjustment leading to socialization in the true sense of the term.

FACTORS RESISTING SOCIALIZATION OF THE CHILD

According to Maslow, the factors, hindering the smooth working of socialization are given below:

1. Childhood situation. For example, lack of parental affection, favouritism, undue punishment, insecurity, conflicts and widowed mother etc.

2. Cultural conditions. For example, caste distinctions, social disparities, prejudices of religion and social status, snobberies, feelings of superiority and inferiority among the sections of society.

3. Current situations. For example, experiences of sufferings, hardships, insult, envy, injustice, despondency and desperations.

4. Other circumstances. For example, experiences of physical hardships, poverty, failure, lack of education, lack of self-reliance, courage and fortitude.

ROLE OF TEACHER IN THE PROCESS OF SOCIALIZATION

Teacher plays a very important role in the socialization of a child. Hence, to reinforce and spread up this process, a teacher should keep in mind the following:

1. Parent-teacher co-operation. The first task of teacher is to come into close contact with the parents of the child and from them try to know about the interests, aptitudes and tendencies of the child and then try to provide suitable facilities for the maximum development of that child in a natural way.

2. Transmission of culture. Teacher should try his best to convey to the children the cultural heritage in the form of customs, traditions, ideals, values and patterns of behaviour in a very imperceptible but effective way. This transmission of cultural values will effectively lead to desirable socialization of children.

3. Social ideals. Teacher should try to put social ideals before children everywhere—in class rooms, on the playgrounds, in cultural and social functions, in all academic activities and diverse programmes. Identification with these social ideals will lead to socialization gradually.

4. Traditions of school. School traditions exert powerful

influences upon the process of socialization. Hence, the teacher should inspire belief and appreciation of those traditions in children encouraging them to follow them in their conduct and other activities.

5. Encouragement of group work. Teacher should devise and launch projects where children work jointly in groups with mutual co-operation, sympathy and fellow-feeling. More and more group activities will develop more and more social qualities which eventually lead to socialization.

6. Development of inter-cultural feeling. Children belonging to different families believing in different cultures mix freely in school. Teacher should try to inculcate inter-cultural feeling in children so that they learn to respect other cultures along with their own culture.

7. Feeling of healthy competition. It leads to effective socialization hence this feeling should be developed by the teacher in children which will lead them to praiseworthy socialization.

8. Healthy human relations. It plays significant role in child's socialization. Hence, all teachers should attempt to build up healthy human relations with all the children. In such healthy social environment, the socialization of a child is must.

QUESTIONS FOR ANSWER

1. Explain the factors leading to child's socialization.
2. How can a teacher promote wholesome socialization in children?

12

The Family and Education

In every part of the world family is the oldest human and social unit which is smallest and basic in nature, hence everywhere family activities are child bearing and initial induction of the child into given culture of the society. Family members are related or associated with each other.

DEFINITION OF FAMILY

(1) "The family is a group defined by sex relationship sufficiently precise and enduring to provide for the procreation and upbringing of children." —*MacIver & Page*

(2) "By family we mean a system of relationship existing between parents and children." —*Clare*

(3) "A family is a group of persons united by the ties of marriage, blood or adoption constituting a single household interacting and intercommunication with each other in their respective social role of husband and wife, mother and father, son and daughter, brother and sister creating and maintaining a common culture."

—*Burgess & Locke*

Each family has its own distinct habits of clothing, eating, thinking, talking and living. These are the items of that family's culture. This culture has to be preserved and transmitted by each family from generation to generation.

MAIN ELEMENTS OF FAMILY

Following are the essential elements of a family:

(1) Sexual intercourse of a man and woman.

(2) Marriage as a basis of these connections by social sanction.

(3) Their progeny known to belong to them and to their family's name by the sanction of state which guarantees their legality and status.

(4) Each member contributing something to the family welfare, joint sharing of income to meet the needs and joint responsibility in all spheres of activities.

(5) Shared use and joint ownership of house and all facilities guaranteed.

CHIEF CHARACTERISTICS OF FAMILY

Following are the chief characteristics of family:

*1. **Universality.*** A family is found in all corners of the world. There is no human society which does not have a family of one kind or the other.

*2. **Limited size.*** The number of the members of a family is limited. It cannot be increased or decreased arbitrarily. In other words, the concept of family denotes a few members.

*3. **Centre of social organization.*** A family is the smallest unit of society. Numerous families constitute a society. Thus, society and its structure is based upon these small units.

*4. **Innate tendencies as basis of family.*** Innate tendencies born out of the sexual relations of husband and wife are essentially the foundations of a family. Such tendencies are mainly innate and inborn.

*5. **Constructive influence.*** The family exerts the most formative and powerful influence on the development of a child's personality. In other words, it is the family which imprints permanent and indelible impressions upon the growing child.

*6. **Responsibility.*** Every member of the family has the responsibility of maintaining the family in one way or the other. Generally, adults have greater responsibility than the minors.

*7. **Cradle of social values.*** A family is the cradle of all social values. It is the set up of the family which inculcates socially desirable values and high qualities of character in its members who ultimately become useful and dynamic citizens devoted to national service and international understanding.

*8. **Permanent institution.*** Family is a permanent institution, because its basis and relationship is permanent. Its members may depart or live apart, their association or living together may be temporary but the basic relationship remains permanent.

FAMILY AND SOCIAL DEVELOPMENT

Human personality develops in a social environment. In the childhood, the personality of an individual is very susceptible to change and variation. He can be turned in practically any desired direction. The famous psychoanalyst Freud has contended that the personality of man is formed in his childhood and the period after that marks only its development.

In view of the fact that the experiences, habits, etc., acquired in childhood are so extremely important, the family situation also becomes important because the childhood of the individual is spent within the precincts of the home. The family situation can be regarded as comprehending three factors:

(1) Relation of parents to child,

(2) Order of the child's birth, and

(3) Presence of brothers and sisters and other members in the family.

The important role played by the family in the formation of the child's personality can be clearly realized after these three aspects have been studied.

RELATION BETWEEN CHILD AND HIS PARENTS

Having affected a psychological analysis of the importance of the parent-child relationship the psychoanalysts have tried to show why the child is influenced to such a great extent by his parents and the relation in which he stands with them.

According to Freud, the parents are particularly present before the child as ideals. They are more powerful and strong and can perform all activities efficiently. The child effects an identification with his father unconsciously. He wants to become as his father. It is often seen that the young child dons the clothes of his father and imitates his manner of walking and talking.

The child behaves precisely as do his mother and father. Besides identification, the second element in this is that of imitation. The child learns much by imitation. There are many activities that the child learns to perform merely by observing and imitating the older members of the family.

For the child, the parents are as examples and it will be very difficult to prevent children from indulging in activity in which the parents themselves indulge particularly when they do so in front of the child. Thus the impact of parents on the child is most vital and lasting.

CRIMINAL TENDENCY AND THE PARENT-CHILD RELATIONSHIP

The misbehaviour of the parents or their neglect of the children are important factors due to which children often become juvenile delinquents. According to the report 'Women of the Street', an important research on the prostitutes of London, the problem of prostitution has its origin in the relationship between the child and the parents.

Often when the child is deprived of parental love and is sternly punished frequently he is filled with the desire to revolt and disgust so much so that he runs away from the home when he gets the opportunity to do so. Once away from the home he falls into criminal ways. If neglected by his parents the child feels helpless and alone as a result of which he develops many kinds of complexes.

The child becomes a delinquent also when the parents try to conceal too much from him. For example, the children are very apt to ask their parents as to where they came from or where the younger child came from and they are often misled. These are the some of the situations which develop criminal tendencies in the child.

Need for Balance

In this way, both excessive neglect and excessive love and affection are not to be desired in the relationship between the child and parents. Both are the origin of difficulties concerning the personality and all kinds of problems take root in the mind of the child.

Similarly, it is harmful both to place absolute control on the child as well as to leave him to his own mechanisms almost entirely. If the child is given too much freedom, he does not develop any respect for authority and cannot be governed. If he is placed under excessive control, his personality is not allowed to develop and he is obsessed with a sense of inferiority and sometimes even turns to crime.

The truth of the matter is that if the child is to be disciplined and educated a bitter pill must be swallowed. It is very difficult to bring up a child. In this connection it is necessary that there should be much balance and understanding.

Influence of Discrimination

Sometimes parents discriminate between their children in behaving towards them. They have unlimited love and affection for one while another receives only scolding and punishment. Sometimes it is the beautiful child that is love while the ugly one is neglected and disregarded. Whatever the reasons at the root of this discriminatory behaviour it is bad because it arouses feelings of hatred for each other among the children.

When the child observes that his brother or sister is being loved more than he is, he becomes anxious to revenge this injustice. Sometimes, he is even seen possessed of aggressive tendencies. He also tries to harm the other children in one way or the other. He is seen to be disappointed, insecure, fearful, etc.

Effect of the Character of Parents

The personality of the child is also appreciable influenced by the moral thoughts and conduct of the parents because usually the child looks upon his parents as ideals on which to mould his life. In order to inculcate morality in the children the parents should place an example before them in the form of their own exemplary behaviour.

There are very few children who can mould their behaviour according to social values and conceptions even when they have seen their parents indulge in theft, sexual immorality, falsehood, deception and other forms of misconduct.

In Miss Eliott's study the parents in 67 percent broken homes and 44 percent unbroken homes were indulging in immoral behaviour. If the mother indulges in prostitution her daughters have no inhibition against it and they would have no difficulty in imitating her and proceeding towards immorality and corruption.

Effect of the Mutual Relation of Parents

The personality of the child is further open to another important influence *viz.*, the mutual relation between husband and wife. If the husband misbehaves towards the wife then the child, particularly the male child, takes exception to it and this increases his hatred for the father.

This can, under certain circumstances, lead to terrible consequences. Similarly, if the wife misbehaves with husband, the female child in particular is likely to dislike it and hence she hates her mother. Constant conflict and quarrelling between husband and wife leads to the creation of an atmosphere of insecurity in the home which is not at all conductive to the development of the child's personality.

If the relations between husband and wife are good the children have a good and encouraging ideal in front of themselves which they can imitate to good effect. They then try to be good themselves. It is only natural for the child to develop some personality defects if the relation between his parents is not good.

Effect of the Broken Family

When the relation between the husband and wife leteriorate, the family is reduced to a broken family. This is because the relations between no two members retain their original charm and goodness. A broken family is one in which the family relations have been severed. Family does not mean the living together of some individuals but rather the intimate and profound relations that exist between them. In the absence of this intimacy the family is disbanded and in the broken family juvenile delinquents are reared and brought up.

In the broken family the children are not looked after or cared for. According to some specialists, the broken family tends to create the criminal tendency in the female children more than it does in the male children.

Effect of the Financial Status

The financial condition of the family also influences the development of the child's personality. If the financial condition is good and the parents can adequately satisfy the needs of the children then the children are generally not possessed with the sense of inferiority and want and they do not turn to crime. But if the financial condition of the family is extremely bad the personality of the child suffers.

Merrill has written that if the income of the family is low the children also have to work and their education is, thus, left incomplete. The child's personality does not react very appreciably to the conditions of work. Many of the desires of the poor children are left unfulfilled in order to satisfy which they turn to criminal activity. Poverty induces feelings of dissatisfaction and inferiority.

Family has a Nuclear Situation

Family is the first institution in the history of man. In the ancient age men lived in small families, which lacked any kind of organisation or permanence. But they served to fulfil simple biological and psychological needs. Generally, the family consisted of husband and wife and their offspring. The powerful men possessed many wives and thus they lived in big families with their wives and children.

When man became oriented in agriculture, many families formed a group and stayed permanently at some place for farming. When these people started partaking of each other's pain and happiness as neighbourly gestures, social relations increased and in this way many families formed a community and the next step was the creation of nation. In this way family is that primary group which slowly evolved into nation.

Family is a fundamental unit of human society. Its foundations rest upon man's biological and psychological needs. In the modern age, many functions of the family have shifted to other institutions but nevertheless, there are many biological and psychological needs which man cannot satiate without a family.

Society Depends upon Family

Proper social organisation depends upon proper organisation

of families. If the families disintegrate in some society, then the society will never be safe. One major cause of social disorganisation is family disorganisation. Families develop the characters of the members of society. Freud and other psychologists have proved that a child, when a man, exhibits the same character and mental tendencies which he acquired in the family. In the opinion of Adler, a man's role in the family determines his role in society.

Family Socializes Individual

In this way, a person is socialized in the family. Defining family, Merrill writes, "Family is an enduring association of parent and offspring whose primary functions are the socialization of the child and the satisfaction of the members."

According to Dewey and Tufts, the family is a social agency for the education and protection of the race. It is in the family that the child acquires such important qualities as sincerity, sympathy, self-submission and realising responsibility etc. It is the character developed in the family which helps the child in becoming an important and responsible member of society.

Wright was quite correct in stating that in every family, the child gets an opportunity for free expression of thoughts and developing his entire personality. Psychologists have incontenstably proved that the proper development of the child is impossible without a good environment in the family.

Family is the Conveyor of Traditions

The family moulds the character and personality of the individual. It is through the family that society imparts its culture to the individual. Thus, the family is very important in the form of socializing agency. In the essay, *The Family Conveyance of Tradition,* Paul Schreker wrote that a particular function of the family is to sanction children. Like marriage, the institution of family is constituted by different elements of culture. It is due to this reason that it has religious, judicial, political, artistic and linguistic aspects. Whenever a new thought impresses itself on an age the family takes a new form in order that the upbringing and mental tendencies may be harmonious to that thought.

Social Control through the Family

A social life is a web of relationships. In order to maintain these relations properly, a system of rights and duties is organised which will avoid any conflict between the members of society and allow them to develop as complements to each other. In order to avoid any breach of this harmony between the individuals in society, the society applies numerous kinds of control on the individual. They are taught to obey the elders, have sympathy for the young and for others. A strict control over sex relationships is necessary for maintaining the social order, otherwise disintegration will spread over the complex social life of today. Relationships between men and women will lose their solidarity. Illegitimate children will be born with no one to look after them.

Although the anthropologists Mead and Malinowski have discovered societies where control over sex relations is inordinately lax without disturbing the social order but such an order is completely contradictory to the thinking of today's cultured person. It is the family which does this work of controlling sex passions for society. In all cultures, the families exercise some degree of control over the unmarried members till they attain the matrimonial state. In the same way, the family acts as a preventive to individual in keeping him from the habits and crimes like drinking, theft, etc.

Not many parents could like their children to embark on careers of crime. Even the worst person tries to prevent his children from adopting similar habits and consequently any objectionable behaviour on the part of children is punished and laudable effort suitably rewarded. They, thus, drop bad habits and learn good things. In this way the making of a good citizen in society depends upon the parents.

Importance of Family in the Education of the Child

In the modern industrial and urban society the age old structure of joint family has been broken down under the stress of industrialization, social, economic and political factors and legal compulsions. This development has led to the establishment of various other institutions for the education and development of children belonging to different families. The importance of family as a powerful informal agency of education has not become less. On the other hand, its role has increased in many other ways.

The infant begins his life under the fostering affection and care of his parents and other near and dear ones associated with his family. As he grows, he receives the first lessons of life in his family and tries to imbibe the habits, ideals and patterns of behaviour of his family members. In this way, the family continues to influence him throughout his life.

VIEWS ON THE IMPORTANCE OF FAMILY IN THE EDUCATION OF THE CHILD

(1) "Education begins at birth and the proper nurse is the mother." —*Rousseau*

(2) "Home—a centre of love and affection, is the best place and the first school of the child." —*Pestalozzi*

(3) "Mothers are the ideal teachers and informal education given by home is most effective and natural." —*Froebel*

(4) "Child learns the first lesson of citizenship between the kiss of mother and the care of father." —*Mazim*

(5) "The home is the soil in which spring up those virtues of which 'sympathy' is the common characteristic. It is there that the warmest and most intimate affection flourish. It is there that the child learns the difference between generosity and meanness, considerateness and selfishness, justice and injustice, truth and falsehood, industry and idleness. It is there that his habitual learning of the one or the other of these is first determined. —*T. Raymont*

Madam Montessori is so much devote to home education that she named her school 'Children's House.' An atmosphere of neatness, love and affection pervades in all 'Children's Houses'.

The opinions of all the above mentioned educationists clearly reveal the importance and value of home or family in the education and development of the child. Great men of India as well as of other countries, learnt the early lessons of greatness from their mothers or from others in the family.

CHILD'S DEVELOPMENT IN THE FAMILY

The facts given in this chapter establish that family develops following aspects of child's personality:

1. Child's physical development
2. Child's mental development
3. Child's emotional development
4. Child's social development
5. Child's religious development
6. Child's transmission in culture
7. Development of child's interests and habits
8. Development of child's language
9. Development of child's morality and character
10. Development of child's innate tendencies
11. Development of child's personality
12. Development of child's practical and vocational knowledge.

EFFECTS OF JOINT FAMILY UPON CHILDREN

Joint family system has been the chief characteristic of Indian family. With the active cooperation, love and sympathy of father, mother, uncle, aunt, grandfather and grandmother together with other close relations, the child imbibes the habits and thoughts of his elders in a natural way.

Due to various reasons the old joint family system is gradually disintegrating into smaller and smaller individual families. The result is that children do not get those all pervading, comprehensive and broad experiences necessary to shape their desirable attitudes and strong good character. Poor families are not in a position to provide adequate diet and other necessities of life to their young ones.

Even the well-to-do families are often found to be quite indifferent towards the proper nurture and education of their children. These conditions need to be changed if the family has to play its shaping and formative role.

AN INDIAN FAMILY

Though a number of defects are found in Indian families but only two deficiencies are prominent from educational point of view. In some families, children are given so much freedom that they become indolent, devoid of self-respect and self-confidence with the result that they become undisciplined and follow no code of conduct or rules of behaviour. They misuse their liberty as licence to do any thing they like and behave in any way they deem fit.

Such children fail to understand and realize the benefits of group dynamics and socialization. Their growth become stunted and they become maladjusted persons in the family as well as in the society. In other families children are subjected to so such rigorous discipline and control that they become snobbish, irresponsible and timid. Their growth remains stunted and often such children become rebellious. The result in such cases is the same maladjustment in the family and in the society.

In the words of Prof. K.G. Saiyidain, "The child fails to establish correct and deep-rooted relation and co-operation with parents and other members of the family. The gulf between the child and parents widens and the Indian family fails in its noble mission."

MEASURES TO MAKE INDIAN FAMILY AN EFFECTIVE AGENCY OF EDUCATION

1. Provision for physical development. Following proper elements are essential for the physical development of the child:

A. Proper residence of the family
B. Good food
C. Proper clothes
D. Provision of play and rest.

2. Development of intellectual, aesthetic, practical interests. Family should develop the intellectual, aesthetic and practical interests of the child from the early childhood. Following measures may be suggested:

A. Intellectual development
B. Aesthetic development
C. Provision for practical knowledge
D. Provision for constructive activity.

3. Development of character and training of responsibility. The character of a child is developed in family by inculcating in him self-confidence and training of responsibility. The parents should encourage children to plan and execute small projects of home decoration, table setting and garden planting etc. This will develop in them self-confidence and a sense of responsibility.

4. Development of individual needs, capacities and interests. Psychology has proved that each individual is not a carbon copy of another. Each individual has his own individuality. Hence, members of family should provide suitable opportunities to each child to develop his individuality according to his needs, capacities and interests. The defect of teaching in school will also be supplemented and complemented by individual development at home under family environment.

5. Impartial treatment. Parents should behave fairly and impartially with all the children of family. There should be no sex discrimination between boys and girls. Both boys and girls of today are the citizens of tomorrow. In their capacity as citizens, they will not only enjoy the fundamental rights equally but also form a sound national government. Hence, the family should break the old artificial walls and provide equal opportunities to boys and girls for their richer, happier and better development.

6. Religious education. The family should provide suitable opportunities to the children to receive religious education. Though child cannot understand the conflicting elements of religion but he can certainly receive religious education in the wider sense through religious books, religious tales and other religious activities. Such religious education shall inculcate in the child all the desirable values namely—love, sympathy, service, sacrifice and fellow-feeling. In a secular state like India, it is the sacred duty of family to provide such religious education to each child so that he may grow into a responsible citizen of the state.

7. All-round development. The family should ensure an all-round development of the child. In India, most of the families are satisfied only with partial development of their children. They neglect the other aspects of development.

In his book 'Total Education', Jacks has classified such families into three categories. In one type of competitive families, children are developed into one set direction upto set limits only while the other aspects are neglected. In an other type of families cultural activities and interests are made fun of with the result that children remain deficient in emotional and cultural aspects of development.

The third type of families are known as emotionally refrigerator families. In such families socially desirable qualities namely—love, affection and sympathy etc., are looked down upon by their members with the result that the behaviour of children belonging to such families becomes static and undesirable.

A family should look to all sides of child's personality—physical, mental, emotional and social. Then only, a wholesome and full development of child will be possible. For this purpose, no aspect of development is to be neglected. Parents should provide all the desirable experiences and activities to their children duly planned and structured in advance.

8. Infant school. If the family is not in a position to cater to the various needs of children, it should admit them in some nursery, kindergarten or boarding school. There, the children will be properly developed under the proper and suitable environment of the school. But such schools are rare and very expensive. Most of them are mere commercial establishments. Hence, the state must come forward and open such schools in sufficient number so that poor and ordinary families are also benefited.

QUESTIONS FOR ANSWER

1. What is family? Enumerate the chief elements and characteristics of a family.
2. Discuss the functions of a family.
3. Discuss the importance of family. How can it be made an effective agency of education?

13

Social Change and Education

Social change means change in the structure and functions of human society. The human life is not static. It is under constant change in the ideals, attitudes and values of an individual which affects social attributes and social structure, which no society in the world can escape.

DEFINITION OF SOCIAL CHANGE

To make the concept of social change more clear, we are giving some definitions as under:

(1) "Social change is a term used to describe variation in or modification of any aspects of social processes, social interactions or social organization." —*Sir Jones*

(2) "Social changes are variations from the accepted modes of life whether due to alterations in geographic conditions, in cultural equipment, composition of the population or ideologies and whether brought about by diffusion or invention within the group." —*Gillin and Gillin*

(3) "Social change means that large number of persons are engaged in activities that differ from those in which they or their immediate fore-fathers were engaged in sometime before. Society is composed of a vast and complex network of patterned relationship, in which all men participate, when human behaviour is in the process

of modification that is only another way of indicating that social change is occurring."

CONCEPT OF SOCIAL CHANGE

There is difference of opinion among scholars about the nature and form of social change. In this connection the views of some famous sociologists namely; Brown, Chopin, Spencer, Lister Ward and Ogburn are as under:

(1) According to Brown, there is no difference between social change and cultural change. Both are interrelated in the sense that cultural change is an important part of social change.

(2) Chopin has divided cultural changes into three categories—*(i)* Those changes which are concerned with material culture; *(ii)* Those changes which are connected with non-material culture; and *(iii)* Those changes which are linked up with composite culture. The examples of these three are serially—social order, ideals, and forms of administration.

(3) According to Spencer, social change and social evaluation are identical. In his opinion social changes are uniform, gradual and progressive. Spencer has further pointed out that as we progress from less painful position to more comfortable positions, the process of social changes also undergoes the essential stages of evaluation.

(4) Lister Ward does not agree with the views of Spencer. According to him, social change is related to the changes in social aims and aspirations of individuals. Hence, it is not based on the principle of evaluation but is planned, intelligent and purposive. Each human being determines those aims according to his intelligence, which he can achieve and this achievement brings about social change.

(5) According to Ogburn, there is no distinction between social change and cultural change. He advocates two forms of culture namely—*(i)* Material, and *(ii)* Non-material. Material culture is concerned with all those things and objects which man has made for his welfare and happiness. Radio, television, means of transport and communication etc., are examples in this connection. Non-material culture is concerned with human ideas, attitudes, values, habits, customs, traditions and our mentalities.

Ogburn asserts that first the change occurs in the material

culture and then in the non-material. When material culture changes and non-material remains the same or lags behind, cultural lag occurs. Indian society is an example of cultural lag. Education is the only means to remove this cultural lag.

FACTORS OF SOCIAL CHANGE

Social change is a continuous process. There are some important factors which help this process. These factors are—(1) The physical environment, (2) Scientific inventions and researches, and (3) Interdynamics. In the above lines, we have mentioned that according to Ogburn, social change first occurs in the material culture and then in the non-material culture. But Ottaways holds that these cultural changes do not take place one after the other, but it is a product of the interdynamics of the two. Ottaway has clearly stated that social or cultural change occurs because of the interaction of technological researches or scientific inventions and the ideals, values and aims of society.

As these factors namely; technology, techniques and values play an essential role in any social change, it is necessary to understand the meaning and significance of these words. Technology is that branch of science which develops various techniques. Techniques are those means which fulfil various basic needs of human beings in a society. In the end values are those objectives, beliefs, thoughts and abstract concepts which make human life dynamic, successful and purposive.

From the above discussion, it becomes quite clear that neither technological techniques alone nor the values in themselves bring about any real social change. It cannot also be determined definitely that which one of the above two has a greater share in achieving social change.

In fact, when technology changes, it affects change in values and when values change, they bring out the corresponding change in technology. In this way, technological techniques as well as values are both the essential basis of social change. Both are equally important and essential. Both actively interact and bring about social changes.

FACTORS RESISTING SOCIAL CHANGE

We have discussed above the factors which promote social

changes, but there are still some factors which resist this change. The factors which resist social change are as under:

1. Cultural inertia. Cultural inertia is the first important factor which resists social change. Cultural inertia refers to those blind beliefs, customs and traditions which come down to us from our forefathers and which we stick to rigidly and blindly thinking them as sacred and indelible. This rigid, conservative and narrow outlook makes us static and averse to any change. The outcome of this inertia is that our society remains backward in many respects and an aversion to modernization is evident. Education should break this inertia and rigidity.

2. Fear of new things. Fear of new things is second factor which stands in the way of any social change. In fact, some minds are always very apprehensive and doubtful about any change. According to Ogburn and Nim-Koff, most of the people show a tendency to stick to traditional routine life and are therefore averse to gain any thing new for fear that these new elements may not turn to be harmful and injurious to them. They are contented with the status quo, the present state of affairs and are always praising the old traditional patterns of thinking and behaviour. This tendency needs to be changed through education. Only then, any social change will be welcomed and adopted by general people.

3. Vested interests. Vested interests is third factor which resists social change. Generally, it has been observed that there are some old traditions and beliefs which satisfy the vested interests of a few privileged section of society. Such people with vested interests, resist any change because of the danger to their self-interests. In other words, people having vested interests vehemently resist social change. Education is the only means to sublimate self-interests and make them welcome any social change.

4. Degree of isolation. Degree of isolation is the fourth factor which resists social change. In fact, there are some people in society who refuse to come into contact with persons of other cultures. They try their best to remain in isolation and insulated from other influences. These people resist any kind of social change. For example, the backward communities and tribal groups resist any outside contacts apprehending danger to their self-centred narrow spheres of life full of special privileges and aids of many kinds.

PROCESS OF SOCIAL CHANGE IN INDIAN SOCIETY

Under the alien rule upto 1947, India remained backward and underdeveloped in comparison with other modern countries of the world. Now, we are free and our Constitution guarantees full freedom to all citizens irrespective of colour, caste, creed and sex. Our national government has enacted laws against untouchability or any kind of social and economic discrimination. We are pledged to a Democratic Socialistic Republic for the welfare, social justice and equality to all based on brotherhood. Not only this, our government has enacted laws to promote widow marriage, secure needed divorce and against dowry together with social discrimination in any way.

Block development officers strive to promote economic development of all the individuals within their area of work. Social legislation provides protection, training and livelihood to abandoned ladies and reformatories to cure the young one's of criminal tendencies. The government is wedded to the ideal of universal, free and compulsory education upto primary standard and is doing its utmost to provide varied educational facilities to more and more boys and girls.Recently a very ambitious project has been launched for the education of the adults and various schemes are working in the land to promote national welfare and development.

In addition to the efforts to the national and state governments, our society itself is showing signs of awakening and striving to achieve more and more progress in various fields of social life. Caste isolation is decaying gradually. Feelings of untouchability and hatred are being removed by education at a rapid speed.

The movement of women liberation from the bonds and restrictions is gaining ground and all blind beliefs, customs and traditions are gradually dying out under the light of reason and modernity. Even the remotest corners of the land are responding to the light of education, uplift and reform. Inspite of all these efforts of the governments and the people, we as a society are still backward and need revolutionary reforms in all fields of life.

It must be borne in mind that the main cause of the backwardness of Indian society is lack of education and moral values which result in frequent caste, communal and language conflicts. There is all-round poverty, economic, social and moral degradation strikes, favouritism and corruption in almost all walks of social, political, economic and national life. Social thinkers and reformers should devise means to stem this degradation and find solutions of the multitude of problems which beset our society today.

In this connection, one thing is clear and universally accepted that education for all at all levels and ages of children is the only remedy to meet these challenges and bring about the desired social change in Indian society. Hence, social engineers should resolutely and confidently remove ignorance and take the nation towards the cherished ideal of national welfare and national glory in the community of world nations.

EDUCATION AND SOCIAL CHANGE

Education fulfils the needs of society and propagates such ideas which promote social change in all fields of life. Education becomes, in this way, a social process by means of which society moulds children according to its needs and approved patterns of behaviour. It is for this end in view that a society organizes its educational activities according to its needs and aspirations. In the light of social change, we are discussing below the functions of education:

1. Perpetualizing eternal values. A society has some eternal values which stabilize and consolidate it. Ralph Litton, while discussing this principle, has stated that whenever these eternal values lose their hold due to social changes, the society begins to decay and degenerate. In such times of crisis, education protects these eternal values, saves them from pernicious effects of social changes and promotes their knowledge and acceptance in such a manner that inspite of social changes, people in general keep faith in these values. In our society, such eternal values are of moral and spiritual nature. Education should protect, preserve and promote these values.

2. Promoting capacity to welcome and accept social change. Education propagates in the society both the materialistic and non-materialistic techniques. It prepares the mentality of people to welcome and adopt desirable social changes easily and gladly.

It may be noted that people will welcome and adopt any technique or pattern only when they become convinced of its utility and desirability. Education, thus, structures a wholesome and conducive environment for these social changes to become acceptable to all.

3. Evaluation of social changes. A society is constantly under a process of transformation of various forms and nature in all fields of human activity. Teachers, by critical evaluation, determine the desirability or otherwise of these social changes.

In other words, education lays down the required standards and criteria of values with reference to which this process of evaluation takes place effectively, and only after that, desirable social changes are propagated whereas the undesirable ones discarded and decried.

4. Aids the coming of new social changes. Education strives to banish social evils, blind customs and traditions through various social reformation projects, political movements, social service schemes and also tries to bring in needed social changes and reforms.

For example, in India, public movements, agitations against child marriage, forced widowhood, caste insulation, untouchability and social injustice resulted in desirable social changes.

5. Transmission of culture. Through its function of transmission of national culture from generation to generation as a continuous process, education lends stability and continuity to the society. Not only this, education prepares society to adopt needed and desirable social reforms.

In this sense, education is the creator, generator and director of all social changes. In short, education is a conservative, consolidating and stabilizing force and in addition, it is a creative force as well.

6. Promotes unity and total integration. When conflicts arise between various groups and sections of a society, education tries to solve those conflicts by advocating thoughts and feelings which bring about unity in diversity and achieve integration of all. Education, in India, has this sacred mission to perform by educating people to rise above petty caste rivalries, communal feuds, linguistic conflicts and regional discords and try to achieve the cherished ideal of national integration and national glory.

*7. **Maintaining human and social relations.*** In an industrial society, development of new techniques and devices, very often, lead of social laxity, disunity and discord among sections of people.

Education strives to maintain and consolidate human relations inspite of these social changes in attitudes and patterns of behaviour of people.

*8. **Education of social changes.*** Education employs various methods to promote knowledge and understanding among people about social changes occurring in society. When the understanding of social changes develops, people gladly welcome and actively co-operate in all the plans to bring about social change.

*9. **Removal of obstacle.*** Various obstacles impede the march of social changes and reformations. Education informs people about their importance and desirability. Not only this, it tries to remove the mental reservations and complexes in the minds of people, which obstruct the progress of change.

*10. **Increasing the areas of knowledge.*** Education promotes in the individuals the capacity to increase their areas and scope of knowledge more and more for their benefit. It opens new vistas for deeper and deeper investigations and researches, which bring about desirable changes in material as well as non-material aspects of culture. Thus, education prepares ground for the advent of social change.

*11. **Leadership role of social-changes.*** By promoting democratic feelings and progressive attitudes in the people, education makes them capable to initiate and guide for needed social changes by fighting successfully against social evils, customs and blind traditions. Thus, people become capable for realizing their own true personality to the full and promote social welfare to greater and greater extent. Education, in this way, prepares people for leadership roles as social reformers and nation builders.

SOCIAL IMPORTANCE OF SCHOOL

In the above lines, we have discussed the functions of education in bringing about social change. To achieve these functions, there is no place better than school. Hence, school, as such, is a social institution of great importance. The role of school in bringing about social change is as follows:

1. Relation with social order. The size, form, nature and organizational set up of a school depend upon the prevalent social order. But social order has some aims, ideals, values and traditions. The school tries its best to realize these ideals and values. In other words, the organization of education conforms to the needs and values of society. This means that school works according to the social order. If social changes occur in society, school is bound to reflect the same changes in its working and operation.

2. Influence of national policy. The current national policy has a powerful influence on the school. In other words, school co-operates wholeheartedly in satisfying the needs and aspirations of the nation. For example, our national need is to increase the production of goods. We see that our schools are extending their hearty co-operation to meet the demand of scientific and technological education.

3. Simplification of socio-cultural patterns. In Indian society, socio-cultural patterns are varied and often complex. Their preservation without the help of school is next to impossible. A school tries to simplify and categorize these bewildering variety of socio-cultural patterns and preserves them for use and understanding by children.

4. Development of capacities and efficiencies. A school is not only concerned with the preservation of cultural heritage, but it looks to the future also. In other words, school tries to foresee the future needs of society and for the purpose of meeting them tries to develop more and more capacities and efficiencies of the individuals.

5. Meeting the economic needs of society. Education promotes the economic efficiency of individuals who achieve their own economic prosperity as well as the prosperity of the society of which they happen to be integral parts. As the school meets the economic needs of individuals, therefore, it plays an important role to add to the prosperity of society.

6. Promoting continuity. A school preserves the cultural heritage of society. Not only this, it transmits this heritage from one generation to another and this promotes continuity of society in a very effective manner.

7. Contact with wide environment. The environment of a school is very wide and varied. In comparison with the narrow and limited environments of a family or neighbourhood, school tries to provide for children a very wide and varied environment to the children by its diverse activities, programmes and experiences.

8. Glorious future. In modern times, a school strives to plan for a very bright and glorious future of society. Thus, it not only preserves the glories of the past but also tries to make society achieve greater and greater heights of glory and fame in future times.

EDUCATION FOLLOWS SOCIAL CHANGE

Education and social change are very intimately related. Hence, education should prepare the background for social change. Not only this, education should also spell out the kinds of desirable changes needed by society and how these changes are to be brought about. For this, education should try to study and understand the various problems of society in specific areas from time to time and should become the integral part of social development. When education will assume this responsibility, society will grow more and more by adopting needed social changes.

But picture seems to be just the reverse. We see that instead of initiating and leading social changes, education today follows social changes. In other words, when changes occur in needs, technology and values, education also adopts itself to these changes. More clearly, education, follows social changes. Below, we are discussing some of the chief factors which compel education to follow social change:

1. Educational changes because of social forces. Social aspirations, social values and social dynamism are some of the social powers. When these forces change, change occurs in the educational process also.

2. Educational changes because of social needs. Society has various needs which affect the process of education for the purpose of their own satisfaction. It means that educational changes occur because of social needs and aspirations. Compulsory, free and universal education, diversification of secondary and higher education, adult education, agricultural, individual, vocational, professional and scientific education are the various forms and varieties of education which have been brought about by the needs of modern Indian society.

*3. **Educational changes because of cultural changes.*** Many changes in education occur because of cultural changes. It may be noted that first the material aspect of culture changes and then the non-material aspect of culture gradually changes. Thus, when cultural changes occur, changes also occur in education.

TEACHER AND SOCIAL CHANGE

Teacher and social change are related as body and soul. As the very thought of body without soul is futile, in the same way, any social change without teacher is a mere figment of imagination. But it should be borne in mind that a teacher can initiate and promote social change only when he knows fully well the needs of society as well as the nature and direction of social change. In fact, social change are of various kinds. They are—(1) Evolutionary, (2) Wave like, and (3) Cyclic order. In the same way, directions of social changes are various. The prominent among them are—(1) Even, and (2) Uneven. Teacher should become well-versed in all kinds and directions of social change and then try to mould the process of social change in such a way that it is acceptable to all people. The teacher should also keep in mind the fact that social changes are not even at all times.

He must know the fact that social changes brought about by such cultural factors which are not acceptable to the people of another culture, will not be welcomed by all people. Such plans and programmes of the teacher and the undesirable social change brought about by him shall be designated as uneven. In other words, when social changes are uneven, the educational changes are also correspondingly uneven. Hence, the teacher should protect society from such unhealthy and harmful changes.

History bears eloquent testimony to the fact that since very early times, teacher has co-operated society whole-heartedly in bringing about desirable social change. That is why, he is known as nation-builder even today.

But it is a sorry state of affairs that teacher of today is mute, inactive and indifferent towards the needful social change. That is why, he has lost his respect in society today. If the teacher wants to achieve the same honour as before, he should try to understand the needs of modern society and bring about the needed social change according to the call of the time.

QUESTIONS FOR ANSWER

1. What is social change? Enumerate the factors which promote and resist social change.
2. How does education bring about social change? Discuss the role of teacher in this connection.

14

Social Control and Education

Social control is the control of the society over the individual to control his undesirable and harmful tendencies. In other words, social control is self-control and keeps on changing in accordance with the changes in society and at times it renders assistance to the individual for his best social adjustment. Thus social control is a comprehensive process for the good of the individual and the society. Definitions of social control are as follows:

"Social control is a collective term for those processes and agencies, planned and unplanned, by which individual are taught, persuaded or compelled to conform to the usages and values of the group to which they belong."

It is clear from the above definition that social control includes those laws by which an individual behaves in concurrence with the mores of group. —*Brearly*

"Social control is that system of measures, suggestion, persuasion, restraint and coercion by whatever means, including physical force, by which a society brings into conformity to the approved pattern of behaviour a subgroup or by which a group moulds into conformity its members."

—*Gillin and Gillin*

"By social control is meant the way in which the entire social order coheres and maintains itself, how it operates, as a changing equilibrium." —*MacIver and Page*

"Social control can be defined as the sum total or rather

the whole of cultural patterns, social symbols, collective spiritual meanings, values, ideas and ideals, as well as acts or processes, directly connected with them, whereby, inclusive of society, every particular group and every participating individual member overcome tensions and conflicts within themselves through temporary equilibria and takes steps for new creative efforts."

—*Gurvitch and Moore*

The definition of social control is adequately comprehensive. It has taken into account both the negative and creative aspects of social control and has indicated the means and processes of social control.

TYPES OF SOCIAL CONTROL

1. Karl Mannheim's View

Different sociologists held differing views upon the types of social control. Karl Mannheim has accepted the following two types of social control:

(i) Direct social control. This is the control exercised upon the individual by the reactions of the people living in proximity. Such control is found existing in the family, neighbourhood, play group, and other primary groups. An individual is deeply influenced by the opinion and views of his parents, colleagues, neighbours and those who work with him. His behaviour is determined or controlled by their criticism, derogation, praise, suggestion or persuasion, etc. This is direct control.

(ii) Indirect social control. This is the control exercised upon the individual by factors which are separated from him. Control of the individual by secondary groups is of this type. Its prominent means are traditions, institutions, customs, rationalised behaviour, changes in situations and social mechanism, etc. The means of social control are invisible and subtle. In the existing complex society, the influence of the opinion, law, custom, etc., is controlled in this way. It is not that there are no individuals behind this control but these individuals are not seen by the persons affected.

2. Kimball Young's View

Kimball Young has divided social control into the following two types:

(i) Positive. Reward has an immense values upon the activities of an individual. A large part of the population of society desires to be rewarded by the society. And, consequently, they constantly endeavour to conform to the traditions, mores, values and ideals accepted by the society. For this, they are rewarded in the form of social recognition, fame, respect, etc.

(ii) Negative. Under this, those types of social controls are comprehended in which a person is prevented from doing something by threat of punishment, while it encourages the people to indulge in certain types of activity by promising reward. Fear of punishments helps to prevent people from violating the socially approved customs, traditions, values and ideals, etc.

3. Other Views

In addition to the above-mentioned form of social controls, two other forms: formal and informal have also been recognized. The formal types are those which are specifically designed for control, and include government, law, police, army, jail, penal, code, etc. Informal social control includes those methods which develop by themselves according to the needs of society such as, mores, traditions, customs, social ideals, etc. Hayes has accepted two forms of social control:

(a) Control by sanction. In this, social control is effected by awarding the obedient and punishing the miscreant.

(b) Control by socialization and education.

AGENCIES OF SOCIAL CONTROL

It would have become evident from the foregoing description of the various types of social control, that there are many direct and indirect, formal and informal means of social control. Among the important means of social control, Ross has enumerated family, educational system, belief and religion, social suggestion, social ideal, ritual and festival, art, leadership, law and administration besides physical force.

Giddings has accepted the importance of belief, social direction or guidance, religion, social ideals, social festivals, art, leadership, intellectual factors, education and propaganda, law and administration and force, as means of social control.

SOCIAL CONTROL AND EDUCATION

According to Ruskin, "Education consists in making people polite what they ought to be." The ideals and patterns in these are promoted through education. Here, the word "education" is used in a comprehensive sense. It is only in this meaning of the word that the sociologist studies or contemplates it. Education teaches man to live according to Nature. Education gives him ability to succeed in his struggle for existence. Education is an art of adaptation. For man, adaptation is more social than natural. Hence, education adapts man to society. In this way, education is an important means of social control.

Education is in the family, playground, club, office, in fact, everywhere. At every place the individual is taught something and socialized. In the family, in school, on playground, he learns to follow the opinion and advice of others and learns to comply with the traditions and mores. Theoretical education, *viz.*, reading and writing, serves to from the intellectual base for all this and with practical education he learns to put this into practice.

The organization or system of society is disrupted and thrown into confusion when the educational system contradicts or when the activity of education does not function correctly and social control fails to function. Hence, education is a necessary condition for the proper exercise of social control.

Without proper education the harmony of the individual and society is not merely difficult but well nigh impossible. Education makes social control normal. It makes social control self-control and the individual does not experience its burden.

QUESTIONS FOR ANSWER

1. What is social control? How is it achieved through education?
2. Explain social control in the context of educational institution.

15

Education and Culture

In the words of Sorokin and MacIver, "Culture implies man's moral, spiritual and intellectual achievements." Bogardus holds: "Culture is composed of integrated customs, traditions and current behaviour patterns of human group. Culture is the stock in trade of group. It is antecedent complex of value into which every individual is born. It is a medium within which individuals develop and mature." Some other definitions of culture are as below.

DEFINITION OF CULTURE

To make the meaning of culture more clear, the following definitions are given:

1. "In terms of anthropology, culture is a continually changing pattern of learned behaviour and the products of learned behaviour including attitudes, values, knowledge and material objects which are shared by and transmitted among the members of society." —*Cuber*

2. "Culture is that complex whole that consists of every thing we think, do and have as members of society."
—*Bierstedt*

3. "Culture is the complex whole which includes knowledge, belief, art, morals, law, custom and other capacities and habits acquired by man as member of the society."
—*Tylor*

4. "Culture is the expression of our nature in our modes

of living and of thinking in our every day intercourse in art, in literature, in religion, in reaction and enjoyments."

—*MacIver*

KINDS OF CULTURE

According to the subject there are different kinds of culture:

(1) Individual culture,

(2) Communal culture,

(3) National culture, and

(4) World culture.

Every individual has some personal traits and qualities which guide his habits of thinking and behaving in all fields of human activities. These personal likes and dislikes, interests, modes of thinking and patterns of social behaviour constitute his personal culture. In the same way, different communities have their distinct traits of life styles comprising specific modes of community beliefs and styles of living.

All the members of different communities exhibit different traits known as community culture. Likewise, every nation has some distinct national traits and attributes of character which condition its national patterns of ideals, values, modes of thought and behaviour. Such national traits are known as national culture.

Further, a rapid rise in the means of transport and communication has shrunk the whole world into one small unit with the result that different nations of the world live together as members of a world community having common values of life. Such values namely–co-operation, sympathy, social service, social awakening and social sensitiveness etc., constitute world culture.

According to contents there are two types of culture in each society:

(1) Material culture,

(2) Non-material culture.

1. Material culture. Material culture includes all those man-made things and objects which human society has created for its physical welfare in times of peace and war. Items such as clothes, utensils, home, roads, ornaments, T.V., radio, various machines, gadgets and various means of transport and communication are some examples of material culture.

2. Non-material culture. Non-material culture includes all those ideals, attitudes and values which modify the behaviour of an individual. Language, literature, art, music, religion, customs and traditions etc., are some examples of non-material culture.

CHARACTERISTICS OF CULTURE

The following are the characteristics of culture:

*1. **Acquired traits.*** Culture is the sum total of acquired traits. The new born baby is devoid of any trait. As he grows older, he acquires different ideals, attitudes and values by imitation and social contacts. These experiences contribute to the formation of his personal culture.

*2. **Distinct entity.*** Different societies of the world have their distinct cultural patterns which establish the different identities of different nations.

*3. **Transmission.*** Cultural traits and patterns are transmitted from generation to generation. Every generation is free to modify the cultural heritage and then transmits it to the next generation. In this way, cultural patterns are powerfully conditioned and influenced by the trends which appear from time to time according to different circumstances and conditions. In short, transmission is a continuing process.

*4. **Utility.*** A culture is good if it has some utility to the individual as well as to the society. If it does not fulfil this propose, it decays and dies out in the long run. It may be borne in mind that mutual give and take among different cultures is also an essential and conditioning process. Generally, cultural fanaticism and snobbery promote conflict and chaos. Hence, one should see and adopt the cultural beauties and excellencies of all the cultures that exist in the world. Only this vitality and welcoming attitude can promote the development of world culture which leads to international brotherhood. The prime need of our Indian society is this cultural integration.

*5. **Dynamism.*** Culture is not static but dynamic. In other words, it changes and grows. Due to rapid rise in the means of transport and communication a culture invades the other culture. It penetrates, inter-penetrates, changes and grows. That is why, our modern Indian culture is not that old culture which guided the nations of the world in the past. One can notice the fast changing patterns of our cultural beliefs, ideals, values, modes of thinking and behaviour. The different cultures of the world are interacting among themselves and thus a synthesis of cultures is going on in this modern world.

EDUCATION AND CULTURAL LAG

Due to rapid progress of scientific inventions and technological advancement, material aspect of culture has gone ahead and its area has been greatly widened. The modern society is gradually adopting more and more of these techniques and scientific achievements in their day to day styles of living, while the non-material aspect of culture has been left far behind.

This vast difference between the material culture and the non-material culture is known as social and cultural lag. As the pace of material culture cannot be slackened, the need is to speed up the changes in the non-material cultural patterns of thinking and living. Both should proceed together in a corresponding pace as the two wheels of a chariot. Education is the only means to bridge this cultural lag.

We see that through scientific inventions, investigations and discoveries many of our own Indian people are enjoying the fruits of the material culture, yet there are still vast masses of people who are steeped in ignorance, inertia and utter backwardness. Education can do this job of eliminating this cultural lag and inspire the general people to march on the road of progress and modernisation as best they can.

EDUCATION AND CULTURE

Education and culture are intimately and integrally connected. Hence, the cultural pattern of a society conditions its educational pattern. For example, if a society has a spiritual pattern of culture, then its educational procedures will emphasize the achievement of moral and eternal values of life. On the other hand, if the cultural pattern of a society is materialistic, then naturally its educational pattern will be shaped for the attainment of material values which promote pleasures of senses and material comforts. It may be borne in mind that a society devoid of any culture will have no definite educational organization.

Hence, it may be safely asserted that the culture of a country has a very powerful impact on its educational pattern. This mutual influence is being discussed in the following lines.

INFLUENCE OF CULTURE ON EDUCATION

Culture influences the following aspects of education:

1. Influence of culture on aims of education. The meaning and aims of education are determined by the cultural ideals, values and patterns of a society. In other words, as is the culture of a society so shall be its aims of education.

2. Influence of culture on curriculum. The aims of education are achieved through curriculum. As the aims of education are determined according to the culture of society, so the curriculum is conditioned according to the culture of society. In other words, as are the ideas, ideals and values of a society, the educational curriculum of that society is conditioned according to the ideals and needs of that society to realize its cultural values. In short, the system of education tries to realize the cultural needs of society through curriculum which conditions activities and programmes.

3. Influence of culture on methods of teaching. Culture and methods of teaching are intimately connected. It is why, the changing cultural patterns of a society exert powerful influence upon the methods of teaching also. In ancient times education was teacher-centred and tried to force into the minds of children specific dozes of knowledge in quite disregard of their natural interests and needs.

The result of this artificial progress of education was mechanical cramming and rote memorization. In modern times, education has become child-centred. Thus, the interests, inclinations, aptitudes, needs and capacities of children are taken into full consideration before exposing them to specific educational experiences, activities and programmes.

In this way, education is now a method of preparing children for successful and effective living during the present times and for the times to come. In short, cultural and social needs condition the methods and techniques of teaching in a very powerful way.

4. Influence of culture on discipline. Cultural values also influence the concept of discipline. The present cultural patterns of thinking and living are directly linked to our concept of discipline. In ancient and middle ages societies where authoritarianism ruled, the concept of discipline was repressionistic. But in modern times when democratic values of life are being accepted all over the world, the concept of discipline has come to mean impressionistic or emancipatory or self-discipline.

5. Influence of culture on text-books. Curriculum is contained in text-books. We have discussed above the powerful impact of cultural values upon the curriculum. These text-books are written according to the formulated or determined curriculum. It may be borne in mind that only those text-books are welcomed if they foster and promote cultural ideals and values. On the contrary, they are discarded and often banned if they militate against the cultural ideals and values of a particular society.

6. Influence of culture on teacher. Each individual teacher is imbued with the cultural ideals and values of the society of which he happens to be an integral member. Only such a teacher achieves his mission successfully. It is only such a teacher who is able to infuse higher ideals and moral values in children. The idealism and higher ideals of teacher are imbibed by children imperceptibly but definitely. It may be noted here that the idealism and higher ideals of teacher are comprised of the cultural ideals and values of his society of nation.

7. Influence of culture on school. According to the ideology of pragmatism, a school is a miniature of society. The total activities and programmes of the school are organized according to the cultural ideals and values of the society which establishes and organizes the school. Hence, school is the centre of promoting, moulding, reforming and developing the cultural patterns of the society which establishes that school for its own good and welfare.

INFLUENCE OF EDUCATION ON CULTURE

Just as culture influences education, much in the same way education also exerts its powerful influence upon the culture of a country. In the following lines, we are explaining the various ways by which education influences the culture of a country:

1. Preservation of culture. Each country believes and flaunts the superiority of its own culture over the rest. Hence, it tries to preserve its culture in its original form. Education is the only means to complete this task In other words, education preserves the culture of society.

*2. **Transmission of culture.*** The process of preservation includes the process of transmission as well because through transmission of culture from one generation to another is the best guarantee of its preservation. The famous sociologist Ottaway has rightly remarked, "The function of education is to transmit the social values and ideals to the young and capable members of society."

*3. **Development of culture.*** The function of education is not only to preserve and transmit the culture of society, but it also brings about the needed and desirable changes in the cultural ideals and values for the progress and continued development of society, without which social progress will stratify and come to naught. In other words, education culturises individual, modifies cultural processes by research and deeper investigations into all areas of human requirements.

*4. **Maintaining the continuity of culture.*** Culture is the life blood of a society. Without culture a society is bound to decay and die sooner or later. Education upholds the continuity of culture through its diverse activities and programmes. It may be noted that a society establishes schools to preserve and transmit its culture from generation to generation. But some schools try to develop cultural chauvinism and superiority complexes among its children. This is very undesirable. Children should be motivated to learn more and more from cultural interaction among various cultures and develop the qualities of tolerance, adjustment together with mutual give and take, that they are able to benefit themselves from the contribution of all cultures. This cultural integration and cultural synthesis is the dire need of the world society in modern time.

*5. **Helping the development of personality.*** Education aims to develop the personality of the child. For this, it employs diverse cultural patterns of thingking, behaviour and items of cultural values so that children are physically, mentally, socially and emotionally developed to the maximum extent.

*6. **Removing cultural lag.*** When material culture develops at a fast pace due to scientific researches and inventions, non-material culture consisting of ideals, values and norms lag behind creating a gulf between the two. Education is the only means to bridge this cultural lag by its activities and programmes of development.

It is clear from the above discussion that whereas on one hand, education culturises an individual, on the other hand, it preserves, transmits and develops the culture of a society. In short, education and culture are mutually interdependent, complementary and supplementary in all their aspects and activities.

ROLE OF CULTURE IN MAN'S LIFE

Culture plays vital role in man's life. Education of various elements of culture can help man in the following aspects:

1. Adaptation to the natural environment.
2. Adaptation to the social environment.
3. Development in individual's personality.
4. Socialization of the individual.
5. Proper use of leisure.
6. In understanding other cultures and proper meaning of liberality.

Education in culture is imparted by the family, society and school.

QUESTIONS FOR ANSWER

1. What is culture? Discuss its types and characteristics.
2. Discuss the influence of culture on education.
3. Throw light on the influence of education on culture.

16

Education for Religious and Moral Values

NEED FOR RELIGIOUS EDUCATION

The aim of contemporary education is not only the mental, physical and social development of the individual, but also his religious and moral development, that is why modern educationists have stressed the importance of moral education for the country.

Vivekananda said that religion is the basis of education, although here he does not imply his own or some one else's religion. This comment also implies that the aim of religious education is not to propound the theories of any one particular religion but to create faith towards universally accepted religious values.

The presence of religious faith helps the individual to face all kinds of adverse conditions with the belief that he can progress at least a little, irrespective of the darkness of the outlook. Hence, religious faith helps man in his progress, raises him to a high level, and also assists him in developing democratic qualities.

Religion is the foundation of all moral character, because without religion man cannot have faith in truth, beauty and goodness. The freedom that we want to grant the child through education is not possible without religion. Besides, even culture has no meaning in the absence of religion which also acquaints us with the final goal of life. Without knowing this goal, education cannot progress. Religion is the basis of true humanitarianism.

It is evident from the foregoing comments that religion should be given its appropriate place in the curriculum for education. Vivekananda has recommended that modern science should be used to awaken the educand's knowledge. History, geography and literature should be taught to the educand along with the teaching of religion which must be used to teach them the greatest truths.

Dr. S. Radhakrishnan also supported the teaching of religion at the various levels of education. He said that we will have to plan for a rational religion for our conflict ridden emerging humanity, a religion that does not ridicule man's soul filled with unrestrained individualism and hesitation born out of conflict.

We have to present a new philosophy of God with which we can fight against those doubting communities of men who are fighting against each other to establish their supremacy on men's souls. Rabindranath Tagore also expressed sympathy with this viewpoint in granting the greatest importance to a humanitarian religion.

Tagore said that these religions differ from each other in moral value, but each one is inspired by the same tendency. In these religions, man looks for his highest ideal, which he calls God. They try to discover it in some personality of human character.

Mahatma Gandhi has also attached the greatest significance to religious education and he has advocated the educands should be acquainted with the basic elements of all religions. Sri Aurobindo has considered religious education to be the most important aspect of education.

AIMS OF RELIGIOUS EDUCATION

Religious education must not include importance and methods of retuals but aim at the following:

1. Mental development.
2. Refinement of human values.
3. Socialization of the individual.

4. Development of democratic values.
5. Cultural development.
6. Sense of respect for man.
7. Complete development of the child.

V.T. Thayer rightly says, "The school must therefore concern itself with the whole child and no child can become whole without instruction in religion."

PLACE OF RELIGIOUS EDUCATION IN A SECULAR STATE

Some people opine that religious education should not be encouraged by the state in a secular country like India, and they argue that religious education should be given by religious institutions and society, not by the school.

This attitude has no justification because education must aim at the complete development of the individual, an aim that cannot be fulfilled in the absence of religious education.

A secular state does not imply a state which is hostile to or indifferent towards religion, because all that the term secular implies is that the state shall not insist upon the adoption of any particular religion, because there is no state religion.

It is correct to assume that the Government should not try to spread any particular religion, but it also be remembered that religious education cannot be equated with the deliberate campaigning for some particular religion. All that is required in religious education is that the educand should be taught the basic elements which are at the root of every religion, thus, developing the educand's faith in moral character, religious values and humanitarianism.

And, since India is also a democratic country, it has a great stake in the development of democratic values, which also depend upon religious education. Hence, religious education has its significance even in a secular state because it is the most powerful medium for developing democratic values. But religious education in a secular state must be carefully planned so as not to injure the sentiments of any particular sect of religionalists, and also to avoid giving undue importance to any one religions. Every educand must be given the freedom and opportunity to profess his own religion, but he should be accompanied by acquaintances with other religions, since this alone is the way to religious tolerance.

True religious feeling can be evolved in the educand by telling him about the lives of all the great religious leaders and founders. The subject matter of religious education should be designed to conform to the level of training and intelligence of the educands. A religious life is a life with a purpose, the same purpose which religious education has.

MORAL EDUCATION

The aim of education is the complete development of the child a development in which moral development occupies an important place. Man's greatest characteristic is his character. Vivekananda has defined character as the sum total of an individual's instincts, the inclinations of his mind. Man is made by his thoughts. One finds that children develop characters according to the ideas presented to them during their growth. For this reason they should be initiated into the ideals of sacrifice, hard work and contemplation.

Good thoughts lead to a sound determination and this in turn puts the man on the path to good life, and he is filled with strength of soul which inspires him to adhere to this path. In order to form character, it is necessary to pay attention to subtle and small things, for character is manifested through habits. Character can, therefore, only be improved by the habits of the individual.

For this, both determination and courage are required. Vivekananda had said in a resonant voice that one must form one's character and express one's true nature, the enlightened pure element in oneself. One must also look for the same element in every other individual.

According to Sri Aurobindo, moral education is the education of the heart, without which no individual can be completely human. But this moral education cannot be imparted through lectures and textbooks because the basis of this education is proper feelings, proper conduct and the development of proper habits of thought, feeling and action.

The task of education is to guide, direct and suggest to the child, without interfering with his activities in any way. Teachers should present the highest ideals but must also remember that moral education is imparted through imitation and setting examples rather than through discipline. In ancient India, the child acquired moral education only by imitating his teacher. The modern teacher, therefore, must also have the highest ideals. In addition, moral education takes place through moral conversation and behaviour. Senior educands should be required to read literature which encourages the purest emotions in them and inspires them to attempt at the highest ideals. In order to give moral training to the child, the latter should be acquainted with the means of distinguishing between the right and the wrong. The various emotions of the child are not to be suppressed but sublimated.

Mahatma Gandhi, like Sri Aurobindo, believed that development of character is the aim of education, for which, in his opinion also, moral education is essential. Dayanand believed that education of any kind is impossible without the practice of abstinence.

Dr. S. Radhakrishnan also said that moral education is absolutely necessary for any education. In Indian culture, very great importance has always been attached to moral character. No education is complete without moral education, and this morality is the foundation of man's future and therefore the seed of this must be sown in the school.

Dr. S. Radhakrishnan said that we must create the proper social order but we must also keep in mind that the individual does not become complete only by achieving economic prosperity. In order to become a complete individual the pleasure and beauty of the soil is essential. This soul must be brimming with love, faith, and the willingness and ability to serve humanity re-born.

From the foregoing account of the opinions of various philosophers, it is evident that moral education is as much a part of education as religious education is.

In this connection, it is stated in the report of the Secondary Education Reorganization Committee for U.P., "That moral and humanistic education should form an integral part of our education; students should be taught the fundamental truth from all religious and ethical movements with a view to emphasizing their essential unit."

QUESTIONS FOR ANSWER

1. Write short note on 'religious education'.
2. Write short note on 'the effect on education of the principle of religious secularism'.
3. "Religion and education are natural allies." Discuss the implications of this statement and say what steps you would take to introduce religious education in Indian school system.
4. Point out the main issue involved in the problem of Religious Education and suggest a practical solution.
5. What should be the place of religion in the Educational Programme of Secular State?

17

Educational Values and Society

The Definition, Views about Kinds of Educational Values, Hierarchy of Educational Values and Educational Values as Determinants of Educational Aims have been discussed in chapter two of this book, therefore, readers are requested to read them again and hence some very brief account of educational values in social context is given here.

WHAT ARE VALUES?

Values relate to the aims of human life. For the achievement of the aims men frame contain notions and these notions are called values. In the words of W.H. Kilpatrick, "That out of man's capacity for goal seeking behaviour arise his wants and efforts and out of these come in consciously chosen ends (goal) a means. Because ends conflict, man is led to weigh his goals against each other. When this is done critically enough values emerge."

According to Mr. Henderson, "It has been pointed out that man acts to satisfy his wants, anything which satisfies, a human want becomes thereby a value. To say, that our conduct is motivated by our value is another way of saying that we act to satisfy our wants."

DETERMINATION OF VALUES

Educationists have propounded the following principles about the determination of values:

1. *Hedonistic view of life.* The value of a thing is due to the fact that the thing has power to satisfy our wants.

2. *Perfection theory.* Anything has value if it relates to the perfection of life for which a man endeavours in his life.

3. *Utility theory.* Anything which has utility is valuable.

4. *Order theory.* Anything which is helpful in organizing society is called value.

5. *Existence theory.* Value is helpful in existence.

6. *Experimental theory.* Values are experiments in present and past as well.

7. *Part and whole theory.* Values are felt sometimes partly and sometimes wholly.

8. *Objective and subjective theory.* Values are determined by the notions of individuals and also by the circumstances in which he lives.

9. *Emotive theory.* Man's emotions are expressed by his nature. These emotions change according to the circumstances. Thus by virtue of his emotions man determines his values.

These values have certain characteristics like subjectivity, objectivity, material or abstract, elasticity, etc. These values aim at perfection, self-realisation, satisfaction, perfection and development, integrity and cohesion etc.

EDUCATION AND VALUES

According to Reid, "Education is part of life, and clearly our questions about values and education are inseparable from larger question of values in life. Values are embodied in educational practice." Thus education develops a sense of discrimination between good and bad. This discrimination is based on values and these value are tested in schools.

To quote W.H. Kilpatrick, "The teacher must have an essential part of his professional equipment, which is here called 'map of value.' Such a map consists of his hopes, aims, ideals, all the criticised values which he will use as aims in guiding those things. Teaching should aim continually on keeping this aggregate of values, life and growing but especially it should include all that the teacher hopes for students to learn so as life for them becomes as rich and fine as possible."

In other words, "Aims are an end in themselves and values

are the product." Values of education are the same as of life. These educational values are individual as well as social.

CONTRIBUTION OF EDUCATIONAL VALUES

Educational values contribute the following advantages for individual and social life:

1. Development of healthy and balanced personality.
2. Capacity to earn livelihood and acquire material prosperity.
3. Development of vocational efficiency.
4. Creation of good citizenship.
5. Reorganisation and reconstruction of experience.
6. Adjustment with the environment and its modifications.
7. Fulfilment of the needs of man.
8. Development of character.
9. National integration and national development.
10. Leaders and skilled workers.
11. Promotion of social efficiency.
12. Cultural values.
13. Utilisation of leisure.

Therefore, educational values play a significant role in the life of man. Through them, one is able to lead his personal and social life successfully. To sum up in the words of J.S. Brubacher, "Hence, the ultimate aim of education is self-realization, the fulfilment of man's instinctive potentialities for many in addition to the realization of eternal life. All proximate aims of education take their direction from the aim which itself stands imperishable eternal."

According to Adams, education is a bipolar process having two parts:

(1) the teacher, and

(2) the child.

In order to mould and modify the behaviour of the child the teacher employs various strategies and tactics to achieve the desired behavioural changes in him. He performs all these activities as he thinks them valuable for the purpose in view. As the teacher provides an environment of utility and value to the child, in the same manner the child participates only in those activities which he considers useful and valuable to him.

Both the teacher and the child participate only in those

activities which they consider as educationally useful and valuable. According to Cunningham, educational values are aims of education. Through education qualities, abilities and capacities are promoted in the individuals, which are inherent values of life.

SOCIAL VALUES IN EDUCATION

Individuals constitute society which has certain ideals, models and norms about behaviour, conduct, duties and responsibilities towards one another. Love, universal brotherhood, sincerity, honesty and integrity of character, firm attitude of rendering help and performing actions and works of general benefit etc. are some of the constituents of healthy social life. True education aims at developing individuals into social beings having these virtues.

Schooling is a preparatory stage for cultivating the sense of social values. In the laboratories, students work in a co-operative way and develop a scientific attitude towards social life. In libraries, while sitting together for study they practise patience. In the hostels, while leading a corporate life they imbibe the spirit of living together like brothers, behave harmoniously sinking their differences and experiences.

Activities correlated with academic aspects afford opportunities for bringing about their physical and intellectual development and strengthening common bonds of spirit. Activities like N.C.C., N.S.S., Boys Scout and Girls Guide help the students to develop themselves physically. These inculcate patriotic virtues in them and enthuse in them preparedness for safety and security of the country at the time of need.

Thus, teachers impart social values to the students in school systems. Education aims at developing individuals into social beings having these virtues.

Social values have been emphasised at every stage of social development. Ancient Indian educational institutions attached importance to social values. The students in the 'Gurukulas' rendered service not only to their students, community, but to the institution as a whole. They would go to the habitations for collecting meals from worthy householders who took it as their duty to set apart of portion of the cooked meal for the students.

In medieval times, the system continued. But with the occupation of India by the foreigners, new system of education was ushered. Emphasis was laid on Muslim education with Western education. Western education aimed at producing white-collar clerks to help Britishers to run the administrative machinery of the state. From this period onwards, Indian social virtues disappeared from Indian mind.

With the dawn of independence education has been accepted as a nation building activity. India developed a national system of education, to help in the all-round development of the educands. The achievements so far are not satisfactory, social values should be developed both inside and outside educational institutions. Students should learn that love for country means love for nation, and love for the mankind leads to international sympathy.

This paves the way for education for international understanding, which is the cry of the day for world peace.

STRATEGIES FOR INCULCATING SOCIAL VALUES

Social values can be inculcated by introducing a programme for educational values of social service. Social service implies service to society or groups of individuals bound together by rules or conventions or other considerations for achievement of objectives and aims.

The individual has to render service to himself and bring about his growth in such a way as to enable him to prove of use for the society. He should prove himself useful to the members of the family, to the neighbours, to the state, to the country and to the world.

The educative process has to see it that the development of the individual is consistent with this aim of usefulness and fitness in the objectives and aims in general.

Education is a stage of preparation for cultivating the sense of social services in its theoretical aspect through teaching of lessons, dwelling on social virtues and through practical in laboratories where students work developing scientific attitude under the supervision of experts.

The following activities should be undertaken by the schools to impart educational values of social service to the students:

1. Pre-school stage. Education at the pre-school stage consists in the upbringing of infants in home atmosphere. Attempts should be made to cultivate virtues of affection, love, truthfulness and obedience at this stage of education.

*2. **Primary stage.*** At the primary stage, affection for all love for the country, truthfulness in behaviour, obedience to elders, curiosity for knowledge, and appreciation of nature should be cultivated.

*3. **Junior high school.*** At the junior high school stage, straight-forwardness, frankness, uprightness, affection and kindness for all sense of rendering help to others in times of need should be cultivated. Foundation should be laid for the formation of character and cultivation of qualities of leadership.

*4. **Secondary stage.*** At the secondary stage, love for all mankind, preliminary knowledge of different aspects of nature, kindness and help to all living beings, dignity of manual labour, respect for the constitution of the country, sense of maintaining country's independence, freedom of thought, speech and action in the just and right context and interest for the defence of the country should be cultivated.

*5. **College and university stage.*** At the college and university stages, all these virtues should be developed and their practical aspect strengthened.

*6. **Extra-curricular activities.*** Programmes of manual labour as cleanliness of neglected localities picnics, excursion etc. should be arranged to provide opportunities to the students for moving among different people and seeing monmumental achievements in the country for broadening outlook and understanding humanitarian values.

*7. **Campaigns against disease.*** These may be arranged by the students of higher education.

*8. **Education of disabled people.*** Provisions should be made to educate the deaf, the dumb and the blind etc.

*9. **Anti-illiteracy drives.*** Schemes for removing illiteracy should be undertaken out of love for the benefit of mankind.

*10. **Development of aesthetic sense.*** Training in drawing and painting should be arranged in order to develop aesthetic sense.

*11. **Music and dance.*** Music and dancing are parts of the cultural aspect of social service. Hence, necessary training in this respect should be imparted.

12. Social service by girls. Girl students should be encouraged to organize mass-cooking, mass-knitting of woollen equipment, visit orphanages, voluntary service to orphan children such as pairing off their nails, washing and bathing them.

13. Construction work. Students should be engaged in minor construction works like repairing and constructing roads, houses, digging well and tanks etc.

14. Service during calamities. Students should render voluntary service during natural calamities.

TRAINING IN CITIZENSHIP

A citizen feels that he is a part of the community and that he is there to share its burdens. Attempts should be made to give education for citizenship to promote the cause of liberty and democracy. Citizens are not born, they are to be trained. Therefore, the following strategies may be undertaken in order to develop the sense of citizenship among the students.

1. Education for citizenship. It should become a dynamic element in our pattern of education.

2. Development. Attempts should be made to inspire the students to develop a sense of co-operation for worthy causes, capacity for critical thought and freedom to place his point of view reasonably.

3. Debates and discussions. School should provide activities like debates and discussions on the issues and problems of our country. Mock parliament, mock panchayats, mock assemblies etc. should be arranged in order to inculcate proper civic values and attitudes.

4. Excursions. The schools should organize excursions to places of historic, religious and cultural importance.

5. Socialization. Students should learn to work in the social context and to come into contact with their fellow-men and women in a variety of ways in order to achieve their personal desires.

6. Productive work. Every boy and girl should willingly undertake useful productive work which may be mental or manual as a result of which he does not remain a burden or a parasite on others and can render some service to society.

7. Special camps. Special camps like N.C.C. or A.C.C., N.S.S.,

I.V.S.P. (international voluntary services for peace) should be organised to provide a natural environment for the students to develop a sense of comeradership resulting from free group activities in work and play.

8. Self-government. Students should be encouraged to organise self-government in order to learn the art of dividing different activities amongst themselves to carry their duties in a disciplined manner and to obey their freely chosen leaders, so much essential for good citizenship.

9. Relations among students. Teachers should have a good understanding of adolescent psychology and be able to establish sincere and friendly relations among the students.

10. Cooperative society. In order to encourage co-operative group work, schools should organise co-operative societies, where they should actively participate.

11. Pen-friends clubs. Students should be encouraged to organise pen-friends clubs, on national and international level.

12. Celebrate birthdays of great men. The school should celebrate birthdays of great men and women of our country like; Lord Krishna, Gautam the Buddha, Shankaracharya, M.K. Gandhi, Gopabandhu, Tagore, etc., besides the celebration of important days like the Independence Day and the Republic Day etc.

QUESTIONS FOR ANSWER

1. Explain various kinds of educational values and point out their hierarchy.
2. Describe social values in education. What are educational strategies to inculcate them?
3. Write short note on Training in Citizenship.

18

The Community and Education

Definition of community, Community as an Agency of Education, Importance of Community in the Education to the Child, and Educational Functions of Community have already been discussed in the fourth chapter of this book at serial number two, under the heading, Most Important Agencies of Education, therefore, readers are requested to read them again. Hence, here only other aspects of community and education as per need of this chapter, in social context, are given:

The word community combines two words—'Com' and 'Munis': 'Com' signifies togetherness and 'Munis' indicates to serve. Thus, the word community means 'to serve together.' Generally, community indicates a group of people living together on a geographical piece of land having common ways of working and common ideals to achieve. A community may be big or small in size. The size of the community is related to the cultural, economic and political commonness of its members. In this sense, a village, a town, a city, a nation and the whole world may be called a community.

RESPONSIBILITY OF COMMUNITY TOWARDS EDUCATION

It is clear from the foregoing discussion that community has great responsibility towards education, for it itself is a medium of education. As Crow and Crow has commented, "A community cannot expect something for nothing, if it wishes its young people to serve their community well, it must provide whatever educational advantages are needed by the young people, individually and collectively, to prepare themselves for that service." Briefly, the community has the following responsibilities towards education:

1. Educational content
2. Control of schools
3. Co-operation between educators and citizens
4. Providing the informal means of education.

INFLUENCE OF COMMUNITY ON SCHOOL

Since, community establishes schools for the fulfilment of its needs, therefore, it exerts diverse influences upon its schools in the following ways:

1. Influence of ideals and traditions of community on schools. Each community has its own ideals, traditions and cultural values and the purpose of opening schools is to transmit these ideals, traditions and values to the rising generation to keep them alive and growing to higher and higher levels. Children in schools are expected to participate in the activities and experiences embodying these ideals, traditions and values and by their own efforts lead the community to higher levels of development.

2. Influence of the needs of community on schools. The needs, problems, culture and religious beliefs of a community exert powerful influence upon schools. A child when he grows up to adulthood is able to contribute to the development of the community up to the limit, which is set up by the degree of depth upto which he gets education and understanding of the community ideals during his childhood.

Because the needs of a community change according to times, circumstances and situations, so also the philosophy, curriculum and methods of teaching change to suit community changes. In modern times, school is regarded as a society in miniature in the sense that what a community does on a grand scale, a school does on a small scale. This identification leads to better education and adjustment.

3. Influence of evils and values of community on schools. A community has both the good attributes as well as evil factors.

Both the good and bad factors directly influence the working of schools. The corruption and evil ways prevalent in a community are bound to have their impact upon school life. On the other hand, the virtues and good values of a community purify school life in all its aspects and influence the attitudes, character and behaviour of teachers, students and all those persons who are associated with its working.

4. Influence of economic conditions of community on schools. Schools cannot escape from the effect of economic conditions of a community. If the economy of a community is sound and it has faith in democratic ideals, it can maintain more and more schools upto a certain level of education. Much in the same way, a community flaunting capitalistic values conditions the aims, curriculum and methods of teaching according to its philosophy of life.

It may be noted here that under the impact of industrial revolution and craze for advertisement, revolutionary changes have occurred to community's economic conditions which have brought significant changes in the aims, curriculum and methods of teaching in the field of education.

We see that there is now a greater and greater demand for more and more vocational, technical, professional, agricultural and such other types of education to promote the earning capacity of the individuals as well as the social and national plenty. In short, the economic condition of a community greatly influences its schools.

5. Influence of political set up of community on schools. The political set up of a community directly influences the schools and their working very powerfully. In other words, political set up of a nation determines the educational set up of schools. Political set up is of two types—(1) Totalitarian, and (2) Democratic. In a totalitarian set up, the political party or the dictator which monopolizes the governmental machinery, organizes schools according to its political ideology and tries to indoctrinate the minds of children accordingly. In other words, education is centralized. The dictator, under such a climate, tries through education to inculcate the ideals of unquestioning obedience, absolute loyalty, rigid and controlled discipline together with sense of duty, devotion, service and sacrifice to the state. In old Greece and Sparta and even today China, Russia and some other despotic regimes organize education on despotic pattern.

On the other hand, if the political set up of the State is democratic, education is decentralized and schools breathe free and fresh air promoting self-discipline, free growth and development according to one's interests, aptitudes and natural tendencies. The aim of education in such set up is to make all individuals happy, healthy and prosperous.

Full freedom is afforded to all individuals to grow and develop according to their needs, ideals and inherent capacities with the result that these developed individuals contribute their best to the social good and growth. In short, in a democratic set up, schools respect the individuality of a child and thus, provide a clean, conducive and promoting environment for his development to the fullest extent. On the contrary, in a totalitarian set up, schools suppress the individuality of children indoctrinating their minds to dance to the tunes of the state.

EDUCATIONAL IMPORTANCE OF THE COMMUNITY

It is evident from the foregoing account that the community makes important contribution to both formal and informal forms of education. The child develops first within the limited sphere of his own family and then steps out into the larger surroundings of the community which unconsciously influences his language, thinking, modes of living, habits, ideas, etc. In fact, every aspect of his development is consciously or unconsciously influenced by the community.

In the words of Francis J. Brown, "Changing the behaviour of individuals is not enough, education must seek to modify community patterns of behaviour through close and constant interaction with the total culture of the community." From the very beginning, the child's behaviour, habits, his dress, etc., are all determined by the community.

It is the community which determines his attitudes towards various religions, tribes, classes, individuals and objects, and in this way community aids the family in socializing the child but it differs from the family in that it continues to influence the child even after the family has stopped doing so.

The community's approved patterns of behaviour are enforced on the individual through school discipline, while the moral and ethical code of the community is reflected in the personalities of the teachers which also influence the individual.

INFLUENCE OF SCHOOL ON COMMUNITY

School influences community as under:

1. Influence on the needs of community. Each community has its own needs. The school by moulding and transforming its activities tries to meet the needs of community in political, social, economic and other spheres of life.

2. Influence on problems of community. Each community has some problems which confront it from time to time. School identifies itself with the efforts of the community and tries to find solutions to tide over the problems and conveys the earned knowledge together with the conclusions of experiments as tentative solutions of all the problems of the community, which after tiding over the difficulties grows higher and higher.

3. Influence on culture of community. Each community has its own culture. By participating in the various activities and functions organized in the school, children easily understand and are able to practise the cultural values of the community. By this imbibing and translating them into practice, children preserve, modify and transmit these cultural values to others. In this way, schools conserve and transmit culture from one generation to another generation.

4. Influence on the standard of living of community. The styles and standard of living of individuals determine the standard of living of a community. School often improves these styles and standard of living which the whole community adopts gradually. But the rise of standard and life style is possible only when the economic growth keeps pace with them.

5. Influence on vocational and industrial progress of community. School powerfully influences the vocational and industrial efficiency of a community. More and more people become self-reliant and economically well off because of school education and training in crafts or modern techniques of production. In short, vocational pursuits of a community are practised in schools and the feed-back promotes community welfare and prosperity.

6. Influence on the citizens of community. Children of community receive education in schools. The philosophy of the school, its aims and curriculum influence children greatly to the education of wholesome citizenship. More and more children receive this education and become useful citizens. The community is, thus, raised higher and higher towards development and greatness because of such dynamic citizens.

7. Influence on the life of community. Schools effectively and imperceptibly convey to children the aims, ideals and values of the community, Children by their own practice and experimentation mould and purify those ideals and values and then feed-back the community which reforms and inspires itself more and more in the light of the feed-back from the schools.

8. Influence in bringing a change in community. Every community needs progressive change and reformation according to the changes in times and circumstances. School provides the directions and processes of the needed change. For changing the nation, it is necessary to change the minds of the nation.

Hence, the despotic doctrines of Nazism in Germany, Fascism in Italy and Communism in Russia were spread by indoctrinating the minds of children studying in schools.

9. Influence on the reconstruction of community. Schools play an important role in the reformation and reconstruction of a community. It is because in the schools, there is open criticism of the blind beliefs, useless customs, traditions and harmful doctrines prevalent in the community, and in the changed circumstances reconstruction is launched according to new aims, ideals and values. In this way, school brings about the necessary reconstruction of a community.

10. Influence on the policy of state. In a democratic set up, a school is free to criticize and evaluate the policy of Government openly and thus, by this healthy criticism, it tries to improve the administration and change the policies to suit the welfare of the individuals and the state. Under the new laws, schools now send their representatives to the Legislatures and Parliament and thus, direct influence of schools is exerted on the community.

11. Influence on the environment of community. Because of its smallness, a school is able to build a neat, wholesome, healthy and controlled environment. It sets an example for a community to follow and provide the same environment for all members of the community.

MERITS OF COMMUNITY AS AN AGENCY OF EDUCATION

(1) Community education is meaningful.

(2) Education provided by community emphasizes the principle of utility, according to which, education emphasizes those ideals which are useful to the individual as well as to the community itself.

(3) Community education gives real life experiences to the children. They get practical experience of objects and their working. Thus, children get real learning.

(4) Community education lays emphasis upon the principle of activity. Instead of simply hearing the lectures, children learn effectively by doing and manipulating things and processes.

(5) The community imparts its cultural heritage to the children.

(6) The community creates consciousness in children about their rights and duties and thus, develops in them those qualities and capacities which make them active and dynamic citizens.

(7) The community bestows upon children the capacity to think creatively and constructively. This makes them responsible and self-reliant citizens.

DEMERITS OF COMMUNITY AS AN AGENCY OF EDUCATION

(1) The community, for its own narrow ends, manipulates the process of education as a play thing and uses it for its selfish ends.

(2) To maintain its own superior status, the community creates blind faith in children, which makes children aggressive and intolerant towards other people having different beliefs and attitudes.

(3) Community develops communal feelings which lead to chaos in national life and create narrow and blind faith in one's own beliefs and traditions. Indian society is still suffering from this nasty and dangerous poison which vitiates national life.

(4) A community often takes recourse to repression and rigid discipline. It spoils the natural development of children.

(5) As a community develops narrow communal feelings in children, hence, it may hinder the development of democratic ways of behaviour and formation of democratic attitudes.

SUGGESTIONS TO MAKE COMMUNITY AN EFFECTIVE AGENCY OF EDUCATION

*1. **Ideal examples of social values.*** The community should provide ideal examples of co-operation, fellow feeling, social service and sacrifice before children so that they may develop their personality properly and contribute their best to the upliftment of community or the well being of society.

*2. **Wider attitude.*** Wider and liberal attitudes embracing all the persons of all the countries of the world must be inculcated in children so that they may rise above the narrow communal feelings and chavinistic attitudes of caste, creed or religion. They should be allowed full free expression and realization of the self by inculcating in them the spirit of tolerance, adjustment and service.

*3. **Maximum development of personality.*** Each child is born with his own distinct interests, inclinations and capacities. He must be provided full opportunities to develop his unique individuality. But the community compels him to develop on narrow communal lines of cast, creed, religion and vocation, which leads to destructive consequences. Hence, children should be provided full opportunities for the development of their personalities in accordance with their innate tendencies and capacities.

*4. **Educative environment.*** Good or bad environment makes or mars the development of the child. The community should protect children from evil influences of society and provide for them a congenial and conducive environment for healthy and proper development on desirable lines.

*5. **Establishment of community schools.*** The community should establish schools not only for children but also for the illiterate adults and handicapped children. In this connection, the establishment of community schools may cater to the demands of uneducated elders and the handicapped ones.

6. Education according to needs of child and demands of community. The community should impart education according to the needs of child and its own demands. Community development and welfare programmes stimulate children to serve and co-operate with such activities because they are useful for both.

7. Development of critical powers. As community has its own culture, each community confines itself to transmit its own culture to the children who are its integral parts. This is not enough. The community should stimulate the critical powers of children also so that they may evaluate their culture impartially and also modify it, if need be arisen.

8. Co-operation with other agencies. To make the education programme of community successful, it is essential that the community should seek the active co-operation of all the agencies of education, specially the family, the schools and the state. Parents, teachers and authorities of the state should also extend a willing co-operation for the progress and development of the community.

9. Assistance of state. Assistance of state is very much essential to make community an effective agency of education. The state should give grant-in-aid to all the schools run by the community and keep them under its control. The state should launch community development programmes and such other welfare schemes as reading rooms, libraries and other mass-media programmes.

QUESTIONS FOR ANSWER

1. Discuss the meaning and importance of community.
2. Throw light on the educational influences of community.
3. Critically evaluate the educational functions of community.
4. How can you make community an effective agency of education?
5. Discuss the relationship between school and community. Mention some of the important programmes of a community school

19

The School Education and the Society

In the fourth chapter of this book under the heading 'Most Important Agencies of Education' at serial number five following aspects concerning the school education has been discussed, therefore, readers are requested to read them again:

1. Definition of school
2. Need of school
3. Concept of school
4. Distinctive features of progressive school
5. Functions of school
6. School as most important agency of education.

Hence, here, we will discuss other aspects of school education as per need of this chapter in social context.

THE SCHOOL AS A SOCIAL SYSTEM

Sociology of education particularly studies the school as a social system. The social organisation in the school consists of different roles and statuses for the educator and educand. Among the teachers also there are different statuses and roles according to their seniority, qualifications, special skills and the position of the hierarchy of the school. The Headmaster in every school occupies a pivotal position, more responsibility, more administrative power and therefore the most important role.

Similarly, among the educands also different students occupy different statuses and roles in the schools according to their seniority, special skills and allotted responsibilities etc. For example, the chief prefect is overall incharge of the discipline among the students.

Similarly, there are so many prefects who maintain discipline in the school. Every class has a monitor who maintains law and order in the classroom in the absence of the teacher and complains to the teacher about the defaulter student.

As a social system the school aims to prepare the students to occupy social roles according to their capacities after leaving the school. In India, most of the rural youths finish their studies after high school. Some of them do not go beyond the middle schools. Therefore the functions of the middle schools and the high schools in transmitting knowledge, skills and socialisation are very important. As a social system the first function of the schools is to transmit knowledge and skills to the younger generation.

The technical schools transmit knowledge concerning so many traits. The agricultural institutions tell the sons of cultivators about better means of cultivation. All the schools impart knowledge of 3r's, reading, writing and arithmetic. This is necessary in order to help every male and female to skillfully manage the household affairs and also matters concerning every day life.

The younger generation learns future roles by means of perception and identity formation both in the family and in the school. Extra-curricular activities in the school are important to develop individual differences and particular skills of the educands. Thus, some of them may develop social leadership qualities, other political leadership traits and so on.

An important function of education is the development of the individuality of the students. This individuality is developed by the development of individual skill and the allotment of roles and statuses according to it. This schould not be based upon favours and prejudices.

As a social system the school is the best place to teach equality, liberty and fraternity to the younger generation. It is the best preparation around for practice of democratic traits in the wider social situation.

THE CULTURE OF THE SCHOOL

Each school has a particular culture. This can be noticed in the comparison in the private and public schools, the rural and urban schools, the schools in the tribal areas, the boys and the girls schools etc. Culture is constituted of the norms, customs, tradition, rules of behaviour, attitudes etc. All these are reflected in the social life of the school.

While in the outer society culture is transmitted without much change and refinement, in the school particular attention is given to transmit refined elements of culture. This is done through various means of socialisation and the allotment of different roles to different students.

THE SCHOOL AS A SOCIAL ORGANISATION

Social organisation is a network of statuses and roles. In a school, the headmaster is at the top of the hierarchy. His word is the law. He delivers the goods. He is responsible for the smooth functioning of the school. In other words, he is the head of the government of the school. Should he decide to act as an autocrate, the school will not develop democratic traits among the students.

Usually the defacto power of the headmaster is exercised through teachers and responsible students. Every class teacher wields authority in matters concerning his class. He is helped in this process by the monitor, the prefect and other teachers.

Thus the social organisation of the school should be dynamic and well-adjusted. The extra-curricular activities are very important for all-round development of the school as a social organisation. The school management consists of representatives of the public who help the headmaster and the teachers to carry out various functions in the school as a part of general community.

If the parents are invited to the school function, the cooperation between the school and the community as limbs of social organisation increases. This is particularly necessary at the nursery and the elementary level.

The most important task of the social organisation is socialisation. This socialisation requires acting according to allotted roles and statuses. The schools provide scope for the development of leadership qualities among the students particularly through the extra-curricular activities. Under the supervision of the teachers, they gradually learn to carry out responsible activities.

The headmaster and the teachers should allow more and more freedom to the students and it makes them more responsibie. They should follow the principle of least interference in the social relationships among the students. They are responsible for the socialisation of the students towards the community. They should impart the knowledge of social customs and traditions and develop values of society among the students.

The school is an important centre for promoting social mobility. It presents an example of the fulfilment of social justice. It is a place where every social custom and tradition is analysed, evaluated and even questioned before acceptance is granted to it.

Therefore the school presents the forum for bringing about desirable social changes. If the new generation learns the defects of the pernicious customs and traditions, it fights for their change and replacement in the wider society. This is particularly true about the high schools.

THE SCHOOL AND SOCIETY

Society is a system or organisation of mutual relation between human beings, implicit in certain communities and institutions. The school is a group and education is an institution. Evidently, the school is an important part of society. Here we means a specific society, not the general concept of society, which is an abstract notion.

And a specific society implies a group of human beings living within the limits of a definite country and which is characterised by a specific culture. The school is related to this specific society. It is for this reason that different educationists have defined the objectives of education differently for different nations.

Explaining the intimate relationship between society and school, T.P. Nunn, the famous educationist writes, "A nation's schools, we might say, are an organ of its life, whose special function is to consolidate its spiritual strength, to maintain its historic continuity, to secure its past achievement, to guarantee its future. Through its schools a nation should become conscious of the abiding sources from which the best movements in its life have always drawn their inspiration, should come to share the dream of its nobler sons, should constantly submit itself to self-criticism, should purge its ideals, should re-inform and redirect its impulses." This comment clearly indicates that the relationship between society and school is characterised by the following elements:

1. Schools keep the moral power of the society secure, and also maintain the social heritage of society. This social heritage is handed on by the schools to the following generation.

2. Schools also protect the historical continuity of society. Schools perform the function of acquainting the new generation with ancient myths and legends, and maintaining the patterns of behaviour in the form of traditions and customs.

3. Schools also help to keep alive the society's achievements in the past, and transfer it to the younger generation through the teaching of history and the social science.

4. Schools are the guardians of the society's future, because educands are the future leaders of the nation. Schools shape the future of the country by achieving the complete development of these leaders. It is for this reason that the educator is often referred to as the architect of the nation.

5. Through the medium of the school, the members of society are acquainted with those motives and inspirations which formed the basis of all the literary achievements of the past. This is achieved through the teaching of literature.

6. Schools also encourage considerable discussion and exchanges of opinion on the functioning, methods of working, customs, and traditions existing in various parts of society. These elements are analysed and subjected to criticism in order to decide whether they should be retained or thrown out. In this way, schools are the source of social change.

7. Through the medium of the school, leaders in various spheres such as engineering, medicine, legal profession, teaching, literature, etc., are trained. In this sense the progress of society depends upon the progress of the schools.

It is evident from the foregoing account of the intimate relationship between society and school that development and progress of schools is essential for the progress of society. Before introducing any change in society on a large scale, it can be experimented within the school and its nature and consequences observed. It can then be introduced into society.

IMPACT OF SOCIETY ON SCHOOL

It is evident from the intimate relationship that exists between society and school that both influence each other. The various points to be noted in the impact of society on school are as the following:

1. All the individuals, educators and educands, found in schools come from society, and hence it is only natural that their thinking should influence life in the school. It is generally accepted that the kind of family an educand comes from can be judged from his conduct in the school.

2. Society is a dynamic and changeable structure. One can see the effect of various social changes on schools.

3. Social conduct, or conduct in society, also has an influence upon the conduct of educand in schools. If social conduct deteriorates, there is no way of shielding the student from this deterioration and consequently conduct in school will also reflect a fall in standard.

4. The curriculum of the school is determined according to the needs of society, because parents always send their children to school in order to prepare them for society. They are given education so that they may become useful members of the society.

5. The life of the school is profoundly influenced by all the major institutions of society, such as family, religion and economic institutions. From this standpoint one can compare the schools in Communist Russia with the schools of democratic America.

6. All the education that the educand imbibes in school through brooks and lectures, actually emanates from society, because books are little more than the accumulated experiences and thoughts of the greatest figures in society.

IMPACT OF SCHOOL ON SOCIETY

Society is influenced by the school in as great a measure as it itself influences schools. In this respect, the following points are to be considered:

1. Schools produce the future leaders for all the spheres of society. It follows that the type of school will determine the calibre of leaders, and their calibre in turn will determine the

nature of society that they will create.

2. The school, like the family, is a social institution which socializes the individual and provides him some experience in social control. Therefore, the individual will learn to accept the kind of social control that is imposed on him in school, and will also demand similar social control from society. For this reason, there is a great insistence in democratic countries that the atmosphere in school should also be democratic so that the educand can get used to democratic norms of social control.

3. It has already been stated that the school plays an important part in social change because it subjects all the customs, traditions, mores, practices, etc., of society to continuous criticism. As a result of this criticism some of these are maintained and others rejected. This determines the direction of future social change.

4. It is the function of society to provide useful citizens to society, and if society wants to do independent, it is necessary that the school should provide it with citizens who are capable of being independent and self-reliant.

5. By exercising their right of criticism, the educands eliminate the weaknesses of society and thus prepare a blueprint for its future reformation and improvement.

RESPONSIBILITY OF SOCIETY IN MAKING THE SCHOOL EFFECTIVE

The extent to which society can play an active part in making the school a powerful and effective medium of purveying education is evident from the impact it has on the school. It is clear that society has great responsibility in this direction. The following points should be noted in this connection:

1. Society should undertake to construct appropriate buildings for schools and also provide for their decoration and maintenance.

2. It is the responsibility of society to see that educators get respect in society and that their needs are well looked after.

3. When invited by the school, various members of society should attend the school functions and take an enthusiastic part in it.

4. The society should not hesitate in providing any and everything which the teacher demands as essential to the complete development of the educand.

5. Society should also look into the examination system, the curriculum, etc., of schools should subject it to criticism, should examine it from the stand point of contemporary needs of society and should suggest changes if necessary.

RESPONSIBILITY OF THE SCHOOL TOWARDS SOCIETY

Just as the society has certain responsibility towards the school, in the same way the school also has certain obligations to society which it must fulfil.

In this connection Prof. M.V.C. Jeffreys writes, "The school can do nothing better for the education of citizens than to make its boys and girls members of a true community in which are combined liberty and order, freedom and responsibility, in which human personality is respected for its own sake, regardless of age or other irrelevant circumstances; which recognizes the authority of reason and experience, not of fear and status; and where liberty of thought has its complement in the responsibility for making one's own choice of opinions, and love rather than neutrality is the guarantee of intellectual freedom." Broadly speaking, the school can do the following tasks for society:

1. Assisting the progress of society in every possible way.
2. Training the children to live in a community.
3. Providing enough technical or scientific training as will enable them to earn their own livelihood and be independent.
4. Generating all qualities of good citizenship in the student.
5. Setting into motion and further assisting all programmes of social reform.
6. Encouraging the students to purge the society of its bad customs and habits.
7. Contribution to the development of folk culture by participating in and celebrating social occasions and festivals.
8. Developing such high moral characters and balanced personalities in the children that they should become useful members of society.
9. Taking the advice of parents and guardians in order to

help in the complete development of their children, and also to warn and guide the parents about possible future problems.

MEANS OF BRINGING SOCIETY AND SCHOOL CLOSE TO EACH OTHER

The importance of close cooperation between school and society is evident from the foregoing discussion. Following are the means by which this can be done:

1. Schools should frequently organise cultural functions of a kind which can make it possible for various members of the society to attend and participate in them.

2. The relationship between society and the school can be given a more firm foundation by running social welfare schemes or adult literacy schemes in the schools to educate the old and illiterate members of the society.

DRAWBACKS OF INDIAN SCHOOLS

Comparing the traditional and progressive schools according to the criteria explained above, we find a number of drawbacks in traditional schools of our country. Regarding Indian schools Prof. K.G. Saiyidain opines, "In our schools of today, only formal education of geography and science is imparted to children. Some schools are much below the standard where the initiative and enthusiasm for the students for work is crushed."

Thus for Indian schools also applies the same thing what has been said about the non-government schools of England, by H.G. Wells—"If you want to feel the generation rushing to waste like rapids, you should put your heart and mind into a private school." Following are the drawbacks of Indian schools:

1. Nature of schools. Indian schools were organised to meet the needs of British rule. Though our country is now a Sovereign Democratic Republic, yet the pattern of these schools is still the same. Their democratic structure and working is still a far cry. It is a hope against a hope to expect these schools to preserve, purify and transmit the cultural heritage of our country.

2. No co-operation of other agencies. Whatever form, structure and scope of Indian school may be, still it can not replace the family. Thus to carry out its function it should seek the active co-operation of the family, the community and the church. At present that there is no such co-operation, rather, sometimes non-cooperation and hostility is evident.

3. Emphasis on subject matter. In Indian schools too much emphasis is laid on the subject matter to the neglect of child. The natural interests, aptitudes and capacities of the child are more often curbed and dozes of theoretical knowledge are forced down into the mind of child.

4. One-sided development. Our schools do not try to promote the complete development of the personality of child. Only one or the other aspect of personality is randomly emphasized and that too in a haphazard way. There is always undue rush to finish the courses. This leads not even to mental development but makes the child cram the content mechanically without proper understanding and pass out of the examination.

5. Unpsychological environment. The entire environment of Indian schools is lifeless, dull and often repulsive. Most of the schools in villages and towns run in improvised shanty structures containing stools or carpets only. The rooms of such schools are dirty, dark and dingy without proper air circulation and light. Only a very few schools have any library, laboratory, reading room and other essential materials.

The campus of such schools is like a countyard where there is no garden, field and canteen. Only bookish theoretical ready-made titbits of knowledge are imparted to children in such schools without employing proper strategies, tactics, techniques and methodology. Dictation by teachers, cramming by students and passing out in any way is the only objective of such teaching shops run on commercial lines with money motive.

6. Stable and rigid curriculum. The curriculum of our schools is framed by Government and the school carries that into practice. It is stable and rigid. The framers of such curriculum do not take any notice regarding the local conditions, need or requirements of the place and above all the nature of children who are to take that curriculum. Teachers cannot modify it. Such rigid and lifeless curriculum is mechanically doled out to the children who profit very little from it.

7. Defective methods of teaching. Methods of teaching are examination oriented in our schools. They care very little about the inherent interests, aptitudes, needs and capacities of children. Rather they crush the initiative and originality of those for whom they are employed.

8. Negligence of individual differences. Psychological researches have emphatically proved that all children are born with distinct inherent capacities and powers. Education should draw and develop these native endowments. Factory like drilling, moulding and sharpening is done in our schools without any regard to individual differences, needs and aptitudes.

9. Lack of character formation and moral development. The whole atmosphere and working of Indian traditional schools is such that not inculcation of moral values and attitudes in children is possible. As such, character formation remains a distant dream. Our schools do not aim at essential goals and ends of life to be achieved.

10. Lack of vocational education. School education is simply bookish and theoretical without any practical experience. As there is not sufficient provision for vocational education in our schools, children either search table jobs or lead a life dependent upon others after getting certificates and degrees.

11. Emphasis on bookish knowledge. In our schools education is purely theoretical and academic. It starts with books and ends with books. While in progressive schools much emphasis is laid upon games and scientific training through experiments and inventions whereas our bookish education is mainly examination oriented.

12. Lack of constructive and creative activities. Modern education lays emphasis upon creative and constructive activities. But most of our schools neglect such activities. Most of them have even no idea of such desirable activities. Therefore, on growing adults, our children are incapable of participating in any sphere of national reconstruction and international development.

13. Lack of well trained teachers. On account of the population explosion, our schools are over croweded and the teacher training institutions lag behind. Adequate number of trained teachers are not available. Lack of well trained teachers leads to education suffering in quality, precision and proper direction.

14. More academic and monastic. School education is so academic and monastic that it has become quite unrelated to real life situation. The education imparted in our schools is quite dull, lifeless and purely theoretical having no relation with real life.

15. Unable to develop social progress. School is a miniature or society or a small replica of society outside the school. It should face the problems of society and foster such attitudes in the children which may lead to social advancement, progress and development. But education imparted in our traditional schools neither leads to individual progress nor progress of society.

SUGGESTIONS TO MAKE INDIAN SCHOOLS EFFECTIVE

To make Indian schools an effective agency of education following suggestions may be made:

1. Democratic nature of schools. India is now free from foreign alien rule. After careful consideration it has transformed itself into a Secular Democratic Republic. We should scrap the old bureaucratic and authoritarian pattern of our schools by changing their working in confirmity with the democratic ideals and processes so that each child may learn to live democratically.

The nature of Indian schools should, now, be democratic so that children are able to adjust with the environment and bring out a change in them according to the changing needs and situations of society.

2. Co-operation of other agencies. The family, the community and the state together with all other agencies of education should co-operate in the working of the school. Then only the Indian schools will be worthy of being known as progressive schools.

3. Emphasis on child's personality. In addition to curriculum, full attention should be paid to the development of the child in accordance with his innate endowments. Education should be child centered.

4. All-sided development. Personality has various aspects. None is to be neglected. Our schools foster all-round development of personality namely—physical, mental, emotional and social.

5. Congenial environment. Our schools should provide congenial and conducive environment to the children. Then only it will be possible for our young ones to develop their inherent tendencies and capacities to the best of their efforts by their own initiative and creativity.

6. Flexible curriculum. Curriculum followed by our schools should be flexible enough to local needs and situations. Teachers should also have the freedom to modify it according to the requirements of children and social conditions.

7. Dynamic methods of teaching. No doubt, curriculum is important but equally important are the strategies, tactics, techniques and methodology of teaching which work out the curriculum. Dalton Plan, Assignments, projects etc. are some of the important useful methods.

8. Emphasis on individual differences. Keeping into consideration the principle of individual differences, our schools should try to meet individual needs and problems as far as possible. Only then, education will be effective and profitable in developing values that equip children for their future life full of stress and strain.

9. Emphasis on character formation and moral development. Emphasis on the development of moral values is essential for the proper development of character. In a democratic country like India, only those citizens can lead the nation to greatness, who are imbued with moral qualities and firm character.

Hence all the policies, programmes and other activities like scouting and guiding etc. of our schools should develop moral values and strong good character in our children.

10. Provision of vocational education. Our schools should make children self-reliant by training them in some craft or vocation according to their needs, interests and capacities. Vocational education shall enable them to live independently on their own labour and efforts in the capacity of socially efficient citizens.

11. Emphasis on practical knowledge. Our schools should minimize imparting bookish and theoretical knowledge. They should try to give more and more creative, constructive and practical knowledge to children. Our curriculum should be based on life experiences as experiences gained through self-learning prove useful in practical life. The motto of experience, current these days, should be sincerely worked out.

12. Emphasis on constructive and creative activities. Indian schools should emphasize the principle of creativity in the education of children. According to this principle children should themselves plan and structure learning experiences. They should initiate and continue all varieties of constructive activities. Co-curricular activities, exhibitions, competitions, social and cultural programmes may also stimulate children in these directions.

13. Provision for the training of teachers. Trained teachers know their job well and do it efficiently in comparison with those who are not trained professionally. As the number of children increases provision of sufficient teaching staff should be made by the management and the government.

The government should provide more and more facilities for the training of teachers. In service training schemes should also be widened in their scope and facilities. Training should be made inexpensive. Working conditions, security of service, pay scales be increased to invite really intelligent and capable persons to the teaching profession.

14. Centre of community life. Indian schools should serve as community centres for children. They should engage all the children in various developmental and recreational activities in such a way so that on one hand all the desirable values namely morality, strong character, self-reliance, sense of emotional and national unity together with national discipline develop in them in a natural way and on the other hand they actively participate in the development of the community to which they belong.

15. Emphasis on social values. Indian schools should develop children in social environment. They should encourage children to come in contact with social centres and social institutions. They also participate actively in various social functions. It will not only establish a bond between the smaller world of school and the wider world outside but also develop in children all the socially desirable values which are greatly essential for the success of democracy.

QUESTION FOR ANSWER

1. What are the drawbacks of Indian schools? Give suggestions to make Indian schools an effective agency of education.

20

Education and National Policy

According to Kothari Commission (1964-66), "It is necessary to prepare an integral plan of development, a plan which will consist of three parts: family planning, economic development and educational reconstruction."

Each nation has its own national policy. Nations which declare themselves democratic, have their democratic policies in all spheres of human activity. In the field of education, the aims of education, its curriculum and methods etc. all reflect democratic principles and values.

DEMOCRATIC POLICY AND EDUCATION

After the attainment of independence on 15th August 1947, Indian national government declared the adoption of democratic principles and values of liberty, equality and fraternity. In 1950, Indian Constitution proclaimed and adopted the ideal of Sovereign Democratic Republic.

It guaranteed equality, free exercise of fundamental rights and full opportunities to the fullest extent by providing them maximum opportunities for growth and development. It also proclaimed that the government would be based on principles of complete equality, free expression, freedom of religion and social justice irrespective of colour, caste, creed and sex.

It laid down the fundamental provisions as well as the directive principles for the national policy for all kinds of development of all individuals irrespective colour, caste, creed and sex in all areas of human activity.

Since education is the most potent means to achieve all the principles and values of democracy enshrined in our Constitution, the union government appointed the Secondary Education Commission on 6th October, 1952 to consider all aspects of secondary education and suggest recommendations to bring about necessary improvement in them on democratic lines.

EDUCATION FOR MODERNIZATION

India has accepted the goal of modernization with the purpose of marching together with the progressive countries of the world. Modernization is a concept symbolizing a movement of progressive thinking, evolution of better and better techniques of production and scientific advancement with the main objective of removing blind beliefs, destructive attitudes and worthless faiths in order to achieve a modern progressive society.

All progressive and developed nations of the world are marching ahead towards modernization. To move with the progressive countries of the world, India should also strain almost to modernize by developing scientific and technological knowledge and bringing about the desired timely changes in our social-cultural customs, traditions, attitudes and values.

Education is the only vehicle to equip us with the necessary insight, capacity and intelligence to achieve all kinds of scientific and technological advancement to develop our nation in all areas of human activity. We should organize our educational system, so that we are able to achieve this objective without any difficulty.

This urge for modernization was inspired by great people like Raja Ram Mohan Roy and others in the later half of the last century. After the attainment of independence in 1947 this urge has gained tremendous momentum for the allround development of our country. Appointed by the central government, the Kothari Commission (1964-66) has recommended modernization as the most important aim of education.

EDUCATION OF SCIENCE

According to our national policy, it has been decided that

scientific education must be encouraged. For this, the central government has brought into being the department of science in the National Council of Educational Research and Training. Its chief purpose is to bring about the following improvements in the teaching of science at various levels of schools and teacher training institutions:

1. To aid all the agencies engaged in the teaching of science.
2. To provide training facilities to those teachers who are already in service.
3. To provide improved designs for laboratories and models of scientific devices.
4. To improve the technology for teaching and teaching techniques.
5. To provide ideal text-books for students and teachers by making desired changes in the curriculum.
6. To enlarge the knowledge of teachers teaching science by organizing science fairs, science magazines and periodicals.
7. To encourage more and more researches into the realm of science and scientific problems.
8. To stimulate interests and urge of talented students studying science by awarding them scholarships and stipends.

NATIONAL ECONOMIC POLICY

As a national policy of economic growth and development, India has adopted mixed economy. Seventy per cent of its population is engaged in agriculture and its allied vocations. Due to inadequate techniques and poor sources, our agricultural production is unsatisfactory. For industrial growth and development, Governments are encouraging small as well as large scale industries in both private and public sectors.

Under these circumstances, the prime aim of Indian educational policy is to obtain the latest techniques of production in the fields of agriculture, commerce and industry under nationally inspired able experts and field workers.

To ameliorate Indian nation from the moral of economic stagnation and industrial backwardness we need more and more capital, latest technology and an army of science workers, able experts, supervisors, administrators and executives at all levels of production in both areas of private and public enterprises.

There is a dire need of capable supervisors, technicians and administrators. Indian system of education lacks in practical expertise and workmanship.

Hence, theoretical teaching should be linked with practical workshop experience and full facilities be provided for improvement and achievement of higher and higher efficiency by those engaged in actual work in factories and workshops of various types so that they may improve their productive efficiency and capacity for increased output and greater skill in manipulative skills.

NATIONAL POLICY OF EDUCATION

Kothari Commission (1964-66) has recommended that for the development of nation, there should be a well throughout, dynamic and clear cut national policy of education. Hence, our national government, in 1968, declared its national policy of education, the salient features of which are as follows:

1. Free and compulsory education. According to article 45 of the Indian Constitution, provision should be made for free and compulsory education for all children upto the age of 14.

2. Position, salary and training of teachers. Teachers should receive respect and recognition from society. Their salary, grades and emoluments should be adequately raised up. Provision should be made for the in-service training of teachers, ensuring full academic freedom for all.

3. Development of languages. To develop languages, emphasis should be laid on:

(i) Hindi
(ii) Sanskrit
(iii) Regional languages
(iv) Three language formula, and
(v) International languages.

4. Equality of educational opportunities. To provide equality of educational opportunities, following points should be emphasized:

(*i*) Removal of regional imbalance.

(*ii*) Raising the standards of schools and methods of teaching should be improved.

(*iii*) Special provision should be made for the education of girls.

(*iv*) Provision of education to the backward, abnormal and poor children should be made in right earnest.

(*v*) Ample provision should be made for the education of mentally retarded and physically handicapped children.

5. Recognition of talents. Search for talents should be conducted in all areas. Such gifted children should receive all needed and possible encouragement from the state.

6. Work experience and national service. To bring the school and the community in close contact, emphasis should be laid on work experience and national service.

7. Scientific education and research. For the economic uplift of the country, more and more encouragement should be given to scientific education and allied researches.

8. Agricultural and industrial education. For agricultural and industrial education, following points should be emphasized:

(*i*) Each state should establish at least one agricultural university.

(*ii*) Under technological education, experimental and research work should be encouraged.

(*iii*) In agriculture, industry and technical areas of education, there should be a positive correlation between man-power and employment according to the needs and also between the input and output in all areas of development of economy and commerce of the nation.

9. Production of books and allied material. Some books should be published for the use of all people in all areas of the country. Their writers should be rewarded adequately by the state. At the same time, universities should undertake the task of publishing standard books in regional languages.

10. Examinations. There should be a radical reformation in the examination system to have optimum validity and reliability.

11. Secondary education. There should be no regional imbalance in the facilities provided to the people in the areas of primary, secondary, technical and vocational education.

12. University education. In the area of university education, the following points should be kept in bold relief:

(i) While opening new universities, full regard should be kept for maintaining high academic standards and adequate financial provision.

(ii) At these centre, there should be ample provision of good libraries, laboratories, material equipment and educational devices.

(iii) There should be full facilities for research work of high standard at these centres.

(iv) The syllabi of higher classes should be very carefully framed with the dynamic support of great scholars.

(v) Effective provision should be made for teacher training courses for new incumbents as well as in-service candidates.

(vi) Full academic and financial freedom should be given to universities and all centres of higher learning.

13. Part time education and correspondence course. Universities should structure and work out various types of part-time courses. They should also be allowed to launch various types of correspondence courses for specific degrees.

14. Eradication of illiteracy and provision of adult education. For this, nation-wide schemes, help of all teachers, students, factory workers, office clerks and other literate personnel should be harnessed to achieve quick results. Such education should be economically self-sufficient and capable to promote individual and social uplift.

15. Games and sports. Education for games, sports and various kinds of atheletic activities should be launched on a nation-wide scale.

16. Education of minorities. There should be adequate facilities for the education of the minority and backward communities.

17. Pattern of education. There should be some national pattern of education effective and prevalent throughout the length and breadth of the country.

While discussing the national policy of education, the central government have pledged to spend six per cent of the national income on education. It has also pledged to support all states in their educational plans and schemes. The national government will review after every five years the educational state of affairs in the country and bring about the needed reforms in its policies and programmes.

EDUCATION AND NON-ALIGNMENT POLICY

Two powerful groups of nations emerged on the stages: after the second world war which ended in 1946. One was of democratic nations and the other was of communistic nations. USA, England and France etc. belonged to the first group whereas Russia and China etc. formed the second one.

There were some underdeveloped and developing countries also which did not belong to any of the groups. Big nations or groups of nations are now trying to bring such non-aligned countries under their sway.

After the attainment of independence in 1947, India declared that it will not align itself to any of the two groups and will not be subservient to any one of them, but will pursue its own independent policies. Our national education is failing to sustain this spirit in the true sense. Indian education should emphasize the following aims to forge ahead and achieve success in its policy of non-alignment.

1. Knowledge of the meaning and importance of non-alignment policy. Indian education should inculcate in our children the true meaning and importance of non-alignment policy so that they are able to understand the true significance of 'Panch Sheel', the corner-stone of non-alignment policy founded by Pandit jawahar Lal Nehru. Indian education should foster the understanding of these ideals in children belonging to lower classes through textbooks. It should enable children studying in higher classes to understand fully well the achievements of 'Panch Sheel' spirit and non-alignment movement.

2. Knowledge of the utility and results of non-alignment policy. Indian education should enable children to understand and appreciate the usefulness and relevance of non-alignment policy for India. Teachers should discuss with children the proceedings and resolutions of the non-aligned conferences and allow debates about their recommendation and achievements.

Educands should be able to imbibe the true significance, utility and purposefulness of the principle of non-alignment.

These should be able to defend the ideals and values of this principle.

3. Development of physical and mental powers. Only physically capable and mentally devoted citizens will be able to defend the independence, solidarity and unity of the country leading it to the path of progress and development. Self-realization leads to self-confidence and self-reliance which are the basic elements of non-alignment policy. Education should develop the physical and mental powers of our children to the fullest possible extent.

4. Achievement of self-sufficiency. The fourth aim of our Indian education should be to teach Indian children to be self-sufficient, self-reliant and self-confident in their beliefs and behaviour. Diverse types of education such as agricultural, vocational, technical, industrial, professional and commercial should be given. No weak nation can safeguard its independence, integrity and solidarity. Only fully developed individuals can make India strong, self-sufficient, self-reliant and really non-aligned.

5. Inculcation of spirit of social welfare. Education should be able to develop social feelings and international understanding. They should be able to stand against injustice and tyranny and uphold justice, equality, fairplay and human brotherhood. Education should stimulate, encourage and promote democratic feelings, attitudes, ideals, values and norms.

QUESTIONS FOR ANSWER

1. Discuss the role of education in realisation of national policy.
2. Explain the salient features of the National Educational Policy of India.

21

Education for Political Conduct

Politics is a social aspect, because society needs a government to serve it better but, in democracy in particular. The government is as the people are and the people are as per the education they receive, therefore, education and politics and so the social good are inter-related. This consideration has made Secondary Education Commission of India to observe:

"We recognise that education is mainly the concern of states, but in view of its impact on the life of the country as a whole, both in the field of culture and technical efficiency, the Central Government cannot divest itself of the responsibility to improve its standards and to relate it intelligently to the larger problems of national life."

THE RELATION BETWEEN EDUCATION AND POLITICS IN INDIA

*1. **Vedic period.*** During Vedic period, education was popagated by Rishis, Munis and Sanyasis. The schools were then known as Gurukuls and Ashrams where pupils and teachers lived together forming a big family. The state had nothing to do with the curriculum methods and duration of education except helping these centres of learning materially and financially.

*2. **Brahmanic period.*** During Brahmanic period, also the pattern of education continued as before. Gurukuls and Ashrams flourished and provided all kinds of education to the children of the community. The state did not interfere with the working of these centres but helped them in all other ways.

3. Buddhistic period. During Buddhistic period, individually organized and managed educational centres of the Vedic and Brahmanic periods developed into big public institutions like the modern universities. Nalanda, Vallabhi, Vikramshila, Nadia were world renowned centres of higher learning which attracted students from all over the world.

The management by committees of these institutions replaced the old pattern of individual management. Though the state had its say in the organization, maintenance and working of all the centres of higher learning, yet the educational atmosphere and processes remained pure and of high academic standard.

The virus of political corruption did not enter the portals of these world reputed centres of learning. Thus, they enjoyed complete internal and external autonomy.

(4) Muslim period. During Muslim period, the rulers controlled the centres of learning and used education to propagate the state religion which was Islam. Thus, centred the virus of political influence and corruption in the sacred precincts of educational centres.

(5) British period. During the early British rule, East India Company remained quite indifferent towards the education of Indians. But in 1913, under the insistence of some Indian and British scholars, East India Company agreed to shoulder some responsibility of education of Indians. For full twenty two years, the controversy between Western and Oriental education continued to rage giving rise to a number of problems.

Finally Lord Macaulay, with the purpose of consolidating the British Empire in India, decided in favour of English, education and exhorted that 'A single shelf of good European library was worth the whole native literature of India and Arabia'. Lord William Bentnick, who had a prejudice against Indian languages and literature, decided on 7th March, 1935 A.D. in favour of Lord Macaulay's policies and decisions about education to be imparted to Indians.

Gradually, the Government assumed full control over the aims, curriculum, methods and medium of education to be given to Indians. In 1854 A.D., on the recommendations of Wood's

Despatch, the Company Government in India established department of education and four universities on the pattern of London University.

The Hunter Commission of 1882 A.D. recommended the opening of Government model schools and provided a scheme of government financial aid to encourage public initiative for opening more and more privately managed schools. The result of this effort was that government began to open more and more schools, colleges and universities for academic, vocational and professional education of the people. At the same time, charitable persons and endownments also began to provide more and more schools and institutions for public education.

Not only this, in 1910, officers were appointed to supervise educational activities at local, district, commissionary and provincial levels. In 1919, the Central Government transferred its responsibility towards education to popularly elected ministries in all the provinces of India.

Since then, education is a responsibility of the state governments, the role of the centre being advisory and financial help. In other words, the state government got control over education in their states in 1919 A.D.

6. Modern period. On 15th August 1947 A.D., India attained independence from the alien British rule and the Indian people framed their own constitution. Education was assigned to both the state and central control also in some aspects and areas.

Central government controls a few universities and institutes of higher learning, but the rest of the educational institutions in the country are under the full control of their respective states, privately managed educational institutions are awarded recognition by the State governments which also provide to them grant-in-aid and other financial supports for their maintenance and growth. In short, the state government controls all the educational activities and processes including the curriculum of the institutions.

CONTROL OF POLITICS ON EDUCATION

In a separate chapter of this Book—'The State', the control of politics on education as well as the state control on education has been discussed at length. Here some special features are being discussed in a nut shell. In a monarchy or despotic state, the whole educational process remains under the grip of the monarch or the despotic ruler and education is used to bolster up consolidating the rule of the monarch or the despot. On the other hand, in a democracy, the aim is the welfare of the people.

Thus, education develops the individual, the society and the state more and more. The modern age is an age of democratic values and patterns of organization in all human areas of existence and activities.

As a democratic state depends for its growth and existence on able, educated, resourceful, dynamic and enterprising citizens of strong character and responsible conduct in all spheres of human existence and progress, hence each democratic state tries to organize its education effectively by decentralizing it, making more useful and purposive.

India has accepted the democratic and socialistic pattern of government. Hence, to achieve maximum public welfare, the state tries to influence and control the educational processes in the following ways:

*1. **Constitutional control.*** Constitutionally, article 11 of the Indian Constitution empowers and makes each state responsible for the education of people in its territories and area of control.

*2. **Economic control.*** The state governments control all education institutions by means of financial aids and supports. Even the privately managed institutions are kept under close supervision by means of grant-in-aid and recognition by state governments.

*3. **Educational control.*** Educational control operates in the fields of aims, curriculum, text-books and examinations at various levels of education through diverse government controlled agencies and boards.

*4. **Administrative control.*** Government recognition is the most effective means of control besides grant-in-aid. In the field of appointment of principals, head masters and teachers and through the enforcement of educational status together with codes all educational institutions are made to conform to set patterns, rules and policies prescribed by the government. Not only this, private managements have also to fall in line and work according to government statutes and directions.

DIFFERENT FORMS OF GOVERNMENT AND EDUCATION

There are three general forms of government namely—(1) Monarchical, (2) Aristocratic, and (3) Democratic. In the followig lines, we are discussing the educational set up in all the three forms of government respectively.

1. Education in monarchy. In a monarchical form, an individual cannot even dream of his progress and free development. He is expected to sacrifice his all, even his life or the welfare of the monarchy. As such, the aims of education formulated are necessarily not in the interests of the general people but education achieves and fosters the welfare and progress of the monarchy.

Thus, education becomes a very formal and dull process which remains quite indifferent towards the development of an individual. The monarchical rule itself lays down the pre-determined and present pattern of education for the people.

The items of curriculum are indoctrinated rigidly into the minds of children and qualities of self-discipline, obedience, tolerance, service and sacrifice are fostered by government controlled process so that monarchy develops more and more its own welfare and consolidated itself.

2. Education in aristocracy. The government in aristocracy fosters the welfare of the powerful few who enforce absolute obedience and service among the masses. The aims of education are so formulated that they promote the good of the chosen few only to the total neglect of the general people. Qualities which are expressed in the form of toleration, obedience, serivce and self-sacrifice are inculcated by educational processes in this pattern.

3. Education in democracy. In this form of government, the state distributes its governing power among the various institutions of citizens who form the state. The purpose of this decentralization is to develop the individuals and the society more and more and achieve greater and greater welfare of both.

Such a system of government is based upon the principles of equality, fraternity and liberty emphasizing co-operation, fellow-feeling, service and sacrifice. Each individual is provided maximum opportunities to develop himself to the highest possible extent according to his inherent interests, inclinations, aptitudes and capacities.

In democracy, curriculum is organized on the principle of diversity to suit the needs of all the individuals. The teachers provide best possible guidance promoting the development of each and every child according to his capacities and tendencies.

4. Education in socialistic state. A socialistic state emphasizes and promotes the development and welfare of society. Hence, agricultural, technical and vocational education is imparted on scientific lines. Not only this, opportunities are also provided to one and all to profit by education according to their interests, inclinations, aptitudes and capacities. Thus, standard of living is raised up which contributes to the welfare of the nation.

JUSTIFICATION OF CONTROL OF POLITICS ON EDUCATION

The above discussion clearly lays down the fact that in any form of government, politics, in one way or the other, organizes its hold upon educational activities and programmes. In some states, pattern of education is centralized, while in others it is decentralized to the lowest levels.

Locke, Mill, Bentham and other individualist thinkers condemn any sort of control by the State over education. They uphold that such control will result in the destruction of education in its true sense promoting various evils and mal-practices.

On the other hand, Mathew-Arnold, Ruskin, Carbyle and other socialist thinkers assert that State has got every right to control education as much as possible. Both these views namely—The Individualism and the Collectivism, emphasize one-sided truth in their extreme forms.

Modern progressive educationists do not agree with either of these extreme views. They neither ascribe to complete laissezfaire like the individualists nor advocate complete rigid control as is in the fascist and communist regimes in the modern world. They put forth the golden mean, the middle path which upholds that the task of education is so important that all the resources of the State should be harnessed towards its implementation.

But the State should not become the only means of education and rigidly control all educational processes and programmes. The State should decentralize its educational functions to responsible public institutions, be they private or community controlled. In other words, individual efforts and efforts of the community should be more and more encouraged so that they run institutions side by side with the government. At the same time, complete autonomy should be assigned and guaranteed to all the universities and institutes of higher learning in the country.

NATIONALIZATION OF EDUCATION

Our Indian Constitution is pledged to a Sovereign Socialistic Democratic Republic. Thus, the minorities have rights to run their own educational and cultural institution for their own welfare and progress. The Central as well as the State governments encourage private individuals, communities and trusts to open more and more schools for the people. We find such privately managed and maintained institutions throughout the country.

These private institutions are sometimes exploited by unscrupulous persons and politicians for their own selfish ends. Some greedy and dishonest persons run these schools and colleges as business establishments earning huge amounts of money by all sorts of corruption and malpractices. Hence, social thinkers, reformers, educationists and teachers have started the movement of nationalization of education to save institutions from corrupt and unscruplous politicians.

The State governments have swung into action by taking over many educational institutions and in some States book trade has been nationalized. Let us be aware of one important factor at such a critical situation. Is this cry of nationalization a panacca of all evils that afflict Indian education? A comparative study of education reveals the fact that private initiatives run a number of educational institutions quite successfully in America and some other democratic states of the world.

Thus, the movement of nationalization in our country is liable to promote despotic control of education by states. As we find in Russia and China, nationalization may make education a tool in the hands of the despotic rulers. We have to guard against this danger.

PROBLEMS DUE TO POLITICS IN EDUCATION

The entry of politics into the field of education starts a chain of problems which adversely affect education in the following ways:

1. Neglect of general welfare. The group holding the administrative powers in its grips exercises total sway over all the plans and schemes of education so that the welfare of all the people is subordinated to the interests and ends of the dominant group in the government. Thus, general interests are often neglected which adversely affect the people's welfare and progress.

2. Favouritism. The dominant group in the government gets the appointments of its own favourites at all levels of the educational process. Such favourites are generally corrupt, incapable and inefficient as teachers, supervisors, administrative officers and even vice-chancellors. Such corrupt and incapable persons spoil the standards and working procedures of education in all fields because they are always mindful of their personal or group interests.

3. Student politics. Political leaders exploit the energies and resources of students for their personal gains or party interests. These student-leaders create all sorts of problems of indiscipline and choas in all educational institutions. They try to gate-crash all corrupt and malpractices which create headache to the teachers, principals and other educational personnel. They create problems of law and order in the campus of educational institutions. Politics in the institutions creates problems for the up right students so that all their efforts to get good education and attain high standards are set at naught.

4. Lowering of standards. Through undue favours and recommendations, even the most inefficient and incapable students succeed in getting jobs, which they do not deserve in any way. Such inefficient and incapable persons further spoil the educational procedures by their misdeeds, evil-designs and selfish doings. Today, educational institutions are turning out undisciplined law-breaking students rather than dynamic, resourceful, and enterprising citizens.

EDUCATION FOR SECULARISM IN INDIA

The present educational system of India promotes secular attitudes and values through its broad-based aims, curricula, enlightened teachers and appropriate activities, all emphasizing open-mindedness, progressivism, rationality, freedom from bigotry and superstition, and equal respect for all religions. Following traits characterise education for secularism in India:

1. Secular aims. The aims and objectives of such a system are secular. They seek to develop India as a rational, democratic, progressive and modern state. The philosophy of humanism guides such educational objectives. The well-being of all the citizens of the country is the goal towards which India's educational energies are directed.

2. Democratic organization of educational institutions. The organization of most of Indian educational institutions is based on secular principles. It is necessary to observe secular, democratic and rational criteria in appointments, promotions, admission and all such matters.

3. Multiple curricula. The educational curricula at all levels in India lay special emphasis on the promotion of secular values. Lessons in text-books are free from religious bigotry and prejudice while the good ideas and values emphasised in different religions are presented in appropriate forms.

The co-curricular activities aim at promoting harmony and co-operation among different groups and respect for each other's culture in the students. It is not permitted to condemn or unduly praise any one particular religious or cultural system or institution.

It is usual practice in all schools, colleges and universities to celebrate fairs, festivals, birth anniversaries, etc., relating to different religions. While imparting moral education, equal importance is given to different faiths.

4. Science teaching. Secularism stands for scientific rationalism. It stresses logical thinking and abhors superstitions and irrational things. Therefore, Indian education today puts much emphasis on science teaching. Science is taught in a practical manner at all levels of shooling, so that it might influence the attitudes and values of the pupils. The spirit of science with emphasis on inquiry experimentation, proof and critical outlook, permeates the teaching of other subjects also.

*5. **Enlightened teachers.*** In the education for secularism in India, the teachers today are expected to treat pupils in an impartial manner. They eschew all caste, community and class considerations in dealing with students and colleagues. Equal respect is given to all students to all religious groups. Every conscientious teacher behaves in a truly democratic and fair manner.

Thus the present Indian secular educational system is trying to create a social climate in the country in which secular values are sought to be promoted effectively and enthusiastically.

DIFFICULTIES IN SECULAR EDUCATIONAL SYSTEM

In a country like India, in which traditional institutions like religion, caste, untouchability and dowry have been prevailing for thousands of years, the building up of a secular state is a very challenging task.

Despite the best intentions of our Constitution makers and great leaders, it is difficult to establish and promote a really functional climate of secularism in India. The main difficulties in secular educational system are as follows:

1. Traditional bias and narrow outlook. In our country today denominational schools are allowed to function with a lot of freedom. There are D.A.V. Schools, Jain Schools, Vaish Schools, Ahir Schools, Kayastha Pathshalas, Shia Schools, Catholic Schools, Rajput Schools, etc.

In these institutions the children of the respective communities or castes are admitted on preferential basis and also teachers of the same communities are preferred. This creates a serious difficulty in the functioning of Indian education as an integrative and secular force in Indian society.

2. ***Too much emphasis on theoretical learning.*** Our educational system presents many things only in theory. Very little efforts is made to change the values and attitudes of education. Many highly educated people do not hesitate to demand big dowries. They are too much fastidious about gotras

and sub-castes in deciding marriage. They ill-treat women-folk and do not show respect to other religions.

The lack of tolerance and courtesy on the part of educated persons towards villagers, women, poor people, minority community members, old people, etc., in buses, trains and at other public places reveals that our present education has failed to change our value system in a desired manner.

3. Neglect of secular and cultural celebrations. Schools and colleges observe holidays on the days of important religious fairs, festivals and birthdays. The result is that the students do not get enough opportunities to understand or imbibe secular values.

4. Neglect of group activities. Educational institutions do not encourage group activities. Group activities, group methods of teaching and learning are neglected. This is a serious difficulty in the promotion of secular and free values.

QUESTIONS FOR ANSWER

1. Discuss the relation of Politics and Education.
2. Explain the demerits of politicization of education.
3. Write an essay on Secular Education in India.

22

Education for Economic Growth

In good old days education was for the sake of education but now almost all countries are forced to spend huge sums of money on their educational planning and thus, educationists also think that education must aim at social and national economic upliftment by increasing the productive efficiency of the workers and inventing new methods and implements for agro-industrial development and progress of the nation.

Hence, there is an intimate relationship between education and economics. Due to this relationship, whereas on one hand, the economy of a particular society influences its education, on the other hand, the return of education affects the planning of education of that society. In this sense, education and economics are so integrally correlated are the two sides of a coin.

GROWTH OF ECONOMICS OF EDUCATION

Because of the intimate relationship between economics and education, some scholars have started to develop a new field of study which goes by the name of Economics of Education. It should be borne in mind that modern American economist Streemelin, British economist John Vizzy and French economist Michael have contributed a lot in the development of this new field of study. But this does not mean that old economists of the previous generation did not do any thing in this field.

As a matter of fact, Adam Smith, T.A. Malthus and Marshall

etc. had already laid the foundation of Economics of Education, pointing out the directions of further growth and development of this discipline.

Sociological and scientific tendencies influence educational purposes very powerfully. The general thought development that education not only develops the personality to the full but also promotes social attitudes and social service mentality increasing thereby the working efficiency as dynamic and useful citizens contributing their best to social and economic welfare of the country.

This sociological tendency asserted the provision of universal, compulsory and free education for all children. Such schemes entailed vast outlay of funds. It became natural, under these circumstances, for people to think of returns of this huge expenditure on education.

This thinking led to the development of the study of economics of education. In short, economics of education is a new concept which studies in depth the expenditure on education with the corresponding return it brings to the nation which spends so much on it for its own good.

EDUCATION AS A PRODUCTIVE ACTIVITY

It should be borne in mind that there is a great difference between education and other productive activities. In contrast to other investment procedures and productive agencies which contribute directly to economic growth and prosperity, education does this indirectly by producing dynamic, capable and efficient workers who promote more and more national development in all areas and spheres of growth.

In other words, instead of producing goods directly, education improves man-power engaged in production and this improvement achieves higher and higher targets of growth and production in all areas and aspects of industrial development and economic prosperity.

EDUCATION AS AN INVESTMENT AND ITS RETURN

Before the dawn of modern civilization there were many economists who regarded education as an end in itself. To them, it had nothing to do with economics. They regarded any expenditure on education as unproductive and this view prevailed so much that whenever a developing country felt the need of curtailment of the budgetary grants, the axe invariably fell on the educational allotment.

In modern age, economists hold the view that education is an essential expenditure and a productive investment. To them, whatever expenditure is incurred on educational plans, equipment, buildings and other expenses is an investment, the return of which is received in the form of useful, dynamic and efficient citizens who contribute more and more to greater and greater economic welfare of the country which provides them such useful education. Thus, educational expenditure is now regarded by all an investment for national development.

ECONOMIC ASPECTS OF EDUCATION

The following points explain the economic aspects of education:

1. Education as economic goods. A 'goods' can be included under the scope of economic goods only when its availability is limited and it is capable of allocation. Following are two types of economic goods:

(*i*) *Material goods.* A material goods is physical and tangible.

(*ii*) *Non-material goods.* A non-material goods is a service rendered that satisfies a human want.

Education is a non-material economic goods. It is service rendered to satisfy a human want. It is limited and capable of being allocated to individuals.

Education is a producer's and consumer's goods as given below:

(*i*) *Producer's goods.* Producer's goods is a goods used in the process of producing other goods.

(*ii*) *Consumer's goods.* Consumer's goods is a goods used by a consumer to satisfy his wants.

Education is both producer's goods and a consumer's goods. It gives satisfaction to the person who consumed it. It helps in the production of more goods. Education in the form of a producer's goods is acquired for the purpose of becoming a teacher, lawyer, engineer or mechanic, or for any other profession or vocation, the main purpose of which is to produce a material or non-material goods. At the same time, it is consumer by those who receive it in the satisfaction of some for their wants.

Again, education becomes a consumer's goods when the purpose of acquiring knowledge is to enrich a person's life by increasing his capacity to use, enjoy or appreciate any material or non-material goods that satisfies human want.

2. Education as industry. A country's government spends its gross national income on different sectors of the economy such as agriculture, industry and education every year expecting more returns than the previous year. The share for education is increasing every year in both developed and developing economics.

Thus education is indeed a 'growth industry' which provides employment and services needed by the total economy as any other industry contributes to the gross national product of the country. It contributes substantially to the total economy of the country, and without it the economy would be all too poor.

Again, education produces non-material goods which satisfy human wants. Education, as it produces goods necessary for human welfare is amenable to demand supply and cost benefit analysis.

3. Education as human capital. Capital is anything that involves costs but yields a stream of income over time. It is the sky to the production of income and consequently to economic growth. It consists of largely in its power to produce or accumulate income immediately or in the long run. H.G. Johnson classified capital in the following four categories:

(i) Capital goods. These render specific services to production or consumption by the owner.

(ii) Human capital. This is labour. Labour, the important characteristics of which is that both inherently and by legal tradition, control over the use of the capital is vested in the individual embodying the capital, regardless of the source of finance or the investment in it.

(iii) Social capital. This is collective capital, the important characteristic for which is that for reasons of inherent necessity or administrative convenience its services to production or consumption are not charged to individual users but are paid for by taxation of the community at large.

(iv) Intellectual capital. This is knowledge, the important characteristic of which is that, once created it is a free goods,

in the sense that use of it by one individual does not diminish its availability to others.

Essentially, education is human capital as it directly promotes the quality and capability of human beings. It contributes to intellectual and partly at least makes social capital. Economics considers human beings as a form of capital due to following reasons:

1. There are costs associated with development and formation of human capital.

2. The costs of skilled human resources add incrementally to the national product.

3. Expenditure on human resources which increase the national product also increase the national wealth.

Factors affecting human capital formation are investment in formal education, improved health, on the job training, manpower rehabilitation, migration, etc. Formal education raises the economic value of the human capital by raising the future earning power and current asset value of human beings.

IMPACT OF ECONOMICS UPON EDUCATION

Areas of impact of economics upon education are the following:

1. Aims of education. Economics determines aims of education. Besides knowledge aim, cultural aim, character aim, spiritual aim, social aim, harmonious development of personality as an aim, vocational aim is one of the important aims of education.

2. Importance of education. Economics explains the importance of education is so far as the economic growth of the country is largely based on educational development.

3. Education as a means. Economics teaches man to be a better producer: both for his personal good, and for the good of the country. It further points out that education is a means for that end.

4. Education as an investment. Education is itself an investment in economic terms. It removes poverty, as it produces skilled labour and creates right attitude to work and development. It creates awareness for better living.

5. Education as a guarantee of economic security. Education determines professional values, the wage structure, and guarantees economic security of the people.

*6. **Education and economic status.*** Economic status of a person is determined by education. Education helps him in possessing a good earning capacity and leading a good economic life.

*7. **Education and economic prosperity.*** Economic development of the country depends on education. Economic prosperity of the country is directly proportional to the educational development of the people.

EDUCATION AND ECONOMIC GROWTH

What is Economic Growth?

Economic growth is identical with prosperity and better life. Faster economic growth helps the people of country to enjoy higher standards of living. It leads to better social services. It gives more aid to the people of other countries.

Economic growth means increase in the net national income during a given period of time. Some economists take increase in per capita income as an indicator and a measure of economic growth. Following are some definitions of economic growth:

"The result of the labour acting on the natural resources of a country which produce within a given period of time a certain, non aggregate of commodities after avoiding double counting." —*Marshall*

"Gross National Product and per capita income." —*Mayer and Baldwin*

"Economic growth implies a growth in Gross National Product." —*Schumpeter and Hicks*

Role of Education

The system of education and the economic growth in a given social set-up are inter-related. One cannot exist without the other. Deterioration in education results in slow economic development. On the other hand, slow economic development will affect educational system and standards.

According to B.G. Tilak, the relationship between education and economic growth is a two way process—one of a reciprocal nature, of mutual contribution. In his book, *'The Economics of Education'* John Vaizey has humorously and rightly described this relationship like a "chicken and egg".

Harbison and Myers opine that education is both seed and the flower of economic development. To sum up, the role of education in economic growth is as follows:

1. Production of material wealth. According to Alfred Marshall, education makes a man "more intelligent, more ready, more trustworthy in his ordinary work; it raises the tone of his life in working hours and out of working hours; it is thus, an important means towards the production of material wealth." Education is now universally accepted as a very useful productive activity which promotes national prosperity and national welfare in various fields. Thus it produces material wealth.

2. Development of talents and virtues. An accelerated and higher level of economic welfare depends on bringing about fundamental changes in both the mental outlook and technical knowledge and skills. An awakened mind, right knowledge, appropriate skills and desirable attitudes are the great levers of economic development.

Conceived and imparted correctly, education produces these talents and virtues. It yields an automatic bonus in the 'growth process' and the 'change process'. It releases the dynamism and forward flowing energy, which are the assets for a developing country. The constructive urges of man are aroused through education.

Better organizational skill and sharp inventiveness are the direct results of education. It aims at the harmonious development of 3 H's (head, hand and heart). This will produce integrated personalities, who are assets to the economic progress.

3. Development of human resources. The development of human beings is the key resource of economic development. Human resource has both quantitative as well as qualitative aspects—quantitative in terms of effective man-hours and qualitative in terms of skills, knowledge and attitudes of human beings, on whom depends the tempo of development of a country.

In a developing country every man's outlook and his level of education must change. With more investment in human capital (education) there will be more improvement in skills, knowledge and attitudes.

Karl Marx pleaded for education on the ground that, "It

is counter balance to the inhuman results of the division of labour." According to Harbison and Myers the educational process of human resources development is necessary for the transformation of social and political institutions, for which the people of modernizing countries strive.

Economic contribution of education could be interpreted in terms of human capital through education. Education improves man-power engaged in production. This improvement achieves higher and higher targets of growth and production in all areas and aspects of industrial development and economic prosperity.

4. Quantitative and qualitative improvement. The role of education in economic growth has both quantity and quality dimensions. Educational innovations and research are necessary and must be encouraged in planning to provide quality labour, efficient administrators, well trained teachers and various other professionals, with dedication and an experimental outlook. The role of education in discoveries and inventions should be supported further with necessary finance.

Education has the power to improve quality. It adapts human resources and makes them more productive. In USSR in 1920's, "It was estimated that the work of people who had received primary education was almost one-and-a-half-times more productive than that of illiterate workers of the same age doing the same work; and that the work of those who had received secondary education was twice as productive, while that of graduates was four times as productive."

Japan has been able to make very rapid economic progress in the twentieth century, in spite of the late arrival in the field, large density of population and paucity of natural resources.

The explanation may be found at least partly in the fact that she has been stepping up her public expenditure on education since World War II. Compared to Mexico and Brazil (rich in natural resources), Denmark and Switzerland (low in natural resources) have higher per capita income because of the effective system of education in the latter.

By spending more than half of the national wealth on education, the USA has attained great heights of economic prosperity in return. The economic progress of the Netherlands is also due to her educational pattern. Thus, economic prosperity of modern advanced countries has proved that the most effective means for prosperity is education. By their efficiency and dynamism educated persons contribute to national prosperity and growth of national income.

QUESTIONS FOR ANSWER

1. Explain the economic aspects of education.
2. What are the areas of impact of economies upon education?
3. Write short note on Education and Economic Growth.

23

Education and Science

Modern age belongs to science and technology which is the base of economic and social progress. Therefore, we are attempting to advance our scientific knowledge at a faster speed through our emphasis on science education. Mudaliar Commission Report (1952-53) states as follows:

"To be effective, a democratic citizen should have the understanding and the intellectual integrity to sift truth from falsehood, facts from propaganda and to reject the dangerous appeal of fanaticism and prejudice. He must develop a scientific attitude of mind to think objectively and base his conclusions on tested data."

INTRODUCTION

Democracy and education are the two supreme powers of modern age. As a matter of fact, both are complementary mutually. During the 15th and 16 centuries, scientific researches and astonishing inventions in the realm of science started the vogue of teaching science in the 17th century to children in place of mere theoretical and academic learning. The purpose behind this was to achieve effective, complete and well-adjusted living in the ever-changing circumstances and situations of society.

Due to the industrial revolution of the 18th century and under the impact of newer and newer scientific inventions and researches in technology, human life changed to new patterns of beliefs and behaviour as individuals and as social beings.

The result was that in England, Germany, France, America and other progressive countries scientific subjects were added to the curriculum placing them in prominent positions replacing much of the dead wood of mere academic learning. Now, we see that in this age of science it has become greatly essential to impart scientific education to all children of society.

MEANING OF SCIENCE

Knowledge of science is superior to all other types of knowledge. While ordinary knowledge generally does not reflect attributes of validity and reliability, scientific knowledge possesses these qualities. It is open to testing and real life experiences. It is a logically related and clearly arranged knowledge of items about which any one can experiment and apply tests for validity and reliability. Science is the systematic knowledge of a particular thing.

The principles of science are clear, definite, broad-based, valid, pure, real and reliable in all respects. The following steps are gone through as logically related steps of scientific analysis, interpretation and conclusions:

(1) Formulation of hypothesis.
(2) Collection of data.
(3) Analysis of data.
(4) Classification of data.
(5) Observation of relationship between facts and events.
(6) Establishing relationship between cause and effect.
(7) Evaluation of hypothesis.
(8) Establishing a principle.

SCIENCE AND GENERAL SCIENCE

At the secondary stage, science includes Chemistry, Physics, Botany and Zoology. At the higher stage, Geology, Minerology and some other branches of science are taught as separate disciplines. In general science, subjects are not taught as separate disciplines.

It is an integrated curriculum which includes—Chemistry, Physics, Botany, Zoology, Geology in the form of general principles. As general principles of science are related to the everyday experiences of all children. This integrated curriculum is made compulsory for all children.

SCIENCE AND EDUCATION

Before eighteenth century science had not developed so much. Today scientific investigations and researches are being made with such a fast speed that their knowledge needs a complete knowledge of science.

Science has become an integral part of human life. All our means of communication, radio, television, food grains, clothes and medicines depend upon the development of science. As soon as we are deprived of any of these scientific investigations and researches even for a short period of time, we fell unhappy.

ADVANTAGES OF SCIENTIFIC EDUCATION

Following are the advantages of scientific education:

(1) Thinking and memory develops.
(2) Principles are formulated.
(3) Self-confidence and self-reliance develop.
(4) Love for truth enhances.
(5) Confidence regarding unity in diversity increases.
(6) Devotion towards nature increases.
(7) Avenues open for newer and newer vocations.
(8) Science has become the basis of our cultural heritage and social progress.
(9) Like other disciplines, education is placed in the Faculty of Science. Education is not only an art but also Science.
(10) Most of the principles of modern education are scientific. Almost all the strategies, tactics and techniques of teaching are scientific in nature.

SCIENTIFIC ATTITUDE

Scientific attitude includes the following elements:

(1) Identifying causes of the problem.
(2) Establishing relationship between cause and effect.
(3) Believing in intellectual integrity.
(4) Raising above blind beliefs and dogmas.
(5) Having full faith in truth irrespective of one's own likes and dislikes.

(6) Developing the capacity of clear thinking and receptivity to new ideas.
(7) Accepting the authentic ideas even with caution.
(8) Possessing a critical and constructive attitude while solving a challenging problem.
(9) Arriving at no conclusion at all on the availability of incomplete or false data.
(10) Basing conclusions on tested data only.
(11) Keeping certain exceptions into consideration while determining a principle.

SCIENTIFIC EDUCATION IN INDIA

Ours is an age of science. It is essential for every individual to have a correct knowledge of this scientific age. Education should be organized in such a way that each child is inspired to participate actively in the economic reconstruction of society.

They should understand that development of modern society depends upon the development of science and technology. They should try to develop themselves technologically so that technological efficiency and high level competence is developed in them and they are able to enjoy maximum advantages of science in their daily life.

Though scientific education in India started in the beginning of 20th century, yet real advancement in this area was achieved during the second half of this century. Gradually, newer and newer industries started growing. When India attained independence in 1947, national leaders thought of industrial growth side by side with the growth of agriculture and allied vocations.

Demand for engineers and technicians began to grow and more and more children began to receive scientific and technical education. Opening of more and more institutions of this types of education was undertaken by the central as well as state governments. But soon thousands of engineers together with technicians began to swell the ranks of the unemployed.

Lack of practical training in workshops and inefficiency of teachers contributed to these chaotic conditions. To improve this type of education, National Council of Educational Research and Training sponsored by the National Government at the centre re-organized and re-planned the education of science in all areas and fields.

NCERT launched various schemes through its extension services for the improvement of scientific education at all levels and in all fields of human work. Some of its working schemes are as fellows:

1. Schemes of teaching science. Various schemes have been launched to stimulate the urge for scientific education among school children. Class-room teaching is augmented with independent investigations and research at all levels of school and college teaching by providing guidance and equipment for experimental work.

2. Promotion of science clubs. Establishment of science clubs is promoted to popularise scientific education among common people. These clubs are provided with adequate equipment and facilities for experimental and practical work.

3. Organisation of science fairs, seminars and symposiums. Through newspapers, teachers of science are encouraged more and more to develop their knowledge of the subject matter and adopt the most up-to-date devices and techniques of teaching.

4. Selection for science education. Through examinations, talented and gifted children in the field of science are selected and encouraged by the award of scholarships, stipends and appreciations in various ways.

5. Central science workshop. On the advice and under the guidance of talented and learned members of UNESCO, science council has established a central science workshop for imparting effective instruction to science teachers in practical investigations, workshop methods together with techniques of work and instruction.

After such experience and training, teachers as well as students are encouraged to prepare designs, models and scientific instruments for laboratories. The central workshop also tries to improve models and designs prepared by Indian schools besides modifying foreign equipments to suit Indian needs and conditions.

6. Training of science teachers. For laboratory and workshop techniques, a part time curriculum for teacher training has been organized at various important places in the country to prepare efficient science teachers for effective teaching and productive guidance. It is expected that participants will be able to set right the instruments, models and machines lying useless in schools and colleges. Huge wastage of resources will be saved through these schemes and part time courses to teachers, students, laboratory workers and technicians.

TECHNOLOGICAL ADVANCEMENT AND EDUCATION

In modern age progress in the field of production science has been attained only through researches in methods and techniques of production. The supreme gift of science to modern age is technology of various types. Technology is the application of science to satisfy the daily needs and requirements of human beings. Technology is the practical or applied use of scientific knowledge. This scientific knowledge is being applied to all areas and fields of human activity.

Technological advancement opens new vistas of progress in all fields of development in a country. The USA, Great Britain, Russia and Japan have achieved great heights of prosperity because of advanced technology in all areas of human activity.

In India, the use of technology in the areas of industry, agriculture and commerce has revolutionized our productive capacity so that we are in a position to export various consumer articles, goods and even machines to other countries.

Scientific and Technical Research Bureau, Atomic Energy Bureau and National Security Scientific Laboratories have promoted science education to a considerable extent. Central and State Governments have established centres of advanced research in almost all the universities where ample facilities have been provided for higher researches and investigation in various fields of science and technology.

This has promoted industrial, agricultural and technological advancement to a very great extent, its pace is increasing day by day.

Hard work, understanding and insight are greatly essential for technological progress. Following suggestions have been given to promote this capacity:

(1) Technological knowledge which includes application of known technology and provision of further research in the field is essential.
(2) National prosperity and conducive atmosphere are required.
(3) Political and administrative encouragement is a must.
(4) Adequate capital, resources and other material for technological research and progress are needed.
(5) Provision of markets must be made for goods produced.
(6) Efficiency of planning and execution of plans must be taken into consideration.
(7) Education of workers to improve their efficiency must be imparted.
(8) Various efficient agencies are required to run the industries efficiently. A nation which can fulfil all these conditions and pool all its available resources will march ahead on the road of progress and prosperity.

In India, more and more industries are being established in various fields of productive work. But these industries are not being run as efficiently and profitably as they should due to the incapacity of our working and executive personnel. To increase the efficiency of workers and organizing personnel, we need the re-organization of our whole system of education and pattern of giving practical experiences in all aspects of technology.

Our national system of education should be linked with productive workshop experiences so that trained persons work efficiently and intelligently to achieve higher and higher targets of production of all kinds of goods and materials. Technical education should be integrally correlated with practical workshop experiences and most recent techniques of production.

An essential need of our modern education in science and technology is to re-orientate and reorganize it on sound and effective lines. Only then, India will be able to stand in the ranks of the developed and prosperous nations of the world.

QUESTIONS FOR ANSWER

1. What is science? Throw light on the relationship of science and education.
2. How can education promote scientific attitude in children?
3. Discussing the progress of scientific education in India, throw light as to how such type of education can promote technological advancement in the country.

24

Vocational and Technical Education

In the present age of science and technology, social good and welfare as well as upliftment of the society and the nation depends upon vocational and technical education, because our main problem is poverty. Therefore under social compulsion, Government has to plan comprehensive development of industry and for doing so had to provide liberal vocational and technical education. Let us see where do we stand today in this field.

Before the country had become independent, it had already witnessed the establishment of the Mines Institute in Dhanbad, the Cloth Institute at Kanpur, the Engineering College in Bombay, Engineering and Technical College in Jadavpur, Tata Institute in Jamshedpur, Technical College at the Banaras University, the Polytechnic in Delhi, and many other similar institutions.

In 1947, there were 38 technical institutions in the country which provided 2,940 trained persons every years. At the same time there were 53 polytechnic schools in the country from which 3,670 students obtained their diplomas annually. On the 30th November, 1945, the Government of India established the All India Technical Education Board.

In 1947, the Scientific Manpower Research Committee came into existence. This Committee conducted a survey and discovered that by 1947 the country required 54,000 engineers and some 20,000 technicians.

After independence, the attention of the Government was soon drawn to the need for vocational and technical education as an essential means of progress and development in the country. Many programmes for this kind of education were put forward in the five year plans. In more recent years, the effort has been stepped up, and now both the Central and the State Governments are concerned with progress in this direction.

The Central Government makes provisions for technological advance in every part of the country, and provide financial aid to the universities and institutions providing the highest technical education. The Central Ministry of Education is concerned with care of these institutes of higher learning in the field of technical education, although the actual work is done by the All India Board for Technical Education.

This Board also has form regional committees concerned with the organization of the board of study, the national diploma course, short-term courses and postgraduate programmes. In the case of the State Government, the responsibility is primarily one of advancing the cause of technical education through its department of technical education. A Board consisting of 17 members, under the Chairmanship of the Education Minister, makes provision for technical education in the State.

INSTITUTES OF TECHNICAL EDUCATION

In India, the various institutes for technical education can be divided into the following three categories:

1. Degree and postgraduate institutions. Such institutes provide education and facilities for research in such spheres as mines, industry, metallurgy, dam building, road industry, irrigation, land reclamation, instrumentation, production engineering, chemical engineering, electronics and telecommunications, petroleum research, clothes, architecture, etc.

2. Diploma course institutions. Polytechnic institutes for girls and boys provide training in various technical subjects for periods ranging from one to three years, depending upon the curriculum. The successful candidates are awarded diplomas.

3. Institutes for training in specific vocations. Institutions belonging to this category provide training for many handicrafts and cottage industries such as weaving, printing, sculpture, leather work, carpentry, jeweller's work, the work of the blacksmith, etc. In adddition to this many schools and colleges strain individuals to make them skilled and semi-skilled technicians. But such people must be literate.

In 1947, the country had 38 such colleges and 53 schools in which 3,670 students received diplomas and 2,940 received degrees. But over the last three plan periods, the number of technical education institutions has increased manifold. In addition to Warangal, Mangalore, Nagpur, Bhopal, Durgapur, Jamshedpur, Allahabad, Delhi and Srinagar, many other towns also have regional engineering colleges. The Indian Institute of Science at Bangalore provides special facilities for research.

The Kharagpur institute also performs the same function. Indian Institute of Technology have been established in Bombay, Madras, Delhi, Kanpur and Kharagpur. In addition to these, the Government is also establishing centres for training in urban and rural planning, printing, industrial organization, etc.

With the assistance of the Ministry for Community Development, the Education Ministry established 48 science temples in various parts of the country in 1964 in which educands were provided scientific information.

In 1950-51, the number of vocational and technical institutions in the country was 2,339 in which 11,568 educators taught 1,87,194 students. On these students, the Government spend some Rs. 3.69 crores. In 1965-66, the number of such institutions was 2,776 in which 2,47,910 students underwent training. It must be remembered that in 1960-61 the number of schools was 4,145 in which 4,01,274 students were being taught. In this manner there was a downfall in technical education in 1965-66.

In the same period the schools providing training in music, dancing and other arts and social services were 5,939 in which some 23,46,279 students were studying. In 1969, the number of institutions for higher training in engineering and technology in the country was 135, from which 17,800 students obtained degrees while 27,900 students obtained diplomas. In 1968, when unemployment spread to the technically trained sphere, the admission to these institutions was generally reduced. This reduction was to the tune of 30 per cent.

This reduction continued in 1969 also. Even today the country has many thousands of technically trained individuals who have not found employment, although the Government is making strenuous efforts to find employment for them.

PROBLEMS OF VOCATIONAL AND TECHNICAL EDUCATION

It is evident from the brief history of vocational and technical education given above that it faces certain special problems in the country. Some of these problems are as the following:

1. Unemployment among trained individuals. In the recent past, there were loud complaints from many sections of society that there were not enough institutions for technical and vocational training in the country. Even today, there are some demands to open more such institutions in certain parts of the country, but at the same time people are aware that there is widespread unemployment among technically trained graduates and technicians.

Besides, many of the people apparently employed are only inadequately or improperly employed. This has created a very redoubtable situation which suggests that there was no correlation between the increase in technical training and actual industrial progress. It has already been pointed out that all modern progressive nations carry out surveys to determine the number of trained people required in each sphere of industry before entering on a programme of providing institutions for their training.

These institutions are used to fulfil this demand for technical training. Although this idea was accepted in principle in India also, in actual practice no relation was maintained between the demand and supply of technically trained personnel.

In the Fourth Five Year Plan, the Government had decided to provide employment to such people and also to control admission to all such colleges as well as colleges providing general education.

2. Shortage of technicians at the lower level. On the one hand, one finds a large number of qualified engineers without employment while on the other there is an acute shortage of trained technicians at comparatively lower levels of work. Most of the craftsmen and mechanics are not trained individuals.

Even today, one finds acute shortage of properly trained mechanics for maintenance work in motor vehicles, small machines, electrical appliances, etc.

3. Absence of co-operation between the State, industry and education. At the root of both the above problems is the lack of co-ordination and planning between the Government, industry and education, because this imbalance of demand and supply is clear evidence of lack of planning.

If technical education is to be really useful to nation, it is essential that there should be co-ordination between these three sectors so that education should train the right number and right kind of individuals for which there is a demand in industry. The Government can then really accept responsibility for finding employment for these trained personnel.

4. Defects of administration. To a considerable extent, the difficulties and problems of technical and vocational education in this country are enhanced by the administration, where sometimes one finds one man doing the job of three while at other times one finds two or more people engaged on a task which can easily be performed by one person.

In both these conditions, the quality and quantity of work suffer, apart from the unpleasant experiences which the trained individual has to suffer. Many times politicians interfere in the work of highly skilled technicians and specialists, and as a result one finds many industrial and technical programmes suffering unimaginable losses. This also leads to dissatisfaction among the workers. Unless these problems of administration are solved, it will not be possible to create a climate conducive to the trained individuals.

5. Narrow curriculum. As far as possible, the curriculum for technical education should also include teaching of several subjects keeping in mind that the technician is also a human being. In recent years, attention has been paid to this aspect, and one finds that the syllabi of most engineering colleges and technological institutes includes studies of social sciences and the humanities.

6. Problem of the medium of education. It is essential that the mother tongue should be the medium of education at the lower and middle level of technical education because educands coming in at this level do not have sufficient linguistic skill to study through the medium of English. But unfortunately, even today, there is little or no technical literature available in Hindi or any regional language, with the result that it has been impossible to use them as media of technical education.

The Government is engaged in the task of creating a vocabulary of technical terms in Hindi and other regional languages, which encourages one of the hope that it will be possible to grant technical training through this medium in the near future.

7. Shortage of trained teachers. In the sphere of vocational and technical education there is an acute shortage of trained educators. In order to overcome this difficulty, it is necessary to make the profession more attractive by offering high salaries to the staff of institutions engaged in this kind of education.

The possible people may find it more attractive and profitable to stay in the country than to settle abroad. Under the existing circumstances, a very high percentage of the trained talent migrates to foreign countries where the prospects are much better.

8. Education after leaving school. Another difficulty is that fairly soon after leaving school and taking up some job the trained individual finds that he is lagging far behind knowledge because he cannot keep up with more recent advances in knowledge and technology. It is, therefore, desirable that some arrangement for refresher courses for these people should be made so that they can keep up with the growing knowledge.

9. Lack of practice in laboratories. Generally speaking, there is definitely a shortage of good laboratories and workshops in the country, but even where they are available they are not put to sufficient use. Most of the education imparted to the educand is of a theoretical nature, with much less emphasis upon practical work and practice.

But research laboratories can only be increased when the industrialists co-operate with the Government. Another aspect of this problem is that such laboratories should make use of the equipment manufactured within the country instead of depending exclusively upon exports.

10. Insufficient research. Compared to the more progressive nations, India spends far less on research in technology. In Russia and America an amount spent on research is 2.8 per cent of the national income while in India the amount invested in research is only 0.2 per cent of the national income.

In the absence of continuous research and new inventions, both technical education and industrial progress suffer.

Hence, there is every need for encouraging research on the materials available in the country.

There is no doubt that some attention is being paid to the solution of these difficulties of technical and vocational education in the country, but undue interference by politicians and the Government's inherent lethargy have only aggravated the situation. If anything positive is to be achieved, co-operation between the Government, industrialists and directors of education is unavoidable.

Unless some co-ordination is reached in the thinking of these three parties, there is no hope of progress in vocational and technical education. Neither will there be any chance of the trained people finding sufficient and proper employment. The one ray of hope is that the Government has professed a keen interest in the problem of the trained unemployed and has promised some relief.

The future of the country inevitably depends upon producing a large number of technically proficient individuals and upon the proper utilization of their talents in the industrial sphere.

QUESTIONS FOR ANSWER

1. Point out the significance of vocational and technical education. What are the chief sources of such education?
2. Write short note on Vocational Education.
3. What is meant by technological change? Discuss the influence of technology on human attitudes and activities.

25

Education and Modernization

In the words of S.N. Eisenstadt, "Historically modernization is the process of change towards those types of social, economic and political systems that have developed in Western Europe and North America from the seventeenth century to the nineteenth and have been spread to other European countries and in the nineteenth and twentieth centuries to the south American, Asian and African continents." Modernization is the characteristic feature of modern society, which aims at greater social welfare.

CHARACTERISTICS OF MODERNIZATION

The process of modernization becomes evident from its characteristics. Following are its chief characteristics:

1. Social mobilization. Social mobilization is that process by which the old social, economic and psychological elements are transformed and new social values of human conduct are set up. The social mobilization is a peculiarity of modernization.

2. Social differentiation. Another feature of modernization is social differentiation. In this process there is increase in the complexity in social, political and economic activities and there is progress in the activities of individuals in various fields. Industrialization is a result of modernization.

As a result of modernization new trends in philosophy, religion, science and literature become visible. Briefly, an increase in modernization leads to a progress in social, economic, political and cultural fields, there is more differentiation in these.

*3. **Structural differentiation and change.*** Another characteristic of modernization is structural differentiation and continuous change. In the social and economic fields, old organizations break up yielding place to new. In political field new parties emerge. The cottage industries are replaced by big industries. The new means of production develop. Many new professions develop. The production becomes more complex.

*4. **Change in organizational and status system.*** A feature of modern society is the emergence of a number of specialized organizations. Secondly, there is greater division of labour. Thirdly, the organizations based on close kinship lose in importance. With the acceleration in the speed of change the status of individuals and families undergoes change. New classes emerge in society. From the cultural and economic viewpoint, there come into being three classes, namely: upper, middle and lower.

*5. **Urbanization.*** The phenomena of urbanization and modernization are inter-linked, one leads to the other.

*6. **Social and political movements.*** An important feature of modernization is the emergence of new social and political movements which aim at the transformation of society. This transformation becomes imperative in order to make man adjust to fast changing conditions. These movements also aim at casting off orthodoxy and paving the ground for change to modernity. In order to attain the new aims, a change of outlook becomes imperative.

*7. **Comprehensive and multi-sided education.*** An important aim of modernization is the spread of education. In modern society it is tried that all should be educated. Besides academic education under modernization, the need for technical and professional education becomes acute; therefore, many technical and professional institutes spring up to meet this demand.

*8. **Development of international cooperation.*** Lastly, the development of international cooperation is the aim of modernization. The national movements gave birth to many nations. For the development of mutual relations among nations, a League of Nations and later U.N.O. came into existence.

MEANS OF MODERNIZATION

After discussing the characteristics of modernization, the means of modernization are as follows:

1. Industrialization
2. Urbanization
3. Secularization
4. Rise of new social class
5. Social change
6. Westernization
7. Democratization.

EDUCATION AND MODERNIZATION

S.N. Eisenstadt has rightly pointed out, "Perhaps the best starting point for the analysis of the characteristics in the educational institutions in modern societies is the pattern of demands for and the supply of educational services that tended to develop with modernization."

In the words of Yogendra Singh, "...education has been one of the most influential instruments of modernization in India. It has led to the mobilization of people's aspiration for nationalism, liberalism and freedom. It alone has been responsible for the growth of an enlightened intelligentsia which carried forward not only a movements for independence but also a relentless struggle for social and cultural reforms."

The most important function of education is modernization. Modernization is a comprehensive concept aimed at capturing, describing and evaluating profound qualitative and quantitative changes in society. It describes the transition of a society from medieval to modern culture. It stands for progress beyond tradition.

Modernization according to some sociologists is based upon European and American models. As compared to urbanization, industrialization, westernization and Europeanization, modernization presents a more complex process and a more complex result. In the intellectual sphere, it is an awareness that it is possible to see a rational explanation of physical and social phenomena.

Thus, it is represented by positivism and empiricism and rationalism. In the field of religion it is expressed in secularism.

Its approach is this worldly. In philosophy it is expressed in humanist thought. It includes social mobilization and differentiation and specialization in individual and institutional activities.

In political field it stands for democratization. In ecology it is characterised by advancing degree of urbanization. But the most important feature of modernization as related to education is cultural. In cultural sphere its symptoms have been pointed out by A.R. Desai as follows:

1. Growing differentiation of the major elements of cultural systems, "The spread of literacy and secular education: a more complex intellectual and institutional system for the cultivation and advancement of specialized roles based on intellectual disciplines."

2. Emergence of a new cultural outlook characterised by emphasis on progress and improvement, on happiness and spontaneous expression of abilities and feelings, on the development of individuality as a value, and efficiency.

3. Emergence of a new personality orientation, traits and characteristics revealed in greater ability to adjust to the broadening societal horizons: some ego-flexibility; widening spheres of interests; growing potential empathy with other people and situations; a growing evaluation of self-advancement and mobility; a growing emphasis on the present as the meaningful temporal dimension of human existence; a growing awareness of dignity of others and an increased disposition to respect them; a growing awareness in the individual that "his world is calculable, that other people and institutions around him can be relied on to fulfil their delegation and responsibilities," growing faith in sciences and technology and a growing awareness that, "rewards should be according to contribution and not according to either whim or special properties of person not relating to his contribution."

4. Finally, modernization implies, "the ability of society to develop an institutional structure capable of adjusting to continually changing problems and demands." The emergence of such a flexibility constitutes, according to Prof. Eisenstadt, the central issue and challenge of modernization.

Education is the most important instrument of modernization since and modernization includes:

1. Directed change in the system of attitudes, beliefs, and values, and also in the institutional complex, to enhance the acceptability of modern technology and its organizational and operational framework.

2. Growth of the infrastructure essential to the adaptation to technology of foreign origin to specific national needs; and

3. Laying the foundations of institutions and organizations which could, in time, assume responsibility for independent innovation and technological growth to the country's needs and problems.

In view of the above mentioned changes required by modernization the functions of education in this direction may be achieved by the following:

1. By enlarging the congnitive map of those exposed to it, education suggests alternatives to tradition, brings into focus the rewards implicit in them, and indicates—roughly at least—the paths through which the new goals with their attendant regards can be achieved. It broadens mental horizons, raises expectations and predisposes people to make experiments.

2. As an instrument of socialization it can project new images and values. Purposively used, it can be helpful in obliterating attitudes and behaviour patterns that are dysfunctional to programmes of modernization.

3. By providing ideological articulation it can promote the development of national consciousness and can help people see their needs and their problems in a national perspective. This can stimulate the creation of a national consensus at least on major issues.

4. Education provides a highway to elite status on the educated. The educated provide a reference model to the masses, who, in imitation of the former, take the first step away from tradition. Modernizing elites are almost always the products of modern or semi-modern school/university systems.

5. Problems-solving leadership—scientists and technicians, management experts and administration—with the requisite knowledge and skills, can only be expected to emerge out of the educational system. Large-scale programmes of modernization demand specialists of several types at different levels, and look to the educational system for a steady flow of technocrates, planners and managers to operate them.

6. Education is a mobility multiplier. Although its impact is on the immobility of thought—ways, in the long run it does alter rigid forms of social stratification. Modernization requires both types of mobility.

In sum, with proper planning and under efficient direction, education can make a meaningful contribution to the attainment of modernization. It can be harnessed to diffuse attitudes and ideologies required for the adoption of modern technology and its associated values and organizational premises, to provide personnel to operate and sustain the programmes of modernization, and to create capabilities for adaptation and origination of new technology.

MODERNIZATION AND INSTITUTIONAL EDUCATION

Researches have been conducted in West and India about the role of educational institution in bringing about modernization. Most of them have shown a positive correlation between the two. However, Saunders in his study *Education and Modernization* in Brazil has found that it undermines modernity.

He remarks: "Brazilian schools, especially at the primary level where their impact on personality development is greatest, tend to stiffle rather than develop the personality traits on which modernization depends, and from which the society must draw its innovators."

Lerner in his research work *The Passing of Traditional Society; Modernizing the middle East* (1963), on the basis of his study with adult samples of six developing countries, asserted that literacy is the basic personal skill underlying the modernization process. Joseph A. Kahl in his research, *The Measurement of Modernizm: A Study of Values in Brazil and Mexico* (University of Texas Press, 1968), pointed out significant correlation between education and modernization.

Reporting results of the Harward's project on the social and cultural aspects of economic development, covering Argentina, Chili, India, Pakistan, Israel, and Nigeria, Inkeles concluded that, "Education is the most powerful factor in making men modern."

In their study based on five national probability samples of adult age, 20 and older, drawn from the USA, Finland, Japan,

Mexico and Coastarica, Waisanen and Kumata, concluded positive correlationship between education and various indicators of modernity.

Examining the immediate effects of schooling on people's modernity, Armer and Youtz concluded, "Western education leads to the modernization of perspectives in traditional, non-industrial societies." After a study of 591 seventeen year old males in Kano City in Nigeria they maintain, "Western education does, indeed have a definite effect on value orientations of youth that is largely independent on test factor."

This has been collaborated by S.L. Sharma in his work *Modernizing Effects of University Education* published by Indian Council of Social Science Research in 1979. This conclusion has been again supported by articles in a special number of *International Journal of Comparative Sociology* (1974, XIV, 3-4). In this special number, researches conducted independently in various parts of the world, showed remarkable uniformity in concluding that schooling promotes attitudinal modernity in developing societies.

Besides the relation of schooling and modernization researches have been conducted about the effect of higher education on modernity. Williamson studying university students in United States, Germany, Japan and Columbia are at the concluded that while Americans and Columbians are at the conservative end, Japanese are on the other end of the scale of rationalism-traditionalism developed by Kahl.

Similar researches were conducted by some other notable sociologists in the West including Silberman (1970), Greer (1972), Smith and Inkeles (1966), Sack (1973) etc. In India studies concerning schooling and social change were conducted by A.R. Desai (1952), G.S. Bhatnagar (1972) and Margaret L. Cormack (1961).

Cormack made a full length study of Indian students concerning social change. She concluded, "They are not considering values, attitudes and attitudinal change. They are concerned with certificates, degrees and employment."

Thus, Cormack maintained negative correlation between higher education and social change in India. She found little evidence of change orientation among her respondents. Similar conclusion was reached by B.V. Shah (1964) in his study *Social*

Change among College Students of Gujarat (Baroda : Maharaja Shivaji Rao University). Y.B. Damley in his study *College Youth in Poona,* however, found some positive correlation between higher education and individuation, a trait of modernization. But he himself admits, "It is not study of the general body of students. Therefore, no generalizations can be drawn about the nature of the student's behaviour or thinking."

M.S. Gore, I.P. Desai and Suma Chitnis found encouraging evidence of the relation between education and modernization. According to them, "The state, sex and educational level of the respondents were all important variables in determining the modernity of student sample."

Similar conclusion was reached by Malik and Marquette in their study *Changing Social Values of College Students in the Punjab.* They concluded that, "...an overwhelming majority of Punjab youth favours the abolition of such traditional institutions and caste and untouchability and strongly approves of a general social revolution in India."

In his book *Education in Social Change* Sullivan found that, "Factors other than experience at a particular training college appears to be operative in changing the students outlook towards traditional social practices."

The latest study in this connection was however made by Dr. S.L. Sharma published by ICSSR (1979) under the title *Modernizing Effects of University Education.* On that basis of a study of 3437 students in the 34 teaching departments of Punjab University during the academic year 1973-74, Dr. Sharma reached the following important conclusions concerning the relationships of modernization and education:

1. The level of higher education is of no consequence as an explanatory variable of student modernity.
2. There is the lowest percentage of moderns in the humanities, followed by social sciences and professionals with the highest percentage in the science faculty.
3. Males are more modern than females.
4. High status students are more modern than low status students.
5. There is a significant and positive correspondence between level of student modernity and that of their reference teachers, provided the latter preferred character-building role, over other

roles, favoured no social distance in their relations with students and reported greater interpersonal interaction with students.

6. There is a weak though positive relationship between years of hostel exposure and modernity's course.

7. Age is found to be inversely related to student modernity. Boys out scored girls in modernity.

8. Caste has no bearing on modernity.

9. A significantly larger percentage of high modernity cases hails from medium size families with 4 to 6 numbers.

10. Family type has no association with modernity.

11. Socio-economic status of the family has significant though weak positive relationship with modernity.

12. Father's education and occupation are only weakly related to student modernity.

13. Father's income has moderately strong positive association with modernity.

14. There is no relationship between parental modernity and student modernity.

15. Students with early urban background are not more modern than those with rural background.

16. Those who have lived longer in urban setting are more modern than those with fewer years of urban dwelling.

17. The initial exposure to cosmopolitan city like Chandigarh makes not much difference in modernity.

18. Duration of urban exposure is positively associated with modernity.

19. Early residential background and modernism of the city have no influence on student modernity.

20. There is a significant and positive relationship between media exposure and modernity.

21. There is a strong positive relationship between extent of exposure to other cultures and level of modernity.

22. Constant exposure to other cultures significantly increases the negative effect of education on modernity.

23. The convent and/or public school educated students are more modern than the government/and/or aided school educated.

24. The type of schooling is the best predictor of modernity with the convent or public school educated being most modern.

25. Early socialization variables account for greater variance

in student modernity than the later socialisation variables.

26. Developmental variables are more powerful than structural variables in explaining student modernity.

27. Educational variables, particularly schooling background, tops the list of explanatory variables.

On the basis of the above conclusions Dr. S.L. Sharma points out inverse relationship between the level of higher education and the student modernity. He gives the following reasons for this surprising fact:

1. The present higher education stresses mere transmission of information to the neglect of inculcating ability to think for one self. It stresses mere skill acquisition to the neglect of generating this position, for skill formation. It neglects character training and stresses mere certification for white collar jobs.

2. The system of higher education in India lacks an articulate social ideal.

3. The present educational system has not changed in the life of goals set by the Constitution of free India.

4. The present system of education is not a source of characterological transformation.

5. The course content of the present higher education does not lead to modernisation.

6. The cognitive and value content in conjunction with the social context of the present higher education is not relevant to the cultivation of modernity.

7. Our teachers are not so modern as to influence the student. They are not interested in character building and social training. They are unsure of what the community expects from them. The persistent authoritarian orientation limits the power of teachers to act as agents of student modernity.

8. The objective conditions in our educational institutions such as overcrowded classes, low teacher-pupil ratio, impersonal character of teacher-taught relationship, render the task of change orientation on the part of the teacher the more difficult. Small classes are better for such influence than large and unwieldy classes.

9. The lack of freedom for the teacher to design his own courses restricts considerably his potential for induction for social changes. In the words of Dr. S.L. Sharma, "Our teachers thus presented a case of double failure as socializers of student

modernity; first, they lacked strong modernity orientation, and second, they failed to modify their role orientations so as to bring them in line with modern norms."

10. The extra academic component of campus climate restricts its relevance to modernity.

11. Routinization of educational experience is a possible reason for the failure of higher education as a modernizer.

12. The overgrown structural format of higher education is a significant reason for its failure to modernize.

13. The built-in traits of present higher education such as under emphasis on the value element in its course content, are responsible for its poor performance.

Dr. Sharma suggests the following three objectives as the aims of higher education to make it a better instrument of modernization:

1. To prepare skilled manpower for a developing economy;
2. To re-socialize people in the values conducive to socio-economic development; and
3. To inculcate in man a creative self-awareness, an ability to think for himself and a sense of critical judgement.

He suggests that three areas should be particularly modernised: the reorientation of the content, the recasting of the teaching-learning nexus, and improving the quality of education. The quality of early education should be improved. Group extra-curricular activities should be encouraged. A secular-relational and egalitarian man should be created.

To conclude, "Besides providing the highly skilled manpower to a technico-industrial economy, higher education in our view can lay down the foundation of socio-economic development in the following ways: (1) by imparting to the younger generation the requisite psychological dispositions which are regarded as helpful for development; and (2) by instilling in students a reflective ability and a capacity to make rational decisions.

TWO PATTERNS OF MODERNIZATION

In his paper 'Social Change and Educational Policy' published in *The Sociology of Education in India* (NCERT, 1967), Professor A.R. Desai accepts two patterns of modernization of a traditional society pointed out by Don Martindale—exogenous and endogenous. He defines these two patterns by pointing out that, "An exogenous factor is one arising outside the social system, and endogenous is one arising internal to the social system."

Both these factors initiate and shape social change. They determine the nature of leadership and its basic aim. These in their turn determine the objectives of education, the structure of the machinery of education, technical and other means of spread, the allocation of finances of education and the nature of personnel executing it.

POST-INDEPENDENT SOCIAL CHANGE

In contrast to the social change undergone by Indian society during the British rule, the following social changes occurred in post-independent era, exhibiting further modernization.

1. The Constitution declared all citizens to be equal.

2. The State was governed by quasi form of federal constitution with a strong Centre and weak State units.

3. The Indian Constitution introduced fundamental rights and the rights in the Directive Principles of State policy.

4. As the new State aimed at general welfare, it created a massive network for the purpose at Central, State and local levels. The educational facilities were expanded in all directions. A new demand for education particularly technical was created. More communication with foreign countries stated.

5. *Planning*. The Congress Government adopted five year plans with certain important characteristics:

   1. Planning was divided into Public Sector Projects and Private Sector Projects.
   2. The State reserved large scale enterprises for manufacture of necessary goods and amenities.
   3. Manufacture of consumer goods was left to private enterprises.
   4. Agriculture was left in private sector.
   5. Trade, regulated by the Government was left in the private sector.
   6. Financing and money lending was in the hands of individuals or private institutions.
   7. Most of the goods were sold and purchased in the open market.

8. In place of barter system, monitory basis of exchange was adopted.
9. Taxation by the Government was mainly indirect.
10. A major source of finance for the plans was foreign aid.

The above characteristics of planning under the Congress Government show capitalist social system. This was however, on the modernised level, while under British rulers it was on colonial basis. This system however does not suit democracy. Democracy under it becomes plutocracy or oligarchy.

Democracy requires education, social security and employment. All this requires enactment of welfare legislations by the State. It is the duty of a welfare State to provide for the minimum needs of all the citizens. Therefore, most of the thinkers have not supported capitalist system for any underdeveloped country.

As Prof. Marshal has pointed out, "In the twentieth century, citizenship and the capitalist class system had been on war." The Indian Government adopted a mixed economy based upon capitalist system. As Prof. A.R. Desai has pointed out, "The relevance of this point is that the educational system is a part of a wider social system and operates to provide techniques, skills and values which would equip the individual to perform efficiently his adult role in this system."

Since India has been a feudal society, therefore, the Government will have to make special efforts for the establishment of a democratic society. Realising this responsibility the Indian Government framed a new educational policy after independence. This policy had the following characteristics:

1. Concurrent subject. Though in theory, education is a State subject, in practice it is concurrent since and Central Government provides a major portion of finance and other facilities. Therefore, both the Central and the State governments play important role in determining educational policy and its expansion in the country.

2. Diversification. Every modern country requires diversification of educational courses and institutions to provide for a wide variety of specialists, scientists, engineers, doctors and others. Therefore, the Government has undertaken the development of vocational institutions particularly. The institutions for the growth of science are mainly grown by the State help while liberal education is partly financed by the State.

3. Expansion of special education. In every country some part of population lags behind others. These are the handicapped, the retarded, the backward class which require special help and incentive to develop along with others. The Indian Government has, therefore, adopted social education and other special categories for education for the educational advancement of the women, the backward classes, the poor and the mentally and the socially handicapped.

4. Educational finance. Education is a stupendous task. Therefore, neither public nor the Government alone can meet its expenses. Hence, both the private and the public sectors are providing for it. Primary education is mostly governed by Local Self-Government bodies. Secondary education and college education is generally supported by individuals and private trusts. The university education, however, is particularly the responsibility of the Government. Vocational education is also supported by the Government. This is helpful in planning the needs and the supply of trained personnel for planned development of the country.

5. Medium of instruction. Mother tongue has always been and still is the medium of instruction at the primary level. At the secondary level, Indian languages have substituted English after independence. The Central Government and the Indian Constitution have declared Hindi as the national language. Besides, 15 regional languages have been recognised for development.

However, English remains the superior language as it is the medium of technical, scientific and higher education in India everywhere. This has given rise to an English speaking elite class which is separated from the general masses. This is a serious hindrance in the establishment of a democratic society in India. In spite of all Government help and vocal incentive to Hindi and other regional languages, English has grown by leaps and bounds in the last several decades and the present Government, having a young leadership of Doon educated leaders, is set to make English defacto *lingua fanca* of India. It is still the language of administration and economic transaction in most of the parts of the country. It is almost the sole medium of instruction in Engineering, Medical and Higher educational institutions in India.

So long as this trend continues the gulf between the elite and the masses will be further widened. In fact, whatever may be the avowed aim of the Indian leaders, practically capitalism of the West type is fast growing in the country. The society is again returning to the old feudal types in new garbs. The public still respects money, power, high breed, the *Rajas* and the *Nawabs*. This has been clearly demonstrated in the recent elections to the parliament. Seasoned politicians were defeated by Rajas and film stars. And this trend is bound to increase its pace.

Whatever may be the criticism of English as a medium of instruction the number of English medium primary and even secondary schools are growing fast everywhere. There is a scramble in the moneyed section to get their children educated in public schools and in foreign countries as far as possible. The Hindi text-books and general books have no sales in comparison to English textbooks and general books.

Therefore, literature in English language is growing fast and the literature in Indian languages is lagging behind. The students educated through the Indian languages blame their parents for their handicap and face frustrations almost everywhere. The most strange phenomenon we witness today is that even in Indian Parliament an influential section of leaders communicate through English. All these trends are anti-democratic and not in favour of national interest though some might hail them as modernization.

Therefore, there is no wonder that thoughtful persons have severely criticised the present educational policy of the Government. It has been rightly suggested that the administration should be transacted in regional languages. The regional language or the national language alone should be the medium of instruction of primary and secondary education.

The higher education should be limited to few on the basis of merit and they may be given a training in English so that higher education may not suffer. As most of the Indians do not study beyond higher secondary level, therefore, this step will create a wider democratic base. Again, if every child will have primary and secondary education through the mother tongue, he will find himself nearer to the general masses and class distances will be minimised.

However, whatever may be the rationality of these suggestions, the fact is that English as the medium of instruction is being more and more accepted at the primary and secondary level. There is a demand of English medium primary and secondary schools everywhere, however, costly they may be. Clearly, this is a trend towards Westernization.

However, modernization requires democratization on indigenous basis and not aping of the West. Therefore, if India has to be a twenty-first century nation, as aimed at by the new Government, a nationalist policy of education has to be planned and rigorously followed.

QUESTIONS FOR ANSWER

1. What is modernization? Discuss its characteristics. How far education leads to modernization?
2. Explain the impact of modernization on educational institutions.
3. How far education during British period led to modernization?
4. Describe modernization through education in India after independence.

26

Role of Mass-Media in Education

With the development of science and technology 'Information Explosion' is taking place and mass-media instruments such as radio, television, internet and computer are in close reach of common man. Mass-media has effected the personal, social and national life of individuals because their programmes do influence the viewers. Some of the programmes are educative too.

IMPORTANCE OF MASS-MEDIA

Due to "information explosion" and "population explosion", more things are to be learnt and more people are to be taught. There is a cry for "more education to more people in less time." Here educational technology consisting of various media of mass communication are essentially required.

As both qualitative improvement and quantitative expansion of education are facilitated and accelerated with the help of mass media under educational technology, it has come to our rescue to tackle this problem. There are a good number of media for mass communication such as radio, television, newspapers and films etc.

Previously, the mass-media were only put to marginal and individualised uses. There was neither any coherent thinking nor a scientific organisation of these materials in the educational process. Today due to interest and initiative of certain teachers, their use has increased.

A piece of information or knowledge is communicated to us through the communication. This message of great importance, because the same piece of information when conveyed on a printed page or over the telephone, by radio, or television appears different and has entirely a different effect on us.

The effectiveness of piece of information depends upon the medium through which it is imparted. The mass-media is also the massage. It massages the sensory organs and stimulates them to respond actively. It is very important for classroom teaching as a part of the process of instruction. It improves the teaching-learning process. Its main purpose is to benefit more students with fewer teachers or to obtain quality education.

Therefore, the mass-media have entered into all the structures of daily life in the world of today. It is being used as a means of education. To sum up: its role in education is gaining importance every day.

1. Mass-media provides information to the mass within less time.

2. It takes a wide coverage of information regarding what is happening in any corner of the world.

3. It brings the entire world to the individual or to the classroom. Children spend hours together sitting in front of the television and can visualise, hear and acquire knowledge about the world.

4. It easily reaches groups, allows repeated use, gives more reality, influence attitudes, shows cause and effect relationships and ultimately motivates the audience.

5. It sends information to remote places and helps in distant learning.

6. It helps in modification of attitudes, inculcation of desirable values and acquaintance with cultural heritage.

7. It acts as an agency of social change.

8. It is useful for reinforcing group dynamics and interpersonal communication.

9. It is a means of communication to make ideas clear to the children and help them to acquire knowledge. It helps in simplifying and in giving vividness to explanation.

10. It makes the instruction concrete.

11. It stimulates interest and exits curiosity.

MASS-MEDIA IN EDUCATION

"Education today, therefore, has a far greater responsibility than it had ever before. It has to meet the demands of a dynamic world which change its character every day.

Contemporary education has to be more comprehensive and complete than it was ever before. The role of the various agencies of education like home, society, community etc. has consequently increased, so the role of the mass-media like television, radio, cinema, newspaper has increased."

Press, radio, motion-picture, television, etc. are mass-media in education. These are technically called passive agencies of education. They indirectly influence the attitude and behaviour of the people. They cover entertainment, informatory propaganda, historical record, education and improvement of moral judgement and moral tone of people. Following are the role of some important mass media:

1. RADIO

Radio is used mainly to broadcast events to far and wide places of the world. Radio acts as the medium of mass-communication. It is also an important source of entertainment. Students listen various talks, discussions and debates from radio which are extremely important and useful for them.

Many programmes are broadcast over the radio especially for the purpose of teaching. Thus, radio acts as a great recreational and educational force. It broadcasts scientific and cultural facts. It enlightens public opinion. It stimulates curiosity and interests.

The radio is a valuable supplement to class teaching and learning. Educational broadcasting is a new experiment which is catching on well. Expert teaching in such diverse fields of science, social studies, art, music, languages, politics, current affairs and other areas, can provide information and enrichment for pupils and for the teacher through school broadcasts.

Educational programmes broadcast by expert teachers with effective methods demonstrate new ideas and approaches to classroom procedures. In collaboration with the experts, programmes are especially designed for different age groups in the schools.

Advantages

Following are the advantages of using radio as mass-media in education:

1. "Listening participation" in current history. In radio the emphasis is on sound, rather than on picture. Therefore, many programmes are broadcast over the radio especially for the purpose of teaching. Special events and occurrences in the world are immediately brought from the source into the classroom.

An educational programme may be preceded by an introduction by the class teacher and followed by long discussion among students on the subject-matter under the guidance of the teacher. Thus, the teacher requires to have pre-broadcast and post-broadcast discussion. Through radio a talented teacher may teach the students. Important happening—elections, inventions, political developments in other countries and other current topics may be heard and discussed in the classroom.

2. Effective means of presenting music, drama and appreciation. Various talks, debates and discussions held over the radio are extremely informative and useful for the school children. Different items of the school subjects can be presented in the form of dramatised programmes.

Educational radio excels through dramatisation, dialogue, musical features and other creative programmes not possible in day-to-day classroom teaching. School concerts, folk and classical music, drama and discussion programmes of school, local or from other states are broadcast for listening in other schools in India.

3. Team-teaching demonstrations. The radio provides opportunity for student participation in various programmes such as quiz competitions, travel talks, plays, stories, development of lessons, projects and work programmes in the form of team teaching demonstrations arranged by the combined efforts of the best resources in consultation with the specialists and some other subject experts.

While accomplishing the programmes subject content, curriculum validity, suitability for age groups and teaching methods are kept in mind.

4. Participation of local teachers and pupils. Well-planned radio broadcasts are presented to engage the active participation of the local teachers and pupils. Before broadcast time, there should be preliminary study and discussion on the topic.

Through broadcast suggestions the class may be encouraged to carry on follow-up discussion, projects or creative activities. Before presenting the programme, the teachers and the pupils should prepare material thoroughly. They should utilise all possible resources make a very high quality programme from the point of view of content, speech, style, audibility and presentability.

5. Making learning an open system. Educational radio can offer corrective programmes for self-learning by the individuals. Breaking all boundaries and constraints of formal education it can reach the participants while at work, at play, at drawing room, at recreational centres. It has reached villages and is now available in every corner of the society.

There is more emphasis on learning through various mass media, since learning directly from the teacher is minimal and there is increasing stress on a system of open learning to overcome the rigidities of formal education. Educational radio broadcasts play an important role towards a system of open learning.

The non-formal approaches of educational radio supplement the movement for de-schooling society. Its programmes lead to a learning society where everybody can learn at any time, at any place.

At present, radio is not only one of the popular mass-media, but also a potential instructional tool in the formal, informal and non-formal education. It is laying more emphasis on the planning and production of science programmes in both the formal and non-formal spheres of educational broadcasts.

In most of the stations there are special programmes for teacher and teacher educators intended to familiarise methods of teaching on account of large changes in school curriculum and methodology particularly in subjects like science, mathematics. These services have been more necessitated in recent years in Social studies and English.

Secondary School Broadcasts help students and teachers by giving up-to-date content knowledge and providing new approaches and methods of teaching. However, a few non-syllabus programmes are broadcast in order to break away from the stereotyped formal education, for doing away with monotony in the curricular topics and to stimulate awareness and curiosity, in order to reduce wastage and stagnation at the primary school stage.

Primary school programmes have recently assumed greater importance by making the school situation more attractive and interesting. With its vast resources, the radio can organise a series of programmes to bring universalisation of primary education and promote adult literacy.

These programmes are related to education, health, hygiene, nutrition etc. bringing the audience into the mainstream of national life.

As an effective medium radio has occupied a significant place in communication. It is also playing an important role in education. It informs, as well as inspires. It inculcates values and virtues and creates attitudes, interests and appreciation.

2. TELEVISION

Television is an extremely popular source of entertainment among youngsters today. They listen and see the instruction of the speaker from the television. Therefore television is the most important and powerful agency of mass-communication. In it news items are not only read out but the events are also shown. Not only problems are discussed but practical remedies and solutions are also suggested.

There are programmes especially for the school children aimed at educating them and instilling good moral values. Through dances, short-films on historical places, museums etc. television can give an idea of the history of country. Thus, television plays a vital role as a means of mass-media in educating the masses.

Advantages of Educational Television

There are many advantages of educational television. By watching the television, the young people get a good idea about how it really happened. For example, the students can see for themselves how science has advanced by watching the nuclear explosion or the launching of rockets programmes.

Following are the advantages of educational television:

(1) It is capable of making available many so far inaccessible learning experiences.

(2) It brings about continuing co-operative planning by teachers, supervisors, learning materials experts and skillful production teams.

(3) Good and effective educational television broadcasts help in the outgrowth of curriculum planning offer occasion for analysis and of the selection of this most appropriate instrumental media.

(4) A variety of audio-visual aids, motion pictures, film-strips, slides, recordings, drawings, maps and other projected and non-projected aids are demonstrated through television. Video-tapes and recordings on television show us the launching of space rockets, and happening of political and social events.

(5) It brings us a new kind of vision.

(6) It acquaints the children with literature, history and social life.

(7) It motivates both children and adults as it is not only educating but also entertaining.

(8) Televised-lectures are thrilling and entertaining to the listeners not only verbal information and the introduction of the speaker but also the whole of his personality.

(9) National problems like those of population explosion and poverty and illiteracy are highlighted and discussed on the television.

(10) It plays an important role in education of the children on the history and culture of our country. It provides an idea of the history of the country by telecasting various programmes through dances, short films on historical places, museums etc.

(11) As a means of mass-media in education on the masses, television plays a vital part. It is a dynamic medium which influence education. It is based upon fundamental, mental psychological principles of learning. These apply to all successful programmes of learning.

Development of Educational Television

1. Starting educational programmes. A General Conference of UNESCO held in New Delhi in 1956 desired for the development of educational television in India. Experimental television service was started with the objectives of "experimentation, training and evaluation" as a part of the UNESCO Project.

A series of social education programmes were telecast in collaboration with UNESCO during 1960-61. The National Fundamental Education Centre and Indian Adult Education Association, New Delhi evaluated the nature as well as impact of these programmes. Regular T.V. Service was inaugurated in Delhi.

Launching of the 'Krishi Darshan' programme for farmers on 15th August, 1965 was a landmark in the history of television.

2. Installation of TV sets in school. In India, TV Sets were installed in secondary schools by 1985. The experiment of all these projects were significantly beneficial, enlightening and interesting.

3. ETV. After 1982, the use of educational television increased at a rapid rate. Tremendous progress has been made in use of educational television in India. Benefit of ETV programmes were extended to number of students in different subjects like Physics, Chemistry, Hindi, English, Geography and current affairs, as the number of schools equipped with TV sets increased.

4. SITE. Inaugurated by Smt. Indira Gandhi the then Prime Minister of India at Ahmedabad on the 1st August, 1975. The famous Satellite Instructional Television Experiment (SITE) was implemented during 1975-776.

How TV programmes could be telecast with the help of a satellite called ATS-F loaned by the National Aeronautics and Space Administration (NASA), USA. These TV programmes were related to Education, Agriculture, Health, Family Planning, National Integration and so on. Rural population was selected as the target audience for this project.

The scheme was implemented in three districts—Dhenkanal, Sambalpur and Phulbani in Orissa. The scheme was effective in educating the rural people in Andhra Pradesh, Bihar, Karnataka, Madhya Pradesh and Rajasthan.

5. INSAT projects. As India decided to have a Satellite of her own to utilize the INSAT capability for educational development, the Ministry of Education initiated action for preparing plans of operation as early as in July 1979. On the

30th January, 1980 a meeting was convened by the Ministry of Education to discuss the background and all connected issues involved in the satellite utilisation for radio and television programmes.

In collaboration with UNESCO, the Ministry of Education, Government of India convened National Workshop on Educational Broadcasting, at New Delhi from December 1 to 6, 1980. On account of the Nation's renewed emphasis on Educational Broadcasting on the eve of putting INSAT in the orbit, the workshop assumed special significance.

On 10th April, 1982 the first Indian Satellite, INSAT-IA was launched. With modified advanced technical equipment for the use of educational broadcasts through television, the second satellite INSAT-IB was launched on 30th August, 1983.

6. NCERT. Under the NCERT, the Central Institute of Educational Technology at New Delhi, is mainly concerned with the development of innovations and with using various media in school education using television through INSAT has developed an attractive system of education to reach in and out of school children and teachers in rural areas.

It produces ETV programmes which are being telecast via INSAT. In order to implement the INSAT for education project effectively, State Institute of Educational Technology (SIET) has been set up in six states such as Andhra Pradesh, Bihar, Gujarat, Maharashtra, Orissa and Uttar Pradesh.

ETV in Orissa

In the INSAT states Andhra Pradesh, Bihar, U.P., Gujarat, Maharashtra and Orissa, Education TV programmes are telecast for five days in a week for 45 minutes per day during the school hours. A recent study carried out in Orissa by the CIET has brought out that only in 15 per cent of the cases, there has been successful utilisation of the equipment.

All INSAT states were expected to create state Institutes of Educational Technology (SIET) to function autonomously but only Orissa has taken a decision on the creation of SIET Institute. A building for SIET has been constructed at Bhubaneswar. 118 posts for Academic & Production, Engineering and Administration have been released by the Government of India. However Technical and professional posts have remained unfilled in the existing institution.

In Orissa, more emphasis is given to the production of ETV programmes for the children in the age group 5-8 and 9-11 years and teachers of primary schools. The ETV Programmes of Orissa are being telecast for 45 minutes starting from 10.30 a.m. to 11.15 a.m. with 5 minutes for change over.

There are three Advisory Committees, one at the state level for the entire INSAT project another for ETV Programmes and the third one at the district levels. Three districts namely Dhenkanal, Sambalpur and Bolangir in Orissa were selected for ETV programmes through the INSAT. Now more districts like Cuttack, Puri and Balasore are being included in the scheme.

After the expiry of INSAT-IB and the failure of the INSAT-IC. At present ETV programmes are being telecast via INSAT-ID since 1990. The INSAT is a challenging National project and its experiments inter alia, with television programmes provide new light and insight into the viewing problems and conditions of the rural audience deprived of modern sophisticated media.

3. THE PRESS

Reading matter has vast potentialities. It exerts good influence on the individuals. It acts on the intelligence and emotions of the individuals in shaping out attitudes and philosophies of life. The Press covers the printed matter including books, magazines, journals or newspapers.

An educated individual has an open kind, a general awareness and knowledge of the world around him. His field of knowledge is vast and varied. Press gather events, and also present their own views on issues. The reader gets an opportunity to consider an issue from many angles. The knowledge of History, Geography, Science, Literature etc. is supplemented by the newspapers.

By means of the press through newspapers and other journals it is possible to link certain topics with everyday life. It makes pupils aware of what is happening in the world around them. Thus, the press renders an important service to education by imparting knowledge of current affairs to pupils.

News regarding earthquakes, cyclones, new planets and political changes is brought to the notice of the pupils by the press. It provides a great ideal of historical information. Press may elaborate and enhance the pupil's limited knowledge of history. It serves as one of the important medium of education and instruction.

4. THE MOTION PICTURES

Motion pictures exercise great influence on human mind. They create lasting values in the pupils. Educational films meet the challenge of commercial pictures, supplement them and explore new avenues of educating children and adults. They provide reality, influence attitudes, show cause effect relation and motivate the students. Thus, they exercise great instructional force to be used intelligently in the class-room.

Many areas of learning can be wisely dealt with the help of films. One can use these motion-pictures in teaching of geography or science. Topic such as rivers of India, climate of India etc. can be taught effectively with the help of the motion pictures.

Advantages of Motion Pictures

1. They make a concept more clear, durable and realistic.
2. They arouse interest in pupils and satisfy their emotions.
3. They present abstract, and abstruse problems of life and nature in concrete reality, illuminate the hidden meanings of events and mysteries of nature, reconstruct history in a short mirror of life.
4. They bring the past, the distants to the class room. They bring the whole world to the classroom.
5. Events occurring over-days appear in seconds.
6. Through them they can be replayed many number of times when and where required.
7. They can be used for demonstration of skills and experiments.
8. They can serve the purpose better, if they are made for specific age and ability groups.
9. They can be fitted into the school syllabus, if the commentary is simple and straight forward.
10. They can be of great service in teaching the backward children, because they act on their imagination.

PRINCIPLES OF USING MASS-MEDIA

1. Organisation. Mass-media should be organised as an integral part of the educational programmes. They should not be separated from other curricular activities.

2. Selection. Mass-media should be properly selected and co-ordinated by the teacher. An experienced and trained teacher may select the mass-media according to the needs of the students.

3. Planning. Mass-media should be adjusted according to the need of the instructional programme. The teachers should possess skill in its use. They should have special training. All this should be properly planned.

4. Experience. Mass-media should be related to pupil's experience.

5. Preparation. While there should be adequate preparation on the part of pupils, the teacher should prepare himself before using it. He should know what the mass-media teach and where they fit into his plan of teaching. Adequate preparation should be followed by proper presentation and an adequate follow-up.

6. Evaluation. In regards to their use, effect on learning and their functions mass-media should be evaluated at regular intervals.

In classifying oncepts, stimulating group and individual activities developing a collective critical awareness, changing attitudes, imposing a new structure or organisation on certain subjects and encouraging originality and creativeness. Mass-media have proved of help in education.

As we know, good teachers are not born, they are made. Training in the methods, techniques, use of various mass-media help a teacher to be good and efficient. Teacher should be properly motivated and made interested in the use of mass-media. They should be trained and oriented in the adequate use and maintenance of the materials.

QUESTIONS FOR ANSWER

1. Discuss the role of mass-media in education in India.
2. Which is the best mass-media of education? Give arguments to support your choice.
3. Write short note on Educational Television in India.

27

Education for Democracy

Democracy is universally accepted as the pro-people form of government, because it is based on people's will, hence, it works for social good. India is a parliamentary democracy, hence our education should aim at making democracy to work well which is only possible if citizens understand their democratic rights and duties and also exercise them in national interest. Such citizens are to be produced through education.

BASIC ELEMENTS OF DEMOCRACY

According to Sir Stafford Cripps, "By democracy we mean a system of government in which every adult citizen is equally free to express his views and desires, upon all subjects in whatever way he wishes and influences the majority of his fellow citizens to decide according to those views and to implement those desires."

As far as the definition of a democratic state is concerned, the above definition is quite appropriate. But, as Dr. S. Radhakrishnan pointed out in his University Report, democracy is not merely a political system but a way of life which affords equality to every one, irrespective of the differences of race, religion, sex, economic status. This equality implies equal freedom and equal rights.

In fact, democracy is a very comprehensive concept which can be interpreted in three ways—political, social and economic. The creation of democracy depends upon the extent to which the ideals of freedom, equality and brotherhood can be concretized in all the three spheres.

Before going on to a detailed discussion of democracy in these three spheres, it is necessary to clarify these three fundamental elements.

1. Liberty. Liberty is a prerequisite of the success of democracy. John Stuart Mill attached the greatest importance to the liberty of the individual. But liberty does not imply complete wilfulness, for, freedom is not absolute but subject to control imposed by the individual's owned conscience.

Liberty implies the freedom given to the individual to develop his own abilities as he thinks best, without being conditioned or restricted by any external factor. But the freedom of a large number of people is possible only then no single individual has unlimited power and no individual misuses the rights given to him.

2. Equality. If democracy is to be successful it is necessary for every individual to be socially, politically and economically equal. Generally speaking, no privileges or special should be given to any class of people in a democracy. But equality also does not imply a deliberate neglect of individual differences between one person and another.

Stated more accurately, equality actually means an equality of purpose, because equality cannot be used as the basis for ignoring differences between individuals. Lord Haldane was quite correct when he said that one cannot make all people equal because nature is far too powerful. While one woman is born beautiful, another is ugly, and this creates great differences. One man is born with remarkable intelligence, while another is remarkable for the lack of it.

Thus the concept of equality should be abandoned, for it has governed the minds of people long enough, with little good effect. In democracy it is perfectly practical to give certain privileges to a backward class of people in order to give them an opportunity to raise themselves to the levels of others, but all such efforts should be exceptions, not the rule. In this way, offices in the administration or government should be open to all those who have the abilities and qualities required for such jobs.

Every adult should have the right to vote. Every individual

should have the opportunity to get employment which will bring him a wage sufficient to allow him to live well. Unemployment, famine and such conditions can prove fatal to democracy.

3. Fraternity. It is important to achieve the ideal of brotherhood in a democracy because this is the only way of removing the psychological obstacles to democracy. The real difficulty lies not in the establishment of a democratic government but in the creation of a democratic society, to which democratic government is but a means or agency.

Brotherhood is the chief characteristic of a democratic society, and cooperation the basis on which members of such a society work together. If a democratic society is to be created it is essential that every effort be made to increase brotherhood and cooperation.

G.D.H. Cole is correct when he says, "A democrat is someone who has a physical glow of sympathy and love for anyone, who comes to him honestly, looking for sympathy and help; a man is not a democrat, however justly he may try to behave to his fellow men, unless he feels like that."

Hence, the establishment of a democratic society requires a complete change in the ideas, personalities and patterns of behaviour of the people. And for this all these people must develop totally. It is difficult even to conceive of democracy in the absence of a liberal mind, sympathy, love, consciousness of social responsibility, a high character and a developed personality.

ASPECTS OF DEMOCRACY

Following are the important aspects or are as of democracy:

1. Political democracy. As already has been pointed out earlier, the three ideals of democracy have to be translated into reality in the political, economic and social spheres. It is, therefore, important to understand these three aspects.

In its political aspect, democracy can be defined in the words of Lord Bryce, "Democracy is the form of government in which ruling power of a state is legally vested, not in any particular individual or class but in the members of the community as a whole." In a democracy, legally even individual is equal, because law and justice are the same for everyone.

Although a democratic government is the representative of the majority, it takes care to protect every right of the minorities residing within its territories. Every individual has complete right to think as he chooses and to express his opinion. Citizens are not discriminated against on the basis of sex, race, religion or any other ground which distinguishes them from others.

2. Social democracy. In its social aspect, democracy lies in emphasis upon equality and brotherhood between all individual. In the worlds of Dewey, "Such a society must have a type of education which gives individuals a personal interest in social relationship and control, and habits of mind which secure social change without introducing disorder."

The social feeling of a democratic society is best expressed in Kant's famous moral formula, "So act as to treat humanity whether in thine own person or in the of any other, always as an end and never as a means." From this principle Kant derives the practical suggestion, "Try always to perfect thyself and try to conduce to the happiness of others, by bringing about favourable circumstances, as you cannot make others perfect."

The democratic individual, therefore, functions as one member of a special government of ends. And this system of ends is the state of democratic ideals. As Kant puts it, "Act as a member of kingdom of ends."

Implicit in this is the notion that one should treat oneself and every other individual as something having inherent value, one should act as the member of a state in which every person treats the good of another as no less valuable than his own good. In such a state or country, all the others should also behave so that everyone is not a means but an end. Everyone should endeavour to promote the good of another while trying to achieve his own ends.

3. Economic democracy. The economic aspect of democracy comprehends the rights of individuals to economic independence and quality. In democratic societies all individuals have the right to earn wealth without interfering in or obstructing the rights of other people.

This liberty to earn wealth is limited or restricted by the right to equality because, despite the freedom to earn and accumulate wealth, no individual in a democracy has the right to control the means of production in such a way that his possession may obstruct the economic freedom of other people or his wealth may create a chasm between his position and that of others. In order to maintain the right to equality, all democratic societies enact legislation in order to protect the rights of the working class or backgward classes.

Democracy is opposed to capitalism and it does not approve of excessive economic differences between individuals. Because it beilieves in brotherhood, democracy is opposed to any kind of economic exploitation.

NEED FOR EDUCATION IN DEMOCRACY

Aldous Huxley has remarked, "If your aim is liberty and democracy, then you must teach people the arts of being free and of governing themselves." Democracy can never be successful, it has been because of the lack of education. In a democracy the government is composed of the elected representatives of the people and if the people are uneducated they can never elect the right leaders and consequently can never create the right kind of government.

In fact, it is impossible even to hope for democracy in the absence of education. It is difficult to expect a citizen to behave responsibly if he is not even aware of his rights and duties. Bertrand Rusell has commented, "Democracy in its modern form would be quite impossible in a nation where many men cannot read." The truth of the matter is that education is a prerequisite of democracy. Only after proper education should the citizen be invested with his democratic rights.

Fichte, the German philosopher has commented, "Only the nation which has first solved in actual practice the problem of educating perfect men will then solve the problem of the perfect men, will then solve the problem of the perfect state." Although Fichte made this comment in the context of autocratic states, it cannot be doubted that the perfection of even a democratic state can be judged only by the extent to which it contains educated people.

Hetherington puts it, "Democratic government, at least, demands an educated people." Throwing light on the objectives of education in the 1949 meeting of the Universities Commission, Dr. Radhakrishnan stressed the fact that the democratic state recognises the importance of the individual, and it is the process of development of this individual which is called education.

Hence, education is absolutely necessary for establishing a democratic society. Dewey has pointed out that democracy is inconceivable without education, because education can generate and instill the qualities which democracy demands as a prerequisite.

Philosophers of the ancient Greek city state were aware of the significance of education. Both Plato and Aristotle laid stress on the importance of education for the success of democracy. Earnest Barker comments, "To Plato education was the most important function of the state and the department of education the most important state department which was particularly advocated for producing the philosopher kings to improve the men's minds for becoming virtuous being."

Plato, in his famous text, *The Republic,* stressed not only the importance of education for democracy but even formulated a plan for the education of men and women which made all kinds of development—physical, mental, moral and aesthetic—possible.

Aristotle was of the opinion that the aim of the state is to make possible the achievement of the highest moral level and this can be reached through education alone. Thus, education is the most important function of the state. From one point of view, the state itself is a school in which the individual learns citizenship, for Aristotle suggested that the aim of education was to produce good citizens.

These truths were known not only to the ancient Greeks but also to Indian thinkers of ancient times. India has been the home of democratic ideals and principles from ancient times. Hermitages and places of worship were used as schools in which the sages tried to produce ideal citizens who could become useful members of society.

But the modern age needs democratic education far more than was needed in ancient Greece or ancient India because modern democracies are so vast and their problems so complex that the education of citizens is even more imperative today.

IMPORTANCE OF EDUCATION IN DEMOCRACY

This importance of education for a democratic state is fairly evident from the foregoing account. The following things can be stressed in this connection:

1. Knowledge of rights and duties. If democracy is to be a success, it is essential that every citizen should be aware of his rights and duties because only then he can take active and productive part in the affairs of the state. This knowledge of rights and duties can be obtained only through education. Education socializes the individual so that he develops consciousness of duty.

2. Development of humane qualities. If the ideal of brotherhood is to be achieved by a democratic state, it is necessary for it to develop humane members. Kant's moral concepts, quoted earlier, throw important light on this. Only through education can such qualities as a high moral character, sociability, benevolence, patience, pity, sympathy and brotherhood, etc., be developed in the individual.

3. Faith in democratic ideals. In order to make democracy a success, it is essential that its citizens must have faith in the democratic ideals. And this can be brought about only when they are adequately educated because it is only the educated person who realizes that the sole purpose of life is not the satisfaction of gross physical desires.

The ideals of freedom, liberty, brotherhood, are more valuable and necessary. No one but the educated individual can understand the circumstances and needs of another person before passing judgement on him. Only such a person can accept the ideal of equality after recognizing human values as being the end to be achieved.

4. Fulfilment of political duties. In a democracy the government is elected by the people, and hence the responsibility for electing a good government devolves upon them. And, if the people are unable to understand their political rights or to fulfil their political responsibilities, it is foolish to hope for a democratic government.

This ability to recognise where one's duty lies can come only through education. Educated people can properly assess the qualities and shortcomings of the various individuals who are fighting the elections, and of the various political parties and their plans and policies which they profess.

In India, the absence of education is a big handicap in

creating a truly democratic state because during elections the ignorant people are persuaded to vote for the wrong person, with the result that the governance of the country has failed time and again. Corruption is rampant.

The Mudaliar Report points out that if democracy is anything more than voting blindly, then every individual must accept the task of independently thinking about all social, political and economic problems before deciding upon the party he wishes to support. But this is possible only when the entire electorate is educated to think independently.

5. Protection and transmission of culture. In any state, ideals can be achieved only when change is accompanied by a parallel continuity, and this continuity with the past is maintained only through culture, the social heritage, which is passed on the new generation through the medium of education. Hence, education is also required for transmitting culture of future generations and for protecting it.

6. Preventing exploitation. The ideals of democracy are opposed to exploitation of every kind, but if political, social and economic exploitation is to be eliminated from society, it is essential to have universal and compulsory education.

In its absence, the rich and powerful people will never give up their advantage and habit, while the poor will never become sufficiently conscious of their rights or their ability to organize together and counter this exploitation.

Educated people in a country are aware of their rights and they have the intelligence and training to fight exploitation or violation of their rights. Hence, education is the only real foundation on which democracy can be based.

EDUCATION FOR DEMOCRACY IN INDIA

All these important aspects of democratic education hold true in India also. India is not merely a modern democratic state but a country which is traditionally inclined towards democracy. A democratic constitution was adopted after independence.

In 1938, Jawaharlal Nehru had said, "The Indian Constitution seeks to establish a popular government in the country on the basis of democratic principles outlined earlier. For this every citizen must participate in the administration, through his right to vote and to be elected. Every individual is guaranteed and given equal status and opportunity because no one is discriminated against on the basis of religion, race, caste, community, sex, or on any other grounds. The government is responsible to the people and its elected representatives.

In order to achieve this objective of democracy, education is as necessary in India as anywhere else, a truth which the Indian people have been quick to realise. In the words of Dr. F.W. Thames, "Education is no exotic in India. There has been no country where the love of learning had so early an origin or has exercised so lasting and powerful an influence. From the simple poet of the Vedic age to the Bengali philosopher of the present day there has been an uninterrupted succession of teachers and scholars." Not only did the Indian Constitution accept the ideals of democracy, it considered education the prime responsibility of the state.

In Article 45 of the Constitution it has been stated that every state must arrange for the provision of free and compulsory education to all children upto the age of 14, within ten years of the date of inception of the Constitution. After the achievement of independence, a new phase began in the history of education.

Articles 29 and 30 of the Constitution give fundamental rights to every individual in connection with education and cultural development. According to article 29, every Indian national living in any part of India will have the right to maintain his own specific language, script and his culture. No person can be refused right of admission to any educational institution, established by the state, by reason of religion, race, caste, language or any other similar consideration.

According to article 30, every minority community will have the right to establish and maintain educational institutions of its own choice, irrespective of whether the minority is a linguistic or religious one. The state will also not refuse aid to any such institution created by a religious or linguistic minority.

Articles 45 and 46 determine the policy for education as part and parcel of the directive principles. According to article 45, the state will make every effort to provide free and compulsory education, within ten years, to every child below the age of 14.

According to article 46, the state will pay special attention to the educational and economic interests of all backward classes, especially the scheduled castes and scheduled tribes. It also entrusts the state with the duty of protecting such tribes from social injustice and exploitation of every kind.

The Indian Constitution laid the foundation for a federal government in which the functions of the state and central government are distinctly defined. Both the central and state government have some duties with respect to education. It has been realised that there must be coordination between the central and state authority on education for a balanced development of the country.

The modern Indian state is a welfare state whose objective is the complete development of its people. This welfare can be achieved only through education. Little surprise, therefore, if all the leaders of the nation stress the importance of education as a first step to improving the future of the nation.

VIEWS OF SECONDARY EDUCATION COMMISSION

The democratic ideals which the existing educational policy is trying to achieve the outlined most precisely in the Secondary Education Commission's explanation of the objectives of education:

1. Development of democratic citizenship. The success of democracy depends largely upon the people's awareness of their rights and duties and the extent to which people fulfil their responsibilities. Education aims at developing this ability in the people, because education teach the man to think and distinguish between right and wrong. He can understand social, economic and political issues, and reflect on the possibility of solving such problems.

He can decide upon the political party or the leadership which should be entrusted with the task of forming a government and undertaking administration. He does this after thinking of the problems facing the country and considering the ability of each group of leader to face such problems. He can express his ideas and suggestions through lectures, essays, articles etc.

He can organize new movements or constitute various kinds of committees to solve the problems facing the country. It is the duty of the state to insist upon a syllabus which can be expected to generate such democratic awareness among the children being educated.

*2. **Training in skilful living.*** Democracy can be said to have succeeded only if it can translate the democratic ideals to its society. And, for this, socialization of the individual through education is essential. It is desirable to develop such social qualities as collective feeling, cooperation, discipline, tolerance, sympathy, brotherhood, etc. in the individual.

Education must also aim to create faith in social justice and the willingness to rebel against injustice. Education helps in adjusting to each other, and the educated individual is generally tolerant and liberal. Although he may differ from other people in their opinions, he has the ability to adjust to such people because he can understand their attitudes.

Hence, education is the only means of removing the obstacles in the path of democracy, and also of achieving some adjustment between people who differ from each other in respect of language, race, caste, religion, sex, etc.

*3. **Development of personality.*** The success of a democratic society also depends upon whether mature men and women form the majority or minority in its population. Democracy can succeed only if most of its members heave developed mature personalities, because a mature person has gone through physical, mental, social, ethical and spiritual development. Hence, education should (aim) at the development of all aspects of the educands' personality through various kinds of training.

Keeping this in view, most schools and colleges now provide many kinds of extra-curricular training, which supplements all that is taught as part of curriculum.

*4. **Developing vocational skill.*** The Secondary Education Commission has pointed out that another aim of education is to develop some vocational skill in the educand. No nation can progress in the absence of economic progress.

The first duty of the state is to provide a system and means of education which imparts some vocational and professional skills to the educands so that they can earn their livelihood at the same time as they contribute to the nation's economic growth. The country urgently needs skilled craftsmen, engineers, doctors, teachers and administrators.

For this, specialized colleges are required. Every child should be given the right to choose a profession of his own liking, and he should be given the opportunity to acquire the highest training and education in his profession.

5. Developing leadership. The success of a democracy depends upon the capabilities of the leadership. The democratic government is a decentralized government, and for that reason it requires skilled leadership at many different levels of administration.

The democratic government is run by the elected representatives of the people, who should be possessed of special qualities. Expert leadership is required for development and progress in every sphere—political, social, economic, artistic, scientific and cultural.

Education should aim at evolving such leadership, because without doing this education cannot make any real contribution to democracy, for, then it is leaving unfulfilled one of its important responsibilities. The element of leadership can be encouraged through many kinds of curricular and extra-curricular activities in schools and colleges.

Apart from these objectives of education laid down specifically by the Secondary Education Commission, it is desirable to reflect upon some other objectives, which have significance in view of the fact that India is a democracy. In fact, the aims of education vary a little bit with the level of education—the primary, secondary and university education—a fact which has been recognised by the different education commissions established from time to time.

The aim of education, at the primary level, is to develop the child's mind by presenting the fundamental elements in the various areas of knowledge, and also to give him an opportunity to develop all his abilities—physical, mental, moral, motor, creative imagination, etc.

At this stage attention should be paid to physical development no less than mental development, but attention must also be paid to the burden such an education places on the child. The education imparted should not become a burden.

At the secondary level, attention should be focused on discovering the interests and abilities of every adolescent, and then developing such abilities.

Education should be concerned not merely with the general welfare of society but also with the self-realization and personal development of each individual.

RECOMMENDATIONS OF INDIAN UNIVERSITIES COMMISSION

The Indian Universities Commission has laid down the following objectives of university education in the country:

1. Providing leadership in politics, administration, professions, industry and commerce;
2. Training and intellectual leaders of culture and creating inventors;
3. Causing spiritual development in the educands;
4. Protecting the culture and civilization of the country and instilling the youth with the ideals of this culture; and
5. Discovering the inherent qualities of individuals and developing them through training.

Development of Emotional Integration

For the success of democracy, education must have an additional objective of promoting emotional integration among the citizens of this country which has an unlimited variety of races, tribes, languages, religions, communities, etc. Without this the ideal of brotherhood cannot be realized. Besides, such a situation also encourages the growth of disorganizing and disruptive forces which hinder the country's growth.

Promoting Internationalism

Addressing the Indians leaving the country and going abroad, Pt. Jawahar Lal Nehru said that Indians did not have to go to far away lands in search of a rich past, for such a past existed in India. Indians went abroad in search of a present, a search which was absolutely essential because living apart from others in the modern world implied backwardness. The old world has changed, the old bonds have been destroyed and life is becoming steadily more international.

Nehru told the Indians that they would have to play their part in this increasing internationalism, and if they were to make success of it, it was necessary for them to live in close contact with the world. They must go to all parts of the world, travel to the remotest corners, meet other people and learn to live with them.

It is, therefore, necessary that Indian education, particularly at the university level, should seek to create a feeling for internationalism. UNESCO, the international organization, has laid stress on education for international adjustment. Speaking to the American Committee for teacher's training colleges in Chicago in 1956, Walter H.C. Lewis, the former director general of UNESCO said, "In education for international understanding we should try to promote a comprehension of the way of life, the values and the aspirations of the world."

For the development of internationalism it is essential that members of every nation must rise above the considerations of nationalism and culture and learn to appreciate the cultures, values and life patterns of other people. Liberality of mind is very desirable.

Actually the democratic ideal which exists within the bounds of one nation is not different from the democratic ideal comprehending the entire world. Both are based on tolerance and liberality, and both stress the importance of liberty, equality, and fraternity.

PREREQUISITES FOR DEMOCRATIC EDUCATION

In India, it has been recognized everywhere that education must have the foregoing objectives for the success of democracy, although one is aware of the absence of any concrete step in this direction, upto the present. In order to achieve a higher level of democratization in the educational pattern, it is essential to pay attention to the following things:

1. Efforts must be made to put an end to the discrimination practised in educational institutions established by religion. The selection of educands, the appointment of teachers, the fashioning of the syllabi are all apparently influenced by caste and communal considerations. All such things must be prevented. The state should penalize all such institutions by refusing them grants and other financial aid to compel them to give up such undemocratic practices.

2. Regional considerations and affiliations are also seen influencing the selection of candidates and appointment of

teachers in many parts of the country. Such practices cannot be prevented without the intervention of the central authority.

3. Arrangements should be made for the teaching of Hindi, the India language, and English, the international language, in addition to the languages being taught in each region and state. Some people oppose the teaching of English while others are averse to learning Hindi.

But it must be realized that Hindi is essential for developing nationalism while without English we cannot participate in any movement for internationalism. Both of them are important for achieving the democratic ideal, and it is to be regretted that the centre gives little evidence of clear thinking on the issue.

4. The syllabi at all levels of education—primary, secondary and university levels—need to be reformed in order to lay greater emphasis upon democratic tendencies through the proper teaching of history and geography. Democratic tendencies should be actively encouraged.

5. In most Indian schools and colleges, the working conditions and pay scales of teachers are far from satisfactory. Few universities provide sufficient facilities for research and higher studies. Appointments of teachers are made more on the basis of personal considerations than on the actual merits of each individual. So long as such conditions are allowed to exist, there is little hope for democracy. Hence, it is desirable that the government should study the situation, punish the culprits and provide more facilities for teachers and research enthusiasts.

6. In order to achieve the objectives of nationalism and internationalism, students and teachers should be given facilities for domestic and foreign travel, because such facilities are practically non-existent at present.

7. At each level of education, the educand should be acquainted with ancient Indian culture and knowledge. Little has been done in this direction so far.

Improvements in Syllabi

If democratic ideals are to be achieved, the syllabi at every level need to be drastically changed. Following things should be considered in this connection:

1. Wide based syllabi. In order to achieve the democratic ideals discussed earlier, and also to achieve the comprehensive development of child's personality, it is desirable that the syllabi at the primary, secondary and university levels should be wide based. The educational pattern in India has been evolved after keeping this point in view but it is regretted that the shortage of means has made implementation difficult.

2. Variety and flexibility. At the various levels of education, the curriculum should be flexible and varied, not rule-bound and rigid. This is desirable, because only then can the curriculum accommodate the brilliant as well as the average educands.

At the secondary and university levels, this is all the more essential because the syllabi must provide each educand with reasonable choice for selecting subjects that he would like to study. It must also be flexible in order to permit some minor adjustments according to the level of educands studying it.

3. Based on local requirements. India is a large country with a remarkable variety of race and tribes, languages and dress, etc. The syllabi should take into account local requirements. It would be better to give primary education to the children residing in different parts of the country in their respective mother tongues.

At the secondary level and later at the university, the educand should be given an opportunity to learn both Hindi and English. Ignorance of English will handicap them and leave them ignorant of a very big chunk of knowledge.

4. Creating a social consciousness. The curriculum should invariably provide certain programmes which can be expected to create social consciousness and a desire for responsible community life. But this sentiment for community life should be in keeping with the sentiments of nationalism and internationalism.

5. Earning one's livelihood. The syllabus must include the teaching of subjects which the student can study and later on turn to account for earning his livelihood. In deciding the syllabi for the teaching of professional subjects, it is essential to keep in mind the situations the educand will be required to face in practical life and also the extent to which the present syllabus is helping to prepare him for those situations.

Improvements in School Administration

Another aspect of educational reform is introducing the following changes in the pattern of school administration in the country. The pity of it is that little if any work has been done in this direction.

1. More rights to teachers. Educators should have greater say in determining the policy of the school, in preparing the syllabus and in other matters pertaining to the school. The educator must experience a sense of being free from shackles so that he may be able to work enthusiastically.

2. Greater freedom to educators. Educators should be given greater freedom in framing the syllabus, in selecting the methods of teaching, studying, research, etc. Without freedom, little creative and original work can be expected. Only when the educators are given freedom to act and to think for themselves can they be expected to make new discoveries in contemplation, science, literature and art, etc.

3. Democratic environment in schools. Cooperation and brotherhood should form the basis of relations between teacher and taught, between the educator and the administrators or organisers of the school, between the vice-chancellor and the teachers of the university, etc.

The principle of equality should not be sacrificed in the name of discipline, for the latter is perfectly possible even when everyone is treated as equal. Defects should be removed and faults rectified democratically and liberally, not in an authoritarian manner.

4. Improvements in the conditions of the educator. The educator is also an important element in the teaching pattern, like the educand. The working conditions of teachers can hardly be said to be satisfactory in this country. Arrangements should be made for training them adequately, and their selection should be made on merit, not on personal considerations and whims of the powers that be. They should be encouraged to study further and go in for research work. Their scales of pay should be made equal to the scales of pay of people who are as well qualified as they are. Payment should be made on the basis of equal pay for equal work. Their work should be free from officious interruptions from the administrative staff.

Seminars and institutes should be organized from time to time in order to improve their efficiency by informing them of the latest discoveries in their respective spheres.

Improvement in Methods of Teaching

In a democracy, even the teaching methods adopted inside the school should be essentially democratic. In this connection, the following suggestions can be given:

1. Encouraging cooperation. All work should be done with the cooperation of the principal and the head of department, between the head and the educator, between the educator and the educand, and between one educand and another. This helps to evolve the sense of cooperation and sense of community so essential for democracy.

2. Stress on activity. According to John Dewey, one of the most famous exponents of democratic education is that the child should be taught by actually doing some action. By taking an active part in the process of teaching, the educand learns self-control, self-discipline and self-inspiration, all of which are essential for the success of democracy.

3. Independence. Liberty is the fundamental principle of democracy, and hence, the democratic method of teaching also has no place for any external pressures. It permits the educand to ask any questions coming to his mind, to express his own opinion and to make any criticism which suggests itself to him.

Democratic education aims at training this individual to think for himself. Great stress is placed on the child's independence in all modern teaching techniques, such as Montessori method, Project method, Dalton method, Heuristic method, etc.

In all such democratic techniques the teacher serves only as the guide whose task is to encourage, guide and direct the child who learns for himself and moves on the path of knowledge.

4. Based on all-round development. Teaching methods in a democratic society should be so designed as to promote and encourage development of every aspect of the child's personality. Care should be taken to see that no aspect is repressed, so that all-around comprehensive development becomes possible.

The democratic citizen would be handicapped by a lopsided

development of personality because it would render him unfit for performance of duties in one sphere or the other. In proportion to the greater rights given to a citizen in democracy, his duties and responsibilities also tend to be greater than those of an individual in some other society.

Hence, education must be so designed as to create such abilities in the child as self-dependence, self-reliance, dedication to duty, ability to fulfil responsibilities, etc.

Establishing Discipline

Discipline has special value in the democratic pattern of education because the educands passing through the phase of education have themselves to grow up and take part in administration. They have to consider the success of democracy. In other patterns of government, too much discipline and training in discipline are not quite so necessary.

The greatest discipline is self-discipline, it is self-control, it involves changes in one's own tendencies and desires, according to the demands of the community and the society. It is absolutely essential for the members of a democratic society to be disciplined. And this is possible only when school and university students are taught the lesson of discipline. In schools, the educator should be impartial in his behaviour towards all the educands. Most of the work of the school should be performed by the educands under the guidance and supervision of the educators.

Self-governing units such as students unions, students committees, and students parliaments should be created so that the educands may be trained in democratic activities and life. He should be able to take active and intelligent part in such activities. The educand's activities be hindered or obstructed by his own organizations and institutions, not by the official administered.

Social control will, thus, teach them to be disciplined. The teacher must prove himself to be a model of discipline. Even the state should avoid unnecessary interference in the working of educational institutions.

Finally, it can be said that only the voluntary cooperation of the educators, guardians and administrators can help to create a truly democratic environment in schools in which the educand can learn to be disciplined.

QUESTIONS FOR ANSWER

1. What shape does education take in a democracy as opposed to that in a totalitarian country? In what respects does the Indian system today need more democratization?
2. What role can education play in fostering, nurturing and strengthening our secular democracy?
3. What should be the role of education in developing democratic citizenship and bringing about national integration?
4. How can education help in developing democratic citizenship?
5. What should be the educational objectives in India in view of the emerging democracy in the country?
6. Write note on education for democracy.
7. (a) How can education for democracy be imparted in schools?
   (b) "Democracy without education is blind." Discuss.
8. What is Democracy? How does a democratic way of life depend on education?
9. Briefly expound the basic tenets of Democracy. How would you, as an enlightened teacher, try to promote it in the class room? Exemplify.

28

Freedom, Discipline and Responsibility in Education

While some educationists advocate full freedom to a child, others emphasise rigid discipline to be exercised over him during the period of his education. Therefore, this chapter is devoted to study this problem.

IMPORTANCE OF FREEDOM

Full freedom is essential for the full development of a child's individuality. Rousseau gave a clarian call of full freedom to the child for his self-development and advancement. In the absence of this freedom, a child's physical, mental, moral, artistic and spiritual development will not be possible.

In a controlled environment a child finds it difficult to act freely according to his interests and needs. He finds no interest in activities imposed upon him. Thus freedom inspires proper initiative, interest, fearlessness and sense of responsibility in a child.

IMPORTANCE OF DISCIPLINE

While freedom is essential to the full development of a child, discipline is equally essential and important. The advocates of discipline believe that unrestrained freedom develops a child in a haphazard manner and arbitrary ways without inculcation of human qualities so essential to modern culture and civilization.

Such child tends to be extremely selfish and aggressively self-centred.

His indisciplined and greatly selfish activities may lead a child towards inhuman and mischievous behaviour towards other fellow beings. Development of human and moral qualities are essential for a well-adjusted life. These traits make a child cultured and civilized. They help him in leading one's life happily and also contributing to the welfare and society.

Discipline is very essential to achieve this great aim. The raw instincts are sublimated into desirable qualities and habits of behaviour by means of discipline. It is very necessary for allround development of a child as well as fullest development of society.

Discipline makes an individual a dynamic, co-operative, sympathetic and tolerant citizen imbued with social ideals of service and sacrifice at the cost of his own self-interests. The sense of discipline creates such conditions in a school which promote desirable development of a child. In ancient times so much importance was given to discipline that it was regarded as an end in itself.

Both freedom and discipline are essential for the proper and fullest development of a child. Freedom and discipline are both based on two ancient philosophical doctrines. Freedom is based on Naturalism, while Idealism is the foundation of discipline. Naturalism and Idealism are two important ancient philosophies. Both have contributed a great deal to education.

Freedom upholds heredity while discipline advocates environment. One can neither deny heredity nor the environment. Freedom develops individuality while discipline raises personality. Sociology speaks for discipline while psychology lays stress on freedom. Individualism and sociability are also two important aims of education.

Both psychology and sociology are valuable sciences. Both have contributed a great deal to educational aims, processes and programmes. Hence, freedom and discipline are both equally essential and valuable. Both are mutually supplementary and complementary. One cannot exist without the other. They may be regarded as two sides of the same coin. What is needed is a synthesis of the two apparent different concepts.

Meaning of Freedom

'. Narrow sense. In the narrow sense freedom means

unrestrained free operation of the interests and impulses of child. A child does not possess a sense of discrimination between good and bad, proper and improper, right and wrong. He may avoid performing his duties and enjoy his rights arbitrarily. This may spoil him in various ways. He may go against national welfare, security and solidarity.

This will lead to social disintegration and national disaster. Unrestrained freedom creates all sorts of indiscipline and cuts across the qualities of self-discipline, self-control and self-restraint. It may lead to the destruction of social and moral values so essential to proper human development. Hence unbridled and uncontrolled freedom cannot be allowed to any child under any circumstances in the democratic age of today.

2. Wider sense. In its wider sense freedom advocates the principle of live and let live. If an individual desires his freedom to enjoy to its fullest extent, it becomes his bounded duty to respect and provide the same right of enjoyment to other fellow human beings also.

A child should be provided so much freedom that he develops his individuality as much as he can and enjoy happiness to his heart's content by indulging in creative activities according to his interests, inclinations, aptitudes and needs. Proper use of freedom is possible only when each individual allows the same freedom to think, feel and act to others also as he desires for himself. This will lead to the development of individual and welfare of society of which he is an integral part.

Meaning of Discipline

1. Discipline and order. (*i*) According to Rusk, order is the sate of affairs which we find in a family, section or class, while discipline means to keep one's tendencies and properties under submission and control, so that they work out according to set channels and forms laid down.

(*ii*) Order is concerned with only the present, while discipline is meant to regulate the whole life.

(*iii*)Herbert calls discipline as 'Zucht' and order as 'Ragie Rung'. According to him, the chief aim of education is to develop a child morally. For this he prescribes instruction and for effective instruction a high level order is essential. A good order can lead to a good discipline. Thus discipline is an end and order is a means to achieve that end.

To quote Herbart, "To maintain quiet and order in the lessons, to banish every trace of disrespect of the teacher is the business of government, direct action on the temperament of youth with a view to culture is training."

2. Discipline in a narrow sense. In its narrow sense, discipline means the repressionistic discipline in which the natural instincts, impulses and propensities of children are kept under control by force or compulsion. Children are not allowed to develop according to their interests, inclinations, abilities and capacities.

Under the spectre of fear and injury they are compelled to develop according to a pre-determined form. Great educationists like Rousseau, Pestalozzi, Herbart, Froebel, John Dewey and many others have raised firm and loud voices from time to time against such cruel, rigid and terrible form of discipline.

3. Discipline in a wider sense. In its wider sense, discipline means impressionistic influences and emancipatory activities. There is no place for any external force, fear and punishment. The teacher is expected to behave kindly, lovingly and sympathetically with the children keeping in view their needs and demands of society.

He should strive to structure an ideal, inspiring and conducive environment wherein children enjoy freedom to express themselves freely and are able to develop self-discipline and other desirable traits of conduct and character. Under self-discipline, a child will be able to discipline his bodily impulses and develop insight together with capacity for future development to higher and higher levels of achievement of human excellence and social advancement.

PHILOSOPHICAL THEORIES OF DISCIPLINE

In his book, *The Child's Path to Freedom,* Norman Macman and Adams in his book, *Modern Development in Educational Practices* have classified discipline into three categories according to various philosophical doctrines.

(1) Repressionistic Discipline.
(2) Impressionistic Discipline.
(3) Emancipationistic Discipline.

1. Repressionistic Discipline

(i) Meaning. Repressionistic discipline is based on the ancient doctrine of repression. According to Jermiah, a child is basically evil and mischievous. Hence, fear and punishment must be used to control and modify the child. Despotic rulers, in those days, used to enforce obedience through harsh, fearful and rigid laws. In the same way authoritarian teachers took recourse to very hard rules to enforce obedience and discipline in the class.

These educationists believed that to develop a child to a higher stage of life, it was essential to rigidly and absolutely control and modify his basic instincts into predetermined channels of thinking and behaving. Teachers in schools used the hardest and often cruelest means to enforce obedience and discipline among children. Their slogan was *spare the rod and spoil the child.* Such was the practice in Europe and India in old times.

(ii) Arguments in favour.

(1) There is no better medicine to educate a child than fear and punishment.

(2) Punishment can reform even the most mischievous child.

(3) Harshest punishment must be given to reform the indisciplined child.

(4) Fear of punishment keeps children away from unsocial behaviour towards others.

(5) Without fear there is no love. Hence a sense of fear must be inculcated in the child by the teacher.

(iii) Arguments against.

(1) Repression creates a feeling of hatred in the child. He becomes a rebel and more indisciplined.

(2) Constant fear and punishment scares away the child from education and he drops out.

(3) Repression creates mental complexes.

(4) Repression mars the normal development of a child.

(5) Repression creates forgetfulness.

(6) Fear may compel obedience in school, but not outside.

(7) Repression is the antithesis of freedom.

In a democratic set up, feelings of equality, fraternity and social justice are to be developed in children, which cannot be developed through repression. Hence, there is no place for repressionistic discipline in this age of democracy.

2. Impressionistic Discipline

(i) Meaning.

Based upon the philosophy of Idealism, the votaries of impressionistic discipline oppose any kind of punishment in education. They emphasize that to maintain class order, the teacher should exercise the influence of his personality. The teacher should try to structure a model environment before children by means of his own ability, conduct and character, so that they form a character of high order by imitation of the teacher.

Under the influence of the profoundly creative personality of teacher, the problem of indiscipline will not arise at all. The teacher should try to develop discipline by love, affection, sympathy and consideration towards such children by the examples of his own conduct and character.

(ii) Arguments in favour.

(1) The process of educational development goes on smoothly under impressionistic discipline because the relationship of teacher and children is based upon love, sympathy and regard.

(2) Children imitate the achievements of teacher and behave in a desirable way.

(3) Children develop normally and naturally as it is a mid way process between arbitrary freedom and authoritative repression.

(4) The concept of *prestige suggestion* is used in it to promote effective learning and growth.

(5) Impression promotes self-discipline.

(iii) Arguments against.

(1) Impressionistic discipline gives greater importance to teacher who is likely to develop sense of self-conceit and snobbery. He may consider himself to be the sole creater of a child's character which is likely to mar the development of both.

(2) As the child is not able to develop according to his own inherent nature, impression is worse than repression and emancipation.

(3) The child becomes a carbon copy of the teacher and thus loses his own mental freedom.

(4) The child becomes a blind follower of teacher. He loses the capacity of independent thinking, understanding, initiative

and self-assertain.

(5) It is difficult to find model teacher today.

In modern times such teachers are few in number whose character and conduct can be put before children as ideals and examples. Hence, impressionistic discipline remains an ideal far removed from realization.

3. Emancipationistic Discipline

(i) Meaning. The basis of emancipationistic discipline is psychological. Its slogan is freedom. Its protagonists agree neither with repressionistic nor with impressionistic concept of discipline. They believe in the inherent goodness of child. If free environment is provided for development, children will develop like flowers. Moral qualities will develop in them through a natural and divine process of growth.

Rousseau and Herbet Spencer acclaimed emancipatory concept of discipline as the best one. Children should be allowed full freedom to develop according to their natural tendencies interests and tastes so that they freely express their inner urges and develop themselves to the fullest extent possible.

(ii) Arguments for.

(1) As a child does all his activities freely and learns by doing and experiencing, the traits of self-discipline, self-reliance and self-dynamism develop in him naturally.

(2) As freedom is the birth right of a man, it is improper to impose restraints over the child and circumscribe his freedom.

(3) Emancipatory discipline leads to self-discipline in a suitable and smooth way.

(4) Emancipationistic discipline does not create any emotional complex in child. He remains mentally and physically healthy.

(iii) Arguments against.

(1) The innate tendencies of a child are generally animal instincts. If he is allowed to express his raw instincts, he will harm society in various ways.

(2) A child is incapable of distinguishing between good and bad. The interference of some mature person is essential to foster this capacity.

(3) Undue freedom may harm the child himself.

(4) Indentifying freedom with his rights only, a child becomes

indifferent towards his duties and obligations.

(5) Freedom often develops self-interest which in turn gives rise to indolence and indifference towards his responsibilities.

(6) A child is not born with the sense of self-discipline and self-control, which cannot be developed providing him all freedom in the very beginning. It is neither good to the child nor to the society.

Though a child needs freedom for proper development, this does not mean that he should be allowed freedom without limits and control. Only so much freedom should be given to a child as is essential for his development in the right direction.

SYNTHESIS OF FREEDOM AND DISCIPLINE

Thus, both freedom and discipline have their merits and demerits. Neither is right in its absolute narrow and rigid form. Unlimited freedom without restraints may develop a child to evil doing harmful to society and dangerous to the nation. Harsh and rigid discipline may mar a child's normal and natural development with the result that qualities of self-confidence, self-reliance, self-assertion together with initiative and problem solving capacities will not develop in the child.

Thus, both freedom and discipline are essential for proper and full development of personality. Both should jointly co-operate in the development process. A synthesis of impression and emancipation is to be achieved to develop self-discipline. Self-discipline is the bed rock of all developmental activities of the individual as well as the welfare of society.

PROBLEM AND REMEDIES OF INDISCIPLINE AMONGST STUDENTS

In mordern times one finds indiscipline in the classroom as well as outside.

Causes of Indiscipline in the Class

1. Lack of interest. As children in classroom do not get adequate opportunities to receive education according to their interests, they show inattention and indiscipline.

2. Formation of bad habits. As some children develop bad habits in the company of parents, family members, friends and class fellows, they indulge in indiscipline in various ways.

3. Unsuitable curriculum. In the prevalent curriculum, there is little provision for subjects connected with disciplinary habits. Thus, children do not take interest in studies. Thus the unsuitable curriculum is also responsible for the growing indiscipline and disorder.

4. Too much restrictions in the class. Some teachers employ terror and punishment tactics to enforce order in the class. They compel children to remain sitting dumb in the class. These rigid restrictions create reaction in the form of indiscipline as soon as the teacher is away from the class.

5. No attention to individual differences. In the collective teaching of a class no attention is paid to individual differences. Hence, children go astray and show indisciplined behaviour.

6. Unpsychological methods of teaching. Most of the teachers employ unpsychological methods of teaching with the result that children fail to understand to content and indulge in indiscipline.

7. Overcrowding in the class. Classrooms are generally so overcrowded that individual contact of teacher with each child becomes very difficult. Disorderly behaviour of children is a natural reaction to such situation.

8. Over competition among students of the class. When a teacher overemphasizes competitive spirit among children those who score more marks take to self-conceit and snobbery and those who do not do well become frustrated.

Both groups indulge in indiscipline with different motives and in different ways.

9. Lack of right type of teachers. As other considerations rather than merits and academic achievements play a greater role in the selection of the teaching personnel, incapable teachers are selected who are unable to control and guide children properly.

10. Lack of facilities for education. Absense of physical conditions of calss namely rooms of school, area of rooms, pure air, sun light, fans and furniture are responsible to make the educational process unwelcome and uncongenial. Indiscipline among children is often a reaction to the lack of aforesaid facilities.

Causes of Indiscipline Outside the Classroom

1. Poverty. As children from poor families suffer from wants to books, stationery, fees and other essentials of educational process, they remain worried and sometimes in desperation and react in an indisciplined manner.

2. Rejection by parents. When parents show a sense of indifference and rejection towards their own children who are mentally handicapped or physically ugly, such children develop a sense of revolt and revenge towards society in general and show indiscipline in schools and outside of schools.

3. Favouritism by parents. When parents show discriminatory attitude towards their children the favoured ones develop a sense of egoism and snobbery towards those who are less cared for and favoured. Children of both the groups show indiscipline in different manners according to their feelings of hatred and revolt.

4. High ideals and parents. When parents, authoritarian in attitudes and votaries of absolute ideals, force their children to follow those ideals against their wishes, such compulsion generates mental complexes exploding in indisciplined activities.

5. Wrong locations of schools. When schools are located in crowded localities and market places, the effect of these situations is obvious. Outside activities distract the attention of children and they indulge in indiscipline as an unavoidable reaction.

6. Miserable economic status of teachers. When the economic condition of teachers is miserable, they try to supplement their meagre income by tutions or other forms of work. Dejection and fatigue make their teaching lifeless resulting in indiscipline on the part of children.

7. Low social prestige of teachers. Today the respect and recognition is directly correlated to economic status and material plenty. As teachers are economically unsound, they do not receive respect from the rich parents. While children of well to do parents behave in an indisciplined manner, poor teachers keep quiet. Other children also copy this indisciplined behaviour.

8. Schools as teaching shops. Schools of today are teaching shops where knowledge is sold to those who pay. Thus, no ideal is followed with the result that children indulge in various forms of indisipline.

9. Lack of moral education. As there is no provision of moral education in our educational system of today, children fail to discriminate between right and wrong. Lack of moral education leads children to evil habits and indiscipline.

10. Lack of co-curricular activities. Participation in co-curricular activities satisfies the emotions and impulses of children in a healthy ways. As our system of education ignores these activities, impulses of children find indisciplined and undesirable outlets.

11. Impact of political associations. Political parties use students for their political gains teaching them all sorts of indiscipline and disorderly behaviour.

12. Wrong system of examination. The present system of examination is often lures children towards copying and other underhand means to pass out. The success of these unfair means provokes others to take resort to them and thus indiscipline is created.

13. More students, less teachers and limited number of rooms. While more and more children are coming to schools for education today, classrooms are very few and teachers are also not in sufficient numbers. Overcrowded classrooms, overcrowded campus, less free periods and over burdened teachers create chaos, disorder and indiscipline.

14. Pressure of student unions. Student unions in all educational institutions create problems for teachers and administrators leading to open and violent confrontations.

SUGGESTIONS FOR MAINTAINING DISCIPLINE IN SCHOOLS

To remedy the problem of indiscipline in schools of today, W.P. Shoring has advocated three types of disciplinary activities: (1) Constructive, (2) Preventive, and (3) Remedial.

1. Constructive Discipline

Following suggestions should be kept in mind to achieve constructive discipline or self-discipline in a normal and natural way:

(1) Do not prescribe taboos and don'ts to children.

(2) Moral education to children should teach them their duties together with their rights.

(3) More opportunities should be provided to children to participate in co-curricular activities.

(4) Co-operation of children should be sought by persuation

for every work in the school.

(5) Full respect should be accorded to the individualities of all children.

(6) Teachers should try to understand the interests and needs of children and try to meet them as much as possible.

(7) The ideals and traditions of school should be in conformity with the constructive discipline.

(8) The personality of teacher should be so effective as to exert the wholesome influence on all children

2. Preventive Discipline

Following suggestions are relevant to achieve preventive discipline concerned with those restrictions which prevent the indisciplined behaviour of children:

(1) Teacher should know all children of the class by their names.

(2) The teacher should keep an eye over the whole class while teaching.

(3) Seating arrangements for children should be comfortable.

(4) Inattentive children should be warned and pulled up.

(5) Interesting methods of teaching should be used.

(6) Behaviour of teacher should develop in children a sense that the teacher is their well wisher.

(7) Children disturbing teaching should be psychologically dealt with to make them co-operate in the work.

(8) A child should not be harshly treated and pulled up before others because it injures the self-respect of the scolded child.

(9) Teacher should be serious from the start of the session. Laxity in the beginning may spoil the future attitude and behaviour.

(10) Teacher should stand at the head of the class and should not move about unnecessarily as movements distract attention.

(11) School campus should be kept neat, clean, tidy and attractive.

3. Remedial Discipline

Remedial discipline means to reform the child. It requires (1) diagnosis or understanding the cause of indiscipline, and (2) treatment or removal of the causes of indiscipline. Following suggestions may be given in this connection:

(1) Defaulting children should be isolated from others till they are reformed.

(2) They should first be given opportunity to explain their conduct and their explanation should be patiently heard.

(3) They should be clearly told about their guilt and they should not be compelled to apologize at the beginning of talks.

(4) Punishment should be awarded to them after due deliberation and decision.

(5) The talk about their guilt should cease after the award of punishment.

(6) The guilt of a child should not be discussed before others.

(7) The whole class should be warned if the guilty child is not found out.

(8) Guilt of one should not be generalized and no punishment should be given to the whole class.

(9) Help from his parents and guardians should be solicited for reforming a child.

(10) Guilty child should not be severely scolded.

(11) Guilty child should not be laughed at.

(12) Small mistakes should not be taken as indiscipline.

(13) Punishment should be proportionate to the guilt.

(14) Help from senior teachers should be sought when a teacher fails in the task.

(15) Remedy should be made clear to the guilty child.

(16) The teacher must know the background of the guilt.

(17) Full investigation should be made by the teacher before the award of punishment.

(18) If the guilty child has done some good deeds, he should get appreciation for them.

(19) Full precautions should be taken after punishing the indisciplined child so that there is no repetition of the guilt.

(20) All the remedial measures should be well-understood by the child.

QUESTIONS FOR ANSWER

1. Explain the narrow and wider concepts of freedom and discipline. How can a synthesis between the two be established?
2. What are the causes of growing indiscipline among students? Give your own suggestions to remedy these tendencies.

29

Education and Nationalism: A View Point

All human beings belong to society, similarly they also belong to a nation or state and thus alike social responsibility they have to perform some national duties, but in the present day world nationalism is commonly an out-dated philosophy because according to some intellectuals, it hampers internationalism. Yet there are other intellectuals who say that unless someone is nationalist, he cannot be internationalist, therefore, this chapter is devoted to study this subject from Indian viewpoint in respect of education in particulars.

WHAT IS NATION?

Nation can be defined as that human group which lives in an area with clearly defined geographical boundaries, united by common traditions, common interests and common sentiments, possessing a desire for unity and common political ambitions. Elements which go to make up the nation are of two kinds—the objective and the subjective. Among the six elements are—geographical unity, unity of language, unity of race, a common religion, political unity and independence.

According to Renan and Mill, it must also possess consciousness of a glorious past, feelings of pride and shame, happiness and pain, common experience and sacrifice, true glory, allied to this past. The chief among these emotive elements are common interests and traditions, common political ambitions, and most important of all, a community feeling, or we feeling.

CONSCIOUSNESS OF NATIONALITY

Community feeling or we feeling is such an important constituent of nationhood, that MacIver has defined nationality in terms of this feeling. He defines nationality as a kind of community feeling that has its origin in certain historical circumstances, and which is also strengthened by such strong common psychological factors that individuals who experience it, desire to form a specific and even an individual government of their own. Oppenheimer has commented that consciousness of nationality makes the nation.

NATIONALITY AND EDUCATION

This consciousness of nationality is generated in the younger generation through education, and hence, there is a profound relationship between nationality and education. In India, when the revolt against the British government was awakened, all national leaders demanded the formation of a national educational programme.

They argued that the educational programme of the country should be modified to suit the requirements of the nation. In 1921, Mahatma Gandhi expressed his views on this subject in *Young India,* criticising the existing educational pattern introduced by the British people. He too demanded that the educational pattern must be modified to suit the demands of the nation. His reasons for adding manual work to education were sound since he knew that education must in pay its own way in a poor country like India.

Rabindra Nath Tagore conducted an experiment in Shantiniketan to produce a novel kind of human society in which the problems of the individual and the community, the nation and the world, could be solved simultaneously.

Swami Dayanand insisted upon reforming education to suit the educational pattern that existed in ancient times. On the other hand, Annie Besant's educational plan, which included the establishment of primary schools, lower middle schools, higher middle schools, high schools for general education, high schools for general science, commercial schools, technical high schools, agricultural high schools etc., was more directory in touch with the problems of contemporary India.

Madan Mohan Malviya established the Hindu University at Kashi in order to realize the ideals of education which prevailed in ancient India. In addition to these individual and specific efforts, all other educational philosophers of the time, including Sri Aurobindo, Vivekanand, etc., favoured the modification of the educational pattern in order to make it conform to ancient Indian values, ideas and thinking.

In more recent times, in his report of the Universities Commission, Dr. S. Radhakrishnan pointed out the defects of the existing pattern of education, and suggested that it should be refashioned to fulfil national needs. It is only because of the feeling of nationality that most educationists have objected to the use of English as a medium of instruction in the country. Every one has stressed the need for education to be a character building process, because without this the future of the nation will always remain dark.

Dr. S. Radhakrishnan has said that the future of the nation is made by character. No country can be great if its inhabitants have low characters. If we want to create a great nation, we must educate our young men and women in such a manner that they should possess the force of character. We must have men and women who see themselves reflected in other human beings. This has been said in our sacred texts.

Stressing the need for an education for nationality the Kothari Education Commission has said that the objective of our system of education should be to develop national consciousness. For this, we must develop the knowledge of our cultural heritage, but we must also submit this cultural heritage to revaluation. At the same time, we must have faith in the future towards which we are moving.

DEVELOPMENT OF NATIONALISM IN THE NEW GENERATION

Following suggestions can be given for generating nationalism in the younger generation:

1. Development of a national language. The first prerequisite for developing nationalism is the development of a national language in the country. In India, this position can be occupied only by Hindi. When the succeeding generations learn Hindi and use it, the feeling will gradually take root that India is one nation.

*2. **Development of a national literature.*** Development of a national language will lead to the development of a national literature. With the propagation of Hindi in every part of the country, a new literature will be created, which will be read everywhere. Apart from encouraging national unity, it will also enable the people to create a literature which encourages national power and protects the cultural heritage of the country.

*3. **National educational programme.*** In India, the spread of education is the responsibility of both the central and the state governments but as yet, it has not been possible to formulate a national programme of education with the result that one can see considerable disparity in the various parts of the country.

In order to evolve a feeling of nationalism, the country should have unified educational programme which should be flexible enough to take within its purview the differences that exist between one region and another. This will lead to a certain similarity in the education in all parts, and make possible the application of a single curriculum through which national literature on the all India scale can be created.

*4. **Observance of national festivals.*** The feeling of nationalism can also be strengthened by enthusiastic observance of national festivals, independence day, republic day, children's day, teacher's day and the birthdays of all great men.

*5. **Respect for national symbols.*** Another way of fostering the feeling of nationalism is to generate and show respect for national symbols such as the national anthem, the national flag, the national bird, etc. Now-a-days the national anthem is played after every film show and people are required to stand at attention to show their respect for it. This also helps growth of national sentiment.

*6. **Improvements of curriculum.*** In order to help the development of the national sentiment, it is desirable that the teaching of history, civics, etc., should be conducted in such a way that it helps national sentiment. This can be done by preventing the publication of any material in text books and other media of publication which hurts national sentiments and pride. The government seizes all copies of such material and punishes the publishers and authors.

*7. **Cooperation of political parties.*** It is impossible to generate nationalism if the political parties fail to cooperate. Many political parties not only hinder the growth of this sentiment, but actively engage in activities calculated to harm the national interest. Such political parties owe their allegiance to other nations, show no respect for national symbols and spread anti-national feelings among the people. As far as possible, political parties should be prevented from indulging in such activities.

*8. **Cooperation of teachers.*** Education for nationalism can never be really successful without the active co-operation of teachers. For this reason the educators must themselves possess this feeling, because then they can set an example for the educands. It will then be even easier to foster the national sentiment among the younger generation.

SYNTHESIS OF NATIONALISM AND INTERNATIONALISM

Now-a-days many thinkers object to the use of education for fostering the national sentiment because they have come across many bad effects of narrow nationalism in many countries and seen that education for nationalism has stood in the way of the growth of internationalism.

The education for nationalism that was given in Italy and Germany, for example, was completely opposed to internationalism. It is in connection with this one-sided education that Bertrand Russell pointed out that children are taught to exhibit complete devotion and worship to the state of which they are citizens. The lesson taught to them is that worship of the state consists in doing as directed by the state.

For this, they are taught distorted versions of history, politics and economics so that they should not be critical of the blind national faith expected of them. They are acquainted with the evil actions of other nations but not of their own, although the truth is that each nation has been unjust to other nations. It is unquestionably true that if the facts of history are distorted in order to propagate the sentiment of nationalism it is undesirable. But this danger is not peculiar to nationalism alone.

It is true of almost all human relations that as they become deeper and stronger they also become narrower, and that they impede the growth of any liberal attitude. If, for example, an individual has intense love for his family, this may come in the way of his loving his nation, but this does not imply that love for nation can exist only at the cost of love for family.

Proper and healthy love for the family does not impede love for the nation, it helps it to grow. In the same way, healthy nationalism also does not preclude the possibility of internationalism.

As Dr. Louise has said that it is essential to strengthen one's love for one's motherland, but this does not make it proper to violate the cannons of humanity, for the external benefit of one's own nation. It is obvious, therefore, that education must not only propagate nationalism but must also encourage internationalism. The plan for national education presented by such eminent educationists as Mahatma Gandhi, Sri Aurobindo, Vivekanand, Rabindra Nath Tagore, etc. has kept this in view, that nationalism and internationalism should grow harmoniously.

That is the reason why Rabindra Nath Tagore's Shantiniketan turned into an ideal institution for education in internationalism. According to Tagore, the educand's aim is to reach the level at which there is no distinction between nationalism and internationalism.

OBSTACLES IN THE DEVELOPMENT OF NATIONALISM

The progress and growth of nationalism in India is being impeded by certain elements and obstacles, the more important ones among which are the following:

1. Casteism. Casteism is the most restricted form the narrow interests. As a result of this, not only the country but even Hindu society has been fragmented into small pieces, each one of which is concerned only with preserving its own interests, without caring for those of other groups.

In the presence of this casteism, nationalism is a far cry. Even the unity of the Hindu social organisation is difficult to maintain. Hence, it is necessary to get rid of casteism, although it is not necessary for this to destroy the caste system.

*2. **Regionalism.*** In contemporary India, regionalism and regional loyalties have spread so much that even the political unity of the country is being threatened. Some states have expressed the deisre to secede from the Union, because they believe themselves to be separate nations. Such tendencies should be suppressed with a strong hand because otherwise national unity may be damaged beyond repair.

*3. **Communalism.*** In India today, there are still many Muslims who do not accept India as their country. At the root of this is communalism, and because of their blind faith in their own community they believe the country to belong to Hindus, although it belongs to everybody. It is impossible to evolve nationalism without first putting an end to the mutual distrust of the different communities. For this active steps must be taken in educational institutions.

*4. **Linguism.*** Another expression of the disorganizing influences at work in the country is linguism. With independence came the problem of deciding a national language, because a national language is essential for maintaining the unity of the nation.

Compared to other languages, Hindi is best equipped to fulfil this role, but many people object to this because of narrow political interests. In addition, the people of some states are not willing to accept any language but their own.

This controversy turned violent and led to considerable bloodshed. An early solution of this problem is desirable, if nationalism is to foster in the country.

*5. **Classicism.*** Most people in India create distinctions among themselves on the basis of economic and social classes. Communist influence has encouraged class hatred to such an extent that various classes fight for their own interests, even at the cost of the national interest. Class interest is also manifested in the form of untouchability. This class struggle is a serious impediment to the growth of national sentiment, and it must be eliminated from the minds of the younger generation.

The purpose behind recounting these obstacles to national

sentiment is to point out that both negative and positive steps must be taken. Nationalism can be spread among the younger generation by following the suggestions given earlier and also by removing these hindrances. Mutual cooperation between the people, government and educators is of the essence. It is impossible to improve the country's future without increasing the sentiment of nationalism, irrespective of industrial and scientific progress. The future of the nation is dark unless a high national character of the people is formed.

QUESTIONS FOR ANSWER

1. Write short note on place of Nationalism in Education.
2. What is meant by 'national culture'? How can children imbibe it through various agencies of education? Answer the question with special references to the present day needs of India.

30

Education for National Integration

Progress and security of the nation depends upon national unity and emotional integration of its people. Therefore, this chapter is devoted to understand the role of education in fostering the ideal of national integration in India.

NEED FOR EMOTIONAL INTEGRATION

The unity of a nation depends upon the extent to which its various members look upon themselves as members of the same group. National unity or integration does not automatically follow upon living within the same geographical boundaries. Emotional integration is necessary for this unity. As is evident from the term itself, emotional integration is the unity, identity or similarity of emotions. If it exists, then individuals feel related to and concerned with each other. It is emotional integration which keeps members of a family organized. In colleges, this emotional integration is generated which promotes a sense of community and impedes the progress of disorganizing tendencies.

In India, one finds marked differences in the living standards, dress, customs, religion, culture, etc., of the various people existing in different parts. India's large size is emphasized by these differences, but one result of this is that when a person goes from one part of the country to another, he is almost a foreigner there. This has led to regionalism expressed in the desire of people of one region to promote their own regional interests at the expense of the interests of other regions. Regionalism has gained tremendous momentum because it has been linked with linguism.

Casteism or racial distinction between the Hindus and Muslims has led to deterioration of social organization in the country. Untouchability is an offshoot of casteism. Religious communities have been known to come into violent conflict with each other, thus leading to considerable damage to public and private property, and bloodshed on a large-scale. Communalism is responsible for the hatred which one religious group fosters for another. Putting it briefly, regionalism, linguism, casteism, communalism etc., are the disruptive and disorganizing influence which have divided Indian society into various groups. It is impossible to hope for a solution of these problems, without emotional integration.

UNITY IN DIVERSITY

Generally speaking, the extent of diversity found in India tends to create the impression that it is not a country but a subcontinent. But this does not imply that unity or integration is impossible in such a situation. One finds distinct and different racial characteristics among the inhabitants of different parts of the country, because differences of complexion, size, shape, etc., are clearly evident.

In the north, complexion varies from darkly wheatish, dark, yellow to red and even runs into mixtures of these colours. Inhabitants of the Andamans are jet black while those of the South Dravidians is a shining black, in direct contrasts is the rosy white complexions of the Kashmiris.

Turning to languages, one finds that the Indian Constitution has granted recognition to Urdu, Bengali, Assamese, Oriya, Punjabi, Gujarati, Marathi, Sindhi and numerous other languages, in addition to Hindi. Besides, Telugu, Kannada, Tamil and Malayalam have been accepted as the four Dravidian languages. Sanskrit has also been given special consideration as the original Aryan language. Differences exist not only at the level of language but also in respect of dress, religion, culture, etc.

Tribes of the north-east, central districts and the south differ from each other in their modes of life, their social and psychological characteristics, etc., to such a great extent that one can find among them different cultural and social regions. If one travels from east to west, and then back again, one will find clearly perceptible differences in complexion, dress, customs, modes of life, dietary habits and other aspect of culture, even at very short distances.

But despite these differences of region, race, language, tribe, etc., the existence of national unity cannot be questioned. One finds this inner unity or integration in all the people spread over the landmass limited by the Himalayas on the one side and the Indian Ocean on the other, the Burma Hills on the east and Pakistan on the west. This inner unity is the basis of emotional integration. Despite the more obvious and superficial differences, prosperity increases.

It is this inner unity which Sir Herbert Rizley described when he commented that, at the root of the apparent diversity of physical and social type, languages, customs and religion that immediately strikes the observer coming to India, is a definite similarity or identity or inner unity of life from the the Himalayas to Cape Comorin. This inner integration or unity is the basis of Indian culture. All the saints of the past were aware of this unity, although they were no less aware of the obvious differences. It is for this reason that India has always been treated as a single unit, even in the remote past.

It has been customary to refer to all the people residing in different parts of the country as Indians, even though one could see the differences of religion, culture, languages, etc. In fact, the very name *Bharatvarsha* denotes not merely geographical boundaries but actually the ideal of a cultural unity. During the Middle Ages, India was always treated as one unit. That India is accepted as the mother by all Indians is only due to a feeling of oneness and identity.

EFFORTS AT INCREASING EMOTIONAL INTEGRATION

It was the question of emotional integration which inspired the Central Education Ministry in 1961 to organize a Committee for Emotional Integration under the Chairmanship of Dr. Sampurnanand. This campaign to increase emotional integration had the solid foundation, belief in the principle of unity in diversity. All that is needed is that the younger generation should be educated in this direction through various kinds of programmes.

Speaking at the inauguration of the Indian Integration Committee, K.L. Shrimali, explained the significance of education and commented that if we want to generate a national consciousness in our people, we will have to plan our education accordingly. Education must be so designed as to encourage every participant to think of himself as a responsible part of the Indian nation.

Education must take upon itself the responsibility of awakening the younger generation to the turth that, despite obvious external differences, all Indians are emotionally the same.

Keeping in mind the objective outlined above, the Emotional Integration Committee gave the following suggestions.

1. Reorganization of syllabi. In order to reorganize and reshape the syllabi of colleges and the universities to accord with the needs of the nations, the Committee made the following suggestions:

(1) At the primary stage, stress should be laid upon nationalistic stories, poems, songs, etc.

(2) At the secondary stage, in addition to the other subjects being taught, special attention should be given to the study of national literature, social studies, moral and religious guidance and extra-curricular activities.

(3) At the university level, the syllabi should include the various social sciences, languages, literatures, cultures and arts. Teachers and students should be given facilities to travel to various parts of the country.

2. Encouragement to extra-curricular activities. Besides imparting formal knowledge to the students, the teachers must provide them with the opportunity to take part in such extra-curricular activities which are important from the standpoint of emotional integration. Besides, such programmes must also represent the entire nation.

Such programmes help in the development of 'we' feeling, a feeling of unity and sympathy. One example of such programmes is the Inter University cultural festivals, in which teachers and students participate from all parts of the country.

3. Improvement of textbooks. It is desirable that textbooks on various subjects, and especially on history, should be amended and improved. They should be designed to encourage a sense of emotional unity with people living in other parts of the country. This will also help to check the growth of communal feelings.

But it should also be remembered that such amendments should not be made at the cost of truth because such violence to truth is not necessary. That the country is one, is an undeniable truth. What is required is an expression of this truth.

4. Improvement concerning language and script. In this connection, the Committee on Emotional Integration made the following recommendations:

(1) The use of the Roman script should be permitted to increase knowledge of Hindi in certain areas.

(2) International numerals should be used in every part of the country.

(3) Arrangements should be made to teach the Devanagari script where it is not known.

(4) Hindi textbooks should also be provided in the regional scripts. Dictionaries using both Hindi and the regional languages should also be prepared.

(5) At the university level, study of Hindi and English literature should be encouraged so that integration is encouraged and divisive forces checked.

(6) The rights of the minorities should be protected in formulating a language policy.

In addition to the above list of suggestion, the Committee for Emotional Integration also made certain other suggestions. In schools, the daily programme should be started after a community prayer and a ten minute talk, either by the principal or by some respected person, on some subject which may encourage emotional integration. Another way of encouraging emotional integration is to organize a mass meeting of the school once a year and asking the students to take on oath to increase emotional integration.

Besides, all subjects and activities likely to lower awareness of differences should be encouraged. In this manner, it is possible to create a climate in which all people feel that they are members of one nation. On the negative side, all efforts must be made to destroy all elements which tend to obstruct the growth of emotional integration.

SUGGESTIONS FOR IMPROVING EMOTIONAL INTEGRATION

Apart from the suggestions outlined above, education can be used in the following suggested ways for improving emotional integration in the country:

1. Development of an all-India language. The first condition for increasing emotional integration in the country is that an all-India language should be evolved. Hindi is the only language capable of performing this role. Hence, it is desirable that knowledge of this language be made compulsory for every citizen. Government should extend every facility for developing Hindi literature, and the development of regional languages. They should be allowed to pursue their own course.

But all communications between the centre and the state should be conducted in the all-India language. Applicants for administrative jobs in the Government should be required to know Hindi, although they may be allowed to take the examination in their regional language.

2. An all-India educational policy. Education is the most effective tool for spreading emotional and national integration. For this reason, a national educational plan should be devised. This plan should aim at providing every child with knowledge of the ideas of great men, poets, leaders, religious thinkers, etc. Textbooks should be prepared under the supervision of the Central Government and provided by it so that the younger generation may be brought up in an atmosphere of nationalistic fervour.

Rules for the appointment of teachers, their pay scales and their conditions of working should be common all over the country. The same syllabi should be applicable to all institutions in the country at the primary, secondary and university levels. All India organizations like the N.C.C., Scouting, Girl Guides, etc., should be given appropriate encouragement. University education should be through the medium of the national language, even if the students are permitted to answer questions in their mother tongues. In this manner, the objective of national unity or integration can be achieved by evolving an all-India educational plan.

3. Programmes for increasing national unity. Many kinds of programmes can be devised for increasing national unity.

For example, the cinema can be used to spread the feeling of national unity. Radio and television can also be used equally effectively. All-India competitions and meetings can be organized in various parts of the country to increase national unity.

Such programmes help people living in different parts of the country to meet residents of other parts and learn their ideas and understand them. Travel facilities should be made more common and delegations and tours encouraged. During the last few years, special trains made up of farmers of different areas, students and members of Parliament toured the entire country. This helped the cause of national integration. Other programmes similar to these can be organized.

4. Development of inter-cultural understanding. In all the programmes outlined above, inter-cultural understanding will be promoted. This helps people to achieve liberality of attitudes to other cultures, an essential pre-condition of national unity in a country in which there are many cultures.

5. Efforts by teachers. Success of most of these programmes for increasing national unity depends upon teachers. As long as the teachers themselves do not rise above their petty narrow-mindedness and create ideals, there is little hope of the students developing any emotional unity. Hence, it is desirable that national consciousness should first be stirred in the students. For this, teachers from various parts of the country should be encouraged to meet each other.

This can be done through the All-India Teachers Organization. Even otherwise, most of the problems of teachers are common all over the country, and when they meet each other, they will get an opportunity to think over these problems and exchange ideas. At the same time, a national consciousness will be awaken in them. Yet, attention must be paid to forestalling the development of a class-consciousness among the teachers. The Government can make a positive contribution in this direction by organizing lectures from time to time and distributing literature of this kind.

6. Governmental efforts. Governmental efforts is essential for bringing success to all the projects outlined above, because without official blessing, there is little that education can achieve. This cannot be doubted because there are many agencies which are working against the development of emotional integration.

So long as the Government fails to check agencies which encourage linguism, communalism, religious bigotry, and other disruptive forces, education will not be able to achieve the goal. One of the first steps in this direction is control over destructive political parties. In every part of the country laws should be enacted to prevent any individual from giving expression to linguism, communalism, regionalism, casteism, untouchability, etc. This should be followed up by a strict application of these laws.

It is evident from the foregoing description of the measures for increasing emotional integration that these measures must be both positive and negative. Adoption of all these measures would be a positive step. The negative step of destroying all obstacles in the way of emotional integration is no less important. For this, teachers, administrators and guardians will have to work collectively. Then along the country will witness solid national integration in spite of religious pluralism.

QUESTIONS FOR ANSWER

1. How in your opinion can education help National Integration and Understanding?
2. Schools in India had failed to promote emotional integration and mutual understanding. How far do you agree with this? What can schools do in this matter? Give practical suggestions.
3. What is the meaning of National and Emotional Integration? Discuss the part that education can play in bringing about this integration.
4. What contribution can the various educational institutions make towards awakening a nationalist feeling in the students?
5. How can education contribute to national integration in India?
6. Explain the concept of emotional integration. What can a school do to help in this and to fight against the forces of disintegration?
7. What is meant by National Integration? What can we do in schools to foster the national spirit?
8. What do you mean by National Integration? What is the role of education for developing National Integration among school children?
9. How can education help in National Integration?

31

Education for International Understanding

World peace and security as well as welfare of humanity as a whole is essential. Therefore, people of the whole world, particularly of the democratic world must have international understanding. Hence, this chapter is devoted to discuss how Indian education attempts to achieve this objective.

NEED FOR AN INTERNATIONAL ATTITUDE IN EDUCATION

Internationalism implies the awareness of all human beings as members of a single human society, irrespective of national boundaries and other differences. The modern period has seen a remarkable transformation of the means of transport and communication, the tremendous spreading of eduation, the notable increase in the mutual contact between citizens of the world.

As a consequence the world has shrunk in size, which in itself has led to local problems influencing areas and people far removed. For example, it is now being recognized that the excessive increase in poverty in any part of the world is almost certain to affect the economic conditions of other countries as well. If peace and prosperity are to be created in one country, it becomes necessary to create good living conditions all over the world. Now, that man has set foot on the moon, there is an increasing demand for international understanding.

Besides, the two world wars of the century enforced the useful lession that, in this age of nuclear weapons, the people of the world have to live and die together. Communist and non-communist countries both feel that they cannot hope to maintain their status in the world, unless they make efforts to spread their ideology in other countries.

The failure of the League of Nations inspired rather depressed the desire for internationalism. For this reason its successor, the United Nations, is aiming at co-operation not merely in the field of politics but also in the economic, educational and cultural spheres. UNESCO, one specialized body of the UNO is dedicated to the spread of international understanding through the medium of education in every part of the world.

INTERNATIONALISM IN CONTEMPORARY INDIAN EDUCATION

Contemporary educational philosophers in India have supported the notion of internationalism for a specific uniqe reason. This attitude is based on the philosophy of the ancient *Upanishads* which taught that God lives as soul in the bodies of all human beings, irrespective of differences of race, nation, area, sex, etc. The Vedanta philosophy provides the strong foundation for the internationalism found in current thinking in education.

Even, Sri Aurobindo was a staunch internationalist, in spite of his very emphatic expression of nationalism. He expressed the opinion that, just as the ideal nation is one in which the individual's freedom and perfection is harmonized with the development and organization of society, the freedom and development of an international society should be harmonized with the development and perfection of humanity in its entirety.

Of the many contemporary thinkers, Rabindranath Tagore expressed such vehement support for internationalism that people misunderstood him and took him to be opposed to nationalism. His creation, Shantiniketan, is the concrete manifestation of the international attitude in education.

Dr. S. Radhakrishnan, the Chairman of the Indian Universities Commission drew attention to the need for an international attitude in education. He expressed regret at the failure of the current educational system to propagate feelings of internationalism and universal brotherhood. An educational system should be such that it can create a new generation of individuals who believe that all human beings are brothers and that differences of caste, region, community or nation have no significance.

True education is a training in internationalism. Dr. S. Radhakrishnan commented that we must make efforts for the unity of the world. We should try to create a new generation which has faith in the nobility of intellectual life, in purity, in a feeling of brotherhood towards humanity, in love and peace. There should be no national educational plan which proves an obstacle in the growth and spread of this feeling.

In fact, there is no opposition between nationalism and internationalism, but if it becomes necessary to make comparisons, both Rabindranath Tagore and Dr. S. Radhakrishnan inclined towards inter-nationalism. Education must aim at making every man and woman a citizen of the world, by developing within each one such thinking, concentration, insight and intellectuality or spirituality that they can perform useful roles in life.

Peace in the world can be expected only when this ideal is pursued by education in every country. These ideas of Dr. S. Radhakrishnan have found echoes in every part of the world, and there is consensus of opinion among educationsists everywhere that training men and women in internationalism through education is the only way of avoiding a third world war.

PROPAGATION OF INTERNATIONALISM BY UNESCO

The role of UNESCO in spreading internationalism was glanced at earlier. This body is a special organ of the UNO dedicated to the spread of international understanding. It has been said in its constitution, "Since wars begin in the minds of men, it is in the minds of men that the defence of peace must be constructed." The breadth of its scope can be judged from its name, the United Nations Educational Scientific and Cultural Organization. In order to achieve its goal of spreading international understanding, it performs the following functions:

(1) This organization transmits knowledge of the literature, art, science, etc., of one nation to all other nations.

(2) It also provides many opportunities to thinkers, scientists, teachers and artists to meet each other and exchange ideas and put forward creative plans for promoting world peace and justice. Efforts are made to prevent the arts from being influenced too much by narrow parochial thinking.

(3) UNESCO also seeks to improve the mutual relations between various nations and remove fear, suspicion, lack of confidence, between them.

(4) Considerable financial aid is given by UNESCO to improve the teaching facilities in backward and exploited countries.

(5) UNESCO also provides guidance in medifying texts prescribed in various syllabi in order to make the more internationally-oriented. The organization does its best to root out illiteracy and lack of education from the poor countries.

(6) In order to promote international understanding, UNESCO provides facilities to students and teachers to visit abroad and to exchange views and also gain experience in international living.

(7) It also organizes art and literature exhibitions at the international level to promote feelings to love and friendship.

(8) Research is also encouraged by UNESCO, for it provides financial help and other facilities to researchers.

It is evident from the varied function of UNESCO that the organization is particularly aiming at creating an international feeling in education but this objective cannot be achieved by UNESCO alone. For this, it will be necessary to make proper arrangements for education in many countries.

SYNTHESIS OF THE NATIONAL AND INTERNATIONAL POINTS OF VIEW

Here it is essential to understand how the national and international standpoints can be sythesised and reconciled with each other. Nationalistic feeling attaches the great importance to the nation's interests. Inspired by such feelings, individuals are even willing to lay down their lives in order to protect the honour of their nations.

It is only by awakening such feelings that many nations have gathered so much military power and have attempted to extend their own frontiers. But, if carefully examined, it will be seen that this is a disorted form of nationalism. In its best form nationalism does not oppose internationalism. It has helped various nations to collect power in their hands in order to throw off the yoke of a foreign nation.

Nationalism has played a vital role in throwing out colonialism. But despite these great advantages and positive qualities, nationalism underwent a change and became colonialism itself. As a result of the nationalistic feeling, people focused their eyes on their own country and lost interest in anything other than their own sectarian interests.

Just as any interest turns into an ism by becoming narrow and thus harms the more liberal interests, in the same way, this narrow-minded nationalism which inspired many nations of Europe to establish big colonies in Africa and Asia. Later, Germany and Italy became jealous of the English and French colonies, a feeling which manifested itself in the First and Second World Wars.

After the First World War, an international organization known as the League of Nations was established, but it came to a premature end due to the narrow nationalism of its members. It was the precursor of the United Nations Organization which came into being after the second experience of a global conflict.

Despite the lessons learnt earlier, many nations continue to constitute a very grave threat to international peace because of their own interests. One concrete example of this is South Africa which continues to exercise its policy of apartheid, despite the many warnings given by the UNO. It is now universally felt that it is only the distorted form of nationalism which hinders the growth of internationalism.

On the other hand, healthy nationalism is a boon to internationalism. As has already been pointed out, it is only nationalism which has inspired many nations to throw off foreign rule. It is nationalism which has helped even the smallest nations of the world to raise their heads and stand proudly by the side of their mightier brothers.

Thus, nationalism can be used or misused by human beings.

The two international wars of the previous century should be sufficient to teach human beings that there is need for balance and synthesis between nationalism and internationalism. There is a parallel to be drawn here. Individuals sacrifice the interests of family, race, town, etc. for the benefit of the nation, because they realize that these also gain when the nation gains.

In the same way, national interests can be allied with international goals. National interests can be restricted for this and it cannot be questioned that progress of isolated groups also depends very much upon the progress of the world as a whole. This fact must be realized first of all by the rich, powerful and the prosperous nation, because on them lies the onus of the world's development.

In fact, it is the realization of their responsibility which is persuading the rich nations to extend a helping hand to their poor neighbours, but when some political strings are attached to the aid given, it defeats the purpose of encouraging internationalism. It must be remembered that there would be no international feeling in the absence of a national one, for it is the latter which inspires the former.

No nation should become an obstacle to the progress of another nation in trying to achieve greater prosperity for itself. Secondly, progressive nations must help the underdeveloped ones. The principle of *Panchsheel* is a fine example of a synthesis between the nationalism and internationalism, but for this peaceful coexistence itself is not enough. Active co-operation is more important.

MEANS OF INTERNATIONAL EDUCATION

In order to encourage the growth of internationalism, it is necessary to make suitable amendments and modifications in the objectives of education, in the syllabus, and the methods of teaching. The following suggestions have been put forward:

(a) Aims of education. With the intention of spreading international feeling, the following aims of education should be paid special attention:

(i) Development of independent thinking. Education must help every student to think for himself so that he should not blindly accept every statement favourable to his own country, and blindly everything in favour of another. He must be able to

arrive at an independent judgement of the worth of some fact relating to his own country or another.

(ii) Developing a feeling of world citizenship. Education must also seek to teach children that they are citizens of a world State. When this feeling is developed in them, they will have no difficulty in rising above national interests and understanding international interests, which they will try to achieve.

(iii) Creating faith in humanity. Rabindranath Tagore, the strongest supporter of internationalism among the contemporary Indian educational philosophers starts with a background of humanitarianism. Humanity is the true religion of human beings, while all the great religions are only different forms of it.

All great religions have placed great stress upon the equality of human beings. Human perfection has been accepted as the goal of human life. Once this concept is understood, it becomes easy to have faith in humanity and to love all human beings irrespective of their country.

(b) Improvement in syllabi. Following changes in syllabi are suggested, if an international feeling is to be created:

(1) All syllabi should include paintings, literature, music, etc., which are typical of different countries.

(2) The children should be acquainted with all attempts at humanitarian work carried out in every part of the world.

(3) Efforts should be made to overcome narrow-mindedness and blind faith in children through a scientific education.

(4) The teaching of geography should be supplemented with knowledge of the singleness of the world.

(5) The teaching of history should concentrate primarily on the efforts of great figures who have contributed to the history of the world.

(6) In teaching civics, the educator should explain to the students not only the rights of a citizen but also the rights and duties of a person to the international community as a whole.

(7) Teaching should not be restricted to bookish teaching alone, but must also include visits to different parts of the country and also to other countries.

(8) Pen-friendship should also be encouraged.

IMPROVEMENTS IN THE METHOD OF TEACHING

Certain suggestions about the changes and improvements in

syllabi also imply some changes in teaching methods, if education is to have an international impact. The points to be noted in this connection are:

(1) During the process of teaching, it is desirable to stress points which may help in evolving an all encompassing level and world citizenship.

(2) The teaching of history, geography and civics, should concentrate not upon the differences between and tensions among nations but on the similarities so that sympathy for other nations and nationals is awakened in the mind of the educand.

(3) But an international viewpoint cannot be generated in the educand if the educator himself lacks it. When the educator is possessed of it, he will inspire the educand through his conversations, his ideas, training, and by setting an example. Hence, the first step in the process is to educate the educator.

The various committees for the various sciences and arts that are constituted at the university level should be encouraged to develop contact with national and international of the same kind.

In addition to the above suggestions, certain other steps can also help in evolving an international attitude. Actually, this cannot be generated through university or formal education alone.

What is really required is international contact at all levels of life and among people of every walk of life, scientists, scholars, literary figures, teachers, doctors, in fact, every profession. Such contacts can be evolved by international meetings of local committees concerned with different professions, and also through mutual exchange of scholars and learned people.

Finally, it has also been suggested that every national plan of education, in every country, must make a specific provision for developing international feeling through education. Educators and educational institutions should be given specific instructions concerning this. Only this will awaken sufficient enthusiasm in local institutions, and only thus can the aim of international education be fulfilled.

MEANS OF SPREADING INTERNATIONAL EDUCATION

Apart from the formal education of colleges and schools, certain other media can also be useful in spreading international feeling, the major ones being:

1. Pen-friendship. Quite a few of the contemporary magazines, in all parts of the world, carry descriptions of individuals who are keen on forming pen-friends in various parts of the world. More particularly, the magazines meant for children and adolescents carry this kind of information.

Such magazines publish the reader's interests, age, hobies, other relevant information, and sometimes even a photograph of the person interested in pen-friendship. Thus, many children and adolescents from pen-friends in all parts of the world, and later on exchange pictures, postal stamps, books and other things. Pen-friendship is, thus, the most important means of increasing feeling for people of different parts of the world.

2. Exchange of gifts. Another modern practice is sending of gifts by the children of one country to the children of other countries. India, for example, has gifted elephants to the children of other nations. Such actions strengthen international feeling by attracting children of one country to another. Sometimes, some gift packets are also distributed in schools.

These packets contain things that the children can use. It is only natural that when the children get these gifts packets, they harbour kind and friendly feelings for the donor. The American Red Cross distributes such gift parcels among Indian children from time to time.

3. International competitions. Nowadays, cultural competitions over the display of dance, drama, art, music etc., take on an international colour because people from many countries participate in them. This brings people into contact with the result that the world seems like a vast home.

4. International exhibitions. Such exhibitions also play an important part in promoting international uderstanding, because they help to acquaint people with the art and culture of different countries.

5. Cine films. People derive a lot of information by seeing foreign films, because they see their mode of living. Besides it also encourages the feeling that human beings are the same everywhere, in their happiness, pain, pleasure, problems, joys and sorrows. This helps international understanding.

*6. **Radio and television.*** Radio and television play practically the same role as films because foreign programmes help the audience to understand life in other parts of the world.

*7. **Literature.*** Nowadays, the literature of almost every country is available in every other country of the world. This can help in increasing acqaintance with life as it is lived in different parts. In addition to such literature, certain books specialize in compiling the stories of lives, character, interesting incidents and surprising objects in various parts of the world. This is a kind of international literature.

*8. **Contribution of universities.*** Finally, it can be said that universities are the most important medium of propagating international education because they provide opportunities for the meeting of artists, scientists, literary figures and scholars. This creates international understanding at a very high level.

*9. **Various institutions of UNO.*** Many institutions of UNO, more particularly, UNESCO, are engaged in directly and consciously promoting international understanding and the growth of international feeling. It is desirable that their sphere should be further expanded, and that more nations should participate in their programmes so that their objectives can be achieved more easily.

QUESTIONS FOR ANSWER

1. Write short note on 'Importance of Education for Internationalism.'
2. The need of the hour is to lay stress on fostering international understanding in our students. How can it be developed in schools?
3. Write short note on 'Role of education in forstering internationalism'.
4. Write short note on 'Education for citizenship of the world.'
5. Write short note on 'International understanding.'
6. Explain fully the meaning of "education for international understanding." Describe a few activities which can be undertaken in your school for its development.

32

Deschooling Society

In the present day civilized world there are some intellectuals such as Everett Reimer, Poul Freire, Poul Goodman, Charles Weingartner, Neil Postman, John Holt, Ivan D-Illich etc. in their works are firmly convinced that the educational institutions have polluted our consciousness and create greater fragmentation of human society. Therefore, they plead for deschooling on following grounds:

1. Poor students lag behind. Even with schools equal quality a poor child can seldom catch up with a rich one. Even, if they attend equal schools and begin at the same age, poor students lack most of the educational opportunities which are casually available to the middle-class child. These advantages range from conversation and books in the home to vacation travel and a different sense of oneself, and apply, for the child who enjoys them, both in and out of school. So the poorer student will generally fall behind so long as he depends on school for advancement of learning.

2. Over dependence on school. School appropriates the money, men and goodwill available for education. It discourages other institutions from assuming educational tasks. Work, leisure, policies, city living and even family life depend on schools for the habits and knowledge.

3. Neither learning nor justice. Neither learning nor justice is promoted by schooling because educators insist on packaging instruction with certification.

4. Most learning outside the school. A major illusion on which the school system rests is that most learning is the results of teaching. It is true that teaching may contribute to certain kinds of learning under certain circumstances. But most people acquire most of their knowledge outside school.

5. Teachers less skilled than craftsmen. Skilled teachers are made scared by the belief in the values of licences. Certification constitutes a form of market manipulation and is plausible only to a schooled mind. Most teachers of arts and trades are less skilful, less inventive and less communicative than the best craftsmen and tradesmen.

6. Recognition of two faced nature of learning. The deschooling of society implies a recognition of the two faced nature of learning. As an insistence on skill drill alone could be a disaster, therefore, equal emphasis must be placed on other kinds of learning. But if schools are the wrong places for learning a skill, they are even worse places for getting an education.

7. Two realms. The very existence of obligatory schools divides any society into two realms, some time spans and processes and treatments and professions are academic or pedagogic, while others are not. This power of school to divide social reality has no bounds, education becomes unworldly and the world becomes non-educational.

8. Learning in practice. Everyone learns outside school, to speak, to think, to love, to feel, to play, to curse, to politick and to worry without interference from a teacher. Even children who are under a teacher's care day and night are no exception of the rule. Orphans, idiots and school teacher's sons learn mostly outside the educational process planned for them.

Teachers make a poor showing in their attempt at increasing learning among the poor parents who want their children to go to school are less concerned about what they will learn than about the certificate and money they will earn. Middle class parents commit their children to a teacher's care for learning what the poor learn on the streets.

9. Wrong motivations. Pupils have never credited teachers for most of their learning. Bright and dull alike have always relied on rote reading. Both are motivated by the stick or by the carrot of a desired career.

10. Job for school teachers. Schools create jobs for school teachers, no matter what their pupils learn from them.

GENERAL CHARACTERISTICS OF DESCHOOLED SOCIETY

1. Purposes. A good educational system has three purposes. It provides all what they want to learn with access to available resources. It empowers all who want to have what they know to find those who want to learn it from them. It furnishes all who want to present in issue to the public with the opportunity to make their challenge known.

2. Application of constitutional guarantee. Such a system would require the application of constitutional guarantee to education. Learners should not be forced to submit to an obligatory curriculum, or to discrimination based on whether they possess a certificate or a diploma.

The public should not be forced to support a huge professional apparatus of educators and buildings through a regressive taxation which in fact restrict the public's chances for learning by the services the professional is willing to put on the market.

3. Modern technology. It should use modern technology to make free speech, free assembly and a free press truly universal and, therefore, fully educational.

4. Less restrictive educational artifacts. The market for learners would be much more various and the definition of educational artifacts would be less restrictive. There could be tool shops, libraries, laboratories and gaming rooms. Photo labs and offset presses would allow neighbourhood newspapers to flourish. Some storefront learning centres could contain viewing both for closed-circuit television, others could feature office equipment for use and for repair. Film clubs would compete with each other and with commercial television. Museum outlets could be networks for circulating exhibits of works of art, both old and new, originals and reproductions, perhaps administered by the various metropolitan museums.

5. Hidden curriculum and open learning. To understand deschooled society, we must focus on the hidden curriculum of schooling. We are not concerned here with the hidden curriculum of the ghetto streets which brands the poor or with the hidden curriculum of the drawing room which benefits the rich. We are rather concerned to all attention to the fact that the ceremonial or ritual of schooling itself constitutes such a hidden curriculum. Even the best of teachers cannot entirely protect his pupils from it. Inevitably, this hidden curriculum of schooling adds prejudice and guilt to the discrimination which a society practises against some of its members and compounds the privilege of others with a new title to condescend to the majority. This hidden curriculum serves as a ritual of initiation into a growth oriented consumer society for rich and poor alike.

*6. **Open learning system.*** The system accepts the learner and his surroundings as the environment for learning. It concentrates on enriching that environment. The system seeks, obtains and maintains the active cooperation of the community and regional resources which can be important factors in enriching the learning environment. It diminishes the dependence of the learner on a single resource. It treats learning as a continuing activity. It includes living, working, recreating and learning.

*7. **No need of degree.*** The system is capable for enabling learners to participate in the programme of learning and instruction without imposing traditional academic entry requirements, without the pursuit of an academic degree or other certification as the exclusive reward.

*8. **Practical objectives.*** The planning of new educational institutions ought not to begin with the administrative goals of a principal or president, or with the teaching goals of a professional educator, or with the learning goals of any hypothetical class of people. It must not start with the question, 'What kinds of things and people, learners what to be in contact with in order to learn'.

The system requires, formulation of learning objectives in such a way that they can serve the basis of decisions in instructional designs including evaluation and in such a way that it will not only be known to the students but they also be participated in decision-making.

*9. **Role of extra-curricular activities.*** It is a process of learning that is not enclosed or encumbered by barriers that is accessible and available, not confined or concealed and that implies a continuum of access of opportunity. Most learning happens casually, and even most international learning is not the result of programmed instruction. Normal children learn their first language casually, although faster, if their parents pay attention to them. Most people who learn a second language will do so as a result of odd circumstances and not of sequential teaching. They go to live with their grand parents, they travel, or they fall in love with a foreigner. Most people who read widely, and with pleasure, merely believed that they learned to do so in school, when challenged, they easily discard this illusion.

10. Advent of 'brave new world'. Deschooling could mean the advent of a 'brave new world' dominated by well-intentional administrators of programmed instruction. Deschooling could take place in either of two diametrically opposed ways:

(i) The first would be the expansion of the mandate of the pedagogue and his increasing control over society even outside school. With the best of intentions and simply by expanding the rhetoric now used in schools, the present crisis in the schools could provide educators with an excuse to use all the networks of contemporary society to funnel their messages to us, for our own good.

(ii) On the other hand, the growing awareness on the part of governments, as well as of employers, taxpayers, enlightened pedagogues and school administrators, that graded curricular teaching for certification has become harmful could offer large masses of people an extraordinary opportunity: that of preserving the right of equal access to the tools both of learning and of sharing with others what they know or believe.

GOALS OF EDUCATIONAL REVOLUTION

But this would require that the educational revolution be guided by following goals:

1. To liberate access to things by abolishing the control which persons and institutions now exercise over their educational values.

2. To liberate the sharing of skills by guaranteeing freedom to teach or exercise them on request.

3. To liberate the critical and creative resources of people by returning to individual persons the ability to call and hold meetings—an ability now increasingly monopolized by institutions which claim to speak for the people.

4. To liberate the individual from the obligations to shape his expectations to the services offered by an established

profession by providing him with the opportunity to draw on the experience of his peers and to entrust himself to the teacher, guide, adviser or healer of his choice. Inevitably, the deschooling of society will blur the distinctions between economics, education and politics on which the stability of the present world order and the stability of nations now rest.

WORK EXPERIENCE AND SOCIALLY USEFUL PRODUCTIVE WORK

Vocationalization, Work Experience, Socially Useful Productive Work, Basic System—The underlying philosophy behind all these concepts is the same, i.e., relating education to productivity and providing work experiences. These terms provide a redefinition of educational thinking in terms of a society launched on the road to industrialization.

Work Experience

Work experience is a participation in productive work in school, in the home, in a workshop, on a farm, in a factory or in any other productive situation.

Socially Useful Productive Work

According to the Ishwarbhai Patel Committee (1978), "It may be described as purposive, meaningful manual work resulting in either goods or services which are useful to the community. Purposive, productive work and services related to the needs of the child and the community will prove meaningful to the learner." The Committee has further observed, "The purpose of demarcating a distinct curricular area as Socially Useful Productive Work is to emphasize the principle that education should be work-centred, as the concept of Socially Useful Productive Work is to be developed in the light of the Gandhian Philosophy of Basic Education, in and through work."

1. Aim of socially useful productive work. The Committee observes, "The aim of this curricular area is to provide children with opportunities of participating in social and economic activities inside and outside and classroom enabling them to understand scientific principles and processes involved in different types of work and in the setting in which they are found in the physical and social environment."

2. Planning and criteria of selection. The Committee stresses that this work must not be performed mechanically but must include planning, analysis and detailed preparation at every stage, so that it is educational in essence. The criterion for selection of activities should, thus, be that the work involved is:

(*i*) Productive,
(*ii*) Educative, and
(*iii*) Socially useful.

3. Lack of usefulness in work experience. In the view of the Committee, the programmes of work experience which were introduced as a result of the recommendations of the Kothari Commission with the objective of relating education to productivity lacked the component of social usefulness and in practice were not even casually correlated to other subject areas.

4. Three phases. The Review Committee has stated the three phases of the Socially Useful Productive Work:

(*i*) Study of the world of work through observation and enquiry,
(*ii*) Experimentation with materials, tools and techniques, and
(*iii*) Work practice.

5. Six areas of work situation:

(*i*) Health and Hygiene,
(*ii*) Food,
(*iii*) Shelter,
(*iv*) Clothing,
(*v*) Culture and recreation, and
(*vi*) Community work and social service.

6. Merits of the programme:

(i) Reduction of gap in work and education. The Committee feels that if 'Socially Useful Productive Work' is given a central and dominant place in the curriculum, the gap between work and education will be reduced, the schools will not remain isolated from the community and the gulf that divides the affluent from the weaker and poorer section of the community will be bridged. Such a scheme, will provide equality of opportunity for working and learning to all children, irrespective of caste, creed, sex and economic status.

(ii) Control on migration. The Committee further hopes that

those who receive education under the new scheme will not migrate from the village to the towns, deserting the community which had nurtured them and spent money on their education.

(iii) Bridging gulf between rural and urban. The Committee envisages that the new pattern will assist in checking the cleavage that has been created between the so-called educated and the rural masses and which has resulted in lack of harmony.

(iv) Check on educated unemployed. The Committee thinks that the introduction of 'Socially Useful Productive Work' will avert the paradoxical situations in which national resources are spent on the education of the villagers only to help them to join the ranks of unemployed.

(v) Right direction. The Committee strongly feels that the reaffirmation of the Gandhian concept of work education is the very step in giving the right direction to the present system of education. Therefore, it asserts that the work education must find a central place in the school curriculum.

(vi) Education through work. The Committee makes it clear, "We are not advocating education plus work but education in and through work as this is the basis of the Gandhian philosophy of basic education."

(vii) Following natural instinct. The Review Committee points out that the merit of education through work is that it follows the natural instinct of man to translate 'thought into activity and activity into thought'.

(viii) Coordination. The Review Committee has further observed, "At the risk of sounding pedantic we would like to stress the close co-ordination of the senses and thought and also the reciprocal influence between brain activity and material creative activity".

(ix) Socially useful productive work—subjected to related activities. The socially useful productive work should, as far as possible, be allied to the elective chosen by the students, allowing also for any other kind of work depending upon the facilities available in the neighbourhood. The students who are studying Home Science, for instance, work with the community for improvement of the nutritional status of the population, utilizing the local products for developing cheap and wholesome diets. Those of physics may similarly work on rural electrification, improvement of small and cottage industries, etc. Biology

students may serve in primary health centres and promote other health measures or help farmers, horticulturists, etc., for improving productivity. Political Science students may work with Panchayat Administration, local bodies, etc., for purpose of improving various services to the community.

QUESTIONS FOR ANSWER

1. What is deschooling? Why is it recommended?
2. Describe general characteristics of deschooled society.
3. What is work experience? Explain socially useful productive work.

33

Karl Mannheim on the Future of Sociology of Education

The concept of describing the society as discussed in the last chapter is an unwanted, anti-social and anti-educational thought. The points raised by the advocates of this thought are based on their inapt knowledge of the role of individual differences in personality formulation and social as well as academic achievements. Therefore, hereunder, we are discussing the views of Karl Mannheim, a noted American intellectual of Sociology of Education as given by him in chapter 15 of his book "An Introduction to the Sociology of Education."

No educational activity or research is adequate in the present stage of consciousness unless it is conceived in terms of a sociology of education. Apart from the philosophical, psychological and technical approaches, we are gradually becoming aware of the significance of the social context in which education works, and this very awareness produces new insight at every stage.

This need for the sociological approach to education is due to the very simple fact that tradition is fading in the most important spheres of life. In an age of tradition, education was simply one of the unconscious techniques for assisting the infant to grow up into a given social order. The more these silent means of transmission lose their effect, however, the more they have to be replaced by conscious proceses, and these in their turn only improve along with an awareness of the circumstances in which they are expected to operate.

In many spheres of life we can no longer rely upon the spontaneous emanation of a tradition; the main changes taking place do so too quickly to make spontaneous adjustment and unconscious selection reliable.

The principal contribution of the sociological approach to the history and the theory of education is to draw attention to the fact that neither educational aims nor educational techniques can be conceived without a context, but rather, that they are to a very large extent socially directed. Who teaches whom for what society, when and how, as the sociological questions were once framed.

Our investigation into the sociological foundations of education cannot be a purely academic one, piling up facts for their own sake. There is something definite we want to know. We are in search of something which should never be lost sight of in our research. We want to understand our time, the predicament of this age and what healthy education could contribute to a regeneration of society and man.

In this quest for orientation, sociology is a tool and we shall use it in a two fold sense: as a special theory of education and as a new approach to its history. These two means of access will continually draw upon each other. We shall study history in order to have a broader background to the understanding of our own society, but this study of history will be intensified by our desire to be able ultimately to build up a sociological theory of education which can assist us in our present task.

The sociological approach looks at education not as an aim in itself but as a part of the social-historical dynamics. If it is true that the child is never educated in the abstract, but rather, for a given society, then it must be possible for the sociologist to interpret the educational aims of an epoch from the needs and ultimate strivings of that very same society.

But it would lead us too far a field to collect all the possible aims which developed in history and it will, therefore, perhaps be helpful to describe a few main types which could be used as a measuring rod in our historical researches. In this connection, I should like to draw attention to the classification of educational aims by Max Weber. He distinguishes three main types of education throughout history. The first he calls charismatic education, the second aiming at future, and the third specialist education. We are in the age of specialist education.

Specialist education seeks to transfer a special knowledge or skill and is strictly correlated with the growth of division of labour which makes the specialist indispensable in modern industrial society. This education loses sight both of the deeper levels of the self which were the main concern of religious education and of the humanistic many-sidedness of personality which was still the ideal of the educated few.

Although it produces the necessary cogs and wheels in the social machine specialist education disintegrates both the personality and the mental powers for understanding the human situation which has to be mastered.

A thorough-going study of the social origins, the special methods of putting these three educational ideals into practice, will help us to interpret our present situation and will lead to decisions as to whether each of these techniques could be used in different compartments of life, and in different stages of the individual's development.

Because these three different types of education, although they developed in a detectable sequence in history, are no mutually exclusive, but rather complement each other, a continuous awareness of their special significance could enable us to establish their proper place in modern education.

Not only the content of education, its ideals and its ultimate aims, vary from one society to another, but also many of the seemingly universal qualities of man, sometimes even quite imponderable forms of experience, change with the changing time.

The transfer of these changing forms of experience occurs through invisible channels in face-to-face contacts, but they help to determine the way in which people will react spontaneously to both the trivial and the important objectives of life.

Although it appears as if these changing attitudes and minute forms of experience were either innate or produced by spontaneous and unconscious processes of the invisible social texture, even in the past, when there was less theoretical awareness of educational aims than there is today, much care has been given to their procreation. In our society, the symptoms of re-barbarization are perhaps largely due to the neglect of the cultivation of these human attitudes and sentiments or to the fact that they have been left without control.

This negligence on the part of official education in a society in which the family and the community are losing their educational power, ultimately, means that the creation of basic attitudes is left to vulgarizing agencies such as the cinema, television, radio, press, which satisfy the thirst of the masses for basic attitudes and new forms of experience.

Within the framework of the study of basic attitudes, we must of necessity consider the history of fundamental virtues. Some of these are undoubtedly widespread in the world, and this corresponds to the fact that in traditional society the primary groups, like the family, the neighbourhood and the community, will always develop the very same primary virtues, such as love and mutual help.

But apart from these basic virtues there are some equally elementary virtues which vary with society. Courage, for instance, or piety, is not acknowledged to the same degree in all societies. It is characteristic that in China when a general pacification took place the virtue of heroism was rejected by Confucius and that, in history, the changing significance of piety very much depends on the changing role which the various generations play in different societies.

In the same way, restraint and dignity are virtues which are chiefly linked up with the existence of some leading elites to whom self-control has become a basic virtue. The moderation of medieval chivalry is another instance of such a basic virtue bound to time and class. Rhetorical eloquence is a virtue of the market place and of democratic societies, but history very often produces shades and combinations of such basic virtues, such as the Jesuits' ideal of the *sapiens et eloquens pietas*.

The significance of a study of these basic virtues in their genuine historical context consists in helping us to re-establish some of them and to find new ones which conform to our age. Since, we are at last becoming aware that their function is to create that minimum of social conformity without which no society can continue, such a study may reveal to us why these basic virtues disintegrate in the present stage of capitalism. Perhaps it would also show us the educational techniques by which they could be maintained or developed, directly or indirectly.

But not only can the attitudes and the basic virtues, be studied in the social context; even the more comprehensive patterns of life, are subject to change and are the perceptible expression of the ultimate strivings of a society. Only in a society like our own could the idea of fate and life history degenerate into the bureaucratic idea of a life career.

In place of this idea there were, in more meaningful times, the visible symbols of different ways of life. The sage of antiquity, the saint, the monk, the heretic, the martyr, the ascetic in religious culture, the knight in chivalry, etc. were all educational patterns integrating life histories.

We should not be completely blind to some recent trends which work towards the creation of acceptable patterns of living. The youth movement has undoubtedly produced some of the new ideals of the sincere man who wants to find a genuine relation to nature and to his fellow beings.

Psychoanalysis is striving towards a life pattern the ideal of which is to gain a new sense of reality and to escape the distortion created by uncontrolled repressions, fears and anxieties. In the English ideal of never over-stating facts, there is a treasure of self-control, and appreciation of common sense; in the stakhanovite worker of the Russians is to be found the ideal of the pioneer ready to make people efficient, enthusiastic and willing to sacrifice for the community.

Another aspect of a sociological study of education is the problem of synthesizing different trends operating in different social layers and in different ethnological and geographical regions. In periods of high culture there was a partly conscious and partly unconscious balance created between the contributions of the different groups to education.

This balance was sometimes based upon the idea of a hierarchy of separated estates or castes, each one of which produced its own cultural contribution on different levels.

The democratic conception adds to the idea of synthesis the free intercommunication between social layers and their cultural contributions. Its main concern is the access of the gifted members of the lower classes to the elites, the invention of right methods of social selection and the preservation of society from deteriorating into undifferentiated masses.

Its cultural balance is based upon processes more complex than and even antagonistic to segregation and careful isolation of the groups.

Another aspect of synthesizing the different forces operating in a culture consists in harmonizing antagonistic elements, for instance the contrasts between the school and life, work and leisure, action and reflection, self-control and self-expression, individualization and co-operation, change and tradition. Such studies are equally instructive, both when they deal with periods in which a balance has been reached and with periods in which disharmony and destruction follow.

For instance, the study of the consequences of the industrial revolution, which has been the main agency in upsetting the balance of modern society, is still very significant and here we can learn a great deal from the criticisms developed by men like Kingsley, Morris and Ruskin and later by the Socialists.

When approaching the study of our age, we shall have to aim at a general sociological diagnosis able to explain the main educational problems in terms of more fundamental structural changes operating in our society. We are living in an age of planning which is bound to find a new form of co-ordination, we are living in an age in which the forces of both traditions and enlightenment are disintegrating, we are living in an age which passes from the stage of the predominance of limited elites to mass democracy, we are living in an age whose uncontrolled forces bring about dehumanization and disintegration of the personality.

Ultimately, education has to be conceived of as a new form of social control which is neither the inculcation of Fascism nor the complete anarchy of a deteriorated laisser-faire policy.

But all these studies of the historical background of education will be exclusively directed to a better understanding of our immediate task. The number of historical items we will study, and the choice of them, will depend on the means available, and on the practical issues that seem to be most urgent.

Perhaps it would be useful to mention some of those immediate practical issues on which we will have to take a decision sooner or later, and which will necessarily react upon the historical part of our work.

It may be that our first task will be to decide what the educational aims of modern society should be. It may be that our main interest will be to investigate the existing alterations in the balance between the contributions of the home, church, school, factory, and public life towards moulding individual character.

If so, an historical study will have to be supplemented by a survey of the existing educational institutions in this country and their inter-relations, in order to discover the strategic points at which the educational reconstruction ought to begin.

It may be that we will come to the conviction that the cultural decline in our society is mainly due to the disintegration of the leading elites, and that a mass society can only preserve its cultural traditions if, in spite of its democratic basis, it creates a more adequate selection and the right scope for the influence of these elites.

It may be that the crisis of humanistic ideals or of religious life will become the focal point of our interest. Ultimately it may be that the factors making for the disintegration of personality and dehumanization will become central. Then, among others, a study of labour attitudes and the problem of leisure in modern society will have to be stressed.

Thus, the next task should perhaps be to select from these scattered suggestions and others those which are the most urgent and promising ones, and gradually to translate them into even more detailed and specialized research schemes, if we make an appropriate choice.

One could show that the right command of primary sources and of the existing literature on the subject already offers answers to a great number of them. At the moment we have to aim at the creation of a pioneering elite among our best teachers, clergymen, youth movement leaders, and anyone who has to do basic work in the field of education, in order to give them an orientation based upon sociological knowledge, in the hope that this will bring more unity and purpose into their action.

QUESTION FOR ANSWER

1. Write a note on the concept and feature of the sociology of education.

Bibliography

Abbott, T.K., *Kant's Theory of Ethics,* London, Longmans Green, 1909.

Adams, Sir John, *The Evolution of Educational Theory,* London, Macmillan, 1912.

Adamson, J.W., *English Education 1789-1902,* Cambridge University Press, 1930.

Aiyar, S.P., "Education and the Traditional Society in India," *General Education Quarterly* (Vol. III, No. 1), October, 1965.

Altekar, A.S., *Education in Ancient India,* Nawal Kishore & Bros. Varanasi, 1957.

Anderson, C. Arnold, *The Social Context of Educational Planning,* Paris, International Institute of Educational Planning, UNESCO, 1968 (Fundamentals of Educational Planning No. 5).

Appadorai, A., "Integration Council and Its Task," *The Hindustan Times,* June 20, 1968.

Archer, R.L., *Rousseau on Education,* New York, Longmans, Green & Co., 1912.

Armytage, W.H.G., *Civic Universities,* London, Ernest Benn, Ltd., 1955.

Bagley, W.C., *Determinism in Education,* Baltimore, Warwick and York, 1925.

Bagley, W.C., *Educational Values,* New York, Macmillan, 1911.

Barnett, George and Jack Otis, *Corporate Society and Education: The Philosophy of Elijah Jordan,* Ann Arbor, Michigan, University of Michigan Press, 1962, 1961.

Battle, Jean Allen, *Culture and Education for the Contemporary World,* Columbus, Ohio, C.E. Merrill Publishing Co., 1969.

Baudouin, C., *Suggestion and Autosuggestion,* London, Allen & Unwin, 1920.

Bazeley, E.T., *Homer Lane and the Little Commonwealth,* London, Allen & Unwin-Heinemann, 1928.

Biddle, Brue J., *et. al., Essays on the Social System of Education,* Columbia, Missouri, University of Missouri, 1966.

Bode, B.H., *Progressive Education at Crossroads,* Newson, New York, 1938.

Brookover, W.B., *A Sociology of Education,* New York, American Book Co., 1955.

Clarke, Sir Fred, *The Study of Education in England,* London, Oxford University Press, 1943.

Coleman, J.S., (Ed.) *Education and Political Development,* Princeton, Princeton University Press, 1965.

Cooley, C.H., *Human Nature and the Social Order,* New York, Scribner, 1928.

Cuber, F., 'The Cultural Relativity of Education' in Roucek, J.S. (Ed.), *Sociological Foundations of Education,* The Thomas Crowell Co., New York, 1942.

Curtis, S.J., *History of Education in Great Britain,* London, University Tutorial Press, Ltd., 1948.

Curtis, S.J. and Boultwood, M.E.A., *A Short History of Educational Ideas*, London, University Tutorial Press Ltd., 1953.

Damle, Y.B., "Socialisation for an Unknown Future"—paper presented to the Seminar on "Higher Education, Technology and Social Change" (December 1-3, 1966), New Delhi, Indian Institute of Technology, Department of Humanities and Social Sciences, 1966.

Desai, A.R., *Essays on Modernization of Underdeveloped Societies* (Ed.) Vol. I, Thacker & Co., Bombay, 1971.

Deutsch, Martin, "Early Social Environment: Its Influence on School Adaptation" in *The Social Dropout,* Washington, National Education Association, 1964.

Dewey, John, *Democracy and Education,* New York, Macmillan Co., 1916, p. 144.

Dewey, John, *Human Nature and Conduct,* New York, Holt, 1922, p. 128.

Dewey, John, *Reconstruction in Philosophy,* New York, Henry Holt, 1920, pp. 207-08.

Dewey, John, *The School and Society,* Revised ed. Chicago, 1916. See further Sir Fred Clarke, *op. cit.* (note 4 in Chapter I).

Dilthey, Wilhelm, *Selected Readings from His Works and an Introduction to His Sociological and Philosophical Work,* by H.A. Hodges, London, Routledge and Kegan Paul, 1952.

"Education and Social Values"—paper presented to the 'Conference of Indian Sociologists' (October 14-16, 1967), Bombay, Indian Sociological Society, 1967.

Eistenstadt, S.N., *Modernization: Protest and Change,* Prentice Hall of India Pvt. Ltd., New Delhi, 1969.

Elkin, Frederick, *The Child and Society,* New York, Random House, 1960.

Erikson, E.H., *Childhood and Society,* London, Imago, N.d.

Erickson, Erick H., (Ed.) *Youth: Change and Challenge,* New York, Basic books, 1963.

Finney, Ross L., *Sociological Philosophy of Education,* MaçMillan, New York, 1928.

Flugel, J.C., *A Hundred Years of Psychology,* London, Duckworth, 1937.

Freud, S., *Introductory Lectures on Psycho-Analysis,* London, Allen and Unwin, 1923.

Freud, S., *New Introductory Lectures on Psychoanalysis,* New York, Norton, 1933; London, Hogarth Press, 1935.

Fromm, E., *Man For Himself—An Enquiry into the **Psychology of** Ethics,* New York, Rainchast & Co., 1947.

Fromm, E., *The Fear of Freedom,* London, Kegan Paul, Trench, Trubner & Co., 1942.

Garforth, E.W., *Education and Social Purpose,* London, Oldburire, 1962.

Goel, B.S., "Caste and Class Tensions in Indian Education," *Conspectus* (New Delhi, Indian International Centre, Vol. No. 4), 1966.

Goodman, Paul, "The Universal Trap" in *Social Foundation of Education: Current Issues and Research in Education,* Dorothy Westby-Gibson (Ed.) New York, Free Press, 1967.

Gore, M.S., I.P. Desai and Suma Chitnis, *Field Studies in the Sociology of Education,* NCERT, New Delhi, 1970.

Gore, M.S., Desai, I.P. and Chitnis, Suma, *Papers in Sociology of Education in India,* New Delhi, National Council of Educational Research and Training, 1967.

Government of India, *Emotional Integration Committee: Preliminary Report,* New Delhi, Ministry of Education, 1962.

Gwynn, A., *Roman Education from Cicero to Quintilian,* London, Oxford University Press, 1926.

Hansen, Donald A., "The Responsibility of the Sociologist of Education," *Harvard Educational Review* (33), Summer 1963, p. 313.

Harris, P.E., *Changing Conceptions of School Discipline,* New York, Macmillan Co., 1928.

Herriott, Robert E., "Some Social Determinants of Educational Aspirations," *Harvard Educational Review* (Vol. XXXIII, No. 2), Spring, 1963.

Hocking, W.E., *Man and State,* New Haven, Yale University Press, 1926.

Horne, H.H., *The Democratic Philosophy of Education,* New York, Macmillan Co., 1932.

Horney, K., *New Ways in Psychoanalysis,* New York, Norton & Co., 1939.

Horney, K., *The Neurotic Personality of Our Time,* New York, Norton & Co., 1937.

Hunter, W.S., *Human Behaviour,* University of Chicago Press, Chicago, 1928.

India, *Education and National Development: Report of the Commission* (1964-66), New Delhi, Ministry of Education, Government of India, 1966.

India, *Post-war Education Development in India,* Report by the Central Advisory Board of Education, New Delhi, January, 1944.

India, *Report of the National Committee on Women's Education,* Ministry of Education, Government of India, 1959.

Inkeles, Alex and David H. Smith, *Becoming Modern,* Cambridge, Harvard University Press, 1974.

Inkeles, Alex, "The School as a Context for Modernization", *International Journal of Comparative Sociology,* XIV (3-4), 1973.

Isaacs, Susan, *The Intellectual Growth in Young Children,* London, Routledge, 1930.

Jaeger, W., *Paideia—The Ideals of Greek Culture,* 3 Vols., Oxford, Blackwell, 1934-36.

James, William, *Talks to Teachers on Psychology,* London, Longmans, Green & Co., 1899.

Jesselyn, Irene M., *The Happy Child,* New York, Random House, 1965.

Kabir, Humayun, *The Indian Heritage,* London, Asia Publishing House, 1962.

Kant, Immanuel, *Paedagogik* (Kant on Education) Trans. by A. Churton, London, Kegan Paul, Trench and Trubner, 1899.

Kardiner, A., *The Psychological Frontiers of Society,* New York, 1945.

Kimball, Solon T., "An Anthropological View of Learning" in *Social Foundations of Education: Current Reading from the Behaviour Sciences* (ed.), New York, Macmillan, 1966, pp. 266-71.

Klages, L., *The Science of Character,* Allen & Unwine, 1929.

Kohn Melvin L., "Social Class and Parental Values," *American Journal of Sociology* (Vol. LXIV), 1959.

Livingstone, R.W., *Greek Ideals and Modern Life,* London, Oxford University Press, 1935, and Harvard University Press, Cambridge, Mass.

Mannheim, Karl, *Systematic Sociology,* Edited by J.S. Eros and W.A.C. Stewart, London, Routledge and Kegan Paul, 1957.

Mannheim, Karl and Stewart, W.A.C., *An Introduction to the Sociology of Education,* London, Routledge and Kegan Paul, 1962.

Martin, A.V., *Sociology of the Renaissance,* London, Routledge and Kegan Paul, 1944.

Mayo, E., *The Social Problems of an Industrial Civilization,* London, Routledge and Kegan Paul, 1949.

McClelland, David C., *The Achieving Society,* Princeton, D. Van Nostrand Co., 1961.

McDougall, W., *An Introduction to Social Psychology,* Boston, John W. Luce, 1926.

Mead, G.H., *Mind, Self and Society,* Chicago, University of Chicago Press, 1934.

Mead, Margaret and Wolfenstein, Martha (Eds.), *Childhood i Contemporary Cultures,* Chicago, University of Chicago Press, 1955.

Mekeel, Scudder, "Education, Child-Training and Culture" in *Education and the Social Order,* Blaine E. Marcer and Edvin V. Carr (eds.), New York, Rinehart & Co., 1968.

Mill, J.S., "Inaugural Address at St. Andrews," published in Cavenagh, F.A., *James and John Stuart Mill, on Education,* Cambridge University Press, 1931, pp. 132-98.

Morgan, T.H., 'Are Acquired Characteristics Inherited?' *The Yale Review,* Vol. 13, July, 1924.

Mukerji, Shridhar N., *Higher Education and Rural India,* Baroda, India, Acharya Book Depot, 1956.

Munshi, K.M., *Foundations of Indian Culture,* Bombay, Bharatiya Vidya Bhawan, 1962.

Nunn, Sir Percy, *Education: Its Data and First Principles,* London, Edward Arnold, 1930, p. 9.

Ogburn, W.F. (ed.), *Social Change*, Chicago, University of Chicago Press, 1929.

Painter, F.V.N., *Luther on Education*, Philadelphia, Lutheran Publication Society, 1899.

Phillips, H.W., *Sociology and the Planning of Education in Relation to Development*, Paris, UNESCO, 1964.

Piaget, J., *The Language and Thought of the Child*, London, Kegan Paul, 1926.

Poignent, R., *Social Change in Modern India*, Bombay, Allied Publishers, 1966.

Radha Kumud Mukherji, *Ancient Indian Education*, Delhi, Motilal Banarsidas, 1951.

Rai, Lala Lajpat, *The Problems of National Education in India*, Delhi, Publications Division, 1968.

Ramanathan, G., *Education Planning and National Integration*, Bombay, Asia Publishing House, 1965.

Rashdall, Hastings, *The Universities of Europe in the Middle Ages*, 3 Vols., New edition, edited by Sir F.M. Powicke and A.B. Emden, London, Oxford University Press, 1936.

Razran, G.H.S., "Conditioned Responses", A Classified Bibliography, *Psychological Bulletin*, Vol. 34, 1937, pp. 191-256.

"Research Needs in the Sociology of Education" in *Research Needs in the Study of Education*, U. Shanker and S.P. Ahluwalia (Eds.), Kurukshetra, Kurukshetra University, 1968, pp. 17-25.

Richmond, W.K., *The Permanent Value in Education*, London, Society for the Promotion of Christian Knowledge, 1920.

Rodehover, Myles W., Axtell, William B., Gross, Richard E., *The Sociology of the School*, New York, Thomas Y. Crowell Co., 1957.

Ross, J.S., *Groundwork of Educational Theory*, London, Harrap, 1942.

Roucek, J.S. *et al.*, *Sociological Foundations of Education*, New York, Thomas J. Crowell Co., 1942.

Rugg, Harold O., *Culture and Education in America,* New York, Harcourt Brace & Co., 1931.

Ruhela, S.P., *A Note on the Researchable Topics in Sociology of Education in India*—A Paper presented to the Jamia Millia Teachers' College Seminar on 'Educational Sociology,' December 24-26, 1968 (Mimeographed).

Ruhela, S.P., *A Preview of the Seminar on Sociology of the Teaching Profession in India*—A Paper presented to the Seminar held at the Tata Institute of Social Sciences, Bombay, February 5-10, 1968 (Mimeographed).

Ruhela, S.P., *Field Studies in Sociology of Education,* New Delhi, National Council of Educational Research and Training.

Ruhela, S.P., *Sociology of Education: A Review of Researches and Priorities,* New Delhi, National Institute of Education, Department of Foundations of Education, 1967 (Mimeographed).

Ruhela, S.P. (Ed.), *Sociology of the Teaching Profession in India,* New Delhi, National Council of Education Research and Training, 1970.

Saiyidain, K.G., *The Humanist Tradition in Indian Educational Thought,* Bombay, Asia Publishing House, 1960.

Shah, A.B., *Planning for Democracy and Other Essays,* Bombay, Manktalas, 1967.

Shah, B.V., "Sociology of Education—An Attempt at Definition and Scope," *Sociological Bulletin* (Vol. XIV, No. 2), September, 1965, p. 65.

Sharma, R.N., *Philosophy of Education,* Delhi, Atlantic, 1996.

——, *Problems of Education,* Delhi, Atlantic, 1996.

Sharma, S.L., *Modernizing Effects of University Education,* ICSSR, New Delhi, 1979.

Sir Fred Clarke, *Freedom in the Educative Society,* published by the University of London Press in 1948.

Stanley, William O., *Education and Social Integration,* New York, Columbia University, Teacher's College, 1953.

Stow, David, *The Training System,* Glasgow, 1840.

Sullivan, E.E., *Education in Social Change,* Asia Publishing House, Bombay, 1968.

The Individual and His Society with a Foreword and two anthropological reports by R. Linton, New York, Columbia University Press, 1939.

"The Modernization of Education" in *Modernization, The Dynamics of Growth,* Myron Weiner (ed.), Madras, Higginbothams, 1967.

"The Uncomfortable Relation of Sociology and Education" in *On Education: Sociological Perspectives,* Donald A. Hansen and Joel E. Gerstl (eds.), New York, John Wiley & Sons, 1967, p. 22.

Thorndike, E.L., *Human Nature and the Social Order,* New York, Macmillan, 1940.

UNESCO Publication No. 359, Columbia University Press, New Yark, 1949.

Vadekar, D.D., "The Indian Traditional Values and Their Indications for Education in India in the Age of Modern Science and Technology," *The Journal of the University of Poona,* Humanities Section (23), 1965.

Vakil, C.N., "National Integration: The Common Language" (Part I), *Times of India,* July 13, 1961.

Veblen, Th., *The Theory of the Leisure Class,* New York, Macmillan Co., 1912.

Waller, Willard, *The Sociology of Teaching,* New York, Wiley & Sons, 1932.

Westby-Gibson D. (Ed.), *Social Foundations of Education: Current Issues and Research,* New York, Free Press, 1967.

Wheeler, Olive, *The Adventure of Youth,* University of London Press, 1945, p. 12.

Wilkins, A., *Roman Education,* Cambridge University Press, 1921.

Woodworth, R.S., *Contemporary Schools of Psychology,* New York, The Ronald Press, 1948. (First published in Britain in 1931.)

Index